First World War

and Army of Occupation

War Diary

France, Belgium and Germany

6 DIVISION
1 Midland Infantry Brigade Headquarters,
Brigade Duke of Wellington's (West Riding Regiment)
2/4th Battalion,
King's Own (Yorkshire Light Infantry) 2/4 Battalion,
King's Own (Yorkshire Light Infantry) 5th Battalion,
2 Midland Infantry Brigade Headquarters,
Leicestershire Regiment 51 Battalion,
Leicestershire Regiment 52 Battalion,
South Staffordshire Regiment 1/5th Battalion
(Territorial Force), 3 Midland Infantry Brigade
Sherwood Foresters (Nottinghamshire and Derbyshire Regiment)
51st, 52nd and 53rd Battalions
10 January 1918 - 31 July 1919

WO95/1626

The Naval & Military Press Ltd
www.nmarchive.com
Published in association with The National Archives

Published by

The Naval & Military Press Ltd

Unit 10 Ridgewood Industrial Park,

Uckfield, East Sussex,

TN22 5QE England

Tel: +44 (0) 1825 749494

www.naval-military-press.com

www.nmarchive.com

This diary has been reprinted in facsimile from the original. Any imperfections are inevitably reproduced and the quality may fall short of modern type and cartographic standards.

Contents

Miscellaneous		06/06/1919	06/06/1919
Miscellaneous	1st Midland Brigade Defence Scheme No. 2.	06/01/1919	06/01/1919
Miscellaneous	To all recipients of 1st Midland Brigade Warning Order No. 4. App III.	15/06/1919	15/06/1919
Miscellaneous	Message Form. App III		
Operation(al) Order(s)	Amendment No. 1 to 1st Midland Brigade Warning Order No 4.	16/06/1919	16/06/1919
Miscellaneous	Table "B"		
Miscellaneous	1st Midland Brigade Defence Scheme No. 3. (Provisional) Appendix IV	20/06/1919	20/06/1919
Miscellaneous	Appendix 1.		
Miscellaneous		21/06/1919	21/06/1919
Map	Map To Be Attd To 1st Defence Order No 3		
Miscellaneous	War Diary		
Operation(al) Order(s)	1st Midland Brigade Order No. 6. App V	24/06/1919	24/06/1919
Miscellaneous	Table "A" to Accompany 1st Midland Brigde Order No. 6.		
Miscellaneous	1st Midland Brigade Order No. 6.	25/06/1919	25/06/1919
Miscellaneous		25/06/1919	25/06/1919
Miscellaneous	Message Form.		
Heading	War Diary Headquarters 1st Midland Brigade July 1919 Original		
Miscellaneous	Cover for Documents. Nature of Enclosures.		
War Diary	Lechenich	04/07/1919	31/07/1919
Miscellaneous	Fighting & Trench Strength.		
Operation(al) Order(s)	1st Midland Brigade Order No. 7 App V	30/07/1919	30/07/1919
Miscellaneous	Table To Accompany 1st Midland Order No. 7.		
Miscellaneous	Administrative Order No. 7 Issued with reference to 1st Midland Brigade Order No. 7	04/08/1919	04/08/1919
Operation(al) Order(s)	B.M.S. 92. 1st Midland Brigade Order No 8. Appendix II	31/07/1919	31/07/1919
Miscellaneous	Administrative Order No. 8 issued with reference to Ist Midland Brigade Order No. 8.	04/08/1919	04/08/1919
Heading	War Diary. Headquarters 1st Midland Brigade August 1919		
Miscellaneous	Cover for Documents. Nature of Enclosures.		
War Diary	Lechenich	02/08/1919	28/08/1919
Miscellaneous	Fighting & Trench Strength.		
War Diary	Lachquich Germany	04/09/1919	04/09/1919
War Diary	Lechenich Germany	05/09/1919	05/09/1919
War Diary	Kinmel Park N. Wales	08/09/1919	19/09/1919
Miscellaneous	Urgent Postal Telegram.	11/09/1919	11/09/1919
Heading	WO95/1626/2		
Heading	BEF Midland div 1 Mid. Bde 2/4 D.O.W (W. Riding) 1919 Mar to 1919 Sept From 62 Div 186 Bde		
Heading	War Diary of the 2/4th Bn Duke of Wellingtons (WR) Regiment T.F. From 1st March 1919 to 31st March 1919		
Miscellaneous	Cover for Documents. Nature of Enclosures.		
Miscellaneous	2/4 Duke of Wellingtons Regiment Appendix No 1	31/03/1919	31/03/1919
War Diary	Zulpich	01/03/1919	14/03/1919
War Diary	Epp	15/03/1919	31/03/1919
Heading	War Diary of the 2/4th Bn duke of Wellingtons (W R) Regiment (T F) Volume no: 28 April 1919		
Miscellaneous	Cover for Documents. Nature of Enclosures.		
War Diary	Erp	01/04/1919	13/04/1919

War Diary	Herrig	14/04/1919	30/04/1919
Heading	War Diary 2/4th Bn Duke of Wellington's (WR) Regt T.F. Volume no: 29-May 1919		
Miscellaneous	Cover for Documents. Nature of Enclosures.		
War Diary	Herrig	01/05/1919	01/05/1919
War Diary	Germany	31/05/1919	31/05/1919
Heading	War Diary of the 2/4 Bn Duke of Wellington's Regt for June 1919 Volume no: 30		
Miscellaneous	Cover for Documents. Nature of Enclosures.		
War Diary	Herrig	01/06/1919	05/06/1919
War Diary	Gymnich	06/06/1919	17/06/1919
War Diary	Mergamch	18/06/1919	30/06/1919
Heading	War Diary of 2/4th Bn. Duke of Wellingtons (WR) Regt Volume no: 31 July 1919		
Miscellaneous	Cover for Documents. Nature of Enclosures.		
War Diary	Germany		
War Diary	Merzenich	01/07/1919	01/07/1919
War Diary	Gymnich		
Heading	War Diary 2/4th Bn. Duke of Wellington's (W R) Volume No:32 August 1919		
Miscellaneous	Cover for Documents. Nature of Enclosures.		
War Diary	Germany Weilerswist	01/08/1919	05/08/1919
War Diary	Erp	06/08/1919	26/08/1919
Heading	War Diary of the 2/4th Bn. Duke of Wellingtons (WR) Regiment September 1919 Volume-no: 33		
Miscellaneous	Army Form A. 2.		
War Diary	Germany	01/09/1919	01/09/1919
War Diary	Erp	05/09/1919	06/09/1919
War Diary	Koinmel Park	07/09/1919	30/09/1919
Heading	WO95/1626/3		
Heading	B E F Midland Div. 1 Midland Bde 2/4 K.O.Y.L.I 1919 Mar to 1919 Aug From 62 Div 187 Bde		
Heading	War Diary 2/4th Battn. King's Own Yorkshire Light Infantry From 1-3-19 To 31-3-19 Volume 27		
War Diary	Pingsheim	01/03/1919	14/03/1919
War Diary	Gymnich	14/03/1919	29/03/1919
War Diary	Pingsheim	01/03/1919	14/03/1919
War Diary	Gymnich	14/03/1919	29/03/1919
Heading	2/4th Div. K.Q. Yorkshire L.L. Vol 28. From 1-4-19 To 30-4-19		
War Diary	Gymnich	01/04/1919	30/04/1919
Heading	War Diary 2/4th Div. K Q. Yorks L.i. Vol 29 From 1-5-19 To 31-5-19		
War Diary	Gymnich	01/05/1919	31/05/1919
Heading	War Diary 2/4th Div. K.Q. Yorks L.I. Vol 30 From 1-6-19 300-6-19		
War Diary	Gymnich	01/06/1919	06/06/1919
War Diary	Weilerswist Camp.	07/06/1919	18/06/1919
War Diary	Gymnich	19/06/1919	20/06/1919
War Diary	Buir	21/06/1919	30/06/1919
Heading	War Diary 2/4th Div. K.O. Yorks. L.i. Vol. 31 From 1-7-19 To 31-7-19		
War Diary	Gymnich	01/07/1919	01/07/1919
War Diary	Weilerswist	02/07/1919	08/07/1919
War Diary	Bruhl	09/07/1919	31/07/1919

Heading	Confidential War Diary 24th Div. K.O. Yorks. L.i. Vol 32 From 1-8-19 To 31-8-19		
War Diary	Bruhl	01/08/1919	06/08/1919
War Diary	Gymnich	09/08/1919	29/08/1919
Heading	WO95/1626/4		
Heading	Midland Div late 6th 1 Midland Bde 5 Bn Kings own Y L i 1919 Mar-1919 Aug From 62 Div 187 Bde		
Heading	5th Battalion The Kings Own Yorkshire LIght Infantry. War Diary For Month Ended 31st March. 1919.		
War Diary	Gladbach	01/03/1919	14/03/1919
War Diary	Freizheim	15/03/1919	22/03/1919
War Diary	Liblar	23/03/1919	31/03/1919
Miscellaneous	5th. Battalion The King's Own Yorkshire Light Infantry War Diary. For Month Ended 30th April 1919.		
War Diary		06/04/1919	30/04/1919
War Diary		01/05/1919	31/05/1919
Operation(al) Order(s)	5th Battn., King's Own Yorkshire Light Infantry. Operation Order No. 1	30/05/1919	30/05/1919
War Diary		01/06/1919	24/06/1919
Miscellaneous	5th Battn., King's Own Yorkshire Light Infantry. Operation Order No. 1.	30/05/1919	30/05/1919
Operation(al) Order(s)	5th Battalion The King's Own Yorkshire Light Infantry. Operation Order No. 2	07/06/1919	07/06/1919
Miscellaneous	Appendix No. 1 issued With 5th Bn K.O.Y.L.I. Operation Order No. 2/1/2	07/06/1919	07/06/1919
Operation(al) Order(s)	5th Battalion the King's Own Yorkshire Light Infantry. Operation Order No. 3.	18/06/1919	18/06/1919
Miscellaneous	Midland Division "C".	16/06/1919	16/06/1919
Miscellaneous	5th Battalion The King's Own Yorkshire Light Infantry.	14/06/1919	14/06/1919
Operation(al) Order(s)	5th Battalion The King's Own Yorkshire Light Infantry. Amendment To Operation Order No. 1.	17/06/1919	17/06/1919
Miscellaneous	5th. Battalion The King's Yorkshire Light Infantry. Warning Order.	20/06/1919	20/06/1919
War Diary		01/07/1919	28/08/1919
Heading	WO95/1626/5		
Heading	BEF Midland Div 2 Mid. Bde. H.Q 1919 Mar To 1919 Aug		
Miscellaneous	2nd Midland Bde No B.M. 295/6	12/04/1919	12/04/1919
War Diary		01/03/1919	31/03/1919
War Diary		22/03/1919	31/03/1919
War Diary	Zulpich	01/04/1919	17/04/1919
War Diary	Good Friday	18/04/1919	19/04/1919
War Diary	Easter Sunday	19/04/1919	21/04/1919
War Diary	Zulpich	22/04/1919	30/04/1919
Miscellaneous	Special Order Of the Day. Appendix "A"	18/03/1919	18/03/1919
War Diary	1919 (Zulpich Sensenich)	01/05/1919	08/05/1919
War Diary	Zulpich	09/05/1919	19/06/1919
War Diary	Duren	20/06/1919	30/06/1919
War Diary	Germany	00/06/1919	00/06/1919
Operation(al) Order(s)	2nd Midland Brigade Order no. 1. Appendix I	25/05/1919	25/05/1919
Miscellaneous	Addendum No. 1 to 2nd Midland Brigade No. 1.	27/05/1919	27/05/1919
Miscellaneous	Addendum No. 3 to 2nd MIdland Brigade Order No. 1. Dated 25th May 1919.	07/06/1919	07/06/1919
Miscellaneous	Addendum N. 4 to 2nd Midland Bde ORder No. 1. dated 25th May 1919.	17/06/1919	17/06/1919
Miscellaneous	2nd Midland Brigade.		

Operation(al) Order(s)	2nd Midland Brigade Order No. 2. Appendix 2	18/06/1919	18/06/1919
Miscellaneous	2nd Midland Brigade. March Table.		
Miscellaneous	Message Form. Series No. of Messages		
Miscellaneous	Addendum No 2 to 2nd Midland Brigade Order No, 1 of 26th May 1919 Appendix 3	02/06/1919	02/06/1919
Miscellaneous	Duren Defence Scheme. Appendix 4	21/06/1919	21/06/1919
Miscellaneous	Localities to which Guards Will be Sent on Receipt of the word "RIOT" Appendix 1.		
Miscellaneous	Appendix 2. Signal For alarming the Town. Appendix 2.		
Miscellaneous	Signal Arrangements. Appendix 3.		
Operation(al) Order(s)	2nd Midland Brigade Order No. 3. Appendix 5	25/06/1919	25/06/1919
Miscellaneous	March Table "A"		
War Diary	Duren	01/07/1919	07/07/1919
War Diary	Zulpich	07/07/1919	31/07/1919
War Diary	Zulpich Germany.	31/07/1919	31/07/1919
War Diary	(Duren.)	01/07/1919	01/07/1919
War Diary	Zulpich	02/07/1919	31/07/1919
War Diary	Zulpich Germany	31/07/1919	31/07/1919
War Diary	Zulpich	01/08/1919	31/08/1919
Heading	WO95/1626/6		
Heading	BEF Midland Div 2 Mid. Bde. 51 Leics. R. 1919 Mar To 1919 Aug		
Miscellaneous		09/04/1919	09/04/1919
War Diary	Dunkirk	08/03/1919	09/03/1919
War Diary	Goeogre	11/03/1919	11/03/1919
War Diary	Siinth	13/03/1919	18/03/1919
War Diary	Euskirchen	18/03/1919	31/03/1919
War Diary	Surth	14/03/1919	17/03/1919
War Diary	Euskirchen	19/03/1919	22/03/1919
Miscellaneous	Euskirchen Barracks. May 10th. 1919		
War Diary	Guskutchew	01/04/1919	11/04/1919
War Diary	Zulpich	12/04/1919	12/04/1919
War Diary	Euskirchen	13/04/1919	13/04/1919
War Diary	Zulpich	16/04/1919	16/04/1919
War Diary	Euskirchen	03/04/1919	25/04/1919
War Diary	Zulpich	26/04/1919	26/04/1919
War Diary	Cologne	28/04/1919	30/04/1919
War Diary	Euskirchen	15/05/1919	19/05/1919
War Diary	Bruhl	20/05/1919	20/05/1919
War Diary	Euskirchen	21/05/1919	29/05/1919
War Diary	Zinzenich	02/05/1919	02/05/1919
War Diary	Zulpich	05/05/1919	05/05/1919
War Diary	Cologne	07/05/1919	07/05/1919
War Diary	Euskirchen	07/05/1919	09/05/1919
War Diary	Zulpich	11/05/1919	11/05/1919
War Diary	Euskirchen	01/06/1919	12/06/1919
War Diary	Bruhl	13/06/1919	13/06/1919
War Diary	Euskirchen	13/06/1919	20/06/1919
War Diary	Menode	21/06/1919	30/06/1919
Miscellaneous	51st Leicester Mid Div		
War Diary	Euskirchen	01/07/1919	02/07/1919
War Diary	Cologne	02/07/1919	02/07/1919
War Diary	Euskirchen	04/07/1919	22/07/1919
War Diary	Romer hof	24/07/1919	24/07/1919
War Diary	Euskirchen	26/07/1919	31/08/1919

Heading	WO95/1626/7		
Heading	BEF Midland Div 2 Mid. Bde. 52 Leics. R 1919 Mar To 1919 Aug		
War Diary	Brocton Camp	23/03/1919	23/03/1919
War Diary	Milford T Brocotn	23/03/1919	23/03/1919
War Diary	Dover	23/03/1919	23/03/1919
War Diary	Dunkirk	23/03/1919	24/03/1919
War Diary	No 3 Restcamp Sdes. Dunkirk	24/03/1919	24/03/1919
War Diary	St Merris	24/03/1919	24/03/1919
War Diary	Bailloue	24/03/1919	24/03/1919
War Diary	Charleroi	25/03/1919	25/03/1919
War Diary	Huy	25/03/1919	25/03/1919
War Diary	Zulpich	26/03/1919	13/04/1919
Heading	52 Leicesters War Diary May 1st to 31st		
War Diary	Zulpich	01/05/1919	19/06/1919
War Diary	Duren	20/06/1919	29/06/1919
War Diary	Zulpich	30/06/1919	30/06/1919
War Diary	Railway Gd. No. 2 Sector	22/06/1919	22/06/1919
War Diary	Zulpich	01/07/1919	31/08/1919
Heading	WO95/1626/8		
Heading	BEF Midland Div 2 MId. Bde. 1/5 Mar To 1919 Aug From 46 Div 137 Bde		
Heading	War Diary. of 1/5th Bn. South Staffordshire Regt. From 1st March 1919 To 31st March 1919.		
War Diary	Fresnoy Le-Grand	01/03/1919	05/03/1919
War Diary	Liblar Germany	06/03/1919	06/03/1919
War Diary	Gymnich	07/03/1919	13/03/1919
War Diary	Kommern	14/03/1919	31/03/1919
Heading	Confidential War Diary of 1/5th Bn. South Staffs Regt. From 1st April 1919 To 30th April 919		
War Diary	Kommern Germany	01/04/1919	30/04/1919
Heading	War Diary 1/5th. BN. South Staffs Regt. From 1st May 1919 To 31st May 1919		
War Diary	Kommern Germany	01/05/1919	31/05/1919
Heading	War Diary of 1/5th. Bn. South Staffs Regt From 1st June 1919 TO 30th June 1919		
War Diary	Kommern Germany	01/06/1919	17/06/1919
War Diary	Duren	18/06/1919	24/06/1919
Operation(al) Order(s)	1/5th Bn. South Staffs Regt. ORder No 26	17/06/1919	17/06/1919
War Diary	Duren	01/07/1919	02/07/1919
War Diary	Wettveiss	03/07/1919	03/07/1919
War Diary	Kommern	04/07/1919	31/07/1919
Miscellaneous	Headquarters, IV Corps.	25/06/1919	25/06/1919
Heading	1/5th Battalion South Staffordshire Regiment. War Diary. From 1st August, 1919. To 31st August, 1919		
War Diary	Commern	01/08/1919	31/08/1919
Heading	WO95/1626/9		
Heading	Midland Division Late 6th Division B.H.Q. 3rd Midland Infy Bde Mar. Jan-Aug 1919		
War Diary	Eichholz. Germany, Sheet 2.L.	01/03/1919	26/03/1919
War Diary	Rodenkirchen	27/03/1919	31/03/1919
Miscellaneous	71st Infantry Brigade. War Diary For Month of March, 1919.		
Operation(al) Order(s)	71st Infantry Brigade Operation Order No. 411	10/05/1919	10/05/1919
Miscellaneous	Amendment No. 1 to 71st Infantry Brigade Operation Order No. 411	10/03/1919	10/03/1919

Operation(al) Order(s)	7 1st Infantry Brigade Operation Order No. 412.	11/03/1919	11/03/1919
Miscellaneous	Amendment No. 1 to 71st Infantry Brigade Operation Order No. 412.	11/03/1919	11/03/1919
Operation(al) Order(s)	71st Infantry Brigade Operation Order No.413.	13/03/1919	13/03/1919
Operation(al) Order(s)	71st Infantry Brigade Operation. Order No. 414.	17/03/1919	17/03/1919
Operation(al) Order(s)	71st Infantry Brigade Operation Order No. 415	21/03/1919	21/03/1919
Operation(al) Order(s)	71st Infantry Brigade Operation Order No. 416.	26/03/1919	26/03/1919
Miscellaneous	71st Infantry Brigade. Roll Of Officers Serving on 31st March, 1919.		
Miscellaneous	Headquarters "A" Midland DIvision.	03/05/1919	03/05/1919
Miscellaneous	3rd Midland Brigade. War Diary for Month Of APril, 1919		
War Diary	Rodenkirchen	01/04/1919	10/04/1919
War Diary	Marienburg (Cologne).	11/04/1919	30/04/1919
Miscellaneous	3rd Midland Brigade. Action to be taken in the event of civil Riot or Insurrection. Appendix No 1.	15/04/1919	15/04/1919
Operation(al) Order(s)	Amendment No. 1. to 3rd Midland Brigade Order No. 417.	19/04/1919	19/04/1919
Miscellaneous	3rd Midland Brigade Order No. 417. Appendix No 2.	17/04/1919	17/04/1919
Miscellaneous	War Diary. Miscellaneous. Appendix 3.		
Miscellaneous	3rd Midland Brigade. Roll Of Officers. Appendix. 4.		
Miscellaneous	Special Order of the Day. Appendix No 5	10/03/1919	10/03/1919
Miscellaneous	Headquarters "A" Midland Division.	02/06/1919	02/06/1919
War Diary	Marienburg	01/05/1919	31/05/1919
Miscellaneous	Headquarters, 3rd Midland Brigade.		
Miscellaneous	3rd Midland Brigade War Diary For Month Of May, 1919.		
Miscellaneous	3rd Midland Brigade. Provisional Defence Choice in the Event of Civil Disturbance.	08/05/1919	08/05/1919
Miscellaneous	3rd Midland Brigade. Defence Scheme in the event of civil Disturbance. Appendix No 20.	22/05/1919	22/05/1919
Operation(al) Order(s)	3rd Midland Brigade Order No. 418 date 25/5/19 Appendix 3.	25/05/1919	25/05/1919
Miscellaneous	March table issued 3rd Midland Brigade O.No 418		
Miscellaneous	Administrative Instructions Issued In Connection With 3rd Midland Brigade Order No 418 Dated 25th May 1919	25/05/1919	25/05/1919
Miscellaneous	Reference Sheet 59.	26/05/1919	26/05/1919
Miscellaneous	Addenda No. 2 to 3rd Midland Brigade No. 418 dated 25th May 1919.		
Miscellaneous	3rd Midland Brigade. Roll of Officers. Appendix No.4.	08/05/1919	08/05/1919
Miscellaneous	Ration Strength Of 3rd MIdland Brigade On 31/5/19. Appendix No.5.		
Miscellaneous	Headquarters, "A" Midland Division. 3rd Midland Brigade No. G. 31.	03/07/1919	03/07/1919
War Diary	Marienburg	01/06/1919	09/06/1919
War Diary	Schmidtheim	09/06/1919	18/06/1919
War Diary	Lechenich	19/06/1919	30/06/1919
Miscellaneous	3rd Midland Brigade War Diary For Month Of June, 1919.		
Operation(al) Order(s)	3rd Midland Brigade Order No. 419 Appendix I	04/06/1919	04/06/1919
Miscellaneous	Administrative Instructions to Accompany Brigade Operation Order No. 419.		
Miscellaneous	Reference Brigade Operation Order No. 419 and Administrative Instructions.	05/06/1919	05/06/1919

Miscellaneous	Amendments to Administrative instructions to Accompany Brigade Operation Order No. 419.		
Miscellaneous	Sports. Appendix no 2	14/06/1919	14/06/1919
Operation(al) Order(s)	3rd Midland Brigade Order No. 420 dated 10/6/19. Appendix No 3.	16/06/1919	16/06/1919
Miscellaneous	Table "A". to Accompany 3rd Midland Brigade Order No. 420.		
Miscellaneous	Table "B" to Accompany 3rd. Island Brigade Order No. 420.		
Miscellaneous			
Miscellaneous	Administrative Instructions To Accompany Brigade Operation Order No. 420.	17/06/1919	17/06/1919
Miscellaneous	Addendum No. 1 to 3rd Midland Brigade Order No. 420. dated 10/6/19.	17/06/1919	17/06/1919
Miscellaneous	Warning Order. Appendix 4	18/06/1919	18/06/1919
Operation(al) Order(s)	3rd MIdland Brigade Order No. 421 dated 24/6/19. Appen 5.	24/06/1919	24/06/1919
Miscellaneous	Allottment of No. Of Covered Wagons Covered Wagons Train. For men. for horses. Flats. Entraining Station.		
Miscellaneous	Administrative Instructions to Accompany Brigade Operation Order No. 421.	24/06/1918	24/06/1918
Miscellaneous	Amendment No. 1 To 3rd Midland Brigade Order No. 421 Dated 24/6/19	25/06/1919	25/06/1919
Miscellaneous	Reference Para. 10 Of Administrative Instructions To Accompany Brigade Operation Order No. 421.	26/06/1919	26/06/1919
Miscellaneous	3rd Midland Brigade. Roll of Officers. Appendix No. 6.		
Miscellaneous	Ration Strength of 3rd Midland Brigade On 30/6/19 Appendix No. 7.		
War Diary	Lechenich Area.	01/07/1919	02/07/1919
War Diary	Schmidtheim.	03/07/1919	31/07/1919
Miscellaneous	3rd Midland Brigade. War Diary For Month of July, 1919.	00/07/1919	00/07/1919
Miscellaneous	Amendment No. 1. to 3rd Midland. Brigade Warning Order dated 29/7/19.	30/07/1919	30/07/1919
Miscellaneous	Warning Order. Appendix No 1	29/07/1919	29/07/1919
Miscellaneous	3rd Midland Brigade. Appendix of Officers. Appendix No.2.		
Miscellaneous	Ration Strength of 3rd Midland Brigade On 31/7/19. Appendix No.3.	31/07/1919	31/07/1919
War Diary	Schmidtheim	01/08/1919	05/08/1919
War Diary	Cologne-Bruhl Area.	06/08/1919	25/08/1919
Miscellaneous	3rd Midland Brigade. War Diary For Month of August, 1919.		
War Diary	Cologne-Bruhl Area.	26/08/1919	30/08/1919
Miscellaneous	3rd Midland Brigade Order No. 422 dated 1/8/19.	01/08/1919	01/08/1919
Miscellaneous	Administrative Instructions To Accompany 3rd Midland Brigade Operation Order No. 422.	01/08/1919	01/08/1919
Miscellaneous	Train Accommodation. Personnel (allotted)	03/08/1919	03/08/1919
Miscellaneous	Brigadier-General Commanding.	03/08/1919	03/08/1919
Miscellaneous	3rd Midland Brigade. Roll of Officers. Appendix No.2.		
Miscellaneous	Ration Strength Of 3rd Midland Brigade on 28/8/19. Appendix No.3.		
Heading	WO95/1626/10		
Heading	Midland Division (Late 6th Division) 3rd Mid'd Infy Bde 51st Bn Notts & Derby Regt Mar-Jly 1919		

War Diary	Brocton Camp	28/02/1919	28/02/1919
War Diary	Wilford Station	28/02/1919	28/02/1919
War Diary	Daner	28/02/1919	01/03/1919
War Diary	Durbink	01/03/1919	04/03/1919
War Diary	Rodenkirchen	05/03/1919	31/03/1919
Miscellaneous	Roll of Officers. 51st. Bn. Sherwood Foresters.	31/03/1919	31/03/1919
War Diary	Rodenkirchen	01/04/1919	18/06/1919
War Diary	Lechenich	19/06/1919	01/07/1919
War Diary	Schmidtheim	02/07/1919	31/07/1919
Heading	WO95/1626/11		
Heading	Midland Division (Late 6th Division) 3rd Mid'D' Bde (Infy) 52nd Notts & Derbys. 1917 Nov-1919 July		
War Diary	3rd Ashford Kent	17/11/1919	17/11/1919
War Diary	5th Ashford Kent	10/01/1918	15/02/1918
War Diary	Clipstone Camp Nottingham	22/02/1918	22/02/1918
War Diary	Ridmines Camp the shiffeld	11/03/1919	04/05/1919
War Diary	Welbech Camp near Worksop	05/05/1918	12/02/1919
War Diary	Brocton Camp	19/02/1919	03/03/1919
War Diary	Euskirchen	04/03/1919	18/03/1919
War Diary	Cologne	18/03/1919	18/03/1919
War Diary	Cologne	19/03/1919	30/03/1919
War Diary	Cologne	01/04/1919	22/04/1919
War Diary	Prahs	30/04/1919	30/04/1919
War Diary	Bruhl	01/05/1919	22/05/1919
War Diary	Bruhl	26/05/1919	09/06/1919
War Diary	Schmidheim	14/06/1919	18/06/1919
War Diary	Bruhl	19/06/1919	02/07/1919
War Diary	Schmidtheim	13/07/1919	26/07/1919
Heading	WO95/1626/12		
Heading	Midland Division (Late 6th Division) 3rd Mid'd Infy Bde 53rd Bn Notts & Derbys. Mar-July 1919		
War Diary	Catterick	08/03/1919	08/03/1919
War Diary	Dover	09/03/1919	09/03/1919
War Diary	Dunkerque	09/03/1919	10/03/1919
War Diary	En Route	11/03/1919	11/03/1919
War Diary	Bruhl	12/03/1919	18/03/1919
War Diary	Surth	18/03/1919	25/03/1919
War Diary	Catterick	08/03/1919	08/03/1919
War Diary	Dover	09/03/1919	09/03/1919
War Diary	Dunkerque	09/03/1919	10/03/1919
War Diary	En Route	11/03/1919	11/03/1919
War Diary	Bruhl	12/03/1919	18/03/1919
War Diary	Surth	18/03/1919	25/03/1919
War Diary	Catterick	08/03/1919	08/03/1919
War Diary	Dover	09/03/1919	09/03/1919
War Diary	Dunkerque	09/03/1919	10/03/1919
War Diary	En Route	11/03/1919	11/03/1919
War Diary	Bruhl	12/03/1919	18/03/1919
War Diary	Surth	18/03/1919	31/03/1919
War Diary	Surth	26/03/1919	31/03/1919
War Diary	Surth	26/03/1919	09/06/1919
War Diary	Schmidtheim	10/06/1919	18/06/1919
War Diary	Ublar	19/06/1919	01/07/1919
War Diary	Schmidtheim	02/07/1919	31/07/1919

MIDLAND DIVISION(6 DIV)

1 MIDLAND BRIGADE.H.Q.
2/4 DUKE OF WELLINGTONS.
REGT.1919 MAR TO SEPT.

2/4 KINGS OWN YORKSHIRE
LIGHT INFANTRY
5 KINGS OWN YORK'S L'I'
1919 MAR TO 1919 AUG.

2 MIDLAND BRIGADE.H.Q.
51 LEICESTERSHIRE REGT.
52 LEICESTERSHIRE REGT.
1/5 SOUTH STAFFORDSHIRE
REGT. 1919 MAR TO AUG.

3 MIDLAND BRIGADE. H.Q.
1919 MAR TO 1919 AUG.

51 & 53 SHERWOOD FORESTERS
(NOTTINGHAM & DERBY'S RGT)
1919 MAR TO 1919 JULY.

52 SHERWOOD FORESTERS
(NOTTS & DERBYSHIRE REGT)
1917 NOV TO 1919 JULY.

MIDLAND DIVISION(6 DIV)

1 MIDLAND BRIGADE.H.Q.
2/4 DUKE OF WELLINGTONS.
REGT.1919 MAR TO SEPT.

2/4 KINGS OWN YORKSHIRE
LIGHT INFANTRY
5 KINGS OWN YORK'S L'I'
1919 MAR TO 1919 AUG.

2 MIDLAND BRIGADE.H.Q.
51 LEICESTERSHIRE REGT.
52 LEICESTERSHIRE REGT.
1/5 SOUTH STAFFORDSHIRE
REGT. 1919 MAR TO AUG.

3 MIDLAND BRIGADE. H.Q.
1919 MAR TO 1919 AUG.

51 & 53 SHERWOOD FORESTER
(NOTTINGHAM & DERBY'S RG
1919 MAR TO 1919 JULY.

52 SHERWOOD FORESTERS
(NOTTS & DERBYSHIRE REGT)
1917 NOV TO 1919 JULY.

MIDLAND DIVISION(6 DIV)

1 MIDLAND BRIGADE.H.Q.
2/4 DUKE OF WELLINGTONS.
REGT.1919 MAR TO SEPT.

2/4 KINGS OWN YORKSHIRE
LIGHT INFANTRY
5 KINGS OWN YORK'S L'I'
1919 MAR TO 1919 AUG.

2 MIDLAND BRIGADE.H.Q.
51 LEICESTERSHIRE REGT.
52 LEICESTERSHIRE REGT.
1/5 SOUTH STAFFORDSHIRE
REGT. 1919 MAR TO AUG.

3 MIDLAND BRIGADE. H.Q.
1919 MAR TO 1919 AUG.

51 & 53 SHERWOOD FORESTERS
(NOTTINGHAM & DERBY'S RGT)
1919 MAR TO 1919 JULY.

52 SHERWOOD FORESTERS
(NOTTS & DERBYSHIRE REGT)
1917 NOV TO 1919 JULY.

Box 1626

BEF

MIDLAND DIV.

1 MIDLAND BDE H.Q.

1919 MAR to 1919 SEPT

18th

SECRET.

WAR DIARY

Late. 18th Bde

HEADQUARTERS
1st MIDLAND BRIGADE

MARCH.
1919.

DUPLICATE

(392) Wt. W6192/P875 1,500,000 4/18 McA & W Ltd (E 2815) Forms W3091/4. Army Form W.3091.

Cover for Documents.

Nature of Enclosures.

Notes, or Letters written.

Instructions regarding War Diaries and Intelligence Summaries are contained in F. S. Regs., Part II. and the Staff Manual respectively. Title pages will be prepared in manuscript.

WAR DIARY
or
INTELLIGENCE SUMMARY.
(Erase heading not required.)

Army Form C. 2118.

Place	Date	Hour	Summary of Events and Information	Remarks and references to Appendices
LECHENICH	1919 March	6th.	1/5th South Staffordshire Regt arrived from BUSIGNY and went into billets in GYMNICH. It had been originally intended that this Battalion should form part of the new 18th Infantry Brigade as they had been detailed to relieve the 11th Essex Regt.	
			Orders were received on the 6th March for Battalions to be prepared to send away as drafts all officers and men retainable for the New Army of the Rhine, as follows.-	
			Men of the 11th Essex Regt to the 51st Bedfordshire Regt., 34th Division. Men of the 2nd D.L.I. to the 9th D.L.I., 3rd Division and Men of the 1st West Yorkshire Regt to the 1/6th West Yorkshire Regt also in the 3rd Division.	
	"	12th.	Orders received that the Brigade would be reconstituted as follows.;	
			2/4th Duke of Wellington's(West Riding) Regt. 2/4th King's Own Yorkshire Light Infantry. 5th King's Own Yorkshire Light Infantry.	
	"	13th.	The 1st West Yorkshire Regt moved from ERP to DORWEILER.	
	"	14th.	Those men of the 1st West Yorkshire Regt., 2nd D.L.I.., and 11th Essex Regt who were retainable for the Army of the Rhine left by train to join the Battalions in the 34th and 3rd Divisions, as ordered on the 6th March.	
			The 1st West Yorkshire Regt continued demobilisation begun on the 25th February preparatory to reduction to "Cadre" before going home to England to refit for INDIA.	
			The 2nd D.L.I., and the 11th Essex Regt., also carried on with demobilisation with a view to being reduced to "Cadre" strength and sent to England, the first for service at home, and the 11th Essex Regt for disbandment.	

A7092. Wt. W128 9/M1293. 750,000. 1/17. D. D & L. Ltd. Forms/C2118/14.

Army Form C. 2118.

Instructions regarding War Diaries and Intelligence Summaries are contained in F. S. Regs., Part II. and the Staff Manual respectively. Title pages will be prepared in manuscript.

WAR DIARY
or
INTELLIGENCE SUMMARY.

(Erase heading not required.)

Place	Date	Hour	Summary of Events and Information	Remarks and references to Appendices
LECHENICH.	1919. March	14th.	On the 14th March the 1/5th South Staffordshire Regt left the Brigade for KOMMERN and joined the 16th Infantry Brigade.	
			The 5th K.O.Y.L.I. arrived at FRIESHEIM and joined the 18th Infantry Brigade.	
	"	15th.	The 2/4th Duke of Wellington's Regt marched into ERP and joined the 18th Infantry Brigade.	
	"	17th.	Brig-Genl., G.S.G.CRAUFURD C.M.G., C.I.E., D.S.O., A.D.C. relinquished Command of the 18th Infantry Brigade.	
	"	18th.	Brig-Genl., C.W. GWYNN, C.B., C.M.G., D.S.O., assumed Command of the 18th Infantry Brigade.	
	"	22nd.	The 5th K.O.Y.L.I. moved by march route from FRIESHEIM to LIBLAR .	
	"	30th.	Orders were received stating that the Second Army would become an independent Army of Occupation known as the "Army of the Rhine", and that on the 2nd April the Command would pass from Field Marshall Sir DOUGLAS HAIG to the G.O.C., "Army of the Rhine".	
			The 6th Division ceased to exist as such and was known as the Midland Division, and the 18th Infantry Brigade as the 1st Midland Brigade.	

C W Gwynn

Brigadier-General,
Commanding, 1st Midland Brigade.

A7092 Wt. W128.9/M1293 750,000. 1/17. D. D & L. Ltd. Forms/C2118/14.

Army Form C. 2118.

Instructions regarding War Diaries and Intelligence Summaries are contained in F. S. Regs., Part II. and the Staff Manual respectively. Title pages will be prepared in manuscript.

WAR DIARY
or
INTELLIGENCE SUMMARY.

(Erase heading not required.)

Place	Date	Hour	Summary of Events and Information	Remarks and references to Appendices

FIGHTING AND TRENCH STRENGTHS.

	March 1st.				March 8th				March 15th.				March 22nd.				March 29th.			
	Fighting		Trench		Fighting.		Trench.		Bighting.		Trench.		Fighting.		Trench.		Fighting.		Trench.	
	O.	O.R.	O.	O.R	O.	O.R.	O.	O.R	O.	O.R.	O.	O.R.	O.	O.R.	O.	O.R.	O.	O.R.	O.	O.R
1st West York Regt.	36	693	24	425	35	567	25	322	15	282	9	77	14	200	10	117	10	99	9	92
11th Essex Regt.	34	653	21	325	35	627	22	368	17	382	6	207	15	172	10	123	10	147	3	34
2nd D.L.I.	33	750	17	452	31	757	15	449	19	410	7	143	18	319	7	79	13	244	6	59
2/4th K.O.Y.L.I.	-	-	-	-	37	685	82	396	55	1034	40	804	57	1071	42	818	55	1004	42	697
5th K.O.Y.L.I.	-	-	-	-	-	-	-	-	-	-	-	-	57	1150	45	936	54	1122	39	925
2/4th Duke of Wellington's Regt.	-	-	-	-	-	-	-	-	-	-	-	-	34	925	21	461	37	842	19	380
	103	2096	62	1202	138	2576	84	1535	106	2108	62	1231	195	3837	135	2534	179	3458	118	2187

Copy No. 11.

SECRET.

18th Infantry Brigade Order No. 349.

The 2nd D.L.I. will move by march route from LECHENICH to PINGSHEIM on the 26th March, move to be completed by 13.00 hours.

Major,
Brigade Major, 18th Infantry Bde.

25/3/1919.

Copy No. 1 2nd D.L.I.
2 1st West Yorkshire Regt.
3. 11th Essex Regt.
4. Midland Div. "G".
5. Midland Division "Q".
6. No. 4 Co. Train.
7. 18th Field Ambce.
8. 12th Field Co. R.E.
9. Town Major LECHENICH.
10. O.C. Signals.
11. War Diary.
12. File.

SECRET.

Copy No. 11

18th INFANTRY BRIGADE OPERATION ORDER No. 248. 22/3/19

1. In connection with the rearrangement of sub-areas, moves as detailed on the movement table on reverse will be carried out on the 22nd inst.

2. Completion of moves will be reported by wire to Brigade Headquarters.

3. Acknowledge.

[signature]
Major,
Brigade Major, 18th Infantry Bde.

Issued at 19.30 hours.

Copy No. 1. 5th K.O.Y.L.I.
" " 2. 18th Field Co. R.E.
" " 3. 11th Leicestershire Regt.
" " 4. 2nd D.L.I.
" " 5. 24th Bde. R.F.A.
" " 6. 2/4th K.O.Y.L.I.
" " 7. 2/4th Duke of Wellington's Regt.
" " 8. 18th Field Ambulance.
" " 9. No. 4 Co. Train.
" " 10-11. War Diary.
" " 12. File.

MOVEMENT TABLE TO ACCOMPANY 18th INFANTRY BRIGADE OPERATION ORDER No. 348.

Ser. No.	UNIT.	FROM	TO	ROUTE	STARTING POINT.	TIME.
1.	6th Bn.M.G.C.	BRUHL.	KIERDORF, ROGGENDORF, KOTTINGEN.	Via LIBLAR.	At discretion of O.C. Battalion. To be clear of BRUHL by 14.45 hours and not to reach LIBLAR before that time.	
2.	1/5th K.O.Y.L.I.	FRIESHEIM	LIBLAR.	AHREM-LECHENICH.	March at 09.45 hours.	
3.	12th Fld.Coy.	BONN.	LECHENICH.	WEILER-ERP.	Not to enter ERP before 11.15 hours. March to be completed by 13.00 hours.	
4.	1 Coy. 11th Leic.R.	BERZDORF.	LECHENICH.	BRUHL-LIBLAR.	March at 14.15 hours. Follow in rear of Machine Gun Battn.	
5.	43rd Bty.RFA. 110th Bty.RFA.	LIBLAR	FRIESHEIM	LECHENICH-ERP.	Junction of BLESSEM Road and Main Road. Time 09.00 hours.	
6.	112th Bty.RFA.	KOTTINGEN	BONN.	LIBLAR-LECHENICH-ERP-WEILER.	Junction of KOTTINGEN-LIBLAR, LECHENICH-LIBLAR Roads.	14.30 hours
7.	Cadres, 71st Inf.Bde. Battns.		BRUHL	ANY.	Not to enter BRUHL before 10.15 hours.	

30 copies received.

Distributed to 11th Essex
1 W Yorks Regt
2 DLI
18 Fd Amb
12 Fd Co RE

SPECIAL ORDER OF THE DAY.

The 6th Division, as it has been known to England during the great war, is being broken up, the Artillery and Infantry passing to other formations in the Regular Army and the remainder being transferred to the new Midland Division.

Commencing with the victory on the AISNE, the 6th Division, under Major-General Sir JOHN KEIR, K.C.B. took part in the heavy fighting in October 1914 round ARMENTIERES which really formed part of the first battle of YPRES, and which marked the introduction of trench warfare. The Division remained in the vicinity of this town until the second battle of YPRES, when it was brought up to hold that difficult front. During the year spent in FLANDERS the capture of HOOGE by the 16th and 18th Infantry Brigades (the first occasion on which an artillery barrage was used) and a gallant and successful attack of the 1st K.S.L.I. on a position astride the YPRES - LANGEMARCK road were the outstanding features. During this period too, the 71st Infantry Brigade replaced the 17th Infantry Brigade, transferred to 24th Division in October 1915 after the battle of LOOS, and the command changed twice, Major-General Sir WALTER CONGREVE, V.C. K.C.B., M.V.O., succeeding General KEIR, transferred to command of the VI Corps on 27th May 1915, and Major-General C.ROSS, C.B. replacing General CONGREVE on the promotion of the latter to the command of the XIII Corps. From YPRES the 6th Division went to the SOMME, where in September and October 1916 it had very severe fighting at the capture of the QUADRILATERAL near GINCHY, and the actions at LES BOEUFS and GUEUDECOURT, suffering heavy casualties. Then followed a long period of trench warfare in the LOOS - HULLUCH sector, including many brilliant raids and a short period of severe fighting in April at HILL 70, conducted with the greatest determination and gallantry, in aid of larger operations by the Canadian Corps on the immediate South.

On 19th August 1917, the Division came under my command, and the three Infantry Brigades changed commands almost simultaneously, Brigadier-General E. FEETHAM, C.B., C.M.G., Commanding 71st Infantry Brigade being promoted to 39th Division, and Brigadier-Generals R.J.BRIDGFORD, C.B., C.M.G., D.S.O. and W.L.OSBORN, C.M.G., D.S.O. going home for a rest after a long period ~~fighting~~ of service.

The Division first consolidated HILL 70 captured by the Canadians, and then prepared an attack on LENS, which was eventually abandoned in favour of the CAMBRAI offensive, with large numbers of tanks. On 20th November, 1917, the Division attacked and achieved a notable success with light losses, but suffered fairly heavy casualties in holding up the German counter-attack from 30th Nov- 10th Dec.

In this, the 16th Infantry Brigade did splendid work and the 14th D.L.I. made a lasting name at the defence of MARCOING on 3rd December, where also a company of the newly-formed 6th Machine-Gun Battalion greatly distinguished itself.

After a month's partial rest (two Brigades doing short spells in the BULLECOURT Sector) the Division occupied the trench system East of BAPAUME being reduced by the loss of the 9th Suffolk Regt., 8th Bedford Regt. and the 14th D.L.I. to 10 Battalions. On March 21st and 22nd, 1918, the Division on a widely extended front of which LAGNICOURT was the centre, sustained the full brunt of the German offensive, losing very heavily, but holding up the attack till reinforcements could arrive. Then followed five months of prolonged strain in the YPRES - KEMMEL Sector, during which the Division fought alongside the French, trained several battalions of the 27th American Division and built up from its reserves and partly trained men

/ a hardened ....

a hardened force for the final Allied counter-attack. Notable during this time was the detachment of the 71st Infantry Brigade to stem the German advance near NEUVE EGLISE in May, 1918, where the 9th Norfolk Regt. especially suffered heavy casualties; the successful attack of the 11th Essex Regt. on 28th May to restore the broken line of the French on our right flank; the brilliant capture of RIDGE WOOD and ELZENWALLE by the 1st West Yorkshire Regt. and the 2nd D.L.I. on 14th July, and the gallant daylight raid of the 1st BUFFS a little later.

About 1st September, 1918, the Division was moved South to the SOMME and by 14th September came into the line at HOLNON WOOD near ST. QUENTIN, where it commenced the almost continuous two and a half months' fighting, which practically coincided with the cessation of hostilities. From 14th September-8th October, the Division held the post of honour of right of the British offensive. The preliminary operations in HOLNON WOOD were marked by the success of the 18th Infantry Brigade. On 18th and 19th September, the 16th and 71st Infantry Brigades under most adverse conditions attacked the immensely strong positions which dominated ST QUENTIN and suffered very heavy losses, but behaving with the greatest gallantry got their claws firmly embedded in the enemy defensive system which finally yielded to the tenacious fighting of the 16th and 18th Infantry Brigades (with 1st Leicester Regt.) on 24th and 25th September.

On 8th October, the 16th and 71st Infantry Brigades captured the defensive positions East of the HINDENBURG LINE, of which MANNEQUIN HILL and DOON MILL were the tactical points, fighting on this occasion between the French on the right and the 30th American Division on the left. The 1st West Yorkshire Regt. especially distinguished themselves by the capture by a bombing attack after prolonged fighting of MANNEQUIN and CERISE WOODS on the right flank. The advance on and fall of BOHAIN on 9th October, the battle of VAUX ANDIGNY on 17th October and the final battle of ORS RIDGE on 24th October completed a series of operations of which any division might justly be proud.

Throughout the war the Division has had the tremendous advantage of an artillery second to none in the British Army, and which has on all occasions, notably on 21st and 22nd March, 1918, most notably upheld the glorious traditions of the Royal Regiment.

The Division has also been fortunate in its R.E. and Pioneers, both of which took and active and important part in opposing the great German offensive, where also the newly-formed Machine Gun Battalion proved its worth. Both Medium and Light Trench Mortar Batteries - the latter especially - have done common service. The Medical Services have been pre-eminent in their care of the wounded and have paid a heavy toll during the past year in officers and other ranks. The R.A.S.C. have done splendid work both with horse and motor transport; the R.A.V.C. have worked hard and successfully and the Chaplains have set an example of self-sacrifice and gallantry worthy of their high calling.

It is hoped to publish later a short history of the part played by the 6th Division in the great war, but owing to the many changes of command it will necessarily take some time. Information as to its publication will be given in the leading London, Midland and Yorkshire papers.

In saying good-bye to the 6th Division, which it has been my privilege and fortune to command for the past one and a half years, I wish to thank particularly Brigadier-Generals E.F. DELAFORCE, C.M.G., Commanding Royal Artillery, G.S.G. CRAUFURD, C.M.G., C.I.E., D.S.O., A.D.C., Commanding 18th Infantry Brigade, H.A. WALKER, C.M.G., D.S.O. late Commanding 16th Infantry Brigade, and P.W. BROWN, C.M.G., D.S.O. Commanding 71st

/ Infantry Brigade..

Infantry Brigade for their most loyal help, advice and support in all the difficult situations which have arisen during the fifteen months' fighting, and to all the Commanding Officers, especially Lt. Cols. W.H.F. WEBER, C.M.G., D.S.O., Commanding 2nd Brigade, R.F.A., J.A.C. FORSYTH, C.M.G., D.S.O., Commanding 24th Brigade, R.F.A., R.E. POWER, D.S.O., Commanding 1st The Buffs, D.L. WEIR, D.S.O., M.C., Commanding 1st West Yorkshire Regt., F.LATHAM, D.S.O., Commanding 1st Leicestershire Regt., C.H. DUMBELL, D.SO., Commanding 11th Essex Regt., H.M.MILWARD, D.S.O., Commanding 2nd Sherwood Foresters and J.B. ROSHER, D.S.O. M.C., Commanding 14th D.L.I. and 6th Machine Gun Battalion.

My thanks are further due to the Staff and Heads of Departments, especially Lt. Cols. TT. GROVE, C.M.G., D.S.O., G.S.O. I, P. HUDSON, D.S.O., late A.A. & Q.M.G., G. GOLDNEY, C.M.G., D.S.O., late C.R.E. and Colonel H.W. GRATTAN, C.M.G., D.S.O., late A.D.M.S., whose untiring devotion to duty and ready resource have overcome all obstacles and rendered sucessful the planning of the many operations undertaken by the Division.

Few of the original members of the 6th Division now remain with it, but I am sure that all those who, like myself, have been associated with the Division for any length of time, will always cherish proud and happy memories of the time spent with it.

The 6th Division have never gone to a new command without a hearty welcome, nor left a command without an expression of thanks for services rendered and of regret that it was being transferred.

I wish all ranks the best of luck in whatever fate may have for them in the future.

T. Marden.

Major-General,
Commanding 6th Division.

18th March, 1919.

(6392) Wt. W6192/P875 1,500,000 4/18 McA & W Ltd (E 2815) Forms W3091/4. Army Form W.3091.

Cover for Documents.

CONFIDENTIAL

Nature of Enclosures.

WAR DIARIES

FOR

MONTH OF APRIL /19

1ST. MIDLAND BRIGADE.

Notes, or Letters written.

Instructions regarding War Diaries and Intelligence Summaries are contained in F. S. Regs., Part II. and the Staff Manual respectively. Title pages will be prepared in manuscript.

WAR DIARY
or
~~INTELLIGENCE SUMMARY.~~
(Erase heading not required.)

Army Form C. 2118.

Place	Date	Hour	Summary of Events and Information	Remarks and references to Appendices
LECHENICH.	APRIL 7th.		The 52nd K.O.Y.L.I. joined the Brigade and were absorbed in the 2/4th K.O.Y.L.I.	
	8th.		Capt. T.O.M.Buchan, M.C."The Queen's (R.W.S.) Regt. assumed the duties of Brigade Major vice Bt. Major H.C.E.Hull, who departed to England.	
	9th.		IXth Corps Commander inspected 2/4th Duke of Wellington's Regt.	
	10th.		Capt. J.C.O.Marriott, D.S.O..M.C. (Northamptonshire Regt) joined the Brigade as Steff Captain.	
	11th.		IXth Corps Commander inspected the 5th K.O.Y.L.I.and 2/4th K.O.Y.L.I.	
	12th.		53rd Duke of Wellington's Regt. arrived and were absorbed into 2/4th Duke of Wellingtons Regt.	
	16th.		Col. S. Francis D.SO. arrived and assumed command of the 2/4th Duke of Wellington's Regt.	
	17th.		Lt-Col H.E.Trevor C.M.G..D.S.O., arrived and assumed command of the 5th K.O.Y.L.I.	
	30th.		Drafts from the 2/4th K.O.Y.L.I. and 2/4th Duke of Wellington's Regt., were dispatched to join the 51st, 52nd, & 53rd. Battalions Sherwood Foresters. Permission has not yet been received to strike them off strength.	
			Lieut-Col C.A.Chaytor D.S.O. was appointed to command the 2/4th K.O.Y.L.I.	

Army Form C. 2118.

WAR DIARY

or

~~INTELLIGENCE SUMMARY.~~

(Erase heading not required.)

Instructions regarding War Diaries and Intelligence Summaries are contained in F. S. Regs., Part II. and the Staff Manual respectively. Title pages will be prepared in manuscript.

Place	Date	Hour	Summary of Events and Information	Remarks and references to Appendices
LECHENICH.			The month has been principally spent in re-organising battalions, after their absorbtion of Battalions coming out from England. This re-organisation is now practically complete. The training has consisted of simple Platoon Training in Steady Drill, Handling arms and Musketry. The 5th K.O.Y.L.I. are somewhat in advance of the other two Battalions in Training , owing to the fact that they absorbed their re-inforcing Battalion some time ago.	
			The attitude of the inhabitants remains un-changed, and there do not appear to be any signs of trouble.	

Cond. 1st Midland Brig
6.5.19

SECRET

WAR DIARY

HEADQUARTERS
1ST MIDLAND BRIGADE

MAY

1919

ORIGINAL.

(6392) Wt. W6192/P875 1,500,000 4/18 McA & W Ltd (E 2815) Forms W3091/4. Army Form W.3091.

Cover for Documents.

Nature of Enclosures.

Notes, or Letters written.

Army Form C. 2118.

Instructions regarding War Diaries and Intelligence Summaries are contained in F. S. Regs., Part II. and the Staff Manual respectively. Title pages will be prepared in manuscript.

WAR DIARY

or

~~INTELLIGENCE SUMMARY.~~

(Erase heading not required.)

Place	Date	Hour	Summary of Events and Information	Remarks and references to Appendices
LECHENICH.	1919.			
	May 13th.		Captain J.C.O.MARRIOTT D.S.O., M.C., Staff Captain left for ENGLAND.	
	May 21st. to May 31st.		On May 21st Warning received from Midland Division that the Brigade might have to move at short notice to the DUREN Area on May 23rd or on any day afterward. Brigade Warning Orders No. 1 and No. 2 were issued. Later, further orders were received to the effect that if the Germans did not sign the Peace Terms the Allied Armies would advance. The day on which they would advance would be known as "J" day, and on that day all moves of the Brigade would be completed.	See App. 1 See App.11. See App.111 See App. IV
	May 23rd.		Brigade Commander returned from leave, having been recalled.	
	May 24th.		Brevet.Major W.H. RAMSBOTTOM , West Yorkshire Regt., joined the Brigade to take up appointment as Staff Captain.	

[signature]

Brig-Genl.,
Commanding, 1st Midland Brigade.

A7092 Wt. W128.9/M1293 750,000. 1/17. D. D & L. Ltd. Forms/C2118/14.

Army Form C. 2118.

Instructions regarding War Diaries and Intelligence Summaries are contained in F. S. Regs., Part II. and the Staff Manual respectively. Title pages will be prepared in manuscript.

WAR DIARY
or
INTELLIGENCE SUMMARY.
(Erase heading not required.)

Place	Date	Hour	Summary of Events and Information	Remarks and references to Appendices

FIGHTING AND TRENCH STRENGTHS.

	May 3rd.				May 10th.				May 17th.				May 24th.				May 31st.			
	Fighting.		Trench.		Fighting.		Trench.		Fighting		Trench.		Fighting.		Trench.		Fighting.		Trench.	
	Off.	O.Rs	Off.	ORs.	Off.	ORs.	Off.	ORs.	Off.	ORs.	Off.	ORs	Off.	ORs.	Off.	ORs	Off.	ORs.	Off.	ORs.
2/4th Duke of Wellington's	59	1172	47	688	57	1174	44	641	56	1158	42	601	55	1167	42	518	52	1174	39	507.
2/4th K.O.Y.L.I.	73	1409	58	709	70	1391	55	677	67	1373	52	646	66	1350	51	592	65	1328	50	537.
5th K.O.Y.L.I.	45	999	30	763	46	1001	33	728	44	1009	31	708	45	1006	33	651	45	1001	35	600.
1st Mid.Bde L.TMB.	4	39	4	39	4	38	4	38	4	38	4	38	4	38	4	38	4	42	4	42.
Total.	181	3619	139	2199	177	3604	136	2084	171	3578	129	1993	171	3561	130	1799	166	3545	128	1686.

A7092. Wt. W128 9/M1293. 750,000. 1/17. D. D & L. Ltd. Forms/C2118/14.

SECRET. Appendix 1. B.M.S.19.
Copy. No. 5.

1st MIDLAND BRIGADE WARNING ORDER No. 1.

-*-*-*-*-*-*-*-*-*-*-*-*-*-

1. The Brigade will be prepared to move at short notice on or after May. 23rd.

2. Battalions will be prepared to move to the followinf areas.

2/4th Duke of Wellington's Regt.	MERZENICH.
5th. K.O.Y.L.I.	VETTWEISS.
2/4th K.O.Y.L.I.	GOLZHEIM.
1st Mid.Bde. T.M.B.	BINSFELD.

3. (a). Battalions will arrange to reconnoitre the above villages and the routes leading to the villages on May 22nd.

(b). Reconnoitring Parties will meet the Staff Captain at PINGSHEIM at 16.00 hours on May 22nd, after completion of their reconnaissance in order to report the results.

(c). O.C. T.M.B., will detail one officer to accompany the Staff Captain, reporting at Brigade Headquarters at 08.00 hours.

4. In the event of the move taking place Brigade Classes will accompany the Brigade Headquarters. The Brigade Picquet will rejoin their Battalion on the march.

5. Battalions would march in full marching order. There would probably be a halt half way. Halting places should be reconnoitred.

6. Further details and arrangements for transport of surplus kit and T.M.B., will be issued later.

Blankets will NOT be carried on the men.

T. [signature]

ACKNOWLEDGE.

Captain,
Brigade Major, 1st Midland Brigade.

21st.May 1919.

Distribution. Copy No. 1. 2/4th Duke of Wellington's Regt.
2. 2/4th K.O.Y.L.I.
3. 5th K.O.Y.L.I .
4. 1st Mid.Bde.T.M.B.
5. War Diary.
6. War Diary.
7. File.
8.
9.

Appendix 11.

SECRET.

B.M.S. 20.
Copy. No 3

1st MIDLAND BRIGADE WARNING ORDER No. 2.

1. The 1st Midland Brigade with 93rd Field Co. R.E., and 18th Field Ambulance attached will be prepared to move to the neighbourhood of DUREN on May 23rd or any following day.

2. Billetting Areas are being reconnoitred tomorrow and will be notified later.

ACKNOWLEDGE.

T. O. M. Bache [signature]

Captain,
Brigade Major, 1st Midland Brigade.

21/5/19.

Distribution.
Copy No. 1. 93rd Field Co. R.E.
Copy No. 2. 18th Field Ambulance.
Copy No. 3. War Diary.
Copy No. 4. War Diary.
Copy No. 5. File.

B M S 23

Appendix 111.

16

SECRET 1st Midland Brigade Warning Order no. 3.

Copy no.

1. The First Midland Brigade Group may be required to move on/or any day after May 24th to the LINSFELD-GOLZHEIM-DUREN area, with the object of guarding the communications by road and railway along the DUREN-COLOGNE line.

The composition of the Brigade Group is shown on the attached table

2. The day by which all moves are to be completed will be known as J day.

The day before J day will be J-1 day.
Two days " " " J-2 day.
Three days " " " " J-3 day.

The earliest date which could be J-13 day is May 23rd.
The date of J day will be notified later.

3. Units would probably move to the areas shown on the attached table.

4. Units would move in Full Marching Order: caps to be worn & steel helmets carried. The march would commence about 0730 with a halt during the heat of the day, from about 0930 to 1600.

Mobile reserves to be complete.

120 rounds S.A.A. to be carried on the man.

5. Units will be prepared to take over guards on Roads Railways etc. The detail of these guards will be notified later.

6. Division have asked for three Lorries per Battalion. All Kit and Stores which would have to be left behind will be collected at one central Dump in the Battalion Area and an adequate guard be left to protect them. As far as possible, Units should commence forthwith to collect these Stores at the Central Dump.

T.D.M. Buchan

Captain,

22/5/1919 Brigade Major 1st Midl. Bde.

****

Issued at 1600 hours.

Distribution:- Copy no 1. 2/4th Duke of Wellingtons Regt.
2. 2/4th Bn. K.O.Y.L.I.
3. 5th Bn. K.O.Y.L.I.
4. 1st Mid Bde T.M.B.
5. Bde Education Officer.
6. Staff Captain,
7. Civil Staff Office
8. 18th Field Ambce.
9. 93rd Field Coy R.E.
10. 6th Bn. M.G.Corps.
11. C.R.A.
12. C.R.E.
13. A.D.M.S.
14. Midland Division "G".
15. Midland Division "Q".
16. War Diary.
17. War Diary.

Please acknowledge

Table to accompany 1st Midland Brigade Warning Order No. 3.

UNIT.	Moves To.	Day.	REMARKS.
2/4th D. of W's. Regt.	MERZENICH.	J-2	
5th Bn. K.O.Y.L.I.	VETTWEISS.	J-1	
2/4th K.O.Y.L.I.	GOLZHEIM.	J-2	
Bde H.Qs Bde Schools T.M.Bty.	DUREN	J-2	
93rd Field CoyR.E. 18th Fld Ambce.	FRAUVILLERSHEIM	J-2	
1 Coy. 6th M.G.Bn.	BUIR.	J-2	Comes under orders of G.O.C. 1st Midland Bde on arrival
= 1 Bty. R.F.A.	Binsfeld.	J-2	-do- -do-
No. 4 Coy Divnl Train (Proportion)	FRAUVILLERSHEIM	J-2	Are under orders of Midland Divn.

Brigade Picquet will rejoin Battalion on the march.

SECRET.
****

In continuation of
1st. Midland Brigade Warning Order No.3.

B.M.S.25.

Copy No. 12

7. Lorries will be allotted as under :-

Brigade H.Qrs..............2½ Lorries. (to include T.M.B.)
Infantry Battalions.......3 " each.
93rd Field Coy............1 "
18th. Field Ambulance.....1 "
No.4 Coy. Div.Train.......1. "

8. Reference para 6, each Battalion will leave a guard of One Officer, 2 N.C.O's and 9 men to guard their surplus Kit dump. Smaller Units will leave guards in proportion. All guatds will be issued with three full days rations.

As soon as possible after receiving orders to move, Units will wire Brigade Headquarters the amount of Tonage of Stores left in their dump, to enable arrangements to be made to clear these dumps as early as possible.

9. Two G.S. Limbers from the D.A.C. will report at Brigade Headquarters to-day for the carriage of L.T.M. Guns and Ammunition.

10. No.4. Coy Divisional Train will march under orders of the Brigade. Sufficient supply wagons will be attached to this Company to carry rations for the Artillery Battery affiliated to this Brigade.

11. The normal system of supplies will br taken into use the day moves commence The new refilling point will notified later.

12. D.A.D.O.S. will probably move to DUREN.

13. Divisional Canteen and Divisional Hostel Cologne, will remain in their present locations.

14. The Civil Staff Captain of the 2nd. Midland Brigade will be attached to 1st. Midland Brigade and will accompany the Brigade to the new area. The present Civil Staff Captain of the 1st Brigade will remain to hand over to the 3rd. Brigade.

The P.R.O. will accompany the Brigade to its new area.

15. Immediately on receipt of orders to move, all Units will forward their copy of the Brigade Defence Scheme and all copies of Battalion Defence Schemes to Brigade Headquarters.

T.Chas. Buchanan
Captain.
Brigade Major.1st. Midland Brigade.

23.5.1919.

Distribution.:- Copy
1. 2/4th.D.of W.Regt.
2. 2/4th.K.O.Y.L.I.
3. 5th.K.O.Y.L.I.
4. 1st.Mid.Bde.T.M.B.
5. B.E.O.
6. Civil Staff Office.
7. 18th. F. Ambulance.
8. 93rd.Field Coy.
9. No.4.Coy Train.
10. Mid.Division G.
11. Mid.Division Q.
12. War Diary.
13. War Diary.
14. File.

SECRET.
****

1st. Midland Brigade Warning Order No.3.
(Continued)

B.M.S.No.29.

Copy No 16

16. Reference para 3, cancel the table already issued and substitute the attached Table B.

17. Reference para 8, the guard to be left behind on surplus kit, will not be less than 1 platoon per Battalion, and in proportion in the case of smaller Units.

18. In notifying "J" day by telegram, the following code will be used.

25th. May..........A.
26th May..........B.
27th May..........C.
28th May..........D.
29th May..........E.
30th May..........F.
31st May..........G.
1st. June..........H.
2nd June..........I.
3rd June..........J.
etc.,

Thus, if "J" day were to be on June 1st, the following telegram would be sent in clear to all concerned.

"Reference Midland Division Order No.5 dated 2rth May,AAA
J day will be H.AAA"

19. Units of the 3rd Midland Brigade Group will be moved into them present Brigade area as under.:-

1 Battalion..........LIBLAR....on.....J - 1 day.
1 Battalion..........LECHENICH...on....J - 1 day.
D.Coy. 8th.Batt
M.G.C...............GYMNICH....on.....J - 1 day.

20. Units will be prepared to take over guards in the new area as under:-

2/4th. Bn.Duke of Wellingtons Regt......Railway Guard North of MERZENICH..........14 Other Ranks.

2/4th. Bn. K.O.Y.L.I........Guards on Bridges...BUIR to MERZENICH.........17 Other Ranks.

PLEASE ACKNOWLEDGE.
****

[signature]
Captain.
Brigade Major.1st. Midland Bde.

25/5/1919.

Copy No.1 2/4th. D. of W. Regt.
3. 5th. K.O.Y.L.I.
5. Bde.Education Officer.
7. 18th.Field Ambulance.
9. 8th.Batt.M.G.Corp.
11. C.R.E.
13. Midland Div.G.
15. No.4.Coy Train.
17. War Diary.

Copy No. 2 2/4th.K.O.Y.L.I.
4 1st. Mid.Bde.T.M.B.
6 Civil Staff Office.
8 93rd.Field Coy.R.E.
10 C.R.A.
12 A.D.M.S.
14 Midland Div.Q.
16. War Diary
18. Office.

TABLE "B"
****

Table to accompany 1st. Midland Brigade Warning Order No 3.

UNIT.	MOVES TO.	DAY.	REMARKS.
2/4th. D.of W's Regt.	MERZENICH.	J-2	
5th. Bn.K.O.Y.L.I..	VETTWEISS.	J-1.	
2/4th.BN.K.O.Y.L.I.	BUIR.	J-2.	
Bde.H.Qrs.	DUREN		
Bde.Schools. } T.M.Bty. }	GIRBELSRATH.	J-2.	
[illegible] Field Coy.R.E. [illegible] Field Ambul.	FRAUVILLERSHEIM	J-1.	
C. Coy. 8th.Btn.M.G.C.	GOLZHEIM.	J-1.	Comes under Orders of G.O.C. 1st.Mid.Bde on arrival.
= 1 Baty. R.F.A.	NIEDEREAU.	J-1.	do. do.
No.4. Coy Divnl Train. (Proportion)	ESCHWEILER.	J-2	

1st. Midland Brigade Warning Order No.3.
(Continued.)
****

B.M.S. No.30.

COPY No. ________

Reference 1st. Midland Brigade Warming Order No.3. issued under this office B.M.S.29. dated 25th May 1919, delete last sentence of para 18 and substitute the following.:-

"Reference 1st. Midland Brigade Warning Order No.3 dated 22/5/19 AA J day will be M ".

[signature]

Captain.
Brigade Major. 1st. Midland Brigade.

26.5.1919.

Issued to all recipients of 1st. Midland Brigade Warning Order No.3.

Appendix IV.

S E C R E T. 1st Midland Brigade Warning Order No.4. B/M.S.No. 35

Copy No. 21

1. 1st Midland Brigade Warning Order No. 3 is cancelled, and will be destroyed, the following substituted in its place.

2. If the Peace negotiations fail, notice of the Termination of the Armistice in 72 hours will be given to the Germans. The day on which the Armistice ceases will be called "J" day.

3. In this event the First Midland Brigade Group will be required to move to the Area East of DUREN with the object of guarding the communications by road and railway along the DUREN - COLOGNE Line.

4. Moves would therefore take place in accordance with the attached Table "A".

5. "J" Day will be notified by wire, the following code being used.-

28th May.	"D"
29th May.	"E"
30th May.	"F"
31st May.	"G"
1st June.	"H"
2nd June.	"I"
3rd June.	"J"

Thus if "J" Day were to be on June 1st the following telegram would be sent in clear to all concerned.-

"Reference 1st Midland Brigade Warning Order No. 4 dated 28th May AAA "J" Day will be "H" AAA ".

6. Units would move in full marching order, caps to be worn, steel helmets carried.

Mobile Reserves to be complete, 120 rounds S.A.A. to be carried on the man.

All bodies of troops on the march will be preceded by a small advanced guard.

Any transport moving independently from its Unit will be accompanied by an escort.

7. (a) Lorries for carriage of stores will be allotted on the following scale.-

Brigade H.Q's and T.M.B.	2 lorries.	
Infantry Bns.	3 "	each.
93rd Field Co. R.E.	1 lorry.	
18th Field Ambce.	1 "	
No. 4 Co. Divnl.Train.	1 "	

(b). Lorries will probably be able to do double journeys.

(c). Surplus kit which has to be left behind will be collected at one Central Store in Battalion Areas. Battalions must leave an adequate guard for the defence of this kit. In no case should the guard be less than one platoon.

18th Field Ambulance, No. 4 Coy. Train, and all Units in LECHENICH will concentrate their surplus kit in the Store at LECHENICH.

One storeman per Unit will be left with this kit. A guard will be arranged by Brigade Headquarters.

(d). All guards will be issued with three full days rations.

(e). As soon as possible after receiving orders to move, Units will wire Brigade Headquarters the Tonnage of Stores left in their Dumps, to enable arrangements to be made to clear these Dumps.

8. No. 4 Coy. Divnl. Train will march under orders of the Brigade. Sufficient supply wagons will be attached to this Company to carry rations for the Artillery Battery affiliated to the Brigade.

9. Immediately on receipt of orders to move, all Units will forward their copy of the Brigade Defence Scheme, and all copies of their own Defence Schemes to Brigade Headquarters.

10. (a). Guards in the new Area will be taken over as under.-

2/4th Bn.Duke of Wellington's Regt.	Railway Guard North of MERZENICH. One platoon.
2/4th K.O.Y.L.I.	Guards on Bridges. BUIR to MERZENICH. One platoon.

Details of taking over these Guards will be notified later.

(b). In addition to the above Guards the O's.C., 2/4th Duke of Wellington's Regt., and 2/4th K.O.Y.L.I., will be responsible for ensuring that the DUREN - COLOGNE Railway is adequately protected within the following limits.-

2/4th Duke of Wellington's Regt.- from Junction of Railways N.E. of DUREN to point 126 S.W. of LAMBERTSHOF.

2/4th K.O.Y.L.I.- from point 126 to the point where the MANHEIM - BLATZHEIM track crosses the Railway.

(c). Immediately on arrival in New Area Battalions will prepare preliminary Defence Schemes on similar lines to the Defence Scheme for this Area.

11. (a). The Civil Staff Captain of the 2nd Midland Brigade will accompany 1st Midland Brigade to the New Area.

(b). G.O.C., 1st Midland Brigade will administer 1st and 3rd Highland Brigade Areas. G.O.C., 3rd Midland Brigade will administer the present 1st Midland Brigade Area.

(c). The P.R.O., will accompany 1st Midland Brigade.

F.W. Buckan

ACKNOWLEDGE.

Captain,
Brigade Major, 1st Midland Brigade.

28/5/1919.

Distribution.

Copy No. 1. 2/4th Duke of Wellington's Regt.
2. 2/4th K.O.Y.L.I.
3. 5th K.O.Y.L.I.
4. 1st Midland Brigade T.M.B.
5. Brigade Education Officer.
6. Civil Staff Captain.
7. 18th Field Ambce.
8. 93rd Field Co. R.E.
9. 8th Bn. M.G.Corps.
10. 6th Bn. M.G.Corps.
11. C. R. A.
12. C. R. E.
13. A.D.M.S.
14. Midland Division "G".
15. Midland Division "Q".
16. 3rd Mid. Bde.
17. 2nd Mid. Bde.
18. 1st Highland Bde.
19. 3rd Highland Bde.
20. No. 4 Coy. Train.
21. War Diary.
22. War Diary.
23. Office.

TABLE "A" TO ACCOMPANY 1st MIDLAND BRIGADE WARNING ORDER No. 4.

UNIT.	MOVES TO.	DAY.	REPLACED BY	
2/4th D.of W. Regt.	MERZENICH.	J-2.	Nil.	Not to enter MERZENICH before 17.00 hours. Time of starting to be arranged by O.C. Unit.
5th Bn. K.O.Y.L.I.	VETTWEISS	J-1.	53rd Sherwood Foresters on J-1 day.	Time of starting to be arranged by O.C. 5th K.O.Y.L.I. Incoming Battalion will arrive LIBLAR about 10.00 hours.
2/4th Bn. K.O.Y.L.I..	BUIR.	J.	"D" Coy. 6th Bn. M.G.C.	Time of starting to be arranged by O.C. 2/4th K.O.Y.L.I..
Bde.H.Q's.	DUREN.	J-2.	3rd Mid.Bde.H.Q's. 51st Sherwood Foresters.	March under Orders of B.E.O. March off from Village Square 08.00 hours.
Bde.Classes. 1st Mid.Bde.TMB }	BINSFELD.			
93rd Field Co. R.E.	FRAUVILLERSHEIM	J-1.	- do -	March off at 07.30 , under orders of O.C., Coy.
H.Q's Section. 18th Fd.Ambce.	- do -	J-1.	1st Section. 18th Fd.Ambce.	March under orders of O.C., 5th K.O.Y.L.I. who will provide protection.
No.4 Coy. Divnl. Train.	ESCHWEILER.	J-2.	No.3 Co.Train.	March off at 07.30 and join Brigade H.Q's in LECHENICH.
Battery R.F.A.	NEIDERAU.	J-1.		Comes under orders of G.O.C., 1st Midland Brigade who is also responsible for rationing and administration.
"C" Coy. Bn. M.G.C.	KELZ.	J-1.		- do - - do - - do - - do -.

18th Field Ambulance.
6th Bn. M.G.C.

Reference 1st Midland Brigade Warning Order No. 4 attached

Please note that it may be necessary for the 18th Field Ambulance to proceed to KELZ in addition to "C" Coy. 6th Bn. M.G.C.

18th Field Ambulance will consequently reconnoitre KELZ as well as FRAUVILLERSHEIM.

Tom Buchan

Captain,
Brigade Major, 1st Midland Brigade.

28/5/1919.

SECRET.

Copy No.........10

1st. Midland Brigade.

-*-*-*-*-*-*-*-*-*-*-

ADMINISTRATIVE INSTRUCTION No.1 ISSUED IN CONNECTION WITH SECRET ORDER No. 4 B.M.S. No. 35.

---

1. AMMUNITION

(a) DUMPS. R.E. Ammunition, S.A.A., Grenades, etc., are established at :-

VO CHEM
LONGERICH.

(b) All Units will move ~~full~~. with full echelon.

(c) Units will demand by wire on Brigade to reach Headquarters by 12-00 hours daily.

2. SUPPLIES

On receipt of the warning telegram notifying "J" day

(1) Every Officers and man will immediately be issued with an Iron Ration.

(11) RAILHEAD will move to Duren.

(111) REFILLING POINT - FRAUIERLLERSHEIM.

(1v) Petrol Tins will be made up to normal establishment forthwith Indents if not already sent in, to be forwarded at once to Headquarters.

(V) WATER CARTS Each Battalion will be issued with an additional Water Cart on demand., if required.

3. TRAFFIC CONTROL

Whenever weather permits, cross country tracks will be used by Horse Transport and Infantry. All Units will take steps to ensure that when halted, columns are clear of the road, and transport halted as close to the near side of the road as possible.

4. RETURN "A" CASUALTIES. Battalions which have suffered 50 casualties or more, will wire approximate casualties to Brigade H.Q., by 15-00 hours daily. If at least 50 more casualties have occured in the Battalion during the night, a fresh wire will be sent next morning. Casualties will be reported by phases, commencement of the phase will be notified by Brigade H.Q. Daily Casualty wire will include numbers already reported since the commencement of the phase, and will begin with the following words " Estimated Casualties from (here insert date of commencement of phase")

RETURN "B"

An accurate statement will be sent in giving the rank, initial and name of Officers and date of officers'casualty . Also the number of other ranks as soon as the information is obtainable.

5. MEDICAL ARRANGEMENTS. The Division will vacate to No.11 Station Hospital, DUREN, and No. 42 Station Hospital, EUSKIRCHEN. Reserve of Drugs, Dressings, etc., at SERUM obtained from No. 13 Base Medical Stores, ZUINNER STRASSE (near UBER RING) COLOGNE. 1000 Stretchers and 2000 blankets are held in reserve at 47 N.A.C., NORD HOTEL, EUSKIRCHEN, for issue if required.

6. PRISONERS OF WAR CAGE Divisional Cage at KREUZAU. exact site will be notified later.

7. MECHANICAL TRANSPORT

Demands for Lorries must reach these Headquarters by 12-00 hours daily.

8. ACKNOWLEDGE.

W H Ranshall [signature]
Major.
Staff Captain 1st. Midland Brigade.

29/5/1919.

Copies to :-

No. 1. 2/4th. Duke of Wellington's Regt.
2. 2/4th. Bn. K.O.Y.L.I.
3. 5th. Bn. K.O.Y.L.I.
4. 1st. Midland Bde.L.T.M.Battery.
5. Brigade Education Officer.
6. Civil Staff Captain.
7. 12th. Field Ambulance.
8. 93rd. Field Company, R.E.
9. No. 4. Coy.Midland Divisional Train.
10. War Diary.
11. War Diary.
12. File.

SECRET

WAR DIARY

HEADQUARTERS : —

1st MIDLAND BRIGADE

JUNE

1919

ORIGINAL —

(6392) Wt. W6192/P875 1,500,000 4/18 McA & W Ltd (E 2815) Forms W3091/4. Army Form W.3091.

Cover for Documents.

Nature of Enclosures.

Notes, or Letters written.

Army Form C. 2118.

Instructions regarding War Diaries and Intelligence Summaries are contained in F. S. Regs., Part II. and the Staff Manual respectively. Title pages will be prepared in manuscript.

WAR DIARY
or
INTELLIGENCE SUMMARY.
(Erase heading not required.)

Place	Date	Hour	Summary of Events and Information	Remarks and references to Appendices
1919.	June 3rd.		Verbal orders were received from the Division for one Battalion to move to BRUHL on June 9th and one Battalion to Musketry on June 6th. These orders were confirmed later by Midland Division Order No. 6. Battalions were warned of above moves by phone and 2/4th Duke of Wellingtons Regt were warned that they would move to GYMNICH on June 6th.	
	June 5th		Brigade Order No 5 relating to the above moves issued.	See appendix I
	June 6th		2/4th K.O.Y.L.I. moved to WEILERSWIST Camp and 2/4th Duke of Wellingtons Regt. to GYMNICH with one Company at KIERDORF. 1st Midland Brigade Defence Scheme No. 2 issued.	
	June 8th		1 Company 5th K.O.Y.L.I. moved to BRUHL to take over the guard on the Army Ammunition Dump at VOCHEM.	See appendix II
			5th K.O.Y.L.I. less one Company left in LIBLAR moved to BRUHL.	
	June 16th		Amendment No 1 to Brigade Order No. 4 was issued relating to the moves of the Brigade in the event of the Germans not carrying out the Peace Terms.	See appendix III
DUREN.	June 18th to June 20th		Moves were carried out to the DUREN Area in accordance with appendix III. The Brigade was responsible for guarding the DUREN–COLOGNE Railway and for controlling the Brigade area in the event of Civil disturbances. All orders on this subject are shown in 1st Midland Brigade Defence Scheme No 3.	See appendix

(A7092). Wt W12839/M1293. 75,0 0. 1/17. D. D. & L., Ltd. Forms/C.2118/14.

Instructions regarding War Diaries and Intelligence Summaries are contained in F. S. Regs., Part II. and the Staff Manual respectively. Title pages will be prepared in manuscript.

WAR DIARY
or
INTELLIGENCE SUMMARY.
(Erase heading not required.)

Army Form C. 2118.

Place	Date	Hour	Summary of Events and Information	Remarks and references to Appendices
DUREN.	June 23rd		Orders were received from the Division to the effect that if Peace was signed, the Brigade would return to its original area. The first day of the moves back would be known as "A" day.	
	June 24th		1st Midland Brigade Order No. 6. giving instructions to this effect was issued.	See appendix V
	June 28th		Notification was received that Peace had been signed and that Monday June 30th would be "A" day i.e. the first day of the moves back to the original Brigade area.	See appendix VI
	June 30th		2/4th K.O.Y.L.I. moved to GYMNICH. and 18th Field Ambulance to BLESSEM. "C" Coy. 6th Bn M.G.C. moved to MERZENICH and returned to the command of the M.G. Battalion.	
			General Review of the Month	
			With the move of the 2/4th K.O.Y.L.I. to WEILERSWIST and the 2/4th Duke of Wellingtons Regt to GYMNICH, the period of Musketry and Company Training for these two Battalions commenced. The 5th K.O.Y.L.I who moved to BRUHL were chiefly employed in finding guards and duties.	
			The move of the Brigade to the DUREN area between the 18th and 20th June interfered however with this training, and during the remainder of the month, it was impossible to progress with Company Training	

(A7092). Wt W12839/M1293 75,0.0. 1/17. D. D. & L., Ltd. Forms/C.2118/14.

Army Form C. 2118.

Instructions regarding War Diaries and Intelligence Summaries are contained in F. S. Regs., Part II. and the Staff Manual respectively. Title pages will be prepared in manuscript.

WAR DIARY
or
INTELLIGENCE SUMMARY.
(Erase heading not required.)

Place	Date	Hour	Summary of Events and Information	Remarks and references to Appendices
			Whilst in the DUREN area, the 2/4th Duke of Wellington's Regt and 2/4th K.O.Y.L.I. were employed in finding guards for the DUREN-COLOGNE Railway line until June 26th, when orders were received from the Division to the effect that the guards need not be maintained.	
			[signature] Brig-Gen. Commanding 1st Midland Brigade.	

(A7092). Wt W12839/M1293. 75 ,0 0. 1/17. D. D. & L., Ltd. Forms/C.2118/14.

Army Form C. 2118.

Instructions regarding War Diaries and Intelligence Summaries are contained in F. S. Regs., Part II. and the Staff Manual respectively. Title pages will be prepared in manuscript.

WAR DIARY
or
INTELLIGENCE SUMMARY.
(Erase heading not required.)

Place	Date	Hour	Summary of Events and Information	Remarks and references to Appendices

Fighting & Trench Strengths.

	7th June				14th June				21st June				28th June			
	Fighting		Trench		Fighting		Trench		Fighting		Trench		Fighting		Trench	
	Off	O.Rs.	Off	O.Rs.	Off	O.Rs.	Off	O.Rs.	Off	O.Rs.	Off	O.Rs.	Off	O.Rs.	Off	O.Rs.
2/4th Duke of Wellingtons	51	966	35	517	51	1156	34	519	51	1157	32	520	50	1157	30	508
2/4th K.O.Y.L.I.	63	1322	46	574	62	1308	45	579	60	1306	40	521	62	1310	42	583
5th K.O.Y.L.I.	45	1002	35	692	44	998	33	676	43	998	32	649	44	998	31	663
1st Ntd. Coletms	4	41	4	41	4	39	4	39	4	44	4	44	4	46	4	46
Total	163	3331	120	1824	161	3501	116	1813	158	3505	108	1734	160	3511	107	1800

A7092. Wt. W128_9/M1293 750,000. 1/17. D. D & L. Ltd. Forms/C2118/14.

Appendix I.

SECRET.

Copy No.________

1st MIDLAND BRIGADE ORDER No. 5.

1. Moves of the 1st Midland Brigade will take place as under during the period June 6th to June 9th.

(a) June 6th - 2/4th K.O.Y.L.I. to WEILERSWIST Musketry Camp by March Route.

(b) June 6th 2/4th Duke of Wellington's Regt to GYMNICH and KIERDORF by March Route.

(c) June 9th - 5th K.O.Y.L.I. less one company to BRUHL by March Route, relieving 52nd Sherwood Foresters. To enter BRUHL at 11.00 hours.

2. 5th K.O.Y.L.I. will take over the following guards,

(a) Guard on VOCHEM Army Ammunition Dump - 2 officers 58 Other Ranks (with remainder of Company standing by), at present found by 52nd Sherwood Foresters. Relief to take place on Sunday June 8th. Details to be arranged between Commanding Officers concerned. Completion of relief to be reported to Brigade Headquarters.

(b) Guard on HODENKIRCHEN Chemical Factory (9 Other Ranks) at present found by 53rd Sherwood Foresters. Relief to take place as in (a) above.

(c) Guard of one officer and 12 other ranks on COLOGNE - DEUTZ Goods Station at present found by 53rd Sherwood Foresters. Details of relief to be notified later.

(d) Guard of one N.C.O. and four other ranks on Midland Division Pack Train at present found by 51st Sherwood Foresters, on Sunday June 8th at 15.00 hours. Guard to report to D.A.D.R.T., EIFEL TOR STATION, ZOLLSTOCK AREA, COLOGNE.

3. (a). The responsibility for the defence of BRUHL and of the four bridges of the COLOGNE - BONN Railway which lie in BRUHL and immediately North and South of it, will be taken over by O.C., 5th K.O.Y.L.I., on June 9th in addition to his present area.

(b). A revised Brigade Defence Scheme will be issued shortly.

4. Completion of all moves will be wired to Brigade Headquarters.

ACKNOWLEDGE.

T. O. M. Buck

Captain,

5/6/1919.

Brigade Major, 1st Midland Bde.

Copy No. 1. 2/4th Duke of Wellington's Regt.
2. 2/4th K.O.Y.L.I.
3. 5th K.O.Y.L.I.
4. 1st Midland Bde. T.M.B.
5. 18th Field Ambulance.
6. Brigade Signalling Officer.
7. Civil Staff Officer.
8. Midland Division "G".
9. Midland Division "Q".
10. 3rd Midland Brigade.
11. No. 4 Co. Train.
12. A.D.M.S.
13. War Diary.
14. War Diary.
15. File.

App. II

S E C R E T.

1st Mid.Bde.No. B.M.S.58.

HEADQUARTERS 18th INFANTRY BRIGADE No. Date.

All recipients of 1st Midland Brigade Defence Scheme No. 2 dated 6/6/1919.

In Para. 5 (b)(ii) line 3.

For "while not" read "will act"

Please ACKNOWLEDGE.

Major,
A/Brigade Major, 1st Midland Brigade.

12/6/1919.

S E C R E T.

Herewith Copy No. 16 of Scheme "A" of the 1st Midland Brigade Defence Scheme No. 2, for action in the event of Civilian Disturbances.

Map attached for Battalions, L.T.M.B., and Midland Div. " G".

ACKNOWLEDGE.

[signature]

Captain,
Brigade Major, 1st Midland Brigade.

6/6/1919.

Copy No. 1. 2/4th Duke of Wellington's Regt.
2. 3/4th K.O.Y.L.I.
3. 5th K.O.Y.L.I.
4. 1st Mid. Bde. T.M.B.
5. No. 4 Co. Train.
6. 18th Field Ambce.
7. Midland Division "G".
8. Midland Division "Q".
9. C. R. A.
10. C. R. E.
11. Midland Division M.G. Bn.
12. A.D.M.S.
13. Civil Staff Officer.
14. War Diary.
15. War Diary.
16. File.

SECRET. Copy No. 16

1st Midland Brigade Defence Scheme No. 2.

Scheme "A".

1. Dispositions of 1st Midland Brigade Group.-

Brigade H.Q's.	LECHENICH.
1st Mid.Bde. T.M.B.	LECHENICH.
1 Battalion.	BRUHL with detached Company LIBLAR
1 Battalion.	GYMNICH " " " KIERDORF
1 Battalion.	WEILERSWIST CAMP.
18th Field Ambce.	BLESSEM.
No. 4 Coy. Train.	AHREM.

2. Owing to the above alterations in dispositions, the following revised scheme of action in the event of civilian disturbances will be sunstituted for those issued under this Office No. G22/347/1 dated 23/4/19.

3. The general principles laid down in the above quoted 1st Midland Brigade Defence Scheme will hold good.

4. In the event of warning of disturbances being received or of actual trouble occurring the message "Precautionary Action" will be sent out by Brigade Headquarters. The following action will then be taken.

(a). Battalions will be responsible for the maintenance of order and communications within the Area shewn on the attached map.

(b). Battalion at WEILERSWIST will be in Brigade Reserve, ready to move at one hour's notice.

(c). Guards on vulnerable points will be mounted or reinforced on a pre-arranged plan.

(d). Mobile Columns will be organised.

(e). Such concentration of the Brigade as circumstances dictate will be carried out on orders from Brigade Headquarters.
The most probable moves would be

Brigade Headquarters.	to	BRUHL.
GYMNICH Battalion.	to	LIBLAR.
WEILERSWIST Battalion.	to	BRUHL.
No. 4 Co. Train.	to	LIBLAR.
18th Field Ambce, remain	to at	BLESSEM.

5. On receipt of the message "Precautionary Action",

(a). The Battalion at GYMNICH will

(i). Prepare one Company to move at once to LIBLAR to relieve detached company of the BRUHL Battalion.
(ii). Detail one company as a Mobile Column ready to move at 30 minutes notice.
(iii) Detail one Company to be ready to act in support to the Mobile Column Company, or to act as Inlying Picquet.
(iv) Detail one Company to take over all local duties, and to be ready to act as Baggage Guard in the event of the move of Battalion Headquarters to LIBLAR.

NOTE. Two platoons of the support Company may be required to move to LECHENICH to Guard Brigade Headquarters, and to act as escort to supply wagons.

Sheet 2/.

~~(b). Battalion in the BRUHL - LIBLAR Area will.-~~

~~(i). Reinforce VOCHEM Guard with remainder of Company.~~

(ii) Detail one Company for the defence of BRUHL. The personnel of Divisional H.Q's organised under Camp Commandant while not under orders of this Company.

(iii) Detail one Company for the Defence of four bridges shewn in the attached map in the neighbourhood of BRUHL.

(iv). Detail a guard for the Bridges shewn on the attached map East by South of LIBLAR.

(v). Prepare to withdraw the LIBLAR Company to BRUHL on relief by a Company of the GYMNICH Battalion. This Company will then be held as a Mobile Company, ready to move as the circumstances require as 30 minutes notice.

(c) Battalion at WEILERSWIST will hold three Companies ready to move as Mobile Column (one company to be at ½ hour's notice, two companies at one hour's notice)

Remaining Company to form Camp Guard and in readiness to act as escort to Baggage Convoy if Camp is struck.

6. In the event of disturbances occurring without orders for "Precautionary Action" having been sent out by Brigade Headquarters, all measures for precautionary action will be taken and Battalion Commanders will take such action as the situation demands to [illegible] (a) Suppress the disturbances before they can spread (b) To localise the disturbances pending the arrival of reinforcements, should they be on too large a scale to be suppressed immediately.

Disturbances on a large scale must be dealtbwith deliberately after the necessary concentration of force has been carried out.

7. 1st Midland Brigade T.M.B., will be prepared to move to LIBLAR, and to send two sections to ~~cooperate~~ co-operate with Battalions.

8. Battery R.F.A., if placed at disposal will move in first instance to LIBLAR.

9. Company M.G. Battalion if placed at disposal will move in first instanse to LECHENICH.

10. (a). On receipt of the order for precautionary action to the Battalions at WEILERSWIST and GYMNICH and the Company at LIBLAR will establish visual communication with Brigade Headquarters in the SCHLOSS, LECHENICH.

(b). The Battalion at BRUHL will be prepared to communicate with Brigade Headquarters by means of the wireless installation at Divisional Headquarters.

(c). Light signal stations will be established.
The following code will be used.-

Red Verey Lights.	Alarm.
Green Verey Lights.	S.O.S.
White Verey Lights.	Answering Signal.

Brigade Headquarters Light Signal Station will be in the Tower of the SCHLOSS, LECHENICH.

T.E.M. Buckley [signature]

Captain,
Brigade Major, 1st Midland Bde.

6/8/1919.

App. III. B.M.S.68

S E C R E T.

To all recipients of 1st Midland Brigade Warning Order No. 4.

Reference 1st Midland Brigade Warning Order No. 4, para. 5.

The code for notifying "J" day should the latter fall on or after 20th June will be as follows.-

20th June......... "A".
21st June......... "B".
22nd June......... "C".

etc. etc.

ACKNOWLEDGE.

15/6/1919.

Tom Buchan
Captain,
Brigade Major, 1st Mid.Bde.

App III

MESSAGE FORM. Series No. of Message

In CALL v Out v	Recd. At By Sent At By	Army Form C 2128 (pads of 100)

PREAMBLE

Date Stamp

M.M. Offices Delivery v

Origin 1.B.W.Clear.

PREFIX PRIORITY. Words

TO 2/4th D.of W. B.E.O.
2/4th KOYLI. 18th Field Ambce.
5th KOYLI Civil Staff Captain.
1st Mid.Bde TMB. No.4 Co Train.

FROM & Place 1st Midland Brigade

Originator's Number	Day of Month	In reply to Number
B.M.322.	17.	-

Reference 1st Midland Brigade Order No. 4 of 28th May and B.M.S. 68 of 15th June AAA J day will be A AAA Acknowledge.

TIME OF ORIGIN

TIME OF HANDING IN (For Signal use only)

Originator's Signature (Not Telegraphed)

(19514.) Wt. W 5822—G 1276. 51000. 10/18. D & S. (E. 1256.)

War Diary

SECRET. B.M.S.No 69.

Copy No 21

Amendment No. 1 to 1st Midland Brigade Warning Order No 4.

1. Table "A" attached to 1st Midland Brigade Warning Order No 4 is cancelled and Table "B" attached herewith is substituted therefore.

2 No troops of 1st Midland Brigade will use the DUREN - GOLZHEIM - KERPEN Road.

Commanders of Units crossing this road will be responsible that Traffic Control posts under an officer are sent in advance of the Unit to regulate the passing of the Unit across the road.

Troops of 1st Midland Brigade will give way to all formed bodies of troops moving on this road.

3. Reference para. 7 (c) of above order.

O.C. 5th K.O.Y.L.I., will detail a guard of one platoon to report to Staff Captain at Brigade Headquarters, LECHENICH at 08.00 hours on J-2 day to guard surplus stores. This guard on arrival will relieve Brigade Headquarters guard found by 1st Midland Brigade T.M.B.

The guard of 5th K.O.Y.L.I., will rejoin its Battalion on relief by a guard of 3rd Midland Brigade.

4. The following guards will remain in situ until relieved by guards of 3rd Midland Brigade.

(a) VOCHEM Ammunition Dump.
(b) RODENKIRCHEN Chemical Factory.
(c) COLOGNE - DEUTZ Station.
(d) No. 3 Company of Divisional train. BRUHL.
(e) EIFEEL TOR Station.
(f) No. 1 Company Train.

5. Range Wardem and Camp Commandant at WEILERSWIST will remain and will be accommodated and rationed from J-1 day by 509 Field Co R.E. at WEILERSWIST.

6. O.C., 1st Midland Brigade T.M.B., will arrange for a Brigade Headquarters Guard to move with Brigade Headquarters to DUREN, and to mount on arrival. Staff Captain will arrange for this guard to travel on the lorries. The Guard will be relieved as soon as circumstances permit by a Guard from a Battalion.

7. 2/4th K.O.Y.L.I., will hand over the WEILERSWIST RIFLE RANGE to 509th Field Co. R.E., under arrangements to be made between C.O's concerned.

8. Attention is drawn to para 9 of the above warning order.

9. Completion of all moves will be reported to Brigade Headquarters by the quickest means.

10. Amendments and additions to Administrative Instructions No.1 are being issued by the Staff Captain.

11. ACKNOWLEDGE.

[signature]

Major,

16/6/1919. A/Brigade Major, 1st Mid.Bde.

(Distribution as for Warning Order No. 4)

TABLE "B".

1 Serial No.	2 Date.	3 Unit.	4 From.	5 To.	6 Route	7 Remarks.
1	J-2	2/4th D. of W. Regt.	GYMNICH	MERZENICH.	Point 92 - road junction immediately N.W. of "M" in MEILLERHOF -Junction of tracks ½mile S.W. of "M" in MEILLERHOF - WISSERHEIM - NORVENICH.	Not to arrive before 17.00 hrs.
2	J-2	Hdqrs & 3 Coys of 5th KOYLI	BRUHL.	LIBLAR.	Any.	Coys detailed as guard at VOCHEM Ammn. Dump and for defence of BRUHL will not move till relieved by Bn of 3rd. Mid. Bde.
3	J-2	Hdqrs & 3 Coys of 2/4th KOYLI.	WEILERSWIST	GYMNICH	Any.	---
4.	J-2	Bde. H. Qrs	LECHENICH	DUREN.	GIRBELSTRATH -road running through "A" in DISTEZRATH.	March under orders of BEO from Square at 09.00 hours.
5.	J-2	1st. Mid Bde TMB.	LECHENICH	BINSFELD	ESCHWEILER-FRAUWÜLLESHEIM.	- do -
6.	J-2	No. 4 Coy Div. Train.	AHREM.	FRAUWÜLLESHEIM.	-	March off at 08.30 hrs and join Bde. Hqrs in LECHENICH.
7.	J-1	5th KOYLI.	LIBLAR.	VETTWEISS	LECHENICH-ERP-GLADBACH.	To be clear of LECHENICH by 14.00 hrs.
8.	J-1	1 Coy, 2/4th KOYLI	WEILERSWIST	GYMNICH	Via LECHENICH.	Not to enter LECHENICH before 14.15 Hrs.
9.	J-1	Hdqrs Section 18th F.A.	BLESSEM	KELZ	-	To march under orders of 5th. K.O.Y.L.I. who will provide protection.

Continued 2.............

TABLE "B" (CONTINUED)

1. Serial No.	2 Date.	3 Unit.	4 From.	5 To.	6 Route.	7. Remarks.
10.	J-1	Battery R.F.A.	-	NEIDERAU	-	Comes under orders of B-G.C. 1st Mid.Bde on arrival who is also responsible for rations and accommodation.
11.	J-1	"C"Coy; 6th Bn; M.G.C.	MECHERNICH	KELZ	-	- do -
12.	J	2/4th KOYLI.	GYMNICH.	BUIR.	As for Serial No. 1 thence ESCHWEILER - GOLZHEIM.	Not to arrive before 17.00 hrs.

13. 93rd Field Co. R.E., moves under orders of C.R.E. - Details to be issued later.

Appendix IV

SECRET. B.M.S. 85. Copy No________

Reference Map
GERMANY 1/100,000 Sheet 1.L.

1st Midland Brigade Defence Scheme No. 3.(Provisional).

1. 1st Midland Brigade Defence Scheme No. 2 is suspended owing to the move of the Brigade to a new area.

2. 1st Midland Brigade Group is constituted and distributed as follows.-

Brigade Headquarters ----------------	SCHOELLER-STRASSE, DUREN.
2/4th Bn. Duke of Wellington's Regt-	MERZENICH.
2/4th Bn. K.O.Y.L.I. ----------------	BUIR.
5th Bn. K.O.Y.L.I. ----------------	Hdqrs. & 3 Coys. VETTWEISS. 1 Coy. GLADBACH.
1st Mid. Bde L.T.M.B. ----------------	BINSFELD.
A/77 Batty. R.F.A. ----------------	NEIDERAU.
"C" Coy.6th Bn. M.G.C. ----------------	KELZ.
H.Qrs.Section, 18th Field Ambulance-	KELZ.
No. 4 Coy.Divisional Train.---------	FRAUWULLESHEIM.

3. The Brigade area and area of tactical responsibility of Battalions are shewn on attached map.

4. The Brigade Group is disposed as above with a view to:-

(a) Protecting the DUREN - COLOGNE Railway between points J5 95.95 and L3 55.20.
(b) Protecting and keeping open road communications and maintaining order within the Brigade Area.
(c) Being in readiness to support the 2nd Midland Brigade in DUREN. (Headquarters of 2nd. Midland Brigade are in HOLTZ STRASSE).

5. In the event of the termination of the Armistice on account of the refusal of the Enemy to sign peace, a condition of Active Warfare will exist and Unit Commanders will be responsible for their own local protection.

6. From June 21st inclusive the Brigade Group will be organised for operations as follows.-

(a) Each Battalion will hold one Company in readiness to move as a Mobile Column at ½ hours notice, and one Company in support at 2 hours notice.
(b) Each Battalion will detail one Company as an inlying picquet for the protection of its own billetting area.
(c) 2/4th Bn. Duke of Wellington's Regt and 2/4th Bn. K.O.Y.L.I., will each detail one companyfor the protection of the DUREN - COLOGNE Railway in accordance with instructions contained in Appendix 1 attached.
(d) 5th Bn. K.O.Y.L.I., will hold one Company in reserve to furnish escort and duties detailed as required by Brigade Headquarters.
(e) 1st Midland Brigade L.T.M.B., will organise two Mobile sections for allotment to Mobile Column as required.
One section to be at ½ hours notice and the other at two hours notice. Mobile sections will move with 60 rounds per mortar. Remainder of Battery will be in reserve guarding reserve ammunition.
(f) A/77 Battery R.F.A. will hold one section at 1 hours notice and remainder of Battery at 2 hours notice and will be prepared to act with Mobile Columns by sections or as a battery as ordered.

(g) "C" Coy. 6th Bn. M.G.C. will hold one section at ½ hours notice and two sections at 2 hours notice and will be grouped to move sections to co-operate with Mobile column as ordered.

Remainder of the Company will be held in reserve and will be responsible for the local defence of KELZ.

(h) In the event of the warning order "MOBILE COLUMNS" being issued by these Headquarters all troops detailed above for action with Mobile Column will be brought to ½ hours notice and each Battalion will send two cyclist orderlies to report to O.C. Signals at Brigade Headquarters.

7. Whilst employed actively, all troops will move in fighting Order with Steel Helmets, Bayonets fixed and 120 rounds S.A.A.

1st Line Transport will accompany Mobile Columns.

8. Visual Signal Communication will be established forthwith between

2/4th.Bn.Duke of Wellingtons Regt at MERZENICH and Brigade H.Qrs.

" " " ". and 2/4th.Bn.K.O.Y.L.I. at BUIR.

Light Signal Stations will be established ; the following code will be used :-

Red Verey Light ———— Alarm.
Green Verey Light ———— S.O.S.
White Verey Light ———— Answering Signal.

9. ACKNOWLEDGE.

Major.
A/Brigade Major, 1st Midland Brigade.

20th. June 1919.

Distribution :-

Copy No. 1. G.O.C.
" + 2. 2/4th.Duke of Wellingtons Regt.
+ 3. 2/4th.K.O.Y.L.I.
+ 4. 5th. Bn K.O.Y.L.I.
5. 1st Mid.Bde T.M.B.
6. A/77th Battery R.F.A.
7. "C" Coy. 6th Bn M.G.C.
8. No. 4 Co. Train.
9. 18th Field Ambce.
+10. B.M.
11. S.C.
12. O.C. Sigs.
13. Lieut Ball R.E.
14. Civil Staff Captain.
+15. Midland Division "G".
16. C.R.E.
+17. }
18. } War Diary.
19. File .

Maps attached to those marked + .

APPENDIX 1.

1. 1st Midland Brigade is responsible for guarding the DUREN - COLOGNE Railway from Point J5 95.95 to Point L3 55.20.

2. The responsibility for the line will be subdivided as follows.-

2/4th Duke of Wellington's Regt.

From Point J5 95.95 to Bridge at Point 126 (exclusive).

2/4th K.O.Y.L.I.

From Bridge at Point 126 (inclusive) to Point L3 55.20.

3. The line will be guarded by picquets at essential points (e.g., Bridges and level crossings) with patrols (Mounted, Bicycle, or on foot) moving between them.

The following are essential points.-

Bridge at L3 55.20.
" " L3 30.05.
" " L3 22.00.
" " L4 12.98.
" " K4 10.20.
" " K4 02.10.

BUIR BLOCK CABIN is also an essential point.

4. The line will be inspected at frequent intervals by an R.E., Officer or responsible N.C.O., to see that it is not being tampered with or prepared for demolition.

This Officer or N.C.O., will be provided with a pass issued by 1st Midland Brigade Headquarters and bearing the Brigade Stamp.

Guards will be warned of their visits.

SECRET.

1. "J" Day ~~has been postponed~~ to a later date which will ~~be made~~ known later.

In future orders, "I" Day will be used to indicate the day previous to the new "J" Day.

2. In consequence of the above, para. 6 of 1st Midland Brigade Defence Scheme No. 3 will be amended as follows.-

In each case for "one hour" read "two hours".
In all other particulars the orders contained in para 6 will hold good.

3. As from "J" Day onwards troops will be ready to move at the hours notice given in para. 6 of the Defence Scheme.

4. ACKNOWLEDGE.

W Wallace Captain,
Brigade Major, 1st Midland Bde.

21/6/1919.

Distribution.
1. G.O.C.
2. 2/4th Duke of Wellington's Rgt.
3. 2/4th K.O.Y.L.I.
4. 5th K.O.Y.L.I.
5. 1st Midland Bde. L.T.M.B.
6. A/77th Battery R.F.A.
7. "C" Coy. 6th Bn. M.G.C.
8. No. 4 Coy. Train.
9. 18th Field Ambulabce.
10. B.M.
11. S.C.
12. O.C. Signals.
13. Lt. BALL R.E.
14. Civil Staff Captain.
15. Midland Division "G".
16. C.R.E.
17. } War Diary.
18. }
19. File.

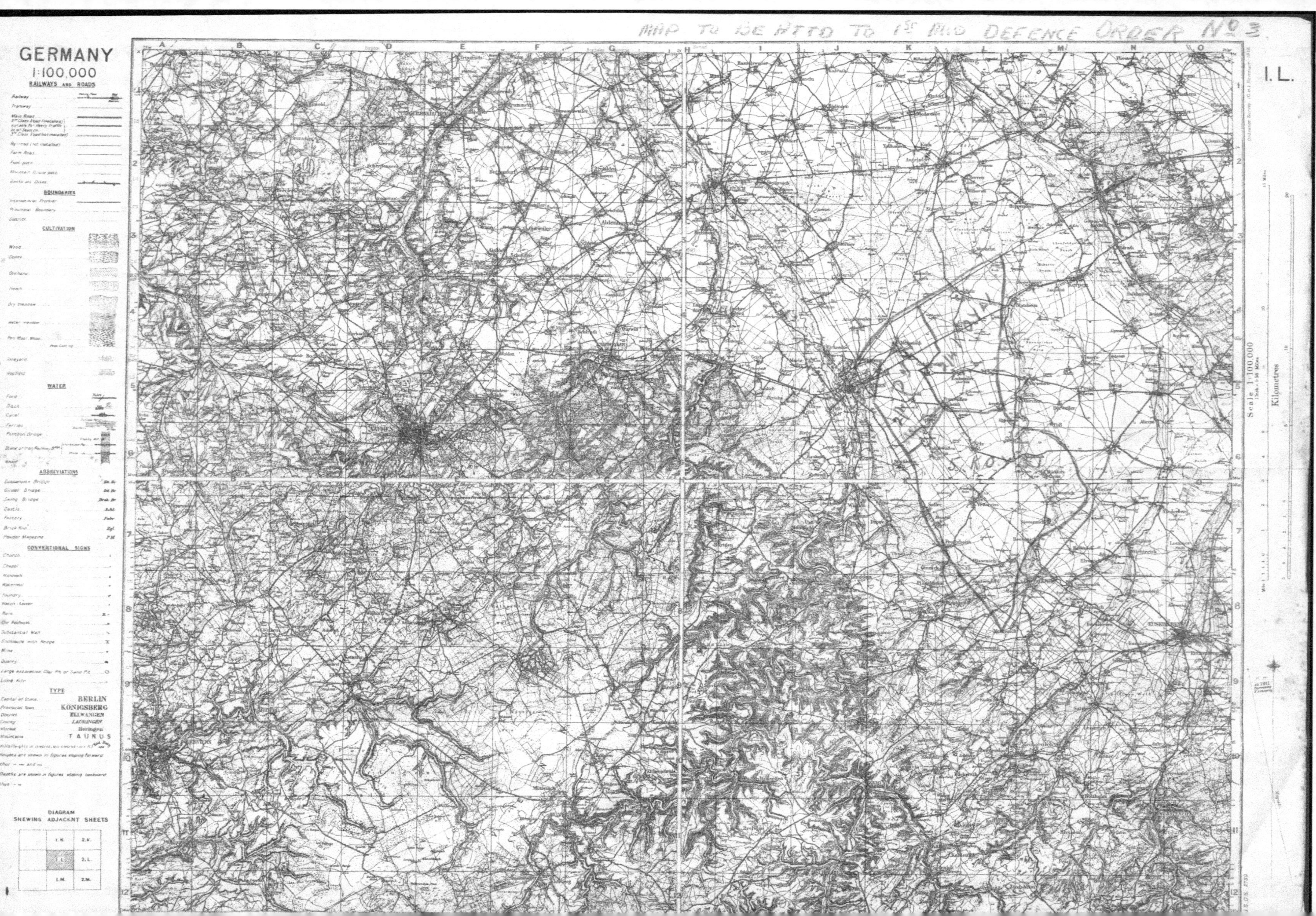
MAP TO BE ATTD TO 1st PAID DEFENCE ORDER No 3
I.L.
GERMANY
1:100,000
RAILWAYS AND ROADS
BOUNDARIES
CULTIVATION
WATER
ABBREVIATIONS
CONVENTIONAL SIGNS
TYPE
BERLIN
KÖNIGSBERG
ELLWANGEN
LAURINGEN
Heringen
TAUNUS
DIAGRAM
SHEWING ADJACENT SHEETS
1.K.
2.K.
1.L.
2.L.
1.M.
2.M.
Scale 1:100,000
Kilometres

War Diary

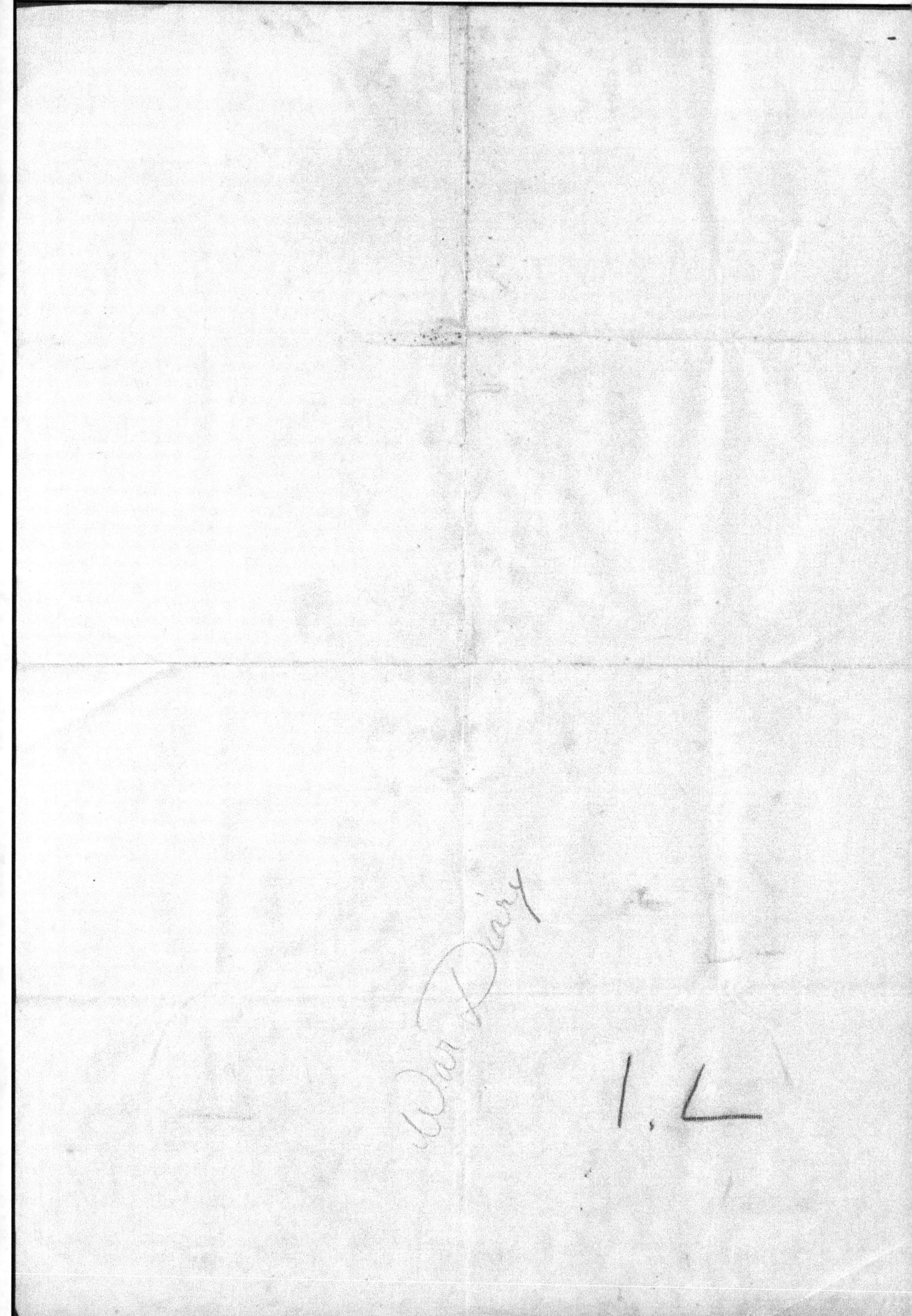

War Diary

1. L

App. V.

SECRET. B.M.S.No. 90. Copy No 18

1st Midland Brigade Order No. 6.

1. In the event of Peace being signed orders may be expected for all troops to resume their normal dispositions, when the organisation of areas and civil administration which existed prior to J-3 day will be resumed.

2. On receipt of the following wire from 1st Midland Brigade, Units will move in accordance with the attached table.-

"Move in accordance with 1st Midland Brigade Order No. 6 AAA ""A" Day will be(date) ---- "

3. 5th K.O.Y.L.I., will take over the following guards.-

(a) VOCHEM Army Ammunition Dump - 2 Officers 58 O.R's. (With remainder of Company standing by) at present found by 52nd Sherwood Foresters. Relief to be complete by 12.00 hours "B" day.
(b) Guard of 1 N.C.O., and 4 O.R's on Midland Divisional Pack Train at present found by 52nd Sherwood Foresters. To mount at 16.00 hours on "B" day, reporting to D.A.D.R.T., EIFEL TOR Station, ZULLSTOCK Area, COLOGNE.
(c) Guard of 1 N.C.O., and 3 men on No. 3 Coy. Train Refilling Point , BRUHL to mount at 18.00 hours on "B" day, at present found by 52nd Sherwood Foresters.
(d) Guard of 1 N.C.O., and 3 men on No. 1 Coy. Train at HAUSWEILER (O.7. 80.50. Sheet 1 L) Guard to mount at 18.00 hours daily commencing on "B" day. Guard at present found by 53rd Sherwood Foresters.
Guards(B), (C), and (D) above will be withdrawn by 3rd Midland Brigade on the moving of "B" day, and will not wait to be relieved.
Guard (D) will be rationed by No. 1 Coy. Train.

4. 1st Midland Brigade T.M.B., will mount a Guard on Brigade Headquarters on arrival at LECHENICH and will find a guard of 1 N.C.O., and three men mounting daily at 18.00 hours on No. 4 Coy. Train Refilling Point, ROMERHOFF commencing on "B" day.

5. 2/4th K.O.Y.L.I., will take over the Range from 509th Field Company R.E., on "C" day.

6. On arrival in old areas, 1st Midland Brigade Defence Scheme No. 2 will again come into force.

ACKNOWLEDGE.

T. M. Buchan

Captain,
Brigade Major, 1st Midland Bde.

24/6/1919.

Issued at 12.00 hours to.-
1. 2/4th Duke of Wellingtons Regt.
2. 2/4th K.O.Y.L.I.
3. 5th K.O.Y.L.I.
4. 1st Mid.Bde T.M.B.
5. B.E.O.
6. Civil Staff Captain.
7. 18th Field Ambce.
8. 6th Bn. M.G.C.
9. "C" Coy.6th Bn.M.G.C.
10. C.R.A.
11. A/77th Bty. R.F.A.
12. No. 4 Coy. Train.
13. A.D.M.S.
14. Mid.Div. "G".
15. Mid. Div. "Q".
16. D.A.P.M.
17. 3rd Midland Bde.
18. War Diary.
19. War Diary.
20. File.
21. Lt. DAVIES.

Table "A" to accompany 1st Midland Brigade Order No. 6.

Serial No.	Date.	Unit.	From	To.	Route.	Time.
1	"A" Day.	2/4th KOYLI.	BUIR	GYMNICH	BLATZHEIM-KERPEN.	Under orders of C.O.
2	-do-	5th KOYLI.	VETTWEISS	LIBLAR.	GLADBACH-ERP.	Move off 08.00 hrs.
3	-do-	A/77th Bty. RFA.	NEIDERAU.	FRIESHEIM	-do- -do-	Move off at 08.00 hrs.
4.	-do-	"C" Coy. 6th Bn MGC.	KELZ.	MECHERNICH	GLADBACH-ZULPICH.	Move off 08.00 hrs.
5.	-do-	H.Q. Sectn. 18th F.A.	KELZ.	BLESSEM.	GLADBACH-ERP.	Move off at 08.15 hrs.
6.	"B" Day.	Bde. H.Q.	DUREN.	LECHENICH	Direct.	Move off 08.00 hrs.
7.	-do-	1st Mid Bde. TMB.	BINSFELD.	-do-	Direct.	Move off 08.00 hrs.
8.	-do-	2/4th KOYLI.	GYMNICH.	WEILERSWIST	LECHENICH-BLIESHEIM.	Under orders of C.O.
9.	-do-	5th. KOYLI less one company.	LIBLAR.	BRUHL.	Direct.	Under orders of C.O.
10.	-do-	2/4th D. of W Regt.	MERZENICH.	GYMNICH.	Direct.	Move off at 08.00 hrs.
11.	-do-	No. 4 Co. Train.	FRAUWÜLLERSHEIM	AHREM.	Direct.	Move off at 08.00 hrs.

Copy No. 18.

[illegible]

B.M.S. 96.

[illegible] No. 1. to 1st. Midland Brigade Order No.6.

1. Owing to Traffic G.H.Q. being unable to provide trains for the move of the 3rd. Midland Brigade until "B" and "C" day, the following alterations will be made in 1st. Midland Brigade Order No.6.

(a) Para 3. In each case delete "B Day" and substitute "C Day".

(b) Para 4. last line. Delete "B Day" and substitute "C Day".

(c) In Table "A", make alterations as under :-
Serial 2. Column 2. for "A" day read "B" Day.
Serial 3. Delete entirely.
Serials 4 and 5. Column 2. read "A" Day.
Serials 6, 7, 9 and 11. Column 2. for "B" Day read "C" Day.
Serials 8 and 10. Column 2. read "B" Day.

ACKNOWLEDGE.

[illegible]
Captain.
Brigade Major. 1st. Midland Brigade.

25th June 1919.

To all recipients of 1st. Midland Brigade Order No. 6.

18.

SECRET.

[illegible] Instruction No. 2 Issued in connection with [illegible] Brigade [illegible] resuming their normal [illegible] following arrangements [illegible]

1. SUPPLIES.

(a) Normal system will continue to be adopted until Units have resumed their original dispositions. No.4 Coy Train will arrange to draw by horse transport for troops of 1st Midland Brigade as soon as the move is complete.

(b) Iron rations now in possession of Officers and men will be re-collected and stored under Units arrangements in the Quartermaster's.Stores.

(c) Advanced Parties for WEILERWIST will take rations up to and including 26th inst. They will subsequently be rationes direct under arrangements to be made by Divionsal Train.

(d) Platoons of 2/4th Duke of Wellington's Regt } at GYMNICH
2/4th K,O.Y.L.I. }
5th K.O.Y.L.I. at LIBLAR
will be rationed by 3rd Midland Brigade up to and including "C" day. P.R.O, 1st Midland Brigade and Staff will be xxxxxxx rationed up to the same date.

(e) Railhead will probably move to WEILERWIST on the 26th inst.

(f) Refilling Pointx. ROMERHOFF.

2. SURPLUS BAGGAGE.

Lorries will be allotted on the following scale:-
Brigade Headquarters:- 2 Lorries.(including L.T.M.B.)
Each Infy Battalion:- 3 Lorries.
"C" Coy 6th Bn. M.G.C.:1 Lorry.
18th Field Ambulance:- 1 Lorry.
No.4 Coy Div. Train:- 1 Lorry.

3. In the event of transport provided being insufficient to complete the move of surplus stores, a guard will be left and a wire sent to Brigade Headquarters xxxxfx xxxxxxxxx notifying transport to complete. Guards will be issued with two days rations.

4. MEDICAL ARRANGEMENT.

All troops on the line of march will be accompanied by a horsed or motor Ambulance.

5. TENTAGE.

All tents drawn from the 2/4th Duke of Wellington's Regt will be returned to them with the exception of those tents lent to WEILERWIST CAMP. The two marquees will be returned by "C" Coy 6th Bn. M.G.C. to D.A.D.O.S.

6. CIVIL ADMINISTRATION.

Sub-Areas will be those prior to the move to DUREN. 1st Midland Brigade Sub-Area Civil Staff Captain will return to LECHENICH on "B" day.

7. LEAVE PARTIES.

Normal Procedure will be resumed.

8. Divisional Reception Camp, D.A.D.O.S., Divisional Clothing Company, Canteen, Clean Clothing Store, Fancies, and Divisional Hostel will reamin in their present position.

25.6.1919.

Major,
Staff Captain, 1st Midland Brigade

Copies to:-

1. 2/4th Duke of Wellingtons Regt.
2. 2/4th K.O.Y.L.I.
3. 5th K.O.Y.L.I.
4. 1st Midland Brigade T.M.B.
5. B.E.O.
6. Civil Staff Captain.
7. 18th Field Ambulance.
8. 6th Bn. M.G.C.
9. "C" Coy 6th Bn. M.G.C.
10. C.R.A.
11. A/77th Bty. R.F.A.
12. No.4 Coy. Train.
13. A.D.M.S.
14. Midland Division "G".
15. Midland Division "Q".
16. D.A.P.M.
17. 3rd Midland Brigade.
18. War Diary.
19. War Diary.
20. File.
21. Leiut. DAVIES.

MESSAGE FORM. Series No. of Message

In CALL v. Out	Recd. At By Sent At By	Army Form C 2128 (pads of 100). Date Stamp.
PREAMBLE		
M.M. Offices: Delivery v Origin I.B.W.Clear.		
PREFIX	Words	

TO 6th Bn. M.G.C. — Camp Adjutant,
Mid.Div. "G". Weilerswist.
Mid. Div. "Q"
3rd Midland Brigade.

FROM & place: 1st Mid. Bde.

Originator's Number	Day of Month	In reply to Number
B.M.375.	29	–

1st Midland Brigde Order No. 6 issued under this Office Nos. B.M.90 and B.M.S.96 is confirmed AAA "A" Day will be Monday June 30th 1919 AAA Completions of moves and reliefs of guards will be wired each day to Brigade Headquarters AAA Addsd all recipients of Order No. 6. except Nos. 10, 11, 13 & 16 AAA Acknowledge

TIME OF ORIGIN

TIME OF HANDING IN (For Signal use only).

Originator's Signature (Not Telegraphed) [signature]

(33620) Wt. W5622/G1276 175,000 pads (36) 1/19 W B & L

SECRET

WAR DIARY

HEADQUARTERS
1ST MIDLAND BRIGADE

JULY
1919

ORIGINAL

(6●) Wt. W6192/P875 1,500,000 4/18 McA & W Ltd (E 2815) Forms W3091/4. Army Form W.3091

Cover for Documents.

Nature of Enclosures.

Notes, or Letters written.

Instructions regarding War Diaries and Intelligence Summaries are contained in F. S. Regs., Part II. and the Staff Manual respectively. Title pages will be prepared in manuscript.

WAR DIARY
or
INTELLIGENCE SUMMARY.
(*Erase heading not required.*)

Army Form C. 2118.

Place	Date	Hour	Summary of Events and Information	Remarks and references to Appendices
LECHENICH	1919 July [illegible]		2/4th Bn Duke of Wellington's Regt moved back to GYMNICH. 2/4th Bn K.O.Y.L.I. moved from GYMNICH to WEILERSWIST CAMP, thus completing the move of the Brigade from the [illegible]	
	July 4th		General Holiday in celebration of Signing of Peace Treaty	
	July [illegible]		Brigadier-General GWYNNE C.B. C.M.G. [illegible] assumed temporary Command of the Division during absence on leave of the Divisional Commander. Col. S.G. Francis D.S.O. 2/4th Duke of Wellington's Regt assumed Command of the Brigade vice Brig Gen GWYNNE.	
	July [illegible]		[illegible] K.O.Y.L.I. moved to WEILERSWIST CAMP and relieved 2/4th Bn K.O.Y.L.I. on completion of their musketry course. 2/4th Bn K.O.Y.L.I. less "B" Coy moved to BRÜHL	
	July [illegible]		"A" Coy 2/4th K.O.Y.L.I. moved to KIERBERG and found Guard for VOCHEM ARMY AMMUNITION DUMP. 2/4th Bn Duke of Wellington's Regt Battalion [illegible] at GYMNICH	
	July [illegible]		The Commander in Chief visited all three Battalions in the morning of this date.	
	July [illegible]		King's Colours presented to 2/4th Bn Duke of Wellington's Regt and 2/4th Bn K.O.Y.L.I. by Lieut. General Sir W.P. Braithwaite K.C.B. Commanding IX Corps British Army of the Rhine.	
	July [illegible]		2/4th Bn Duke of Wellington's Regt moved from GYMNICH to WEILERSWIST CAMP [illegible] relieving 5th Bn K.O.Y.L.I. who moved to LIBLAR on completion of their musketry [illegible]	
	July 19		General Holiday in Celebration of Peace	
	July 2[illegible]		"C" Coy 2/4th Bn K.O.Y.L.I. relieved "A" Coy 2/4th K.O.Y.L.I. in defence of VOCHEM ARMY AMMUNITION DUMP	
	July 2[illegible]		5th Bn K.O.Y.L.I. Sports [illegible] at LIBLAR	
	July 25		2/4th Bn K.O.Y.L.I. Sports Meeting BRÜHL	
	July 26		Verbal information received from Division that the probable date the Brigade would [illegible] SCHMIDTHEIM would be the 14th and 15th August	
			Brigade Preliminary Sports Meeting	
	July 2[illegible]		Brigade Major Capt. [illegible] left the Brigade for a staff appointment in [illegible]	
	July 2[illegible]		Move to SCHMIDTHEIM confirmed by Midland Division Order [illegible]	
	July 30		Brigade Order No [illegible] relating to the move of the 2/4th Duke of Wellington's and 2/4th K.O.Y.L.I. to ERP and GYMNICH respectively on being relieved by Battalions of the 2nd Midland Brigade	See appendix
			Brigade Sports at ROMERHOF. "B" Coy 5th K.O.Y.L.I. won the Cup for the Brigade Standard Competition presented by the Brigade Commander and the staff of the Brigade	
	July 31st		1st Midland Brigade Order No [illegible] issued re move to SCHMIDTHEIM	See appendix

S.G. Francis Colonel
Commanding 1st Midland Brigade

(A7092) Wt W12839/M1293 75 ,0 0. 1/17. D. D. & L., Ltd. Forms/C.2118/14.

Instructions regarding War Diaries and Intelligence Summaries are contained in F. S. Regs., Part II. and the Staff Manual respectively. Title pages will be prepared in manuscript.

WAR DIARY
or
INTELLIGENCE SUMMARY.
(Erase heading not required.)

Army Form C. 2118.

Place	Date	Hour	Summary of Events and Information	Remarks and references to Appendices

Fighting & Trench Strength

	July 5th				July 12th				July 19th				July 26th			
	Fighting		Trench		Fighting		Trench		Fighting		Trench		Fighting		Trench	
	Off	ORs	Off	ORs	Off	ORs	Off	ORs	Off	ORs	Off	ORs	Off	ORs	Off	ORs
2/4th Duke of W. Regt	51	1158.	30	534.	50	1143	29.	507.	50	1145.	26.	498.	50	1108	25.	490.
2/4 K.O.Y.L.I.	59.	1303.	36	544	59.	1303	37.	542.	61.	1300.	38.	539.	61	1279	38.	551
5th K.O.Y.L.I.	44.	1004.	31.	672.	44.	1016.	26	683.	44.	1014.	28.	681.	44	971.	32.	664.
1st [illegible]	3	46	3	46	3	43.	3	43.	4	45.	4	46.	4	45.	4	45
	157.	3511.	100.	1796.	156.	3505.	94.	1775.	159.	3504.	96.	1763.	159.	3403.	99.	1750

(A7092). Wt W12839/M1293. 75,0 0. 1/17. D. D. & L., Ltd. Forms/C.2118/14.

APPENDIX I.

S E C R E T. B.M.S. No. 91. Copy No. 20

1st Midland Brigade Order No. 7.

1. 3rd Midland Brigade Group will move from SCHMIDTHEIM Training Camp, transport by road, on August 4th, staging at ROGGENDORF and LECHENICH, personnel by rail on ~~August 6th and 7th~~ August 6th and 7th to the Area SOUTH - BRUHL, WEILERSWIST Camp.

2. On relief by 3rd Midland Brigade at BRUHL and WEILERSWIST Camp, 1st Midland Brigade will move to Area LIBLAR-GYMNICH-ERP.

3. The moves of the Units affected of the 1st Midland Brigade Group will take place in accordance with attached ~~[illegible]~~ table.

4. Units will send in all requisitions for lorries by 18.00 hours 2nd August.

5. Units will wire completion of the moves to these Headquarters by 18.00 hours 6th August.

6. The Camp Adjutant, WEILERSWIST Camp will hand over the Camp, including all tents, stores, ammunition etc., to the incoming Battalion of the 3rd Midland Brigade, and obtain a receipt. The original receipt will be sent to 1st Midland Brigade Headquarters. He will rejoin his Unit after the completion of handing over the Camp.

7. ACKNOWLEDGE.

W.H. Ramsbottom.
Major,
A/Brigade Major, 1st Midland Brigade.

30/7/1919.

Distribution.

Copy No. 1. 2/4 Duke of W.Regt.
2. 2/4th K.O.Y.L.I.
3. 5th K.O.Y.L.I.
4. Civil Staff Captain.
5. Brigade Signal O.
6. P.R.O. 1st Mid.Bde.
7. 18th Field Ambce.
8. No. 4 Co. Train.
9. Mid.Div. "G".
10. Mid.Div. "Q".
11. 3rd Midland Bde.
12. Camp Adjutant, WEILERSWIST.
13. Commandant Divisional School.
14. 1st Mid.Bde T.M.B.
15. A.D.M.S.
16. D.A.D.O.S.
17. C.R.A.
18. C.R.E.
19. O.C. Divisional Signals.
20. War Diary.
21. War Diary.
22. File.

TABLE TO ACCOMPANY 1st MIDLAND BRIGADE ORDER No. 7.

Battalion.	Date.	Destination.	Route.	Remarks.
2/4th K.O.Y.L.I.				
Advanced Party.	4th August.	GYMNICH.	BRUHL-LIBLAR-BLESSEM DIRMERZHEIM- GYMNICH	Any Stores that can be sent early forward should go.
" "	5th. August	-	- - - - - - - - -	More stores if needed can be sent.
Remainder of Battalion and Transport	6th August.	-	- - ditto - - -	
2/4th Duke of Wellingtons Regt.				
Advanced Party.	4th August.	ERP.	WEILERSWIST-FRIESHEIM - ERP.	Any Stores that can be sent forward early should go.
	5th August.			More stores if needed can be sent.
Remainder of Battalion & [illegible]	6th August.	ERP.	- ditto.	

SECRET. Copy No. 22

Administrative Order No. 7 issued with reference to
1st Midland Brigade Order No.7.

1. LORRIES.

The following lorries will report for move to ERP as follows.-

09.00 hours	4th inst.	2/4th Duke of W.Regt	WEILERSWIST CAMP.	3 lorries.
09.00 "	5th	" " "	" "	6 "
09.00 "	6th	" " "	" "	3 "

The following lorries will report for move to GYMNICH.-

09.00 hours.	6th inst.	2/4th K.O.Y.L.I.	SEMINAR BRUHL.	1 lorry.
09.00 "	5th	" " "	" "	6 lorries.
09.00 "	6th	" " "	" "	3 "

2. GUARDS.

The 52nd Sherwood Foresters will take over the following guards from the 2/4th K.O.Y.L.I. Relief to be complete by 12.00 hours, 6th inst.

(a) Guard of 1 N.C.O., and 4 O.Rs on Midland Divisional Pack Train, to mount at 10.00 hours on 6th inst reporting to D.A.D.R.T. EIFEL TOR STATION, ZULLSTOCK AREA, COLOGNE.
(b) Guard of 1 N.C.O., and 3 O.Rs on No. 3 Coy Train Refilling Point, BRUHL to mount at 10.00 hours 6th inst.
(c) Guard of 1 N.C.O. and 3 O.Rs on No. 1 Coy Train at HAUSWEILER(C.7 80.50 Sheet 1.L). Guard to mount at 10.00 hours 6th inst.
(d) Guard on VOCHEM ARMY AMMUNITION DUMP - 2 Officers 58 O.Rs - Will be issued with 3 days rations on the departure of the 2/4th K.O.Y.L.I. and will be taken over by the 52nd Bn Sherwood Foresters at a later date.

The 2/4th K.O.Y.L.I. will be responsible for the accommodation of the personnel of guards of 3rd Midland Brigade mentioned in para. 2, sub-paras (a) (b) (c) for the night of the 5th/6th who will report to them on the 5th inst.

3. Refilling Point - POMERHOF for all Units in the Brigade.

4. ACKNOWLEDGE.

W. W. Ramsbottham Major,
A/Brigade Major, 1st Midland Bde.

4/8/1919.

~~4/8/~~

Distribution.

Copy No. 1 2/4th Duke of W.Regt.
2 2/4th K.O.Y.L.I.
3. 5th K.O.Y.L.I.
4. Civil Staff Captain.
5. Brigade Signal O.
6. P.R.O. 1st Mid.Bde.
7. 18th Field Ambce.
8. No. 4 Coy.Train.
9. Mid.Div. "G".
10. Mid Div "Q".
11. File.
12. Camp Adjutant WEILERSWIST.
13 Commandant Divisional School.
14. 1st Mid.Bde T.M.B.
15. A.D.M.S.
16. D.A.D.O.S.
17. C.R.A.
18. C.R.E.
19. O.C.Divisional Signals.
20. D.A.D.R.T. EIFEL TOR STN, COLOGNE
21. 3rd Midland Brigade.
22 & 23. War Diary.

APPENDIX II

SECRET. B.M.S.92. Copy No. 21

1st MIDLAND BRIGADE ORDER No 8.

1. 1st Midland Brigade Group will move to SCHMIDTHEIM CAMP - all transport by road staging at ROGGENDORF on 17th - personnel by rail on 18th and 19th August.

2. 1st Midland Brigade Group consists of,-

H.Q. 1st Midland Brigade.
1st Mid.Bde L.T.M.B.
2/4th Duke of Wellingtons Regt.
2/4th K.O.Y.L.I.
5th K.O.Y.L.I.
459th Field Co. R.E.
H.Q. 18th Field Ambulance.
No. 4 Co. Train.

3. Advanced parties consiting of one platoon from each Battalion in this Brigade will move by rail under Battalion arrangements on the 6th August to SCHMIDTHEIM CAMP where they will come under the orders of the Camp Commandant and will find the necessary guards for the Camp under his orders.

Arrangements concerning the rationing of these platoons will be notified later.

4. ACKNOWLEDGE.

W.H. Ramsbotham Major,
A/Brigade Major, 1st Midland Brigade.

31/7/1919.

Distribution.

Copy No.
1. O.C. 1st Midland Bde.
2. 2/4th Duke of W Regt.
3. 2/4th K.O.Y.L.I.
4. 5th K.O.Y.L.I.
5. 1st Mid.Bde T.M.B.
6. 1st Mid.Bde Transport Officer.
7. H.Q. 18th Field Ambce.
8. No. 4 Co. Train.
9. Mid.Div. "G".
10. Mid.Div. "Q".
11. Sivil Staff Captain.
12. P.R.O. 1st Midland Brigade.
13. O.C. Brigade Signals.
14. C.R.A.
15. C.R.E.
16. A.D.M.S.
17. Camp Commandant, SCHMIDTHEIM.
18. 3rd Midland Brigade.
19. 459 Field Co. R.E.
20. O.C. Divisional Signals.
21. War Diary.
22. War Diary.
23. File.

S.E C R E T.   Copy No. 22.

Administrative Order No. 8 issued with reference to
1st Midland Brigade Order No. 8.

1. TRAIN ARRANGEMENTS.

(i) For Advanced Party.

Advanced parties for SCHMIDTHEIM will leave on Wednesday 6th inst by passenger train leaving KIERBURG 12.28 hours, arriving SCHMIDTHEIM 14.26 on the same date.

Battalions will arrange that their Advance Parties and Baggage arrive at KIERBURG STATION by 12.00 hours.

(ii) For Remainder of Brigade Group.

Train arrangements will be notified later.

2. SUPPLIES.

(i) Advanced Party entraining on the 6th inst will carry rations for consumption 7th inst.

(ii) Troops entraining on 18th and 19th will carry rations for consumption 19th. Rations for the 20th will be sent down by lorry to the Camp on the 19th, and drawn by a representative of each Unit at the Camp.

3. The 3rd Midland Brigade will be responsible for the transport ~~fa~~ of the baggage of the 1st Midland Brigade Advanced Party from SCHMIDTHEIM STATION to the Camp.

4. Lorries available for the Brigade to take baggage to LIBLAR STATION from the 17th inst to 19th inst will be notified later.

5. 6 lorries~~x~~ will be available at SCHMIDTHEIM on August 18th and will remain till detrainment of the Brigade is complete.

6. ~~EN~~TRAINING STATION.
459th Field Co. R.E., EUSKIRCHEN. All other Units in the Brigade Group, LIBLAR.

7. ACKNOWLEDGE.

W.H. Ramsbotham Major,
A/Brigade Major, 1st Midland Brigade

4/8/1919

Distribution.

Copy No. 1. O.C. 1st Midland Bde.
2. 2/4th Duke of W.Regt
3. 2/4th K.O.Y.L.I.
4. 5th K.O.Y.L.I.
5. 1st Mid.Bde T.M.B.
6. 1st Mid B.T.O.
7. H.Q. 19th Field Ambce.
8. No. 4 Co. Train.
9. Mid.Div. "G".
10. Mid Div "Q".
11. Civil Staff Captain.
12. P.R.O. 1st Midland Bde.
13. O.C. Brigade Signals.
14. C.R.A.
15. C.R.E.
16. A.D.M.S.
17. Camp Commandant SCHMIDTHEIM.
18. 3rd Midland Brigade.
19. 459 Field Co. R.E.
20. O.C. Divisional Signals.
21. D.A.D.R.T. EIFFEL TOR STN, COLOGNE.
22) 23) War Diary.
24. File.

SECRET

WAR DIARY.

HEADQUARTERS

1ST MIDLAND BRIGADE

AUGUST

1919

ORIGINAL.

(6414) Wt. W3906/P1607 2,500,000 7/18 McA & W Ltd (E 3591) Forms W3091/4.

Army Form W.3091.

Cover for Documents.

Nature of Enclosures.

Notes, or Letters written.

Instructions regarding War Diaries and Intelligence Summaries are contained in F. S. Regs., Part II. and the Staff Manual respectively. Title pages will be prepared in manuscript.

WAR DIARY
or
INTELLIGENCE SUMMARY.
(Erase heading not required.)

Army Form C. 2118.

Place	Date	Hour	Summary of Events and Information	Remarks and references to Appendices
	1919			
Lechenich	August 2nd		Brigadier-General Gwynn C.B., C.M.G., D.S.O., R.E. proceeded on Leave to England.	
"	5th		Warning Order received from Midland Division that Midland and Western Divisions were to be held in readiness to proceed to U.K. complete on or about 25th August	
	6th		2/4th Bn. Duke of Wellingtons Regt having completed G.M.C. proceeded to ERP and 2/4th Bn. K.O.Y.L.I. proceeded from BRUHL to take over billets in GYMNICH.	
			Advance Parties left for SCHMIDTHEIM TRAINING CAMP, but returned on Camp being Struck.	
"	9th		First Preliminary Parade for Inspection by the Army Council.	
"	13th		Second Preliminary Parade for Inspection by the Army Council	
"	19th		Brigadier-General Gwynn C.B., C.M.G., D.S.O., R.E. returned from Leave	
"	"		Brigade Inspected by the Army Council.	
"	20th		All S.A.A., Grenades, Fireworks and Explosives handed into ARMY AMMUNITION DUMPS, at VOCHEM and LONGERICH.	
"	23rd		All D.A.D.O.S. Stores handed in.	
			Wire received from Midland Division to the effect that all Units of Midland Division other than those for Ireland will on arrival in U.K. ~~to~~ will be dispatched to KIMMEL PARK CAMP, RHYL, Authority :- D.O. Telegram G.185 S.H.I.B. of 22nd August	

(A7092) Wt W12839/M1293 750,000 1/17. D. D. & L., Ltd. Forms/C.2118/14.

Instructions regarding War Diaries and Intelligence Summaries are contained in F. S. Regs., Part II. and the Staff Manual respectively. Title pages will be prepared in manuscript.

WAR DIARY
or
INTELLIGENCE SUMMARY.
(Erase heading not required.)

Army Form C. 2118.

Place	Date	Hour	Summary of Events and Information	Remarks and references to Appendices
CONTINUED	1919			
LECHENICH	Aug.	24th	All Equipment (G1098) loaded up and forwarded to ANTWERP for embarkation to GEORGETOWN.	
	"	26th	All remaining Animals returned to ARMY ANIMAL COLLECTING CAMP and No 24 VETERINARY HOSPITAL.	
	"	28th	All "T" Horses sent for entrainment at WEILERSWIST STATION.	

[illegible signature]
Brigadier-General
Commanding 1st Midland Brigade

(A7092). Wt W12839/M1293. 750,000. 1/17. D. D. & L., Ltd. Forms/C.2118/14.

Army Form C. 2118.

Instructions regarding War Diaries and Intelligence Summaries are contained in F. S. Regs., Part II. and the Staff Manual respectively. Title pages will be prepared in manuscript.

WAR DIARY
or
INTELLIGENCE SUMMARY.
(Erase heading not required.)

Place	Date	Hour	Summary of Events and Information	Remarks and references to Appendices

Fighting & Trench Strength.

UNIT.	August 2nd.				August 9th.				August 16th.				August 23rd.				August 30th.			
	Fighting		Trench		Fighting		Trench.		Fighting		Trench.		Fighting		Trench		Fighting		Trench.	
	Off	O.R's	Off	O.R's	Off	O.R's	Off	O.R's	Off	O.R's	Off	O.R's	Off	O.R's	Off	O.R's	Off	O.R's	Off	O.R's
2/4 Duke of W's Regt.	48	1047.	19	521.	46	1044	15	486	44	1032.	18	538	43	1035.	26	618	43	1018	29	631.
2/4. K. O. Y. L. I.	55	1253.	30	543.	57	1206	28	516	56	1193.	32.	584	55	1179.	32.	614	55	1152	34.	638.
5 K. O. Y. L. I.	43.	941.	32.	649.	48	926.	34	604	43	916.	32	650	44	916	34	738	41	894	35.	802.
1st Mid. Bde. T. M. B.	4	40.	4	40	4	46.	4	46	4	46	4	46	4	46	4	46	3	41	3	41.
TOTAL..	150	3281.	85.	1753.	150	3222.	81.	1655.	147	3187	86	1821	146	3146	96	2016	142.	3108	101.	2112.

(A7092). Wt W12839/M1293. 75 ,0 0. 1/17. D. D. & L., Ltd. Forms/C.2118/14.

Army Form C. 2118.

Instructions regarding War Diaries and Intelligence Summaries are contained in F. S. Regs., Part II, and the Staff Manual respectively. Title pages will be prepared in manuscript.

WAR DIARY
or
INTELLIGENCE SUMMARY.
(*Erase heading not required.*)

Place	Date	Hours	Summary of Events and Information	Remarks and references to Appendices
Lechenich. GERMANY.	Sept 4th	~~1332~~	5th Bn KOYLI & advance parties 1st Midland Bde entrained LIBLAR STATION for KINMEL PARK CAMP. N. WALES.	
LECHENICH. GERMANY.	Sept 5th		Brigade Headquarters & remainder of 1st Midland Bde entrained for same destination.	
KINMEL PARK N. WALES	Sept 8th 9th		1st Midland Brigade arrived at KINMEL PARK. N. WALES.	
"	Sept. 12th		Orders received to disband 9/4 Bn Duke of WELLINGTON REGT. Reduce 5th Bn KOYLI to cadre strength, & then demobilize cadre. Retain 2/4 Bn KOYLI, & all non-demobilizable men belonging to the 5th Bn KOYLI to be absorbed by the former Battalion. (Copy of War Office Postal Telegram 538 A.G.2 dated 11th attached.)	
"	Sept. 15th		All demobilizable personnel commenced being sent for dispersal.	
"	Sept 18th		Despatch of all demobilizable personnel completed with the exception of a few men whom it has been found necessary to retain temporarily, but will be sent for demobilization within a few days.	
	Sept 19th		Headquarters 1st Midland Bde at T.I.u.B. disbanded.	

[signature]
Brigadier General
Comdg 1st Midland Bde

A7092 Wt. W128,9/M1293 750,000. 1/17. D. D & I. Ltd. Forms/C2118/14.

URGENT POSTAL TELEGRAM.

Ref. No. 103/239/19. From. War Office
(A.G.2.A.) To. Commandeth, Chester.

Date. 11th September, 1919

538 A.G.2. 11th aaa

(1) Disband 2/4th West Riding Regiment. All personnel other ranks eligible for demobilization is to be sent for dispersal as soon as possible Other Ranks not eligible for demobilization will be posted to 2nd Bn. West Riding Regiment.

(2) Retain 2/4th Yorkshire Light Infantry having sent for dispersal all other ranks eligible for demobilization.

(3) Reduce to Cadre 1/5th Yorkshire Light Infantry. All personnel other ranks eligible for demobilization is to be sent for dispersal forthwith. Other ranks not eligible for demobilization will be posted to 2/4th Bn. Yorkshire Light Infantry. Finally demobilize Cadre in your Command.

(4) Dispose of Officers as follows.

(a) Attach all regular officers of the 2/4th West Ridibg Regiment, 1/5th Yorkshire Light Infantry and any who may becom surplus in 2/4th Yorkshire Light Infantry to their home service regular battalions

(b) Send to dispersal Stations forthwith for demobilization non Regular Officers of 2/4th West Riding Regiment,

(c) Consider as a whole the claims of all non- regular officers of 2/4th and 1/5th Yorkshire Light Infantry. Post those selected to 2/4th Yorkshire Light Infantry which will retain present Commanding Officer and Adjutant. Send direct to dispersal stations for demobilization all surplus officers of bith Battalions.

(d) Separate instructions will be issued regarding Quartermasters.

(5) Ensure that there personnel is sent from one Battalion to another has sufficient numbers of regular officers, or if regular officers are not available non regulars are retained to take that personnel and hand it over to the Battalion concerned. When such officers have completed this duty they will, if regular, join home service battalions if non regular be demobilized at once.

(6) Report dates 2/4th West Riding Regiment is disbanded, and 1/5th Yorkshire Light Infantry is reduced to Cadre and finally demobilized.

(7) Acknowledge.

(Sgd) Eustace Stocker, Rank. Major.
D. A. A. G.

Copies to G.H.Q., Gt.Britian and Infantry Record Offices concerned.

BEF

MIDLAND DIV

1 MID. Bde

2/4 D.O.W
(W. RIDING)

1919 MAR TO 1919 SEPT

From 62 DIV 186 BDE

Secret
Original

No:- 27

M. 2020

War Diary
of the
2/4th Bn Duke of Wellingtons (WR) Regiment T.F

"Midland Divn."
Army of Ocpn.

From
1st March 1919
to
31st March 1919

F. J. Wilson (?)
Lt-Colonel
O.C. 2/4 Duke of Wellingtons Regt

31/3/1919

(6414) Wt. W3906/P1607 2,500,000 7/18 McA & W Ltd (E 3591) Forms W3091/4.

Army Form W.3091.

Cover for Documents.

Nature of Enclosures.

Notes, or Letters written.

Secret

2/4 Duke of Wellington's Regiment

Appendix No I

Honours & Awards

ROUMANIAN – CROISE DE VIRTUE MILITAIRE (2nd Class)

200860 C.Q.M.S. BROOKE P.

[illegible signature]

Lt-Colonel

31/3/19 OC 2/4 Duke of Wellington's Regt.

Secret

Instructions regarding War Diaries and Intelligence Summaries are contained in F. S. Regs., Part II. and the Staff Manual respectively. Title pages will be prepared in manuscript.

WAR DIARY
or
INTELLIGENCE SUMMARY.

(Erase heading not required.)

Army Form C. 2118.

Place	Date	Hour	Summary of Events and Information	Remarks and references to Appendices
Germany				
ZULPICH	1/3/19 14/3/19		The Bn remained in billets in the ZULPICH Area in the 16th Infantry Brigade until the morning of 15/3/19	
EPP	15/3/19 31/3/19		On instructions received from 16th Infantry Brigade, the Battalion moved to ERP and on arrival joined the 18th Infantry Brigade Midland Division (formerly 6th Division).	
			31/3/19 J. P. Wilson Lt-Colonel OC 2/4 Duke of Wellingtons Regt.	

T2134. Wt. W708-776. 500000. 4/15. Sir J. C. & S.

Original

Secret

War Diary

of the

2/4th Bn Duke of Wellington's (W.R.) Regiment (T.F.)

Volume No:- 28 April 1919

Colonel

Cmg 2/4 Bn Duke of Wellington's (W.R.) Regt

28 T
3 sheets

(6392) Wt. W6192/P875 1,500,000 4/18 McA & W Ltd (E 2815) Forms W3091/4.

Army Form W.3091.

Cover for Documents.

Nature of Enclosures.

Notes, or Letters written.

Secret.

Instructions regarding War Diaries and Intelligence Summaries are contained in F. S. Regs., Part II. and the Staff Manual respectively. Title pages will be prepared in manuscript.

WAR DIARY
or
INTELLIGENCE SUMMARY.
(Erase heading not required.)

Army Form C. 2118.

Place	Date	Hour	Summary of Events and Information	Remarks and references to Appendices
ERP	1/4/19 to 11/4/19		The Battalion remained in Billets in ERP	LC.
ERP.	12/4/19		The 53rd (Service) Battalion Duke of Wellington's (West Riding) Regiment arrived in ERP and were absorbed by the 2/4th Battalion Duke of Wellington's (West Riding) Regiment (TF). Strength of 53rd Battalion, 32 officers, 484 other ranks.	LC
ERP	13/4/19		The villages of PINGSHEIM and DORWEILER were taken over by "C" and "D" Companies respectively for accommodation	LC.
HERRIG	14/4/19 to 30/4/19		Battalion Headquarters moved to the village of HERRIG	LC.
			1/5/1919 J S Francis Colonel O.C. 2/4th Battalion Duke of Wellington's (West Riding) Regiment	

T2134. Wt. W708–776. 500000. 4/15. Sir J. C. & S.

Original

Secret

War Diary

of

2/4th Bn Duke of Wellington's (W.R.) Regt T.F.

Volume No: 29 - May 1919

S G Francis Colonel

O.C. 2/4 Duke of Wellingtons (W.R.) Regt T.F.

29 T. 3 sheets

(6392) Wt. W6192/P875 1,500,000 4/18 McA & W Ltd (E 2815) Forms W3091/4.

Army Form W.3091.

Cover for Documents.

Nature of Enclosures.

Notes, or Letters written.

Instructions regarding War Diaries and Intelligence Summaries are contained in F. S. Regs., Part II. and the Staff Manual respectively. Title pages will be prepared in manuscript.

WAR DIARY

~~or~~

~~INTELLIGENCE SUMMARY.~~

(Erase heading not required.)

Army Form C. 2118.

Place	Date	Hour	Summary of Events and Information	Remarks and references to Appendices
Herrig Germany.	1-5-19 to 31-5-19	–	The Battalion remained in Billets in the Erp Area, with Headquarters in Herrig.	
			J S Francis Colonel O/C. 2/4th Bn. Duke of Wellingtons (West Riding) Regt.	

T2134. Wt. W708–776. 500000. 4/15. Sir J. C. & S.

Secret

Original

War Diary

of the

2/4 Bn Duke of Wellington's (WR) Regt

for

June 1919

Volume No:- 30

S S Jones

Colonel

Commanding 2/4 Duke of Wellington's Regt

30 [illegible]

(6392) . Wt. W6192/P875 1,500,000 4/18 McA & W Ltd (E 2815) Forms W3091/4.

Army Form W.3091.

Cover for Documents.

Nature of Enclosures.

Notes, or Letters written.

Army Form C. 2118.

Instructions regarding War Diaries and Intelligence Summaries are contained in F. S. Regs., Part II. and the Staff Manual respectively. Title pages will be prepared in manuscript.

WAR DIARY
or
INTELLIGENCE SUMMARY.

(Erase heading not required.)

Place	Date	Hour	Summary of Events and Information	Remarks and references to Appendices
Herrig	1/6/19 5/6/19	–	The Battalion remained in billets in the Erp-Herrig-Pingsheim area with Headquarters at Herrig.	
Gymnich	6/6/19 17/6/19	–	The Battalion moved to the Gymnich-Kierdorf Area, 3 Companies & Headquarters billeted in Gymnich and one Company in Kierdorf.	
Merzenich	18/6/19 to 30/6/19	–	The Battalion, equipped for active operations, moved to the Duren area, and took over billets in the village of Merzenich, 3 Kilos. N.E. of Duren.	

S. S. Harris [signature]
Colonel.

Commanding 2/4th Bn: Duke of Wellingtons (W.R.) Regt:

D. D. & L., London, E.C.
(10340) Wt W3300/P713 750,000 3/18 E 2688 Forms/C2118/16

Original

Secret

War Diary

of

2/4th Bn. Duke of Wellingtons (W.R.) Reg't

Volume No: 31 - July 1919

J. C. Burnett Major

OC 2/4th Duke of Wellingtons Reg't

31..T
3 sheets

(6392) Wt. W6192/P875 1,500,000 4/18 McA & W Ltd (E 2815) Forms W3091/4.

Army Form W.3091.

Cover for Documents.

Nature of Enclosures.

Notes, or Letters written.

Army Form C. 2118.

Instructions regarding War Diaries and Intelligence Summaries are contained in F. S. Regs., Part II. and the Staff Manual respectively. Title pages will be prepared in manuscript.

WAR DIARY
or
INTELLIGENCE SUMMARY.

(Erase heading not required.)

Place	Date	Hour	Summary of Events and Information	Remarks and references to Appendices
GERMANY				
MERZENICH	1/7/19		The battalion moved by route march to the GYMNICH Area into billets previously vacated.	
GYMNICH			A Kings Colour having been received, was officially presented to the battalion by Lieut-General Sir Walter P. Braithwaite, K.C.B, Commanding IX Corps, British Army of the Rhine.	
GYMNICH			The battalion proceeded by route march to the Musketry Camp, WEILERSWIST for firing the annual G.M.C.	

J. C. Burnett. Major
OC 2/4 Duke of Wellingtons Regt

D. D. & L., London, E.C.
(10340) Wt W5300/P713 750,000 3/1 E 2688 Forms/C2118/16

Original

Secret

Mid Dr

War Diary

of

2/4th Bn. Duke of Wellington's (W.R.) Reg't

Volume No: 32 August 1919

D S Fra[illegible]

31.8.1919

Colonel
O.C. 2/4 Duke of Wellington's Regt

32 T
3 sheets

(6392) Wt. W6192/P875 1,500,000 4/18 McA & W Ltd (E 2815) Forms W3091/4.

Army Form W.3091.

Cover for Documents.

Nature of Enclosures.

Notes, or Letters written.

Instructions regarding War Diaries and Intelligence Summaries are contained in F. S. Regs., Part II. and the Staff Manual respectively. Title pages will be prepared in manuscript.

WAR DIARY
or
INTELLIGENCE SUMMARY.
(Erase heading not required.)

Army Form C. 2118.

Place	Date	Hour	Summary of Events and Information	Remarks and references to Appendices
GERMANY				
WEILERSWIST	1.8.19 to 5.8.19		The battalion remained in Camp at WEILERSWIST completing G.M.C.	LC
ERP	6.8.19		The battalion having completed firing G.M.C. proceeded by route march to billets in ERP.	LC
ERP	26.8.19		In view of the battalion proceeding to the United Kingdom, all battalion Mobilization Equipment & Transport Vehicles were entrained at LIBLAR for transportation to GEORGETOWN, SCOTLAND via ANTWERP on 26.8.1919.	LC

ERP, Germany
31.8.1919

[signature]
Colonel
O.C. 2/4 Duke of Wellingtons Regt.

T2134. Wt. W708-776. 500000. 4/15. Sir J. C. & S.

Secret. Original

War Diary

of the

2/4th Bn. Duke of Wellingtons (W.R.) Regiment

September 1919

Volume - No: 33

S G Francis

Colonel

1/10/1919 Cmg 2/4 Bn Duke of Wellington's (W.R.) Regt

D. D & L. London, E.C.
(A11229) Wt. W2951/T1311 500,000 7/13 Sch. 2 Forms A. 2. / 43

Army Form A. 2.

PROCEEDINGS of a* ____________________

*N.B. — The Form being applicable to any Board of Officers, or Committee, or Court of Inquiry, this blank to be filled in accordingly.

The proceedings should be signed by each Officer composing the Board, etc.

assembled at ____________________

on the ____________________

by order of ____________________

____

for the purpose of ____________________

____

____

____

PRESIDENT.

MEMBERS.

IN ATTENDANCE.

The ____________ having assembled pursuant to order, proceed to

Instructions regarding War Diaries and Intelligence Summaries are contained in F. S. Regs., Part II. and the Staff Manual respectively. Title pages will be prepared in manuscript.

WAR DIARY
or
INTELLIGENCE SUMMARY.
(Erase heading not required.)

Army Form C. 2118.

Place	Date	Hour	Summary of Events and Information	Remarks and references to Appendices
GERMANY. ERP	1/9/19 – 5/9/19		The Battalion remained in billets in ERP, Germany.	LC
	6/9/19		Having received instructions to move to the United Kingdom, the battalion entrained at LIBLAR on the 5th September arriving CALAIS France in the early hours on the morning of the 7th September and embarked for DOVER same day.	LC
Kinmel Park	7/9/19 – 16.9.19		The battalion entrained at DOVER and arrived KINMEL PARK CAMP in the early hours on the morning of the 8th Sept. taking over hutments in No 4 Camp.	LC
"	17.9.19 to 22.9.19		All personnel for demobilization were despatched to their respective dispersal stations for disembodiment or demobilization.	LC
"	21.9.19		A King's Colour which had been presented to the battalion was officially handed over for safe custody to the O/c 90th T.F. Depot Halifax.	LC
"	22.9.19		All personnel not for demobilization transferred to the 2nd Bn Duke of Wellington's (WR) Regiment, 300 of whom were despatched to No I Concentration Camp, Ripon for duty, balance of officers & other rank remaining pending instructions.	LC
"	30.9.19			LC
	1/10/19		S G Francis [signature] Colonel Cmg 2/4 Duke of Wellingtons Regiment.	

T2134. Wt. W708–776. 500000. 4/15. Sir J. C. & S.

BEF

MIDLAND DIV.

1 MIDLAND Bde

2/4 K.O.Y.L.I

1919 MAR TO 1919 AUG

FROM 62 DN 187 BDE

Confidential

War Diary

2/4th Battn. King's Own Yorkshire Light Infantry

From 1-3-19 To 31-3-19

Volume 27

Instructions regarding War Diaries and Intelligence Summaries are contained in F. S. Regs., Part II. and the Staff Manual respectively. Title pages will be prepared in manuscript.

WAR DIARY
or
INTELLIGENCE SUMMARY.
(*Erase heading not required.*)

Army Form C. 2118.

Place	Date	Hour	Summary of Events and Information	Remarks and references to Appendices
PINGSHEIM	1-3-19		Battalion in billets at PINGSHEIM.	
PINGSHEIM	8-3-19		1 Other Rank to U.K. for Demobilization	
PINGSHEIM	9-3-19		1 Other Rank to U.K. for Demobilization	
PINGSHEIM	14-3-19		Battalion moved from PINGSHEIM to GYMNICH	
GYMNICH	14-3-19		Draft of 18 Officers and 489 Other Ranks taken on strength of Battalion from 2nd Bn K.O.Y.L.I.	
GYMNICH	26-3-19		MAJOR G. BEAUMONT, M.C., 2nd Lieut J.E. ROBY and 71 Other Ranks left Unit to proceed to U.K. for Demobilization	
GYMNICH	27-3-19		Draft of 15 Other Ranks joined Battalion from 2nd Bn K.O.Y.L.I.	
			7 Other Ranks proceeded to U.K. for Demobilization	
GYMNICH	29-3-19		4 Other Ranks joined Battalion from 2nd Bn K.O.Y.L.I.	

C.A. Clayton
Lt. Colonel
Comdg 2/4th Bn K.O.Y.L.I.

D. D. & L., London E.C.
(10341) Wt W5300/P713 750,000 3/18 E 683 Forms/C2118/16.

Instructions regarding War Diaries and Intelligence Summaries are contained in F. S. Regs., Part II. and the Staff Manual respectively. Title pages will be prepared in manuscript.

WAR DIARY
or
INTELLIGENCE SUMMARY.
(Erase heading not required.)

Army Form C. 2118.

Place	Date	Hour	Summary of Events and Information	Remarks and references to Appendices
PINGSHEIM	1-3-19		Battalion in billets at PINGSHEIM	A.B.
PINGSHEIM	8-3-19		1 Other Rank to U.K. for Demobilization	A.B.
PINGSHEIM	9-3-19		1 Other Rank to U.K. for Demobilization	A.B.
PINGSHEIM	14-3-19		Battalion moved from PINGSHEIM to GYMNICH	A.B.
GYMNICH	14-3-19		Draft of 18 Officers and 489 Other Ranks taken on strength of Battalion from 2nd Bn K.O.Y.L.I.	A.B.
GYMNICH	26-3-19		MAJOR G. BEAUMONT, MC, 2nd Lieut J.E. ROBY and 71 Other Ranks left Unit to proceed to U.K. for Demobilization	A.B.
GYMNICH	27-3-19		Draft of 15 Other Ranks joined Battalion from 2nd Bn K.O.Y.L.I.	A.B.
			7 Other Ranks proceeded to U.K. for Demobilization	A.B.
GYMNICH	29-3-19		4 Other Ranks joined Battalion from 2nd Bn K.O.Y.L.I.	A.B.

F.A. Chaytor
Lt. Colonel
Comdg 2/4th Bn K.O.Y.L.I.

D. D. & L., London E.C.
(10342) Wt W5300/P713 750,000 3/18 E 688 Forms/C2118/16.

Confidential.

2/4th. Bn. K. O. Yorkshire L. I.

From 1-4-1919 Vol. 28. To 30-4-1919.

Army Form C. 2118.

WAR DIARY
or
INTELLIGENCE SUMMARY.
(*Erase heading not required.*)

Instructions regarding War Diaries and Intelligence Summaries are contained in F. S. Regs., Part II. and the Staff Manual respectively. Title pages will be prepared in manuscript.

Place	Date	Hour	Summary of Events and Information	Remarks and references to Appendices
GYMNICH	1-4-19		Battalion in Billets at GYMNICH.	[illegible initials]
GYMNICH	6-4-19		37 Officers and 560 Other Ranks joined Battalion from 52nd (Graduating) Battn.	[illegible initials]
GYMNICH	7-4-19		"A" Coy moved into billets at DERMERZHEIM and KONRADSHEIM.	[illegible initials]
GYMNICH	9-4-19		Five Officers left Unit to proceed to U.K. for demobilization.	
GYMNICH	11-4-19		Battalion inspected by Corps Commander.	
			8 Officers and 90 Other Ranks left Unit to proceed to U.K. for demobilization.	[illegible initials]
GYMNICH.	13-4-19		4 Officers and 46 Other Ranks left Unit to proceed to U.K. for demobilization.	[illegible initials]
GYMNICH.	14-4-19 to 30-4-19		Battalion in training.	[illegible initials]

[illegible signature] Major
for Lieut-Col.
Commdg 2/4th Bn. K.O.Y.L.I.

D. D. & L., London E.C.
(10340) W1 W5300/P713 750,000 3/18 E. 688 Forms/C2118/16.

Confidential

War Diary

2/4th Bn. K. O. Yorks. L. I.

From 1-5-19 Vol: 29 To 31-5-19

P. 29

Army Form C. 2118.

Instructions regarding War Diaries and Intelligence Summaries are contained in F. S. Regs., Part II. and the Staff Manual respectively. Title pages will be prepared in manuscript.

WAR DIARY
or
INTELLIGENCE SUMMARY.

(Erase heading not required.)

Place	Date	Hour	Summary of Events and Information	Remarks and references to Appendices
GYMNICH	1-5-19		Battalion in billets at GYMNICH	
GYMNICH	2-5-19		Brigade inspected by Army Commander.	
GYMNICH	3-5-19 to 21-5-19		Training carried out	
GYMNICH	22-5-19		Capt. & Adjt. A. E. Earle M.C. proceeded to U.K. for demobilization	
GYMNICH	22-5-19 to 31-5-19		Battalion in training	

H W Franks Capt. & Adjt
for Major
Commanding 2/4th K. O. Y. L. I.

D. D. & L., London E.C
(10346) Wt W5300/P713 750,000 3/18 E 688 Forms/C2118/16.

KA 7 3 0

Confidential

War Diary

2/4th Bn. K. O. Yorks L. I.

From 1-6-19 Vol. 30 To 30-6-19

P. 30

Army Form C. 2118.

WAR DIARY
or
INTELLIGENCE SUMMARY.
(*Erase heading not required.*)

Instructions regarding War Diaries and Intelligence Summaries are contained in F. S. Regs., Part II. and the Staff Manual respectively. Title pages will be prepared in manuscript.

Place	Date	Hour	Summary of Events and Information	Remarks and references to Appendices
GYMNICH	1/6/19.		Battalion in billets at GYMNICH.	
GYMNICH	2/6/19.		Lieut-Col. C.A. CHAYTOR, D.S.O. proceeded to U.K. to join 1st Battn. K.O.Y.L.I.	
GYMNICH	4/6/19		Lieut-Col. H. Milward, D.S.O. proceeded on leave to U.K.	
			"A" Coy moved to WEILERSWIST CAMP.	
GYMNICH	5/6/19		"B" Coy moved to WEILERSWIST CAMP.	
	6/6/19		Remainder of Battn. moved to WEILERSWIST CAMP.	
WEILERSWIST CAMP.	7/6/19 & 8/6/19		In training at WEILERSWIST CAMP.	
WEILERSWIST CAMP.	9/6/19 to 17/6/19.		Firing practices on Range.	
WEILERSWIST CAMP	18/6/19		Lieut-Col. C. E. Heathcote C.B., C.M.G., D.S.O. joined Battalion and assumed Command	
	18/6/19		Battalion (less "B" Coy) moved to GYMNICH.	
GYMNICH	19/6/19		"B" Coy moved to GYMNICH.	
			Lieut-Col. H. Milward, D.S.O. returned from leave.	
			Lieut. B. G. Trevor M.C. proceeded to U.K. for demobilization.	

D. D. & L., London E.C
(10340) W1 W5300/P713 750,000 3/18 E 688 Forms/C2118/16.

Instructions regarding War Diaries and Intelligence Summaries are contained in F. S. Regs., Part II. and the Staff Manual respectively. Title pages will be prepared in manuscript.

WAR DIARY
or
INTELLIGENCE SUMMARY.

(Erase heading not required.)

Army Form C. 2118.

Place	Date	Hour	Summary of Events and Information	Remarks and references to Appendices
GYMNICH	20/6/19		Battalion moved to BUIR. Lieut-Col. H. Milward D.S.O. returned to U.K. Posted to 2nd Notts & Derby Rgt.	
BUIR	21/6/19		Battalion took over the protection of the DUREN-COLOGNE Railway from the 2/4th Duke of Wellington's Regt.	
BUIR	24/6/19		"C" Coy moved to WEILERSWIST CAMP.	
BUIR	25/6/19		Capt. T. E. F. Penny M.C. Adjutant proceeded on leave to U.K. Lieut. J. M. Green took over duties of Adjutant.	
BUIR	30/6/19		Battalion (less "C" Coy) moved to GYMNICH	

[illegible signature]
Lieut-Col.
Commdg 2/4th Bn. K. O. Y. L. I.

D. D. & L., London E.C
(10342) Wt W5300/P713 750,000 3/18 E 688 Forms/C2118/16.

Confidential.

War Diary.

2/4th Bn. K. O. Yorks. L. I.

From 1-7-19.　　Vol. 31.　　To 31-7-19.

Army Form C. 2118.

Instructions regarding War Diaries and Intelligence Summaries are contained in F. S. Regs., Part II. and the Staff Manual respectively. Title pages will be prepared in manuscript.

WAR DIARY
or
INTELLIGENCE SUMMARY.

(Erase heading not required.)

Place	Date	Hour	Summary of Events and Information	Remarks and references to Appendices
GYMNICH	1/7/19		Battalion moved from GYMNICH to WEILERSWIST MUSKETRY CAMP.	[illegible]
WEILERSWIST.	2/7/19		Battalion firing Part III G.M.C.	[illegible]
	3/7/19.		General holiday in celebration of signing of Peace Treaty.	[illegible]
	4/7/19 5/7/19		Firing Part III G.M.C.	[illegible]
	6/7/19 7/7/19		Lewis Gunners firing classification practices.	[illegible]
	8/7/19		Battalion, less "A" Coy, moved to BRUHL. "A" Coy moved to KIERBERG and formed Guard for VOCHEM ARMY AMMUNITION DUMP	[illegible]
BRUHL.	9/7/19		Battalion, less "A" Coy in training at BRUHL.	[illegible]
	11/7/19		Commander in Chief visited Battalion.	
	13/7/19		Capt. T. E. F. Penny M.C. returns from leave and resumes duties of Adjutant.	
	17/7/19		King's Colour presented to the Battalion by Lieut-General Sir W. P. Braithwaite K.C.B.	
	20/7/19		General holiday in Celebration of Peace. "C" Coy went on Rhine Trip.	
	21/7/19		"C" Coy relieved "A" Coy in defence of VOCHEM AMMUNITION DUMP. "A" Coy moved to BRUHL.	

D. D. & L., London E.C
(10342) Wt W5300/P713 750,000 3/18 E 688 Forms/C2118/16.

Instructions regarding War Diaries and Intelligence Summaries are contained in F. S. Regs., Part II. and the Staff Manual respectively. Title pages will be prepared in manuscript.

WAR DIARY
or
INTELLIGENCE SUMMARY.
(Erase heading not required.)

Army Form C. 2118.

Place	Date	Hour	Summary of Events and Information	Remarks and references to Appendices
BRUHL.	22/7/19		LIEUT-COL. C.E. HEATHCOTE C.B., C.M.G., D.S.O. proceeded on leave to U.K.	
			MAJOR W. H. BROOKE M.C. assumes command of Battalion.	
	25/7/19		Battalion Sports Meeting.	
	28/7/19		CAPT. T.E.F. PENNY M.C. takes over command of "C" Coy, vice LIEUT. H. W. SPINK	
			LIEUT. J. M. GREEN takes over duties of Adjutant.	
	29/7/19.		LIEUT-COL. C.E. HEATHCOTE, C.B., C.M.G., D.S.O., returns from leave & assumes command of Battalion.	
			Divisional Horse Show.	
	30/7/19		Brigade Sports Meeting. 2/Lieut. G. K. Riddle, O.B.L.I. attd 2/4th K.O.Y.L.I. wins Brigade individual championship.	
			Lieut. F. G. Lovell proceeded to U.K. for demobilization.	
			Lieut. S. Fraser proceeded to U.K. on leave prior to Educational Course at OXFORD.	
	31/7/19.		2/Lieuts F. E. Semper (Y & L), W. G. Wilkinson (O.B.L.I.), H. F. Alsworth (O.B.L.I.) } proceeded to join Chinese Labour Corps. Struck off strength.	
			Lieut. A. Morris reported as Assistant to D.A.D.R.T. EIFEL TOR Station COLOGNE	

C. E. Heathcote
Lieut Col.
Commdg 2/4th K.O.Y.L.I.

D. D. & L., London E.C
(10340) W1 W5300/P713 750,000 3/18 E 688 Forms/C2118/16.

Med ^{Bn}

Confidential

War Diary

2/4th Bn. K. O. Yorks. L. I.

From 1-8-19 | Vol. 32 | To 31-8-19

Instructions regarding War Diaries and Intelligence Summaries are contained in F. S. Regs., Part II. and the Staff Manual respectively. Title pages will be prepared in manuscript.

WAR DIARY
or
INTELLIGENCE SUMMARY.
(Erase heading not required.)

Army Form C. 2118.

Place	Date	Hour	Summary of Events and Information	Remarks and references to Appendices
BRUHL.	1-8-19		Minden Day. General holiday.	[illegible]
BRUHL.	4-8-19		Bank Holiday.	[illegible]
BRUHL.	6-8-19		Battalion moved to GYMNICH.	[illegible]
GYMNICH.	9-8-19		Practice Parade at LIBLAR for inspection by Army Council.	[illegible]
GYMNICH.	13-8-19		Second Practice Parade at ROMERHOF for inspection by Army Council.	[illegible]
GYMNICH.	19-8-19		Inspection by Army Council at ROMERHOF.	[illegible]
GYMNICH.	23-8-19		2/Lieut. T. H. Briggs M.C. proceeded to U.K. for demobilization.	[illegible]
GYMNICH	29-8-19		Lieut. J. E. David & 2/Lieut. C. L. Douthwaite proceeded to U.K. for demobilization.	[illegible]

[illegible signature]
Lieut Col.
Commanding 2/4th Bn. K.O.Y.L.I.

A5834 Wt. W4973/M687 750,000 8/16 D. D. & L. Ltd. Forms/C.2118/13.

Midland DIV
late 6th

1 MIDLAND BDE

5 BN Kings Own Y L I

1919 MAR - 1919 AUG

FROM 62 DIV 187 BDE

5th Battalion The Kings Own Yorkshire Light Infantry.

WAR DIARY

FOR MONTH ENDED 31st MARCH, 1919.

INTELLIGENCE SUMMARY. 5TH BN. K.O. YORKS. L.I.

Date	Place		
MARCH. 1st 1919 2 3 4 5 6	GLADBACH " " " " " "	16TH INFANTRY BRIGADE. TRAINING	JT
7	GLADBACH.	ORDERS RECIEVED FOR THE ABSORBTION OF 51ST BN. (G) K.O.Y.L.I.	JT
8 9 10 11 12 13	GLADBACH	TRAINING	
14.	GLADBACH.	MOVED BY ROUTE MARCH TO FREIZHEIM INTO 18TH I.B. MIDLAND DIVISION.	JT
15 16 17 18 19 20 21	FREIZHEIM.	TRAINING	JT

INTELLIGENCE SUMMARY.

5TH BN K.O. YORKS. L.I.

Date	Place	Summary	Remarks
MARCH. 22ND 1919	FREIZHEIM.	MOVE BY ROUTE MARCH TO LIBLAR. 1 COMPANY BILLETED AT LIBLAR STATION	[illegible]
23 " 24 " 25 " 26 " 27 " 28 " 29 " 30 " 31 "	LIBLAR.	TRAINING " " " " " " " " MARCH. 27. 1919 INSPECTION OF BATTALION BY BRIG. GEN. C.W. GWYNN C.B. C.M.G. D.S.O.	[illegible]
		DEMOBILIZATION OFFICERS --- 2 CAPT P. BENTLEY M.C. CAPT C.E. TOWNEND M.C. OTHER RANKS -- 80	[illegible]
		[signature] Lieut Col Commdg 5 K.O.Y.L.I.	

15 M.
2 sheets

5th. Battalion The King's Own Yorkshire Light Infantry.

WAR DIARY.

FOR MONTH ENDED 30TH APRIL 1919.

INTELLIGENCE SUMMARY 5TH BN. K.O.Y.L.I.

APRIL 6th 1919	'C' Company moved into KÖTTINGEN	H.T.
APRIL 11th 1919	MAJOR T. SHEARMAN. D.S.O. proceeds to ENGLAND for demobilization	H.T.
APRIL 17th 1919	LT COL. TREVOR. CMG. D.S.O. arrives at the battalion	H.T.
APRIL 18th 1919	LT COL. TREVOR CMG D.S.O. takes over command of the battalion	H.T.
APRIL 29th 1919	LT COL F.H. PETER. DSO. MC. proceeds for an interview	H.T.
	DEMOBILIZATION 6 officers 109 ORs	H.T.
APRIL 1st - 30th	TRAINING (Platoon Training)	H.T.

H.E. Trevor

Lt Col.

Commanding

5th Bn K.O.Y.L.I.

2.5.1919.

INTELLIGENCE SUMMARY. 5TH Bn K.O.Y.L.I.

Date	Summary	
MAY 1919		
1st to 31st	Platoon Training Recreation	H.1.
	Demobilization - Officers	
	Lieut. W. Crow. M.C. 10.5.1919.	
	1st Lieut. I.V. Laudeutcher. M.R.C. 8.5.1919.	H.
	Other Ranks 11.	H.
	Taken on the Strength	
	Lieut. E.H.O. Keats 21.5.1919.	
	Capt. C. Dean M.C. 26.5.1919.	H.
	Attached please find Copy No 14 of the 5th Battalion Kings Own Yorkshire Light Infantry Operation Order No 1.	H.
	H. Tryon Lieut Colonel Commanding 5 KOYLI	

16.M.
3 sheets

SECRET. Copy No. 14

5th Battn., King's Own Yorkshire Light Infantry.

OPERATION ORDER NO. 1.

May 30th 1919.

REFERENCE MAP :- EUSKIRCHEN.

1. If the Peace Negotiations fail, notice of the termination of the Armistice in 72 hours will be given to the Germans. The day on which the Armistice ceases will be called "J" Day.

2. In the event of this the 1st Midland Brigade will move to the Area East of DUREN with the object of guarding the communications by road and Railway along the DUREN - COLOGNE Line.

3. The 5th Bn., K.O.Y.L.I. will move to the VETTWEISS AREA and will be accomodated in billets there.
This move will take place on J - 1 day. J day will be notified to all concerned later.

4. Starting point for the move will be the Bridge over the River ERFT which is 800 yards S.E. of the Church at LIBLAR. The Battalion will rendezvous there "infours" facing S.E. at a time to be notified later, in the following order, H.Q., "D" Coy, "C" Coy, Band, Cased Colours, "A" Coy, "B" Coy.
Transport will move in rear of the Battalion and Field Kitchens and L.G. Limbers will move with the Transport. The distances named in "Notes on March Discipline" will come into force from marching off from the starting point.

5. The Colour Party consisting of Lieut. W.R.Laidlaw, 2/Lt. H.F. Andrews M.M., one Sergeant and two Corporals from "A" Coy, will report to the Adjutant at a time to be notified later at Battn., Headquarters. Colours will be carried cased.

6. Advanced billeting parties under Lieut. H.E.Sharp and consisting of the undermentioned will proceed to take over billets in the new area on J - 2 day.
4 C.Q.M.S., representatives from H.Q., Q.M., and T.O., Sgt.Ploss, and two O.R's per Company will report to the Adjutant at Battalion Headquarters on receipt of instructions to do so.

7. ROUTE - LIBLAR, LECHENICH, ERP, GLADBACH, VETTWEISS.

8. Dress - Marching order, S.D. Caps to be worn, with steel helmets fastened to the valise. Water bottles filled.

9. On Companies being notified of J day all O.R's will be issued with the extra 60 rounds S.A.A. and any surplus after this has been done will be sent to the Q.M. Stores.
Indents will be submitted immediately by Os.C. Companies and Headquarters to the Q.M. to complete all Officers and O.R's with iron rations.

10. Previous instructions have been issued with regard to surplus baggage which is now under the control of the Quartermaster. Three lorries will be placed at the disposal of the Battalion for the move and will do double journeys, and are allotted to Companies as under:-
1st journey - 1 lorry each to "B", "C" and Headquarters.
2nd journey - 1 lorry each to "A", "D" and Quartermaster.
All lorry drivers will be instructed to report to the Quartermaster before leaving LIBLAR.
On receipt of the warning order to move, Canteen goods, dining hall utensils, sports equipment, surplus Orderly Room boxes, Company Education boxes, etc., will be collected at Company H.Q's.
Transport Officer will collect this baggage and convey it to the Q.M. Stores.

11. Surplus baggage which cannot be moved, will be stacked at the

(continued).

11. Q.M. Stores. O.C. "D" Company will detail one platoon, and the Q.M. personnel not going forward to the New Area, as a guard over this baggage. This party will be issued with three full days rations.

12. The H.Q. Section 18th Field Ambulance will move under the orders of O.C. 5th Bn., K.O.Y.L.I. and will proceed to billets in FRAUWULLESHEIM. O.C. "D" Company will detail a strong Platoon as escort to this Section. Further instructions re Rations, billets, and orders to move for this Platoon will be notified later.

13. The two Platoons of "C" Company finding the Town Picquet of LECHENICH will rejoin the Battalion on the march.

14. Special attention is directed to the handing over of billets and latrines in a clean and sanitary condition.

15. Orders will be issued at a later date with regard to rear parties for handing over billets and all Garrison fittings and R.E. Stores.

16. Acknowledge.

[signature]
Captain.
Adjutant, 5th Bn., K.O.Y.L.I.

Issued at 2100 hours.

Copies to :- No.1 Commanding Officer.
2 2nd in Command.
3)
4)
5) Os.C. Companies
6) & H.Q.
7)
8 Quartermaster.
9 Transport Officer.
10 Lieut. H.R.Sharp.
11 Medical Officer.
12 1st Midland Brigade.
13 R.S.M.
14 War Diary. ✓
15 File.

5TH Battalion The Kings Own Yorkshire Light Infantry

Intelligence Summary June 1919

5th BATTN.
THE
KING'S OWN YORKSHIRE
LIGHT INFANTRY.
No. 276.
Date.

Date	Summary	
June 1st to 30th.	Platoon Training. Organized Games.	H.T.
June 9th	The battalion (less D Coy) move from LIBLAR to BRUHL.	H.T.
June 18th	The battalion (less D Coy) move from BRUHL to LIBLAR.	H.T.
June 19th	The battalion move to VEITWIES.	H.T.
June 12th	Lt. Col. C. E. Heathcote CB. CMG. D.S.O. reported his arrival to the battalion	H.T.
June 18th	Lt Col. C. E. Heathcote CB. CMG. D.S.O. takes over command of 2/4 Batt The Kings Own Yorkshire Light Infantry	H.T.
June 20th	2/Lt JH. Williamson reported his arrival to the battalion	H.T.
June 24th	2/Lt JH. Williamson attached 2/4 KOYLI.	H.T.
	Demobilization Officers NIL ORs 10	H.T.

H.E. Twan Lt Colonel
Commanding 5. KOYLI

L.B.

7.11.
13 sheet

SECRET Copy No..4....

5th Battn., King's Own Yorkshire Light Infantry.

OPERATION ORDER No. 1.

May 30th 1919.

REFERENCE MAP :- EUSKIRCHEN.

1. If the Peace negotiations fail, notice of the termination of the Armistice in 72 hours will be given to the Germans. The day on which the Armistice ceases will be called "J" Day.

2. In the event of this the 1st Midland Brigade will move to the area East of DUREN with the object of guarding the communications by road and railway along the DUREN - COLOGNE Line.

3. The 5th Bn., K.O.Y.L.I. will move to the VETTWEISS AREA and will be accomodated in Billets there.
This move will take place on J - 1 day. J day will be notified to all concerned later.

4. Starting point for the move will be the Bridge over the River ERFT which is 800 yards S.E. of the Church at LIBLAR. The Battalion will rendezvous there "in fours" facing S.E. at a time to be notified later, in the following order, H.Q. "D" Coy, "C" Coy, Band, Cased Colours, "A" Coy, "B" Coy.
Transport will move in rear of the Battalion and Field Kitchens and L.G. Limbers will move with the Transport. The distances named in "Notes on March Discipline" will come into force from marching off from the starting point.

5. The Colour Party consisting of Lieut. W.E.Laidlaw, 2/Lt. H.F.Andrews M.M., one Sergeant and two Corporals from "A" Coy, will report to the Adjutant at a time to be notified later at Battalion Headquarters. Colours will be carried cased.

6. Advanced billeting parties under Lieut. H.E.Sharp and consisting of the undermentioned will proceed to take over billets in the new area on J - 2 day.
4 C.Q.M.S, representatives from H.Q., Q.M., and T.O., Sgt. Pless, and two O.R's per Company will report to the Adjutant at Battalion Headquarters on receipt of instructions to do so.

7. ROUTE - LIBLAR, LECHENICH, ERP, GLADBACH, VETTWEISS.

8. Dress - Marching Order, S.D. Caps to be worn with steel helmets fastened to the valise. Water bottles filled.

9. On Companies being notified of J day all Other Ranks will be issued with the extra 60 rounds S.A.A. and any surplus after this has been done will be sent to the Q.M. Stores.
Indents will be submitted immediately by Os.C. Companies and Headquarters to the Q.M. to complete all Officers and O.R's with iron Rations.

10. Previous instructions have been issued with regard to the surplus baggage which is now under the control of the Quartermaster. Three lorries will be placed at the disposal of the Battalion for the move and will do double journeys, and are allotted to Companies as under :-
1st journey 1 lorry each to "B", "C" and Headquarters,
2nd journey 1 lorry each to "A", "D" and Quartermaster.
All lorry drivers will be instructed to report to the Quartermaster before leaving LIBLAR.
On receipt of the warning order to move, Canteen goods, dining hall utensils, sports equipment, surplus Orderly Room boxes, Company Education boxes, etc., will be collected at Company H.Q's.
The Transport Officer will collect this baggage and convey it to the Q.M. Stores.

11. Surplus baggage which cannot be moved, will be stacked at the

(contin[illegible]).

11. Q.M. Stores. O.C. "D" Company will detail one Platoon, and the Q.M. the personnel not going forward to the new Area, as a Guard over this baggage. This party will be issued with three full days rations.

12. The H.Q. Section 18th Field Ambulance will move under the orders of O.C. 5th Bn.,K.O.Y.L.I. and will proceed to billets in FRAUVILLERSHEIM. O.C. "D" Company will detail a strong Platoon as escort to this Section. Further instructions re rations, billets, and orders to move for this Platoon will be notified later.

13. The two Platoons of "C" Company finding the Town Picquet of LECHENICH will rejoin the Battalion on the march.

14. Special attention is directed to the handing over of billets and Latrines in a clean and sanitary condition.

15. Orders will be issued at a later date with regard to rear parties for handing over billets and all Garrison fittings and R.E. Stores.

16. Acknowledge.

P.J. Farnish

Captain.

Adjutant, 5th Bn.,K.O.Y.L.I.

Issued at 2100 hours.

Copies to :- No.1 Commanding Officer.
2 2nd in Command.
3 }
4 }
5 } Os.C. Companies.
6 } & H.Q.
7 }
8 Quartermaster.
9 Transport Officer.
10 Lt. H.E.Sharp.
11 Medical Officer.
12 1st Midland Brigade.
13 R.S.M.
14 War Diary.
15 FILE.

SECRET. COPY NO. 8

5th Battalion The King's Own Yorkshire Light Infantry.

OPERATION ORDER No. 2.

Ref. Map : EUSKIRCHEN. June 7th 1919.

1. Operation Order No. 1 of May 30th, 1919 is cancelled.
The 5th Bn K.O.Y.L.I. (less "B" & "D" Coys) will move to BRUHL, and take over the billets occupied by 52nd Sherwood Foresters on the 9th June.
Orders for "B" and "D" Coys will be issued separately.

2. Starting Point 500yds EAST of the Railway Level Crossing on the LIBLAR-BRUHL Road. The Battalion will rendezvous at this point "in fours" facing East, in the following order at 10 hrs :-
Band.
H.Q. Coy.
"A" Coy.
Cased Colours.
"C" Coy.
Transport.
Transport including L.G. Limbers and Field Kitchens, less that detailed for "B" & "D" Coys, will move in the rear of the Battn.
DRESS :- Marching Order, S.D. Caps will be worn. Steel helmets fastened to valise.

3. Colour Party consisting of Lieuts. W.E. Laidlaw & G.H. Taylor, MC?MM, and 1 Sgt and 2 Cpls from "C" Coy will report to the Adjutant at 9.30 hrs. Colours will be carried cased.

4. Companies of 5th Bn K.O.Y.L.I. will take over from Companies of 52nd Sherwood Foresters as below.
"A" Coy, 5th K.O.Y.L.I. takes over from "A" Coy, Sherwood Foresters.
"B" " -do- -do- "C" " -do-
(Ammunition Guard, VOCHEM).
"C" " -do- takes over from "D" Coy, Sherwood Foresters.
Bn H.Q. -do- -do- Bn H.Q. -do-

5. "D" Coy is detailed as the Garrison of LIBLAR, and will remain there. This Coy will take over the following Guards of which full details have been issued.
(a) RODENKIRCHEN, Chemical Factory.
(b) COLOGNE DEUTZ Goods Station.
(c) EIFEL TOR Station, ZULLSTOCH AREA, COLOGNE. found by C Coy
(d) Guard over Baggage Dump, LIBLAR.
"D" Coy will take over the present Bn H.Q. and 1 platoon will be sent as Garrison to take charge of the Compound at LIBLAR STATION.
The Transport Officer will issue instructions for the following Transport horsed, and necessary personnel to be attached to "D" Coy.
1 Charger.
1 L.G. Limber.
1 Field Kitchen.
1 Mess Cart for S.A.A.
1 Pack Animal for S.A.A.
The Q.M. will arrange for Rations for this Coy and the Transport Animals.

6. Advance billetting Parties under Lieut. H.E. Sharp and consisting of the following will proceed to the new area on Sunday, June 8th to take over billets.
2 C.Q.M. Sgts.
Sgt Ploss H.G.
Representatives from H.Q. T.O. Q.M. and
2 O.R's per Company,
will report to the Adjutant at 1400 hrs.
The Billetting Officer will detail Guides from the Advance Party to meet the Battn in the Southern outskirts of BRUHL on the BRUHL-LIBLAR Road.

7. Three lorries will be placed at nthe disposal of the Battn for the move, and will report to the Q.M. at 08.00 hrs, who will arrange for the removal of all baggage.

8. Officers' Valises, Mess Kit, Medical Equipment, Orderly Room Boxes and all surplus baggage will be stacked at Bn H.Q. and Coy H.Q. ready for removal by hrs. Blankets securely tied and labelled, rolled into bundles of ten will be stacked at Bn and Coy H.Qrs. ready for removal by 08.00 hrs.
N.B. Surplus baggage not going forward should be handed in to Q.M. Stores by 1800 hrs June 8th.

9. The responsibility of the Defence of BRUHL and of the four Bridges of the COLOGNE-BONN Railway which lie in BRUHL and immediately North and South of it will be taken over by O.C. 5th BN K.O.Y.L.I. on June 9th in addition to his present area.

10. Special attention is directed to leaving billets and latrines in a clean and sanitary condition.

11. Completion of the move will be notified to Bn H.Q.

12. Battn H.Q. will close at LIBLAR at 10 hrs, and re-open at BRUHL on arrival.

13. ACKNOWLEDGE.

P. J. Jarrett
Captain,
Adjutant, 5th Bn K.O.Y.L.I.

Issued at ..0900..... hrs.

COPIES TO :-

1. Commanding Officer.
2. 2nd in Command.
3. Capt. T.A.H. Oliphant, MC.
4.)
5.)
6.) O.C. Companies & Bn H.Q.
7.)
8.)
9. Q.M.
10. T.O.
11. Lieut. H.E. Sharp.
12. M.O.
13. 1st Mid. Brigade.
14. R.S.M.
15. War Diary.
16. FILE.

@@@@@@@@@@

SECRET. COPY NO....8.....

Appendix No. 1 issued with 5th Bn K.O.Y.L.I.
Operation Order No.2½

Ref. Map : EUSKIRCHEN. June 7th 1919.

1. "B" Coy, 5th Bn K.O.Y.L.I. will relieve "C" Coy, 52nd Sherwood Foresters, who are on Guard over the VOCHEM Army Ammunition Dump, on Sunday June 8th, 1919. Relief to be completed by 1530 hrs.

2. O.C. "B" Coy will arrange all the details of the relief. i.e. moving off, posting of sentries, taking over defence scheme, duties, advance billetting party etc with O.C. "C" Coy 52nd Sherwood Foresters

3. One lorry will be placed at the disposal of O.C. "B" Coy for the move and the time of its arrival will be notified later. All baggage will be stacked at Coy H.Q. by 0900 hrs ready for removal Sunday June 8th. N.B. Surplus baggage not going forward will be dumped at the Q.M. STores not later than 1800 hrs June 7th. The T.O. will detail limbers to remove this baggage if necessary.

4. The T.O. will issue instructions for the following horsed transport and personnel to report to O.C. "B" Coy at 1100 hrs Sunday June 8th.
   1 Charger.
   1 L.G. Limber.
   1 Field Kitchen.
   1 S.A.A. Limber.
   1 Pack Animal S.A.A.

5. O.C. "B" Coy will arrange direct with the Q.M. for Rations for the Coy, and for the Transport Animals.

6. The Signalling Officer will attach 3 extra Signallers to this Coy by 0900 hrs June 8th.

7. Completion of move will be notified to Bn H.Q.

8. ACKNOWLEDGE.

P.J. Farnish[?]
Captain,
Adjutant. 5th Bn K.O.Y.L.I.

Issued at ..0900.... hrs.

Copies to :-
1 Commanding Officer.
2 2nd in Command.
3 Capt. T.A.H Oliphant, MC.
4)
5)
6) O.C. Companies and Bn H.Q.
7)
8) ✓
9. Q.M.
10. T.O.
11. Lieut H.E. Sharp.
12. M.O.
13. 1st Mid. Brigade.
14. R.S.M.
15. War Diary.
16. FILE.

SECRET. COPY NO....8.....

5th. BATTALION THE KING'S OWN YORKSHIRE LIGHT INFANTRY.

OPERATION ORDER NO. 3.

Ref. Map EUSKIRCHEN. 1/100000. **18th. June. 1919.**

1. The 5th. Battn. K.O.Y.L.I. will move by route march to VETTWEISS, tomorrow and will be accommodated in billets.

2. **STARTING POINT.** - Bridge over River ERFT, 800 yards S.E. of LIBLAR at 0930 hours "in fours" facing S.W. in the order Battn. H.Q., "D" Coy., Band, Colours, "C" "A" & "B" Coys., Transport. The distances named in "Notes on March Discipline" will come into force from marching off at the starting point.

3. The Colour Party, consisting of Lieut. E.H.O. Keates. M.C. and 2/Lieut. G.H.Needham, 1 Sergt. and 2 Corpls from "A" Coy., will report to the Adjutant at Battn. H.Q. at 0900 hours. Colours will be carried cased.

4. Advanced Billet Party under Lieut. H.L.Sharp, and consisting of 4 C.Q.M.S's, Sergt. Floss, representatives from H.Q., Q.M., and Transport Officer and 1 O.R. per Coy. and H.Q. will proceed by train from LIBLAR Station at ~~[illegible]~~ 0920 hours and take over billets. Rations will be taken. Guides will meet the Battalion at entrance to VETTWEISS to guide Coys., to billets.

5. The H.Q. Section, 18th Field Ambulance will move under the orders of O.C. 5th. K.O.Y.L.I. to billets in KELZ. This Section will move in the rear of the Battalion and will be drawn up on the BLESSEM - LIBLAR road, facing E by 09.20 hours, and will not emerge from that road until the last Coy. of the Battalion has passed. O.C. "D" Coy. will detail 2 Sections to report to O.C. 18th. Field Ambulance at 09.20 hours at BLESSEM as escort.

6. O.C. "D" Coy., will detail a guard over the surplus Baggage Dump at LIBLAR of 1 Platoon. This Platoon will be issued with 3 days rations. The guard of 1 Platoon at present at Brigade H.Q. at LECHENICH will rejoin the Battalion on the march.

7. Lorries will be placed at the disposal of the Battalion for the move, and will report to the Q.M. at LIBLAR CHURCH at 07.30 hrs. All Baggage and Blankets will be stacked at Battalion and Coy. H.Q's. by 08.00 hrs., and the Q.M. will arrange all details for its removal.

8. Completion of move will be notified to Battalion H.Q.

9. Battalion H.Q. will close at LIBLAR at 0930 hrs. and re-open at VETTWEISS on arrival.

10. Acknowledge.

P.J. Fairnish
Captain.
Adjutant.
5th Bn. K.O.Y.L.I.

Copies to -

1. Commanding Officer.
2. 2nd in Command.
3. Capt. T.A.H.Oliphant.M.C.
4., 5., 6., 7., & 8. O's.C. Coys. and Bn.H.Q.
9. Q.M.
10. T.O.
11. 1st. Midland Brigade.
12. Signalling Officer.
13. M.O.
14. R.S.M.
15. War Diary.
16. O.C. 18th Field Amb.
17. File.
18. File.

SECRET.

To. Midland Division "G".
Midland Division "Q".
Camp Commandant, Midland Division.
1st Midland Brigade.
Town Major, BRUHL.
D.A.P.M. BRUHL.
Os.Companies.
Bn.,H.Q.
Quartermaster.
War Diary.
File.

5th BATTN.
THE
KING'S OWN YORKSHIRE
LIGHT INFANTRY.
No. KB349.
16.6.19

Reference Defence Scheme in the event ofCivil Disturbances, dated June 14th 1919.

Please insert the following :-

Reference Maps Nos. 3 and 4, COLOGNE, 1/25,000.

Adjt. for P.A. Jamieson Capt.
Lt.-Colonel.
Commanding, 5th Bn.,K.O.Y.L.I.

June 16th 1919.

SECRET.   Copy No......13.

5th Battalion The King's Own Yorkshire Light Infantry.

DEFENCE SCHEME IN THE EVENT OF CIVIL DISTURBANCES.

Ref. Map: June 14th, 1919.

1. Extracts from Scheme "A" of 1st Midland Brigade Defence Scheme issued under this Office No. 2 are suspended, owing to the move of the Battalion from LIBLAR, and the following substituted.

Warning. 2. In the event of warning of Civil Disturbances being received or of actual trouble occurring, the message "CIVIL DISTURBANCE PREPARE" will be sent out to all concerned by Battn. H.Qrs.

Action to be taken on receipt of warning. 3. On receipt of the above message the following precautionary measures will be taken forthwith.

(a) O.C. "D" Coy will re-inforce the Guard at VOCHEM ammunition dump with the remainder of the Company and will take all measures for the defence of the dump in accordance with Appendix I hereto.

(b) Buglers will sound the "ALARM" at Bn H.Qrs and Coy H.Qrs. The "Alarm" will be taken up by all Buglers who hear it.

(c) All troops at Training, Games or on Working Parties will be recalled to billets.

On hearing the "Alarm" or becoming aware of the imminence of Civil Disturbances all individual Officers and O.R's away from their units will rejoin them at once.

(d) "A", "C" & "D" Coys and Bn H.Qrs personnel will be prepared to move at 30 minutes notice in Marching Order with 120 rounds S.A.A. and bayonets fixed, as follows :-

BRUHL AREA.

(i) "A" Coy. for the defence of the Bridges near BRUHL shown on attached map in accordance with Appendix II attached.

This Coy will maintain touch with the Units on its North and South flanks, viz.

53rd Bn Northumberland Fusiliers, H.Q. [illegible].
6th Bn Welch Regiment.   H.Q. [illegible].

(ii) "C" Coy will be responsible for the defence of the BRUHL - LIBLAR Road from Bruhl to Railway Crossing South of GROSS BRUHL exclusive.

This Coy will be relieved by "D" Coy as soon as the latter has been relieved in the LIBLAR Area, and will then be in Battn. Reserve, available to act (a) in the defence of BRUHL, (b) in the defence of [illegible]-[illegible]-PINGSDORF Area, (c) in the defence of KIERBERG, or otherwise as may be required.

(iii) Bn H.Qrs.Personnel of Bn H.Qrs (less guard for H.Q. Mess) under O.C. H.Q. Coy will be organized at the SEMINARY, for the defence of BRUHL. The anti-aircraft L. Guns will be available for this purpose.

(iv) Details of Divn H.Q. under the Camp Commandant, Capt H.J. Spicer, will assemble at the SEMINARY and will act under the orders of the O.C. 5th/Bn K.O.Y.L.I.

LIBLAR AREA.

(v) "D" Coy. 1 platoon less 2 sections for the defence of t the railway bridge East by South of LIBLAR, and 1 platoon and 2 sections to guard LIBLAR - BRUHL Road to Railway crossing South of GROSS BRUHL inclusive. Remainder of Coy in Reserve.

On relief by a Company of the [illegible] Battn this Coy will take over the defence of the BRUHL - LIBLAR Road from "C" Coy as detailed in para 3 (d) (ii).

(e) L.G. and S.A.A. limbers will be packed and all other transport loaded ready to move at 30 minutes notice. Horses harnessed but not hooked in.

(f) Surplus Stores and heavy baggage in the BRUHL Area will be collected in a central spot in each Company area under a guard of 1 N.C.O. and 3 O.R's with a view to its removal to the Seminary, BRUHL, as early as possible.
At LIBLAR it will be similarly collected at the Theatre, and at the Compound.

Communi-
cations.

4. The Battalion Signalling Officer will be responsible that on receipt of the warning message mentioned in para 2, the following signalling arrangements are put into force at once.

(i) Visual Stations are manned ensuring the communications between :-
"D" Coy at LIBLAR and Brigade H.Qrs at the Schloss, LECHENICH.
"A", "B" & "C" Coys with Bn H.Qrs at the Seminary, BRUHL.

(ii) Wireless communication is established between Bn H.Qrs and Brigade H.Qrs through Divisional H.Q at BRUHL.

(iii) Light Signal Stations are manned at Bn H.Qrs and each Coy H.Qrs.
The following Light Signals will be used.

Red Verey Light.	...	Alarm.
Green Verey Light.	...	S.O.S.
White Verey Light.	...	Answering Signal.

(iv) H.Qrs sign and panel for communication with aircraft are put out and runners told off to watch for and collect messages dropped from aircraft on Battn. Dropping Ground.

Action.

5. On receipt of message "CIVIL DISTURBANCE - TAKE ACTION" Companies and Guards detailed in para 3 will parade on their Alarm Posts, and after drawing additional rounds of S.A.A. will move at once to their positions by the quickest routes.
L.G. limbers and Cookers will accompany their Companies.
S.A.A. carts and Water Carts will not move without further orders.

Distur-
bances
arising
without
warning.

6. In the event of disturbances arising without either or both the messages contained in paras 2 & 5 having been sent out such measures as the situation demands, including re-inforcements of Guards, and picquetting roads leading to the disturbed area, will be taken by the Company Commander concerned, or other senior Officer on the spot, with a view to

(a) Localising the disturbances,
(b) Suppressing them,
(c) If too large to be suppressed by the troops available on the spot, localising them until the arrival of re-inforcements.

Ringleaders will be arrested: any action taken will be reported at once to Bn H.Qrs.

7. Whilst engaged in suppressing Civil Disturbances troops will always parade with fixed bayonets and steel helmets.
Fire will be controlled, and if an Officer is present will only be opened on the orders of that Officer.
Fire if opened is to be effective, but as far as possible directed against actual rioters.

8. Company Commanders will make the necessary reconnaissances of the positions they will occupy and of the quickest routes to them and will prepare and submit, as soon as possible, to Bn H.Qrs for approval, orders for the carrying out of the tasks allotted to them respectively.

9. ACKNOWLEDGE.

Lieut-Colonel,
Commanding 5th Bn K.O.Y.L.I.

Issued at .... hrs.

Copies to :-

1. Midland Division "G".
2. Midland Division "Q".
3. Camp Commandant, Midland Division.
4. 1st Midland Brigade.
5. Town Major, [illegible].
6. A.P.M., [illegible].
7. }
8. }
9. } O.C. Coys & H.Qrs.
10. }
11. }
12. Q.M.
13. } War Diary.
14. }
15. File.

SECRET. COPY NO..8.......

5th Battalion The King's Own Yorkshire Light Infantry.

AMENDMENT TO OPERATION ORDER No. 1.

Ref. Map MUSKIRCHEN. June 17th, 1919.

1. Tomorrow being "J-2" Day, the Battalion will move by route march to LIBLAR and take over the billets vacated on June 9th. "J" Day will be June 20th.

2. "A" & "B" Coys will remain in their present positions until relieved by Companies of the 3rd Midland Brigade. All guards at present found by the Battalion will remain until relieved by guards from 3rd Midland Brigade. O.C. "B" Coy will detail a Guard of 1 platoon to report to the Staff Captain, 1st Midland Brigade H.Q., LECHENICH, at 0800 hrs, on "J-2" Day to guard surplus stores.

3. On relief, Coys and Guards detailed in above para will rejoin thexx Battalion.

4. Staring point for H.Q. Coy and Transport - Level Crossing over Light Railway on KIERBERG-PINGSDORF Line, on BRUHL-LIBLAR Road at 0930 hrs, in fours facing West, in the order Band, H.Q., Colour Party, "C" Coy, Transport. Transport of "A" & "B" Coys will move with their respective Coys.

5. Colour Party consisting of 2/Lieut. R.A. Young, 2/Lieut. H.E. Bunting, one Sgt and two Cpls of "C" Coy will report to the Adjutant at Battn. H.Q. Mess at 0830 hrs. Colours will be carried cased.

6. Lorries will be placed at the disposal of the Battalion for the move, and will report to the Quartermaster at the SEMINAR at 0730 hrs. All baggage and blankets will be stacked at Battn. and Coy H.Qrs. by 0730 hrs, and the Q.M. will arrange all details for its removal.

7. Completion of move will be notified to Battn. H.Qrs.

8. ACKNOWLEDGE.

P.J. Fannish
Captain,
Adjutant,
5th Bn K.O.Y.L.I.

Copies to :-

1. Commanding Officer.
2. Second in Command.
3. Capt. T.A.H Oliphant, MC.
4.)
5.)
6.) O's C. Coys and Bn H.Q.
7.)
8.) ✓
9. Q.M.
10. T.O.
11. 1st Midland Brigade.
12. Signalling Officer.
13. M.O.
14. R.S.M.
15. War Diary.
16. File.
17. File.

SECRET.

COPY NO.....4......

5th. Battalion The King's Own Yorkshire Light Infantry.

WARNING ORDER.

Reference Map Germany 1/100000. Sheet 1L. 20th June. 1919.

1. 1st. Midland Brigade Defence Scheme No 2. is suspended owing to the move of the Brigade to a new area.

2. In the event of the termination of the Armistice on account of the refusal of the enemy to sign Peace the conditions of Active Warfare will exist and Unit Commanders will be responsible for their own protection.

3. From June 21st. inclusive, the Battalion will be organised for operations as follows;-

(a) "A" Coy. will be in readiness to move as a Mobile Column at 1 hour's notice.

(b) "B" Coy. will be in readiness to move in support of "A" C- oy at 2 hours notice.

(c) "C" Coy. will hold itself in readiness in reserve to furnish escort and duties as required by Brigade H/Q . .

(d) "D" Coy. and Battn. H.Q. will hold themselves in readiness as an inlying picquet for the protection of the Battalion billeting area.
Field Kitchens with rations and Lewis Gun Limbers will accompany their respective Companies as detailed in above para.

4. Whilst employed actively, all Companies will move in Fighting Order with Steel Helmets, Bayonets fixed and with 120 rounds S.A.A. Packs will be dumped at Coy. H.Q. The T.O. will arrange to collect these and convey them to the Q.M. Stores. O.C. Battn. H.Q. will detail a loading party for this duty.
Iron Rations to the scale of 1 per Officer and man will be drawn by 10.00 hrs. tomorrow.

5. Visual Signalling communication will be established forthwith between 2/4th Duke of Wellington's Regiment/and Brigade Headquarters. (at MERZENICH)
2/4th Duke of Wellington's Regiment and 2/ 4th.K.O.Y.L.I. at BHIR.
Light Signal Stations will be established.
The following code will be used;-

Red Verey Light	-	Alarm.
Green do.	-	S.O.S.
White do.	-	Answering Signal.

6. ACKNOWLEDGE.

P. F. Samuel
Captain & Adjutant,
5th. K.O.Y.L.I.

Copies to;-

1. Commanding Officer.
2. Second in Command.
3.
4.
5. O's. C. Coys. and Bn.H.Q.
6.
7.
8. Signalling Officer.
9. Transport Officer.
10. Quartermaster.
11. R.S.M.
12. File.

5th K.O.Y.L.I.

Intelligence Summary. July. 1919

July 1st to 7th.	Platoon Training at BRUHL.	H.T.
July 8th.	The battalion move by march route to WEILERSWIST. Musketry Camp.	H.T.
July 9th	The battalion firing General Musketry Course on the Rifle Range at WEILERSWIST.	H.T.
July 18th.	The battalion move by march route to LIBLAR.	H.T.
July 23rd	5Bn K.O.Y.L.I. Sports festival at LIBLAR. Lady Robertson, wife of the Commander in Chief, presented the prizes.	H.T.
July. 30th.	1st Midland Brigade Sports at ROMERHOF. "B" Coy 5 Bn. K.O.Y.L.I. won the cup presented by Brig General. C.W. Jeayes. C.B. C.M.G. D.S.O. and Staff of the 1st Midland Brigade for the Brigade Standard Competition	H.T.
Mentions in Dispatches	Captain P. Beilby M.C. 5 K.O.Y.L.I. London Gazette 22.7.1919 Captain P.F. Farnish " " " " " " " Company Sgt Major W. Pavee " " " " " " "	H.T.
Demobilization	Officers. NIL. ORs. 5.	H.T.

5th BATTN. THE KING'S OWN YORKSHIRE LIGHT INFANTRY. 295. 31.7.19

H. Trevor Lt. Colonel.
31.7.1919. Commanding 5Bn K.O.Y.L.I.

AUGUST. 1919. 5TH Bn. K.O.Y.L.I. INTELLIGENCE SUMMARY.

AUGUST. 1st - 31st.	Training as usual. LIBLAR.	H.I.
AUGUST. 19th	Inspected by Army Council at ROMERHOF GERMANY. MR WINSTON CHURCHILL took the salute.	H.I.
AUGUST. 27th.	Regimental Equipment proceeds by rail from LIBLAR GERMANY to ANTWERP en route for GEORGETOWN.	H.I.
AUGUST 28th.	ANIMALS proceed by rail to CALAIS.	H.I.

P.J. Tannick(?) Capt.
Adjt. for Lt Colonel
Commanding
5 KOYLI.

BEF

MIDLAND DIV

2 MID. BDE. H.Q

1919 MAR to 1919 AUG

2nd. Midland Bde No. B.M. 295/6.

Midland Division.

War Diaries for month ending March 31st 1919. are forwarded herewith.

[illegible] Capt.
for Lieut-Colonel,

12th Apl. 1919. Commanding, 2nd Midland Bde.

Army Form C. 2118.

WAR DIARY

or

~~INTELLIGENCE~~ SUMMARY.

(Erase heading not required.)

Instructions regarding War Diaries and Intelligence Summaries are contained in F. S. Regs., Part II. and the Staff Manual respectively. Title pages will be prepared in manuscript.

1156

Place	Date	Hour	Summary of Events and Information	Remarks and references to Appendices
March	1		The Brigadier was present at farewell parades of 2/Y.& L & 1st.The Buffs. Lecture at Zulpich on "Cape to Cairo" by Rev. W.A.Elliot. 5/K.O.Y.L.I. moved one company from Bessenich to Vettweiss. 2/4 Duke of Wellington's moved two companies from Dovenich & Nemmenich to Bessenich	
	2		2/4 Y.& L arrived and were accommodated in Dovenich, Nemmenich, Durscheven. Transport of 2/Y.& L left for Cologne to be handed over to 53rd. Royal Sussex Regt.	
	3		Brigadier inspected Guard of 2/4 Duje of Wellington's prior to relieving Corps Commander's Guardd at EUSKIRCHEN found by 1/Buffs. Brigadier went to Cologne with view to selecting a car.	
	4		Lecture by Mr. Roberts on "Panorama Sketching". 52nd. Battalion Notts & Derby Regt. joined the Brigade, but were accommodated in EUSKIRCHEN. owing to Brigade Area being full. Brigadier was present at farewellparade of 1/K.S.L.I., & then visited 52nd, Notts & Derby in afternoon.	
	5		Divl. Race Meeting. The Brigadier and Staff Captain attended.	
	6		The Brigade Commander visited 52nd. Sherwood Foresters at EUSKIRCHEN, & then attended Divisional Race Meeting.	
	7		Lecture by Lieut. Hake on "The Contending Forces in Europe to-day". The Army Commander held an inspection of the 52nd. Sherwood Foresters (Young Soldiers Battalion) at which the Divisional and Brigade Commanders were present.	
	8			
	9			

2353 Wt. W2544/1454 700,000 5/15 D. D. & L. A.D.S.S./Forms/C. 2118.

Instructions regarding War Diaries and Intelligence Summaries are contained in F. S. Regs., Part II. and the Staff Manual respectively. Title pages will be prepared in manuscript.

WAR DIARY
or
~~INTELLIGENCE SUMMARY.~~
(Erase heading not required.)

Army Form C. 2118.

Place	Date	Hour	Summary of Events and Information	Remarks and references to Appendices
March	10		The Brigade Commander addressed the officers of the 52nd. Sherwood Foresters in the morning, & then proceeded to Divsl. H.Q's where he was the guest of the Divisional Commander for the night.	
	11		Rev. F.J.Paradise lectured to the Brigade on "The part played by America during the war". The Brigade Commander returned with the Divisional Commander to lunch, & then visited the Schwerfen Area.	
	12		The Brigade Commander addressed the officers of the 5/K.O.Y.L.I. at GLADBACH in the morning, & returned via The Buffs.	
	13		Brigade Major visited KOMMERN with view to finding out training facilities etc. 8th. Battalion West Yorkshire Regt.(LEEDS Rifles of 62nd.Division)	
	14		Complete reorganisation on the Brigade took place. The men retainable in The Army of Occupation of 1st. The Buffs, 2/ Y.& L ,& 2/4Y.& L Regt. proceeded to join the 6th. Battalion West Kents (34th. DIVN) and 1/4 Y-& L Regt. (3rd. Divn.) respectively. The Cadres of The Buffs, Y & L, & K.S.L.I. (together with the retainable men of the last named) moved: The Buffs & Y & L to SINZENICH, the K.S.L.I. to SCHWERFEN. The 5th.K.O.Y.L.I. left the Brigade for the 18th.Brigade and proceeded to GYMNICH. No.2 Coy. Divl. Train moved from FROITZHEIM to ULPENICH, establishing refilling point at ULPENICH. A Special Train was run to Bonn for spectators at Football Match between 1st. & 6t. Divsns. resulting in a win for 1st. Divn. 1st. Leicester Regt. represented 6th. Divn. The 1/5 S Staffs joined the Brigade and replaced the Leeds Rifles in KOMMERN.	
	15		The 2/4 Duke of Wellingtons left the Brigade to join the 18th Brigade at ERP. The Brigade Commander visited the latter before they went, and then rode down to SINZENICH & SCHWERFEN.	

2353 Wt. W2544/1454 700,000 5/15 D. D. & L. A.D.S.S./Forms/C. 2118.

Instructions regarding War Diaries and Intelligence Summaries are contained in F. S. Regs., Part II. and the Staff Manual respectively. Title pages will be prepared in manuscript.

WAR DIARY
or
INTELLIGENCE SUMMARY.
(Erase heading not required.)

Army Form C. 2118.

Place	Date	Hour	Summary of Events and Information	Remarks and references to Appendices
March	10		The Brigade Commander addressed the officers of the 52nd. Sherwood Foresters in the morning, & then proceeded to Divsl. H.Q's where he was the guest of the Divisional Commander for the night.	
	11		Rev. F.J.Paradise lectured to the Brigade on "The part played by America during the war". The Brigade Commander returned with the Divisional Commander to lunch, & then visited the Schwerfen Area.	
	12		The Brigade Commander addressed the officers of the 5/K.O.Y.L.I. at GLADBACH in the morning, & returned via The Buffs.	
	13		Brigade Major visited KOMMERN with view to finding out training facilities etc. 8th. Battalion West Yorkshire Regt. (LEEDS Rifles of 62nd.Division)	
	14		Complete reorganisation on the Brigade took place. The men retainable in The Army of Occupation of 1st. The Buffs, 2/ Y.& L , & 2/4Y.& L Regt. proceeded to join the 6th. Battalion West Kents (34th. DIVN) and 1/4 Y.& L Regt. (3rd. Divn.) respectively. The Cadres of The Buffs, Y & L, & K.S.L.I. (together with the retainable men of the last named) moved: The Buffs & Y & L to SINZENICH, the K.S.L.I. to SCHWERFEN. The 5th.K.O.Y.L.I. left the Brigade for the 18th.Brigade and proceeded to GYMNICH. No.2 Coy. Divl. Train moved from FROITZHEIM to ULPENICH, establishing refilling point at ULPENICH. A Special Train was run to Bonn for spectators at Football Match between 1st. & 6th. Divsns. resulting in a win for 1st. Divn. 1st. Leicester Regt. represented 6th. Divn. The 1/6 S Staffs joined the Brigade and replaced the Leeds Rifles in KOMMERN.	
	15		The 2/4 Duke of Wellingtons left the Brigade to join the 18th Brigade at ERP. The Brigade Commander visited the latter before they went, and then rode down to SINZENICH & SCHWERFEN.	

Instructions regarding War Diaries and Intelligence Summaries are contained in F. S. Regs., Part II. and the Staff Manual respectively. Title pages will be prepared in manuscript.

WAR DIARY
or
~~INTELLIGENCE SUMMARY.~~
(Erase heading not required.)

Army Form C. 2118.

Place	Date	Hour	Summary of Events and Information	Remarks and references to Appendices
March	15th		where the Divisional Commander gave a farewell address to the cadres of the 1st Buffs, 2nd Y & L, & 1st K.S.L.I respectively The B, G, C. afterwards rode to Kommern to welcome the 1/5 th South Staffs.	
	16th			
	17th		Brigade Major visited 2nd Y & L, & 1th South Staffs with viewo to proposals for recreational grounds and Training areas. The Brigade Commander went to Cologne. Rev.Hunter Boyd s t ayed the night with the Brigade.	
	18th		Rev. T.Hunter Boyd lectured to the Brigade on "The New Republic of the Czecho - Slovaks" .The Brigade Commander attended the lecture. 52nd. Sherwood Foresters left the Brigade for Cologne. 5 st. Leicesters joined the Brigade and were quartered in EUSKIRCHEN barracks vacated by 52nd. Sherwood Foresters. 489 Fld. Co. R.E. & 1 Coy. 11 Leicester Regt.(Pioneers) joined Brigade and were billeted in Durschaven & Lovenich respectively.	
	19th		The Brigade Commander visited the 51st. Leicester Regt. Brigade Major visited the 2/4 Y.& L and 5th . S.Staffs with reference to Training Areas.	
	20 th.		The new Commander of the new Midland Division (Major- Gen. Sir C.P.A.Hull K.C.B.) visited the Brigade Commander in the afternoon. Captain D. MacCallum M.C. joined the Brigade to take over the duties of Brigade Major.	
	21st.		Capt. D.McCallum M.C. took over the duties of Brigade Major & Capt.A.G.G.Stainforth M.C. rejoined cadre of 1/The Buffs.	

2353 Wt. W2544/1454 700,000 5/15 D. D. & L. A.D.S.S./Forms/C. 2118.

Instructions regarding War Diaries and Intelligence Summaries are contained in F. S. Regs., Part II. and the Staff Manual respectively. Title pages will be prepared in manuscript.

WAR DIARY

or

~~INTELLIGENCE SUMMARY.~~

(Erase heading not required.)

Army Form C. 2118.

Place	Date	Hour	Summary of Events and Information	Remarks and references to Appendices
March	15th		where the Divisional Commander gave a farewell address to the cadres of the 1st Buffs, 2nd Y & L, & 1st K.S.L.I respectively The B, G, C. afterwards rode to Kommern to welcome the 1/5 th South Staffs.	
	16th			
	17th		Brigade Major visited 2nd Y & L, & 1th South Staffs with views to proposals for recreational grounds and Training areas. The Brigade Commander went to Cologne. Rev.Hunter Boyd s t ayed the night with the Brigade.	
	18th		Rev. T.Hunter Boyd lectured to the Brigade on "The New Republic of the Czecho - Slovaks" .The Brigade Commander attended the lecture. 52nd. Sherwood Foresters left the Brigade for Cologne. 5 st. Leicesters joined the Brigade and were quartered in EUSKIRCHEN barracks vacated by 52nd. Sherwood Foresters. 489 Fld. Co. R.E. & 1 Coy. 11 Leicester Regt.(Pioneers) joined Brigade and were billeted in Durschaven & Loven ich respectively.	
	19th		The Brigade Commander visited the 51st. Leicester Regt. Brigade Major visited the 2/4 Y.& L and 5th . S.Staffs with reference to Training Areas.	
	20th.		The new Commander of the new Midland Division (Major- Gen. Sir C.P.A.Hull K.C.B.) visited the Brigade Commander in the afternoon. Captain D. MacCallum M.C. joined the Brigade to take over the duties of Brigade Major.	
	21st.		Capt. D.McCallum M.C. took over the duties of Brigade Major & Capt.A.G.G.Stainforth M.C. rejoined cadre of 1/The Buffs.	

2353 Wt. W2544/1454 700,000 5/15 D. D. & L. A.D.S.S./Forms/C. 2118.

Army Form C. 2118.

Instructions regarding War Diaries and Intelligence Summaries are contained in F. S. Regs., Part II. and the Staff Manual respectively. Title pages will be prepared in manuscript.

WAR DIARY
or
~~INTELLIGENCE SUMMARY.~~
(Erase heading not required.)

Place	Date	Hour	Summary of Events and Information	Remarks and references to Appendices
March	22		Major General G.F.BOYD, C.B., CMG. DSO, DCM. (late Commanding 46th N.Midland Division T.F.) arrived to take over command of the Brigade. On its platoon training .	
	23		Brigadier General G.F.Boy d assumed command of the Brigade. Church services held by Units .	
	24		LECTURE by Prof. ADKINS on "What Belgium means to us" in the SCHUTZENHALLE, ZULPICH.	
	25 26 29		Units carrying on platoon training. 52nd Leicester Regt arrived by train from England on 26th inst to join the Brigade and occupied accomodation in ZULPICH, Battalion H.Q. in the SCHLOSS.	
	30		Church services held by Units.	
	31		Lecture by Mr Wing on "The Navy's part in the War" given in ZULPICH.	

[signature]

Captain,

ZULPICH. April 1st 1919 Brigade Major, 2nd Midland Brigade.........

2353 Wt. W2544/1454 700,000 5/15 D. D. & L. A.D.S.S./Forms/C. 2118.

Army Form C. 2118.

WAR DIARY
or
INTELLIGENCE SUMMARY.
(Erase heading not required.)

Instructions regarding War Diaries and Intelligence Summaries are contained in F. S. Regs., Part II. and the Staff Manual respectively. Title pages will be prepared in manuscript.

Place	Date	Hour	Summary of Events and Information	Remarks and references to Appendices
March	22		Major General G.F.BOYD,C.B.,CMG.DSO.(late Commanding 46th N.Midland Division T.F.) arrived to take over command of the Brigade. Un its platoon training .	
	23		Brigadier General G.F.Boy d assumed command of the Brigade.Church services held by Units .	
	24		LECTURE by Prof.ADKINS on "What Belgium means to us" in the SCHUTZENHALLE, ZULPICH.	
	25 26 29		Units carrying on platoon training. 52nd Leicester Regt arrived by train from England on 26th inst to join the Brigade and occupied accomodation in ZULPICH, Battalion H.Q. in the SCHLOSS.	
	30		Church services held by Units.	
	31		Lecture by Mr Wing on "The Navy's part in the War" given in ZULPICH.	

ZULPICH. April 1st 1919

[signature]
Captain,
Brigade Major, 2nd Midland Brigade.........

2353 Wt. W2544/1454 700,000 5/15 D. D. & L. A.D.S.S./Forms/C. 2118.

Army Form C. 2118.

WAR DIARY
or
~~INTELLIGENCE SUMMARY.~~

(*Erase heading not required.*)

Instructions regarding War Diaries and Intelligence Summaries are contained in F. S. Regs., Part II. and the Staff Manual respectively. Title pages will be prepared in manuscript.

APRIL.1919.
2nd Midland Infantry Brigade.

Place	Date	Hour	Summary of Events and Information	Remarks and references to Appendices
ZULPICH,	April 1st		Units platoon training.-51st Bn.Leicester Regiment.Inspected at EUSKIRCHEN by Brigadier.	
	2nd		" " " -52nd Bn. " " " " ZULPICH by Brigadier.	
	3rd		" " " -Lecture by Major Dugmore on "Animal Life in Africa" given in SCHUTZENHALLE. ZULPICH.	
	4th		Units platoon training.-1/5th Bn.S.Staffs Regiment inspected at KOMMERN by Brigadier.	
	5th		" " " -Capt.J.Mc D.Latham,M.C. arrived to take over duties of Brigade Major to the Brigade.	
	6th		Church Services held by Units.	
	7th		2nd Midland L.T.M.Battery formed and established in BESSENICH- 53rd Bn.Leicester Regiment arrived by train from England to join the Brigade-accomodated in NEMMENICH, ROVENICH,BESSENICH, and LOVENICH. Capt.J.Mc D.LATHAM.M.C. took over duties of Brigade Major from Capt.D.Mc CALLUM.M.C.	
	8th		The Corps Commander inspected the South Staffords at KOMMERN, full marching order with first line transport; he afterwards inspected the 52nd Leicesters at ZULPICH.	
	9th		The Corps Commander inspected the 51st Leicesters at EUSKIRCHEN.	

2353 Wt. W2544/1454 700,000 5/15 D. D. & L. A.D.S.S./Forms/C. 2118.

Instructions regarding War Diaries and Intelligence Summaries are contained in F. S. Regs., Part II. and the Staff Manual respectively. Title pages will be prepared in manuscript.

WAR DIARY
or
~~INTELLIGENCE SUMMARY.~~
(Erase heading not required.)

Army Form C. 2118.

Place	Date	Hour	Summary of Events and Information	Remarks and references to Appendices
	April.			
Zulpich	10th		Consecreation of Colours of 2/4th Y & L and presentation of Colours to them by Divisional Commander at NEMMENICH.	
	11th		Brigadier General C.F.Boyd C.B.C.M.G.D.S.O.left the Brigade and joined the 2nd Army Headquarters as Inspector General of Training.	
			Lecture for Officers by Mr Roberts on"PANORAMA SKETCHING" in the SCHUTZENHALL. ZULPICH.	
	12th.		Lt.Col.White.O.C.1/5th South Staffords Commanded the Brigade pending the arrival of new Brigadier General.	
			Units platoon training and Sportsin the afternoon.	
			53rd Bn. Leicesters ceased to exist being divided up between 51st and 52nd Leicesters. "B"Company 53rd Leicesters transferred to 51st Leicesters and A.C.& D.Coys transferred to 52nd Leicesters. Headquarters and surplus personnel of 53rd remaining at NEMMENICH.	
			L.T.M. moved from BESSENICH to ROVENICH.	
	13th.		Church Services and sports in the afternoon.	
	14th.		Units platoon training.- Capt D.Mc CALLUM.M.C. left the Brigade to take up duties of Staff Captain 3rd Midland Brigade. The "Cadre" of the 2nd Battalion York & Lancaster Regiment left BENSENICH for BRUHL. The Band of 1st Buffs played "Auld Lang Syne" as the lorries STARTED off.	

2353 Wt. W2544/1454 700,000 5/15 D. D. & L. A.D.S.S./Forms/C. 2118.

PAGE 3

Army Form C. 2118.

Instructions regarding War Diaries and Intelligence Summaries are contained in F. S. Regs., Part II. and the Staff Manual respectively. Title pages will be prepared in manuscript.

WAR DIARY

or

~~INTELLIGENCE~~ SUMMARY.

(Erase heading not required.)

Place	Date	Hour	Summary of Events and Information	Remarks and references to Appendices
	April.			
ZULPICH.	14th		Headquarters of 53rd Leicesters move into ZULPICH. In the evening the 1/5th South Stafford's Concert Party "The Knots" gave a Concert in the SCHUTZENHALLE. ZULPICH.	
	15th		Units platoon training. The South Stafford's Concert party gave another Concert in the SCHUTZENHALLE. ZULPICH.	
	16th		Units platoon training. 52nd Leicesters went on a route march.	
	17th		Lt.Colonel Morgan.C.M.G.D.S.O. took overCommand of 1/5th South Staffords and also temporary command of the Brigade in lieu of Lt.Colonel White.D.S.O.	
Good Friday.	18th		Church Services held by Units. The "Cadre" of the 1st K.S.L.I. departed from Cologne on route to England. Lecture in theevening by Dr.J.W.Tyson on"The British Empire .- A Doctor's point of view" in the SCHUTZENHALLE. ZULPICH .	
	19th		Units platoon training. The"Cadre" of the 2nd Y & L departed from Cologne on route to England .	
Easter Sunday.	20th		Church Services held by Units.	
	21st		Units platoon training. Sports in the afternoon. In the evening the 52nd Leicesters gave a Concert in the SCHUTZENHALE. ZULPICH.	

PAGE 4

Army Form C. 2118.

Instructions regarding War Diaries and Intelligence Summaries are contained in F. S. Regs., Part II. and the Staff Manual respectively. Title pages will be prepared in manuscript.

WAR DIARY
or
~~INTELLIGENCE SUMMARY.~~
(Erase heading not required.)

Place	Date	Hour	Summary of Events and Information	Remarks and references to Appendices
	April			
ZULPICH	22nd		Units platoon training. ~~[illegible]~~ A Concert by the 52nd Leicesters in the SCHUTZENHALLE. ZULPICH.	
	23rd		Un its platoon training and sports in the afternoon.	
	24th		" " " " " " " "	
	25th		" " " " " " " "	
	26th		" " " " " " " "	
	27th		Church Services held by Units. Brigadier General G.S.G.Crauford CMG.C.I.E.D.S.O.A.D.C. arrived and took over command of the Brigade.	
	28th		Units platoon training,. G.O.C. visited the 51st Leicesters at EUSKIRCHEN. London Divisional Races were held near COLOGNE.A Special train was arranged to take those wishing to attend from Units. The G.O.C. and Brigade Major went in the car to reconnoitre a ground for an inspection to be held by the Commander in Chief(General Sir William Robertson). Lecture at 5.15 p.m. in SCHUTZENHALLE by Commander Viscount Broome. R.N. on "Naval Subjects" illustrated with Lantern Slides.	
	29th		Units platoon Training. Sports in the afternoon. A Special train was arranged to take those wishing to attend from units to the second day's Meeting of the London Divisional Races.	

2353 Wt. W2544/1454 700,000 5/15 D. D. & L. A.D.S.S./Forms/C. 2118.

Army Form C. 2118.

Instructions regarding War Diaries and Intelligence Summaries are contained in F. S. Regs., Part II. and the Staff Manual respectively. Title pages will be prepared in manuscript.

WAR DIARY
or
INTELLIGENCE SUMMARY.
(Erase heading not required.)

Place	Date	Hour	Summary of Events and Information	Remarks and references to Appendices
	April.			
ZULPICH.	30th.		Units platoon training and sports in the afternoon. The IX Corps Concert party " The Robin Hoods" gave a concert in the SCHUTZENHALLE . ZULPICH.	
			"Special Order of the Day" attached gives a short history ofthe 6th Division throughout the War in which this Brigade formed part.	"A"

ZULPICH. MAY.1st.1919.
GERMANY.

[signature] Capt.
for Brigadier General,
Commanding,2nd Midland Brigade......

2353 Wt. W2544/1454 700,000 5/15 D. D. & L. A.D.S.S./Forms/C. 2118.

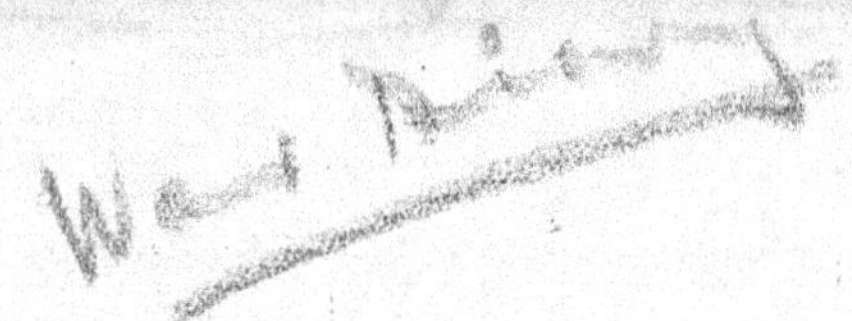

APPENDIX "A"

SPECIAL ORDER OF THE DAY.

The 6th Division, as it has been known to England during the great war, is being broken up, the Artillery and Infantry passing to other formations in the Regular Army and the remainder being transferred to the new Midland Division.

Commencing with the victory on the AISNE, the 6th Division, under Major-General Sir JOHN KEIR, K.C.B. took part in the heavy fighting in October 1914 round ARMENTIERES which really formed part of the first battle of YPRES, and which marked the introduction of trench warfare. The Division remained in the vicinity of this town until the second battle of YPRES, when it was brought up to hold that difficult front. During the year spent in FLANDERS the capture of HOOGE by the 16th and 18th Infantry Brigades (the first occasion on which an artillery barrage was used) and a gallant and successful attack of the 1st K.S.L.I. on a position astride the YPRES - LANGEMARCK road were the outstanding features. During this period too, the 71st Infantry Brigade replaced the 17th Infantry Brigade, transferred to 24th Division in October 1915 after the battle of LOOS, and the command changed twice, Major-General Sir WALTER CONGREVE, V.C. K.C.B., M.V.O., succeeding General KEIR, transferred to command of the VI Corps on 27th May 1915, and Major-General C.ROSS, C.B. replacing General CONGREVE on the promotion of the latter to the command of the XIII Corps. From YPRES, the 6th Division went to the SOMME, where in September and October 1916 it had very severe fighting at the capture of the QUADRILATERAL near GINCHY, and the actions at LES BOEUFS and GUEUDECOURT, suffering heavy casualties. Then followed a long period of trench warfare in the LOOS - HULLUCH sector, including many brilliant raids and a short period of severe fighting in April at HILL 70, conducted with the greatest determination and gallantry, in aid of larger operations by the Canadian Corps on the immediate South.

On 19th August 1917, the Division came under my command, and the three Infantry Brigades changed commands almost simultaneously, Brigadier-General E. FEETHAM, C.B., C.M.G., Commanding 71st Infantry Brigade being promoted to 39th Division, and Brigadier-Generals R.J.BRIDGFORD, C.B., C.M.G., D.S.O. and W.L.OSBORN, C.M.G., D.S.O. going home for a rest after a long period of harassing fighting.

The Division first consolidated HILL 70 captured by the Canadians, and then prepared an attack on LENS, which was eventually abandoned in favour of the CAMBRAI offensive, with large numbers of tanks. On 20th November, 1917, the Division attacked and achieved a notable success with light losses, but suffered fairly heavy casualties in holding up the German counter-attack from 30th Nov- 10th Dec.

In this, the 16th Infantry Brigade did splendid work and the 14th D.L.I. made a lasting name at the defence of MARCOING on 3rd December, where also a company of the newly-formed 6th Machine-Gun Battalion greatly distinguished itself.

After a month's partial rest (two Brigades doing short spells in the BULLECOURT Sector) the Division occupied the trench system East of BAPAUME being reduced by the loss of the 9th Suffolk Regt., 8th Bedford Regt. and the 14th D.L.I. to 10 Battalions. On March 21st and 22nd, 1918, the Division on a widely extended front of which LAGNICOURT was the centre, sustained the full brunt of the German offensive, losing very heavily, but holding up the attack till reinforcements could arrive. Then followed five months of prolonged strain in the YPRES - KEMMEL Sector, during which the Division fought alongside the French, trained several battalions of the 27th American Division and built up from its reserves and partly trained men

/ a hardened ....

a hardened force for the final Allied counter-attack. Notable during this time was the detachment of the 71st Infantry Brigade to stem the German advance near NEUVE EGLISE in May, 1918, where the 9th Norfolk Regt. especially suffered heavy casualties; the successful attack of the 11th Essex Regt. on 18th May to restore the broken line of the French on our right flank; the brilliant capture of RIDGE WOOD and ELZENWALLE by the 1st West Yorkshire Regt. and the 2nd D.L.I. on 14th July, and the gallant daylight raid of the 1st BUFFS a little later.

About 1st September, 1918, the Division was moved South to the SOMME and by 14th September came into the line at HOLNON WOOD near ST. QUENTIN, where it commenced the almost continuous two and a half months' fighting, which practically coincided with the cessation of hostilities. From 14th September-8th October, the Division held the post of honour of right of the British offensive. The preliminary operations in HOLNON WOOD were marked by the success of the 18th Infantry Brigade. On 18th and 19th September, the 16th and 71st Infantry Brigades under most adverse conditions attacked the immensely strong positions which dominated ST QUENTIN and suffered very heavy losses, but behaving with the greatest gallantry got their claws firmly embedded in the enemy defensive system which finally yielded to the tenacious fighting of the 16th and 18th Infantry Brigades (with 1st Leicester Regt.) on 24th and 25th September.

On 8th October, the 16th and 71st Infantry Brigades captured the defensive positions East of the HINDENBURG LINE, of which MANNEQUIN HILL and DOON MILL were the tactical points, fighting on this occasion between the French on the right and the 30th American Division on the left. The 1st West Yorkshire Regt. especially distinguished themselves by the capture by a bombing attack after prolonged fighting of MANNEQUIN and CERISE WOODS on the right flank. The advance on and fall of BOHAIN on 9th October, the battle of VAUX ANDIGNY on 17th October and the final battle of ORS RIDGE on 24th October completed a series of operations of which any division might justly be proud.

Throughout the war the Division has had the tremendous advantage of an artillery second to none in the British Army, and which has on all occasions, notably on 21st and 22nd March, 1918, most notably uphold the glorious traditions of the Royal Regiment.

The Division has also been fortunate in its R.E. and Pioneers, both of which took and active and important part in opposing the great German offensive, where also the newly-formed machine gun Battalion proved its worth. Both Medium and Light Trench Mortar Batteries - the latter especially - have done/yeoman service. The Medical Services have been pre-eminent in their care of the wounded and have paid a heavy toll during the past year in officers and other ranks. The R.A.S.C. have done splendid work both with horse and motor transport; the R.A.V.C. have worked hard and successfully and the Chaplains have set an example of self-sacrifice and gallantry worthy of their high calling.

It is hoped to publish later a short history of the part played by the 6th Division in the great war, but owing to the many changes of command it will necessarily take some time. Information as to its publication will be given in the leading London, Midland and Yorkshire papers.

In saying good-bye to the 6th Division, which it has been my privilege and fortune to command for the past one and a half years, I wish to thank particularly Brigadier-Generals E.F. DELAFORCE, C.M.G., Commanding Royal Artillery, G.S.G. CRAUFURD, C.M.G., C.I.E., D.S.O., A.D.C., Commanding 18th Infantry Brigade, H.A. WALKER, C.M.G., D.S.O., late Commanding 16th Infantry Brigade, and P.W. BROWN, C.M.G., D.S.O., Commanding 71st

/ Infantry Brigade.

Infantry Brigade for their most loyal help, advice and support in all the difficult situations which have arisen during the fifteen months' fighting, and to all the Commanding Officers, especially Lt. Cols. W.H.F. WEBER, C.M.G., D.S.O., Commanding 2nd Brigade, R.F.A., J.A.C. FORSYTH, C.M.G., D.S.O., Commanding 24th Brigade, R.F.A., R.E. POWER, D.S.O., Commanding 1st The Buffs, D.L. WEIR, D.S.O., M.C., Commanding 1st West Yorkshire Regt., F.LATHAM, D.S.O., Commanding 1st Leicestershire Regt., C.H. DUMBELL, D.SO., Commanding 11th Essex Regt., H.M.MILWARD, D.S.O., Commanding 2nd Sherwood Foresters and J.B. FOSTER, D.S.O., M.C., Commanding 14th D.L.I. and 6th Machine Gun Battalion.

My thanks are further due to the Staff and Heads of Departments, especially Lt. Cols. T.T. GROVE, C.M.G., D.S.O., G.S.O. I, P. HUDSON, D.S.O., late A.A. & Q.M.G., G. GOLDNEY, C.M.G., D.S.O., late C.R.E. and Colonel H.W. GRATTAN, C.M.G., D.S.O., late A.D.M.S., whose untiring devotion to duty and ready resource have overcome all obstacles and rendered sucessful the planning of the many operations undertaken by the Division.

Few of the original members of the 6th Division now remain with it, but I am sure that all those who, like myself, have been associated with the Division for any length of time, will always cherish proud and happy memories of the time spent with it.

The 6th Division have never gone to a new command without a hearty welcome, nor left a command without an expression of thanks for services rendered and of regret that it was being transferred.

I wish all ranks the best of luck in whatever fate may have for them in the future.

T. Marden.

Major-General,
Commanding 6th Division.

18th March, 1919.

Instructions regarding War Diaries and Intelligence Summaries are contained in F. S. Regs., Part II. and the Staff Manual respectively. Title pages will be prepared in manuscript.

WAR DIARY
or
~~INTELLIGENCE SUMMARY~~.
(Erase heading not required.)

2nd Midland Brigade
ZULPICH

Army Form C. 2118.

May 1919.

Place	Date	Hour	Summary of Events and Information	Remarks and references to Appendices
1919 ZULPICH (SENSENICH)	May I		The Commander-in-Chief ~~Sir~~ General Sir William Robertson inspected the Brigade. The parade was held at SENSENICH where the three battalions were formed up in Mass. The first line transport was also on parade. The Inspection took place at II45 am in the morning. The Brigade gave the General Salute "Present Arms" on arrival of the Commander-in-Chief. After the inspection each unit with transport marched past the General, and then proceeded to their billets independently.	
	2		Very wet day. Units carried on with training in doors.	
	3		Units Training. Sports in the afternoon. 52nd Leicesters held a Cross Country Run.	
	4		Church Services held by Units. Sports in the afternoon.	
	5		Units Training. A Conference of Commanding Officers at Brigade Headquarters at II00hours Sports in the afternoon, Lecture at I715 in the SCHUTZENHALLE by Commander Everard R N on 'Naval Subjects'.	
	6		Units Training. Sports in the afternoon.	
	7th		Units Training. Sports in the afternoon. A Lecture in the evening by Major Hayward on "Citizenship" in the SCHUTZENHALL, ZULPICH.	
	8th		Units Training. A Lecture by the Brigadier in the morning in the SCHUTZENHALLE, ZULPICH at II30 on "The Army and the Nation", to the 52nd Leicesters and T M BATTERY,	

(A9175) Wt W2355/P36 600,000 12/17 D. D. & L. Sch. 52a. Forms/C2118/15.

2nd Midland Brigade

Army Form C. 2118.

WAR DIARY

or

~~INTELLIGENCE SUMMARY.~~

(Erase heading not required.)

MAY 1919

Instructions regarding War Diaries and Intelligence Summaries are contained in F. S. Regs., Part II. and the Staff Manual respectively. Title pages will be prepared in manuscript.

Place	Date	Hour	Summary of Events and Information	Remarks and references to Appendices
	1919			
ZULPICH	May 9th		Units Training. A Lecture by the Brigadier to the 51st Leicesters in the Morning at EUSKIRCHEN on "The Army and the Nation"	
	10th		Units Training. A Lecture by the Brigadier to the 1/5th South Staffords in the Morning at KOMMERN on "The Army and the Nation". Sports in the afternoon	
	11th		Church Services held by Units Sports in the afternoon.	
	12th		Units Training. Sports held in the afternoon. There was a Brigade Sports Meeting under the presidency of Major A J Newell (52nd Leicesters) at which the Battalion Sports Officers attended. A programme of Football, Basket Ball, Cricket, Tug of War &c was drawn up and dates decided on which to play.	
	13th		Units Training. Brigadier General S G Crawford C M G. D S O. C I E. A D C. took over temporary Command of the Division. Lt Colonel Mc Crosby Commanding 51st Leicesters assumed temporary Command of the Brigade. The Cadres of 1st The Buffs, and 2/4th York and Lanc. left SENSENICH & NEMMENICH for England. The Staff Captain, Signalling Officer and Intelligence Officer represented the 16th Infantry Brigade Headquarters and bid them farewell.	
	14th		Units Training. Sports in the afternoon. Lecture in the evening in the SCHUTZENHALLE by Mr Sandon Perkins on " U S A "	

Instructions regarding War Diaries and Intelligence Summaries are contained in F. S. Regs., Part II, and the Staff Manual respectively. Title pages will be prepared in manuscript.

WAR DIARY
or
~~INTELLIGENCE SUMMARY.~~
(Erase heading not required.)

2nd Midland Brigade
ZULPICH
MAY 1919

Army Form C. 2118.

Place	Date	Hour	Summary of Events and Information	Remarks and references to Appendices
	1919			
ZULPICH	May 15th		Units Training. Sports in the afternoon. Lecture by MrJMc Cabe on "Life in Past Ages" to the 51st Leicesters at EUSKIRCHEN	
	16th		Units Training. Sports in the afternoon. Lecture to the 52nd Leicesters by Mr Saxton Mills on "Panama Canal" in the SCHUTZENHALLE, at 1715	
	17th		Units Training. Sports in the afternoon.	
	18th		Church Services held by Units. Sports in the afternoon.	
	19th		Units Training. First round of the Inter-Coy Brigade Football Competition played between "A" Coy 1/5th South Staffords and Brigade Headquarters.	
	20th		Units Training. Sports in the afternoon. Lecture at night by Mr Eardley Brian on "The League of Nations" to the 1/5th South Staffords at KOMMERN.	
	21st		Units Training. Sports in the afternoon. Football Matches were played in the Inter-Company Brigade Competition, 52nd Leicesters V 16th Field Ambulance and Brigade Headquarters V 1/5th South Staffords.	
	22nd		Units Training. Sports in the afternoon. A "Warning Order" from Division was received to the effect that the Brigade had to be ready to move to occupy another area on or after May 23rd.	
	23rd		Units Training. The Staff Captain and representatives from Units went over to DUREN to make	

(A9175) Wt W2358/P36 600,000 12/17 D. D. & L. Sch. 52a. Forms/C2118/15.

Instructions regarding War Diaries and Intelligence Summaries are contained in F. S. Regs., Part II, and the Staff Manual respectively. Title pages will be prepared in manuscript.

WAR DIARY
or
INTELLIGENCE SUMMARY.
(Erase heading not required.)

2nd Midland Brigade.
Zulpich,.
May 1919.

Army Form C. 2118.

Place	Date	Hour	Summary of Events and Information	Remarks and references to Appendices
	1919.			
ZULPICH.	May23rd.		necessary arrangements for bulleting in case the Brigade moved. Brigadier General Crauford CMG AIE DSO ADC. resumed Command of the Brigade.	
	24th.		Units training. 52nd Leicesters held their sports in BESSENICH on Saturday afternoon. The Brigadier General distributed the prizes to the successfulf competitors. The band of the South Staffords gave selections during the afternoon.	
	25th.		Church Services held by Units.	
	26th.		Units Training. Sports in the afterhoon.	
	27th.		Units Training. Brigadier General and Brigade Major visited 51st Leicesters at EUSKIRCHEN during the morning. Sports in the afternoon.	
	28th.		Units Training. Sports in the afternoon.	
	29th.		Units Training. The Midland Divisional Train held a Race Meeting at ROMER-LOF between LECHENICH and LIBLAR. A Special train was provided to take representatives from units. The G.O.C. Brigade Major and Staff Captain attended.	
	30th.		Units Training. Sports in the afternoon.	
	31st.		Units Training. Sports in the afternoon. Football Match between"B" Coy. 51st Leicesters and "C" Coy.52nd Leicesters in the Inter Brigade Coy Competition played at DURSCHAVEN on the	

(A9175) Wt W2355/P565 ... D. D. & L. ... Forms C2118/13.

Instructions regarding War Diaries and Intelligence Summaries are contained in F. S. Regs., Part II. and the Staff Manual respectively. Title pages will be prepared in manuscript.

WAR DIARY
or
INTELLIGENCE SUMMARY.
(Erase heading not required.)

2nd Midland Brigade.
Zulpich.
May.1919.

Army Form C. 2118.

Place	Date	Hour	Summary of Events and Information	Remarks and references to Appendices
	1919.			
ZULPICH.	May31st.		459th Field Company's Ground. A Whist Drive and Concert was given by the Brigade Headquarters Personnel in the SCHUTZENHALLE, ZULPICH.	
			ZULPICH. GERMANY.	

Captain.
Brigade Major.
Second Midland Brigade.

Instructions regarding War Diaries and Intelligence Summaries are contained in F. S. Regs., Part II. and the Staff Manual respectively. Title pages will be prepared in manuscript.

WAR DIARY
or
~~INTELLIGENCE SUMMARY~~
(Erase heading not required.)

2nd Midland Brigade.

JUNE. 1919.

Army Form C. 2118.

Place	Date	Hour	Summary of Events and Information	Remarks and references to Appendices
ZULPICH. (~~[illegible]~~)	1919.			
	1st,.		Church Services held by Units. Sports in the afternoon.	
	2nd.		Units Training. Sports in the afternoon.	
	3rd.		King's Birthday. Short Ceremonial Parades held by Units at 10.00 hours. The Brigade Commander and Staff attended parade of 52nd Leicester Regiment. Remainder of the day was observed as a General Holiday.	
	4th.		Units Training. Sports in the afternoon.	
	5th.		Units Training. Sports in the afternoon.	
	6th.		Units Training. Sports inthe afternoon. Southern Division Race meeting at KALK. The Brigade Commander attended.	
	7th.		Units Training in the morning. Final of the Brigade Inter Company Football Competition was played at OBERGARTZEN at 18.00 hours. Teams "A" Company, 1/5th South Staffords V "C" Company 52nd Leicesters. Result. Draw 0 - 0. A very hard and exciting match.	
Whit-Sunday.	8th.		Church Services held by Units in the Morning. Usual sports in the afternoon.	
Whit-Monday.	9th.		A General Holiday. Captain.J.M.Latham.M.C. (H.L.I.) Brigade Major proceeded to join the Light Division as G.S.O. 2. Captain J.Blower 53rd Leicester Regiment took over duties of Brigade Major temporarily.	

2353 Wt. W2544/1454 700,000 5/15 D. D. & L. A.D.S.S./Forms/C. 2118.

Army Form C. 2118.

Instructions regarding War Diaries and Intelligence Summaries are contained in F. S. Regs., Part II. and the Staff Manual respectively. Title pages will be prepared in manuscript.

WAR DIARY

or

~~INTELLIGENCE SUMMARY~~

(Erase heading not required.)

2nd Midland Brigade.

JUNE. 1919.

Place	Date	Hour	Summary of Events and Information	Remarks and references to Appendices
	1919.			
ZULPICH.	10th.		Units Training. Replay of Final of Brigade Inter/Company Football Competition at OBERGARTZEN at 17.30 Hrs resulting in another Draw. 3 - 3 . Extra time was played without result. It was decided to play extra time again and the 1/5th South Staffords scored a goal winning the match. Result "A" Coy 1/5th South Staffords 4. "C" Coy 52nd Leicesters 3. The Brigade Commander presented the Challenge Cup to the winning team after the match. Mr .J.Best lectured at the Officers Club, ZULPICH on "Big Game" . A proportion of men from all Units of the Brigade attended.	
	11th.		Units Training. Sports in the afternoon.	
	12th.		Units Training. Sports in the afternoon. Miss KEEN and party gave a demonstration of Old English Dancing at 17.00 hrs at Gymnasium ,ZULPICH. Beigade Commander and Capt Blower attended.	
	13th.		Units Training. Sports in the afternoon.	
	14th.		Units Training. Sports in the afternoon.	
	15th.		Units held Church Services in the morning. Sports in the afternoon.	
	16th.		Units Training. 51st Leicesters held their Athletic Sports Meeting at EUSKIRCHEN. The Brigade Commander attended and presented prizes after the sports. First day of Sports of the 1/5th South Staffords held at KOMMERN.	

Army Form C. 2118.

Instructions regarding War Diaries and Intelligence Summaries are contained in F. S. Regs., Part II. and the Staff Manual respectively. Title pages will be prepared in manuscript.

WAR DIARY
or
~~INTELLIGENCE SUMMARY~~.

(*Erase heading not required.*)

2nd Midland Brigade.

JUNE.1919.

Place	Date	Hour	Summary of Events and Information	Remarks and references to Appendices
	1919.			
ZULPICH.	17th.		Brigade ordered to move to DUREN Area to releive 2nd Highland Brigade. Moves to be completed by 20th. 1/5th South Staffords moved by lorry to DUREN to releive 4th Gordon Highlanders in billets in the town ,and took over guards and other details. Captain J.R.Cowan DOUGLAS.D.S.O. M.C. H.L.I. joined Brigade as Brigade Major.	See Appendix.1
x				
	18th.		Units preparing for move.	Appendix.2
	19th.		Brigade Headquarters and Units moved by march route to DUREN Area. 51st Leicesters(less 2 Companies) stayed at FUSSENICH. Units accomodated as in Appendix 1. 2 Companies 51st Leicesters proceeded by Train to HERBESTHAL to releive a detachment of 6th Black Watch Highland Division. Brigade Commanders visited guards in town and on railway.	Appendix.3
DUREN.	20th.		2 Companies 51st Leicester Regiment moved from FUSSENICH to SCHLICH.,SCHLOSS & MERODE. Brigade Commanders visited guards in the morning with Lt.Col.Morgan.C.M.G. D.S.O. 1/5th South Staffords. ~~xxx~~ Lt.Col. Becher.D.S.O. 52nd Leicesters visited 51st Leicesters at SCHLICH in the afternoon.	Appendix.4
	21st.		Units taking over guards and other details. DUREN defence Scheme issued to Units.	
	22nd.		Church Services held by Units.	
	23rd.		Units Training. Wire received from Division that Enemy have notified officially intention to sign Peace. Places for resumption of operations to be held in obeyance.	

2353 Wt. W2544/1454 700,000 5/15 D. D. & L. A.D.S.S./Forms/C. 2118.

Instructions regarding War Diaries and Intelligence Summaries are contained in F. S. Regs., Part II. and the Staff Manual respectively. Title pages will be prepared in manuscript.

WAR DIARY
or
~~INTELLIGENCE SUMMARY.~~
(Erase heading not required.)

2nd Midland Brigade.
JUNE.1919.

Army Form C. 2118.

Place	Date	Hour	Summary of Events and Information	Remarks and references to Appendices
	1919.			
DUREN.	24th.		Units Training. Sports in the afternoon.	
	25th.		Units Training. Sports in the afternoon.	
	26th.		Units Training. Sports in the afternoon. Brigade Commander visited detachment of 51st Leicesters at HERBESTHAL with Lt.Col.Dumbell. D.S.O..	
	27th.		Units Training. Sports in the afternoon.	
	28th.		Units Training. Sports in the afternoon. News that Peace Terms had been signed came through at 19.00 hours. Brigade ordered to move back to ZULPICH Area. Move to commance on Monday 30th, 1919.	
	29th.		Church Services held by Units in the morning. Brigade Commander attended service of 1/5th South Staffords held in Garrison Church, DUREN. Brigade Headquarters played IV.Corps Signals at Cricket.	
	30th.		51st Leicesters less 2 companies moved to FUSSENICH. 52nd Leicesters, 459th Field Coy., 16th Field Ambulance, No.2.Coy.Train, 2nd Midland L.T.M.Battery and "A" Coy.6th.Bn.M.G.C. moved back to ZULPICH Area. Conference at Divisional Headquarters at 15.00 hours. Brigade Commander Three Commanding Officers, and Brigade Major attended.	See. Appendix. 5.

DUREN.
GERMANY.
JUNE.1919.

[signature] Capt. Bde Major
Brigadier General.
Commanding, 2nd Midland Brigade.

2353 Wt. W2544/1454 700,000 5/15 D. D. & L. A.D.S.S./Forms/C. 2118.

APPENDIX 1

SECRET.

Copy No. 16

2nd MIDLAND BRIGADE ORDER No. 1.

25th May 1919.

1. If the peace negotiations fail, notice of the termination of the Armistice in 72 hours will be given to the Germans. The day on which the Armistice ceases will be called J day. On that day the three leading British Corps advance into neutral territory.

2. In this event, the preliminary moves, detailed in Warning Order of the 22nd May will take place as follows :-

1 Unit.	2 Destination.	3 Day of arrival at Destination.	4 Remarks.
Brigade H.Q.) 2nd.Mid.L.T.M.B.)	DUREN	J - 1	Bde H.Q. in billets. 2nd M.L.T.M.B. in Barracks.
I/5th S.Staffs.	DUREN	J - 3	By lorry from KOMMERN Relieve 4th Gordon Highlanders.
5Ist Leicesters.	SCHLICH & MERODE.	J - 2	By lorry from EUSKIRCHEN, Relieve 53rd Gordon Highlanders.
52nd Leicesters.	DUREN.	J - 1	By march route. Relieve 5Ist Gordon Highlanders in Barracks.
459th Fld.Coy, R.E.	STOCKHEIM	J - 1	By march route.
I6th F.Amb.	LEHRER SEMINAR DUREN	J - 1	Ditto
"A" Coy.6th Bn. M.G.C.	DUREN Barracks.	J day.	By march route staging in SOLLER J - 1 day.
No.2 Coy Train.	DISTELRATH	J - 1	By march route.

3. The I/5th South Staffs will take over the following Guards on arrival at DUREN :-

GUARD	STRENGTH	FURNISHED BY
Inlying Picquet.	1 Company	4th Gordon Highlanders.
Railway Station Guard	2 Offrs 48 O.R.	4th, 5th & 5Ist Gordon Highlanders.
Captured Vehicle Park	1 N.C.O. & Six men.	5Ist Gordon Highlanders.
Railhead Supplies & Corps & Div.Pack Train.	2 N.C.O's & I2 men.	" " "
Post Office	2 N.C.O's & 6 men.	" " "
Ammunition Dump	1 N.C.O. & 3 men.	To be notified later
Prison Guard.	1 N.C.O. & 6 men.	To be notified later
R.A.S.C. Guard	2 N.C.O's & 6 men.	To be notified later
Salvage Dump.	IO Other Ranks.	To be notified later

para 4. In case of the move taking place, O.C. 5Ist Leicesters will arrange for all guards on IX Corps Headquarters to be relieved by the IX Corps ----- Cyclists. On relief guards of the 5Ist Leicesters will rejoin their Unit.

5. Each Battalion leaving a store in their Battalion area will detail a guard over the store of not less than one platoon.

Other units will leave guards in proportion should they store any surplus kit in their present areas. One Officer per Battalion will also be left behind in charge of Details and Unit property, etc.

6. In notifying J day by telegram to all concerned the following code will be employed :-

25th May	A.
26th May	B.
27th May	C.
28th May	D.
29th May	E.
30th May	F.
3Ist May	G.
Ist June	H.
2nd June	I.
3rd June	J.
etc.	

Thus if J day were to be on June Ist, the following telegram would be sent in clear to all concerned :-

"Reference 2nd Midland Brigade Order No. 1. dated 25th May AAA J day will be H.AAA

7. It is probable that 3 lorries per Battalion will be available to assist in moving stores, etc. One blanket per man only will be taken. The second suit of S.D. clothing will not be taken.

8. On day of moving Battalions will refill on Supply Wagons. Changes of Refilling Points will be notified.

9. Arrival in new areas and location of Headquarters will be reported to Brigade Headquarters. O.C. I/5th South Staffs will also report when all guards detailed in para 3 have been mounted.

IO. ACKNOWLEDGE.

[signature]
Captain.
Brigade Major.
Second Midland Brigade.

Distribution to :-
- I/5th South Staffs.
- 5Ist Leicesters.
- 52nd Leicesters.
- 2nd Mid.L.T.M.Battery
- 6th Bn.M.G.C.
- 459th Field Coy R.E.
- I6th Field Ambulance.
- No. 2. Coy Train.
- Sub-Area Staff Captain.
- O.C. Signals.
- D.A.P.M.
- 2nd Highland Brigade.
- Midland Division (2 copies)

COPY No 16

S E C R E T.

ADDENDUM No. 1 to 2nd MIDLAND BRIGADE ORDER No. 1.

1. One Battery R.F.A. to be detailed by G.O.C. R.A. will move to DUREN Barracks on a date to be notified later and come under the orders of G.O.C. 2nd Midland Brigade on arrival.

2. Lorries carrying the 5Ist Leicesters to SCHLICH must not go through DUREN town.

If lorries are not available to convey the 5Ist Leicesters to SCHLICH this Battalion will march to FUSSENICH and FROITZHEIM on J - 1 day and on to SCHLICH on J day.

3. IV Corps Heavy Artillery are taking over the following guards from the 2hd Highland Brigade as soon as the message giving J day is received:-

(a)	Electric Power Station	WEISWEILER,	1 Off. I00 O.R.
(b)	R.A.S.C.Supply Dump	BERVIL,	2 N.C.O's,6 men.
(c)	Railway Station Guard	DUREN.	2 Off. 48 O.R.
(d)	Captured Vehicle Park	DUREN.	1 N.C.O. 6 men.
(e)	Railhead Supplies and Corps & Div.Pack Trains.	DUREN.	2 N.C.O's,I2 men.
(f)	Post Office,	DUREN.	2 N.C.O's, 6 men.

The I/5th South Staffords moving by lorry to DUREN will, therefore, take over (c), (d), (e) and (f) from IV Corps H.A. on arrival, (a) and (b) will be taken over by the 5Ist Leicesters after their arrival in SCHLICH by arrangement with G.O.C. IV Corps H.A.

4. No guards of less than one platoon are to be left as this is the minimum necessary for defence.

In consequence the surplus stores of Brigade Headquarters the 2nd Midland Brigade L.T.M.Battery and I6th Field Ambulance will be concentrated and stored with the surplus kit of the 52nd Leicesters at ZULPICH.

Surplus stores of the 459th Field Coy,R.E. and No.2 Coy Train will be stored at EUSKIRCHEN Barracks with the 5Ist Leicesters.

This will be arranged direct between O's C. concerned.

The Platoon guards of the 5Ist and 52nd Leicesters will be responsible for the protection of all these stores.

5. Until I8.00 hours on 'J' day all troops of the 2nd Midland Brigade arriving in DUREN will be under the tactical command of the G.O.C. IV CORPS H.A. for purposes of defence of the town. At above hour command will pass to G.O.C. 2nd Midland Brigade.

6. ACKNOWLEDGE.

[signature]
Captain.
Brigade Major.
Second Midland Brigade.

27th May I919.

Distribution to :-

1 I/5th South Staffs.
2 5Ist Leicesters.
3 52nd Leicesters.
4 2nd Mid.L.T.M.Battery.
5 6th Bn.M.G.C.
6 459th Field Coy,R.E.
7 I6th Field Ambulance.
8 No.2 Coy Train.
9 Sub-Area Staff Captain.
10 O.C.Signals.
11 D.A.P.M.
12 2nd Highland Brigade.
13&14 Midland Division (2 copies)

S E C R E T .

Copy No. 15.

ADDENDUM No. 3 to 2nd MIDLAND BRIGADE ORDER No.1.

DATED 25th May 1919.

-o-o-o-o-o-o-o-o-o-

Add to para 5 of Addendum No. 1 of the above quoted Order :- O's C. Battalions, 2nd Midland Brigade reaching DUREN before 18.00 hours on J day will report immediately on arrival to the B.G.C. H.A. at the Catholic Lyceum, DUREN.

Battlions to acknowledge.

Captain.
Brigade Major.
Second Midland Brigade.

7th June 1919.

Distribution to :-

1/5th South Staffs.
51st Leicesters.
52nd Leicesters.
2nd Mid.L.T.M.Battery.
459th Field Coy R.E.
16th Field Ambulance.
No.2. Coy Train.
6th Bn.M.G.C.
Sub-Area Staff Captain.
O.C.Signals.
D.A.P.M.
2nd Highland Brigade.
Midland Division (2 copies)

S E C R E T.

ADDENDUM No. 4 to 2nd Midland Bde Order No.1.

dated 25th May 1919.

The attached table shews the movements of Units in the event of "J" day being ordered.

1. Table A. 2nd Midland Brigade and attached Train Company and Field Ambulance.

In the above case the Train Company and Field Ambulance will move under orders of the G.O.C. Brigade to which they are attached.

2. The 11th Leicester Regiment (P) will move in two marches to ZULPICH.

On arrival they will take over from 2nd Midland Brigade the guard of the Corps Ammunition Train by direct arrangements to be made with 2nd Midland Brigade in addition to the guard on the Ammunition Factory at JONTERSDORF.

[signature]

Captain.
A/Brigade Major,
Second Midland Brigade.

17th June 1919.

2nd MIDLAND BRIGADE.

	UNIT	FROM	TO	REMARKS.
J - 3 day	1 Battn	KOMMERN	DUREN	By lorry.
J - 2 day				
J - 1 day.	Bde H,Qrs.	ZULPICH	DUREN	
	1 Battn (less 2 Coys)	EUSKIRCHEN	FUSSENICH Area	
	2 Coys	"	To HERBESTHAL by Train	
	1 Battn	ZULPICH	DUREN	
	1 Fld. Amb.	ZULPICH	LEHRER SEMINAR DUREN	
	1 Train Coy	ULPENICH	DISTELRATH	
J - day	1 Battn. (less 2 Coys)	FUSSENICH Area	SCHLICH	

APPENDIX 2

SECRET. Copy No. 20.

2nd MIDLAND BRIGADE ORDER No. 2.

18th June 1919.

Reference EUSKIRCHEN Sheet 1/100,000.

1. The attached March Table shews the moves of Units of the 2nd Midland Brigade on "J" - 1 day.

2. All moves will be made by march route.

3. "Q" instructions will be issued seperately by Staff Captain.

4. At 18.00 hours on "J" day all troops of the Second Midland Brigade in DUREN will be under the [illegible] command of G.O.C. 2nd Midland Brigade.

5. H.Q. 2nd Midland Brigade will close at ZULPICH at 05.30 hours on J - 1 day and re-open at DUREN on arrival.

6. ACKNOWLEDGE.

R Cowan Douglas
Captain.
Brigade Major.
Second Midland Brigade.

18th June 1919.

Distribution to:-

1 51st Leicesters.
2 52nd Leicesters.
3 2nd Mid.L.T.M.Battery.
4 6th Bn. M.G.C.
5 459th Field Coy R.E.
6 16th Field Ambulance.
7 No. 3 Coy Train.
8 Sub-Area Staff Captain.
9 O.C.Signals.
10 D.A.P.M.
11 2nd Highland Bde.
12, 13 Midland Division (2 copies)
14 B/77th Battery R.F.A.

15 6 20 Office.

2nd MIDLAND BRIGADE.

MARCH TABLE.

Date	Unit	From	To	Starting	Route	Remarks.
J - 1 day	52nd Leicesters	ZULPICH	DUREN	03.00	ZULPICH - SOLLER-DUREN.	
- do -	15th Field Ambulance	ZULPICH	DUREN	03.30	ditto	
	459th Field Coy R.E.	DURSCHEVEN	STOCKHEIM	05.00	DURSCHEVEN -ZULPICH - SOLLER - STOCKHEIM.	
	2nd Mid.Bde H.Qrs.	ZULPICH	DUREN	05.30	via SOLLER	
	2nd Mid.L.T.M.Battery	ZULPICH	DUREN	06.45	- ditto -	
	51st Leicesters (less 2 Coys)	EUSKIRCHEN	FUSSENICH	09.30	via ZULPICH	
	"A" Coy, 8th Bn.M.G.C.	MECHERNICH	SOLLER	05.30	via SINZENICH & JUNTERSDORF.	
	B/55th Battery R.F.A.	FRIESHEIM	DUREN	09.30	FRIESHEIM - ERP - KELZ - DUREN.	

MESSAGE FORM. Series No. of Message

In CALL Out	Recd. At By Sent At By	Army Form C 2128 (pads of 100).
PREAMBLE		Date Stamp
M.M. Offices Delivery / Origin		
PREFIX	Words	

TO COPY.

51st Leicesters.
52nd Leicesters.

FROM & Place: 2nd Midland Brigade.

Originator's Number	Day of Month	In reply to Number
B.M.693.	16th.	B-M.225/19

Reference Addendum No.2 of 2nd June to 2nd Midland Brigade Order No.1 dated 25th May aaa Para 1 should read AAA 51st Leicesters will detail etc.etc. and not as therein stated AAA Para 2 should read Company or Companies detailed will proceed by train from EUSKIRCHEN to HERBESTHAL etc.etc.AAA Amend accordingly AAA ACKNOWLEDGE AAA Addressed 51st and 52nd Leicesters AAA

SECRET

TIME OF ORIGIN 15.00 | TIME OF HANDING IN (For Signal use only)

Originator's Signature (Not Telegraphed) (sgd) S.H.Chamier. Capt.

4063. Wt. W5622/G1276. 937,500 pads(4?). S.O., F.B.

APPENDIX 3

SECRET.

Copy No..15..

ADDENDUM No 2 to 2nd Midland Brigade Order No,1
of 28th May 1919.

1. The 52nd Leicesters will detail one Company of strength not less than 5 officers and 170 other ranks to relieve a similar detachment at present found by the 6th Black Watch, Highland Division at HERBESTHAL on J - 3, 2 or 1 day as may be ordered later.

If necessary, two companies will be detailed to make up the above numbers.

2. The Company, or Companies, detailed will proceed by train from ZULPICH to HERBESTHAL. Train arrangements will be notified later.

3. It is hoped that it may be possible to reduce the strength of this detachment to some extent in the event of an advance taking place, but no guarantee can be given that this will be done,

4. 52nd Leicesters to acknowledge.

[signature]
Captain.
Brigade Major.
Second Midland Brigade,,

2nd June 1919.

Distribution to .-

1 I/5th South Staffs.
2 51st Leicesters.
3 52nd Leicesters.
4 2nd Mid.L.T.M.Battery.
5 8th Bn. M.G.C.
6 459th Field Coy R.E.
7 16th Field Ambulance.
8 No 2 Coy Train.
9 Sub-Area Staff Captain.
10 O.C.Signals.
11 D.A.P.M.
12 2nd Highland Brigade.
13+14 Midland Division (2 Copies)

APPENDIX 4

SECRET.

Copy No. 14

DUREN DEFENCE SCHEME.

1. GENERAL OBJECT.

The following arrangements have been drawn up with a view to maintaining order in the town and outskirts of DUREN in the event of a riot or local disturbance being caused by the civil population.

Any disturbance which is not of a serious nature will be dealt with by the Sub-Area Commandant. His Headquarters are situated opposite the RATHAUS. One Company of Infantry is put at his disposal for this purpose. (See para IO, In-lying Picquet)

2. CHIEF PROBABLE SOURCES OF DISTURBANCE.

It is probable that a riot or disturbance will first arise, either in BIRKESDORF, the group of factories south of NIDEGGENER STRASSE, or in the centre of the town. It seems unlikely that a disturbance will take place except during the hours of daylight.

3. RESPONSIBILITY FOR QUELLING ANY RIOT OR SERIOUS DISTURBANCE.

The G.O.C. 2nd Midland Brigade will be responsible for quelling any riot or serious disturbance, and will work in close co-operation with the Sub-Area Commandant.

The town of DUREN has been divided into three areas, A, B, and C as shewn on attached map. (Map only distributed to Battalions affected). A Battalion of Infantry is quartered in each area, and will be responsible in the event of a riot, for the provision of guards, and for the maintenance of order in its own area.

Periodically it will be necessary to transfer the responsibility for holding certain posts from one Battalion to another, but in general, the 52nd Leicesters will be responsible for "A" Area, the 1/5th South Staffs will be responsible for "B" Area, and the 5th Royal Irish Regiment (billeted at BIRKESDORF) will be responsible for "C" Area.

4. PROCEDURE IN THE EVENT OF A RIOT OR SERIOUS DISTURBANCE.

Should a riot or serious disturbance arise in any quarter of the town, Corps Headquarters, the Sub-Area Commandant, and the G.O.C. 2nd Midland Brigade will at once be informed of its locality and nature. Should military precautions be deemed necessary, the Sub-Area Commandant will order the "Alarm" (swelling sounds of two minutes duration) to be sounded on the syrens from the RATHAUS (see Appendix 2) and will send by telegraph or other means the word "RIOT" to the G.O.C. 2nd Midland Brigade.

As an alternative means to the syrens, the Sub-Area Commandant will warn the nearest guard to sound the "ALARM" on the b bugles. This will be taken up by all guards within hearing.

5. ACTION BY CIVIL POPULATION.

The local authorities have been informed that immediately the syrens sound the "ALARM" all civilians are to quit the streets. This applies equally to the syren which is sounded every evening to warn the civilians to keep indoors.

6. THE FOLLOWING TROOPS WILL BE AT THE DISPOSAL OF THE G.O.C. 2nd MIDLAND BRIGADE FOR THE PURPOSE OF THE DEFENCE OF DUREN.

One Battalion	DUREN Barracks.
One Battalion	19 HOLZ STRASSE DUREN.
One Battalion	BIRKESDORF.
Details of Highland Division.	DUREN Area.
IV Corps Troops.	DUREN Area.
All Cavalry at - - -	DUREN Barracks
Artillery Units stationed in -	DUREN.
In-lying Picquet	The School, DENKMAL STRASSE

7. ACTION BY THE TROOPS.

(a) On the syrens or bugles sounding the "ALARM", all troops as detailed in Para 6 will at once "STAND TO" and prepare to move to their allotted stations.

(b) Troops of other Units quartered in DUREN will at once proceed to their Unit Parade Ground.

(c) Those not quartered in DUREN will proceed to the ramp leading to the Station, where they will be organized into parties by an Officer who has been specially detailed for this purpose.

8. POLICY WHICH WILL BE ADOPTED WHEN TROOPS HAVE TAKEN UP THEIR ALLOTTED POSTS.

(a) The posts are so situated that the town of DUREN can be divided off into various localities by lines of posts. (The location, strength, and the name of Units generally responsible for holding these posts is contained in Appendix 1).

(b) No civilians will be allowed to move about the Streets. This will prevent parties of rioters moving from one locality to another.

(c) Officers Commanding Battalions will hold the remainder of their Battalions, not detailed to posts, in readiness to reinforce any line of posts on receipt of orders from Brigade Headquarters.

(d) Each post must be manned as fully as possible, i.e., at least 25 men to each Platoon, with an Officer in charge of each post.

(e) O's.C. Battalions will ensure that posts allotted to them are thoroughly reconnoitred by the Officers who have to take charge of them, that sites for Lewis Guns are carefully chosen with a view to covering all the approaches of the posts, and that communication by runner between the posts and Battalion Headquarters can be maintained at all times.

(f) Troops will carry 60 rounds of S.A.A. per man. Lewis Guns with 8 drums per gun will be manhandled to the posts.

(g) Troops will not fire unless :-

(1) Rioters adopt a menacing attitude.
(2) Attempt to force the posts.
(3) Looting or destruction of shops or houses is being resorted to.

NOTE. A few rounds fired by Lewis Guns or rifles in any of the above cases would most probably nip in the bud a disturbance which might otherwise assume serious proportions and lead to much bloodshed.

(h) Ringleaders will be arrested and confined in a house near where the posts is situated. No attempt will be made until the disturbance has subsided, to hand these ringleaders over to the Sub-Area Commandant, as this might entail attempts to rescue them.

(i) By the above means it is hoped to confine the rioters to one portion of the town. If it is then found that other means of dispersing the rioters are of no avail, the G.O.C. 2nd Midland Brigade can order a Battery of Field Artillery at the Barracks, DUREN, to fire on that quarter of the town. For this purpose the Battery will establish an O.P. at the Water Tower, COLN PLATZ, and will be prepared to fire on any portion of the town as ordered by the G.O.C. 2nd Midland Brigade.

(j) The Cavalry in DUREN Barracks will "STAND TO" and will be prepared to move on receipt of orders from G.O.C. 2nd Midland Brigade.

(k) Artillery Units quartered in DUREN will "STAND TO". In the event of the whole Battalion quartered in BIRKESDORF being ordered elsewhere, the Artillery Units in that Area will man posts Nos 4 and 5.

Close liaison must be maintained between the O.C. Battalion and the O.C. R.A. Units in BIRKESDORF.

9. SOUNDING OF THE "ALL CLEAR".

As soon as he considers that the disturbance has been quelled the G.O.C. 2nd Midland Brigade will give the order for the "ALL CLEAR" to be sounded, i.e., a succession of short b lasts on the syren.

10. INLYING PICQUET.

One Company of Infantry will be billeted in, in the SCHULE in the centre of the town and will act as INLYING PICQUET. One Platoon will always be available to turn out at 5 minutes notice, and the remainder at half an hour after the sounding of the "ALARM" by the syrens or the bugles, or unless other_wise ordered.

It can be called upon direct by the Sub-Area Commandant to deal with any minor local disturbance, or to support the Military Police, and the Company Headquarters will be connected to his office by a direct telephone line.

The Sub-Area Commandant will at once inform Corps Headquarters and the G.O.C. 2nd Midland Brigade should he call upon this In-Lying Picquet.

Every evening when the "ALARM" sounds for civilians to clear the streets, the In-Lying Picquet will send patrols round the town to assist the Military Police. The routes taken by these patrols will be varied in consultation with the Sub-Area Commandant.

An Officer from the Company supplying the In-Lying Picquet will visit the Sub-Area Commandant each day at 10.00 hours to arrange these routes and times.

H. Cowan Douglas
Captain,
Brigade Major.
Second Midland Brigade.

21st June 1919.

APPENDICES ATTACHED.

Appendix 1. Location and strength of posts with map.
(Map issued only to 1/5th South Staffs, 52nd Leicesters and 5th Royal Irish Regt.)

Appendix 2. Signal for alarming the town.

Appendix 3. Signal arrangements.

DISTRIBUTION OF DUREN DEFENCE SCHEME.

1. IV Corps H.Q.
2. Midland Division 'G'.
3. Midland Division 'Q'.
4. Sub-Area Commandant.
5. G.O.C. R.A. IV Corps for R.A. Units.
6. Commandant DUREN Barracks for Cavalry.
7. 51st Leicesters (For information)
8. 52nd Leicesters)
9. 1/5th South Staffs) With maps.
10. 5th Royal Irish Regt.)
11. Signal Officer.
12. Staff Captain.
13. File.
14. War Diary.
15. Corps Squadron R.A.F.
16. No 2 Coy Train.
17. 459th Field Coy R.E.
18. B/77 Battery, R.F.A.
19. R.T.O. DUREN.
20 to 24. Spare.
25. Camp Commandant, IV Corps.
26. H.Q., Highland Division.

APPENDIX 1.

Localities to which Guards will be sent on receipt of the word "RIOT"

			At present furnished by.
Serial No. 1. Railway Station	2 Platoons (O.C. to report to the R.T.O)		1/5th South Staffs.
Serial No. 2. Electric & Gas Works (GLASHUTEN STRASSE)	1 Platoon.		5th Royal Irish Regt.
Serial No. 3. Junction of EFFERLGASSE & DURENER STRASSE, BIRKESDORF	2 Platoons.	1 Coy.	5th Royal Irish Regt.
Serial No.4. The Church, BIRKESDORF.	2 Platoons.		
Serial No.5. RATHAUS.	2 Platoons.		1/5th South Staffs.
Serial No.6. 2nd Midland Bde H.Q.	1 Platoon.		Unit supplying guard.
Serial No.7. BURG STRASSE.	1 Platoon.		52nd Leicesters.
Serial No. 8 STADT WASSERWERK.	1 Platoon.		52nd Leicesters.
Serial No,9. Water Tower, COLN PLATZ.	1 Platoon.		52nd Leicesters.
Serial No.10. Junction of HORT STRASSE & PHILIPP STRASSE	1 Platoon.		1/5th South Staffs.
Serial No 11. FREDRICK PLATZ	1 Platoon.		52nd Leicesters.
Serial No. 12. CLODWIG PLATZ	1 Platoon.		52nd Leicesters.

-o-o-o-o-o-o-o-o-o-o-o-o-o-

APPENDIX 2.

Signal for alarming the Town.

A. The following is the translation of a notice which has appeared in the local newspapers:-

"The British Military Authorities ,in order to clear the streets of all people foe any reason whatsoever,will forthwith use the Alarm Syrens which formerly were ~~xxxx~~ worked by the Town Municipality with the view to advise the inhabitants of air raids.

With regard to the alarm:the Sub-area Commandant of DUREN has issued the following orders:-

1. ALARM will be sounded in the same manner as was done when air raids were reported,i.e. by swelling sounds of two minute duration.

2. As soon as the"Alarm" is sounded,all people walking in the streets must take refuge in the nearest house,and householders must give refuge to all entering their houses for safety.

3. The streets must be cleared at once by all civilians. Anyone not under cover within five minutes is liable to be fired on as a disturber of the peace.

4. "ALL CLEAR" will be given as formerly,after the danger is over,i.e. short sounds on one minute duration.

5. The signal will be tested every evening until further notice,i.e. short sounds of quarter minute duration,just in the same manner as formerly at 18.00 hours.

6. Alarm Syrens are already installed in the following positions:-

ST.ANNES CHURCH(1) ST.JOACHIMS CHURCH(1) OLD WATERWORKS.(1) NEW WATERWORKS.(1)	Inside DUREN.
ISOLA WORKS,BIRKESDORF(1) POWDER FACTORY,GURTZENICH(1)	Suburbs.

These are worked by one switch which is affixed at the Police Officer,RATHUS, DUREN.

-o-o-o-o-o-o-o-o-o-o-o-o-o-o

APPENDIX 5.

SIGNAL ARRANGEMENTS.

1. The Headquarters, 2nd Midland Brigade is connected by direct line telephone to all Units of Brigade Group, Divisional Headquarters, Corps Headquarters, Sub-Area Commandant, O.C. D/310 Battery Mess at COLN PLATZ.

2. A direct line runs between Sub-Area Commandant and In-Lying Picquets.

3. The Water Tower, COLN PLATZ, the O.P. D/310 Battery is in visual and wireless communication with the Brigade Headquarters.

4. The Mess of D/310 Battery is connected by telephone with its O.P. and with the Battery at DUREN BARRACKS.

-0-0-0-0-0-0-0-0-0-0-0-0-0-

APPENDIX 5

SECRET.

Copy No.......

2nd MIDLAND BRIGADE ORDER No. 3.

Ref. Germany 1.L.
1/100,000

25th June 1919.

1. In the event of Peace being signed without further advance, orders may be expected for all troops to assume their normal dispositions when the organisation of areas and civil administration, which existed prior to J - 3 day will be resumed.

2. On receipt of the orders from 2nd Midland Brigade H.Q. "Move in accordance with 2nd Midland Bde Order No.3 AAA 'A' day will be (date) ". Units will move in accordance with the attached March Table 'A'.

3. The detachment of the 51st Leicester Regt., at HERBESTHAL will be relieved on 'D' day by the Highland Division. Train arrangements for the return of the detachment to EUSKIRCHEN will be notified later.

4. Reliefs of guards will be carried out in accordance with instructions in Table 'B'.

5. Completion of moves and reliefs of guards will be reported to Brigade Headquarters daily by wire.

6. ACKNOWLEDGE.

C. J. [signature]
for Captain,
Brigade Major,
Second Midland Brigade.

H.Q., 2nd Midland Bde.,
25th June 1919.

Distribution to :-

1/5th South Staffs.
51st Leicesters.
52nd Leicesters.
2nd Mid.L.T.M.Battery
6th Bn. M.G.C.
459th Field Coy R.E.
16th Field Ambulance.
No. 2 Coy Train.
Sub-Area Staff Captain. ZULPICH.
O.C.Signals.
D.A.P.M. ZULPICH.
2nd Highland Brigade.
Midland Division. (2 copies)
11th Leicesters (P)

MARCH TABLE "A"

Serial No.	Date.	Unit.	From	To.	Time starting	Remarks
1.	"A" day	52nd Leics.	DUREN (Barracks)	ZULPICH	07.30 hrs.	Will relieve guard 1 N.C.O. & O.R. of 11th Leic.Post.at Ammunition Factory JUNTERSDORF on 'E' day. Guard of 11th Leics. will then move by lorry to rejoin its Bn. Guard will be relieved by Highland Div.at a date to be notified later.
2	"B" day	459th Fld Coy R.E.	STOCKHEIM	DURSCHEVEN.	07.30	
3	"A" day	51st Leics. (less 2 Coys)	SCHLICH	FUSSENICH	07.30	
4	"A" day	Coy.6th Bn.MGC.	DUREN.(Barracks)	SOLLER.	07.45.	
5.	"A" day	16th Fld.Amb.	DUREN	ZULPICH.	08.00	
6.	"A" day	No 2 Coy Train.	DISTELRATH	ULPENICH	08.15.	
7.	"B" day	Bde H.Q.	DUREN	ZULPICH	05.30	After handing over to Bde of Highland Division.
8.	"B" day	2nd Mid.L.T.M.B.	DUREN.	ZULPICH	09.15	
9.	"B" day	Coy,6th Bn.MGC.	SOLLER	MECHERNICH	08.00	
10.	"E" day	51st Leics(less 2 Coys)	FUSSENICH	EUSKIRCHEN.	07.30	Will relieve guards found by IX Corps Cyclist Bn in EUSKIRCHEN on "C" day.
11	"C" day	1/5th S.Staffs	DUREN	VETTWEIS.	09.30	
12	"D" day	1/5th S.Staffs.	VETTWEIS	KOMMERN.	09.30	

N.B. In the event of hot weather, times for starting marches will be 4 hours earlier.

Instructions regarding War Diaries and Intelligence Summaries are contained in F. S. Regs., Part II. and the Staff Manual respectively. Title pages will be prepared in manuscript.

WAR DIARY
or
~~INTELLIGENCE SUMMARY~~.
(Erase heading not required.)

2nd Midland Brigade.

ZULPICH. J U L Y .1919.

Army Form C. 2118.

Place	Date	Hour	Summary of Events and Information	Remarks and references to Appendices
	1919.			
DUREN.	1st.		Brigade Headquarters moved from DUREN to ZULPICH. Office opened at 10.30 hours.	
			51st Leicesters moved from FUSSENICH to EUSKIRCHEN Barracks.	
	2nd.		1/5th South Staffords moved from DUREN to VETTWEISS arriving at VETTWEISS at 13.00hours.	
			Brigade Commander and Brigade Major visited 51st Leicesters at EUSKIRCHEN. Detachment of t he 52nd Leicesters left for ANTWERP. Major L.H.P.HART.,D.S.O. in Command.	
	3rd.		1/5th South Staffords moved from VETTWEISS to KOMMERN. Concert in the evenibg by a Lena Ashwell's party at ZULPICH.	
	4th.		A General Holiday to Celebrate Peace. Brigade Headquarters played the D.A.C.at cricket at NEIDER ELVENICH. The "OWLERS" Concert party gave a concert in the evening.	
	5th		Units Training and Sports in the afternoon. Brigade Commander visited the 1/5th South Staffords at KOMMERN.	
	6th.		Units held Church Services. Brigade Commander attended service held by 52nd Leicesters. Sports in the afternoon.	
	7th.		Units Training in the morning. Sports in the afternoon. Brigade Commander visited the 51st Leicesters at EUSKIRCHEN Barracks. Brigade Headquarters played Divisional Headquarters Signal Company at BRUHL at 1500 hrs. Divisional Headquarters Signal Company won by an Innings and 21 runs.	

2353 Wt. W2544/1454 700,000 5/15 D. D. & L. A.D.S.S./Forms/C. 2118.

Instructions regarding War Diaries and Intelligence Summaries are contained in F. S. Regs., Part II. and the Staff Manual respectively. Title pages will be prepared in manuscript.

WAR DIARY
or
~~INTELLIGENCE SUMMARY~~
(Erase heading not required.)

Army Form C. 2118.

2nd Midland Brigade.
ZULPICH. JULY 1919.

Place	Date	Hour	Summary of Events and Information	Remarks and references to Appendices
	1919.			
ZULPICH.	7th.		South Staffords commenced firing G.M.C on KOMMERN RANGE.	
	8th.		Units Training in the morning. Sports in the afternoon. Practice Hockey Match at 15.00 hours . Teams picked from Brigade Headquarters, L.T.M.Battery and 52nd Leicesters.	
	9th.		Units Training in the morning. The Brigade Commander visited 1/5th South Staffords at KOMMERN. The ZULPICH Hockey XI played the 51st Leicesters at EUSKIRCHEN. Result ZULPICH 2. 51st Leicester 1. The Revd.G.H.Haslett C.F. lectured to 52nd Leicesters, Brigade Headquarters, 2nd Midland L.T.M.Battery and 16th Field Ambulance in the Hall at Officers Club, ZULPICH at 17.30 hours on "Venereal Diseases" .	
	10th.		Units Training in the morning. COLOGNE Races. The Brigade Commander and Staff attended. The Staff Captain had a gallop in one race. Miss Sarah Sylvers (the only Y.M.C.A. Lady who has performed before the Grand Fleet) entertained the soldiers in the evening at 17.30 hours in the Hall, ZULPICH.	
	11th.		Units Training in the morning. 1/5th South Staffords held their Sports in the afternoon. The Brigade Commander and Staff attended.	
	12th.		Units Training in the morning. COLOGNE RACES in the afternoon. First Race at 13.00 hours. The Brigade Commander abd Staff attended.	

2353 Wt. W2544/1454 700,000 5/15 D. D. & L. A.D.S.S./Forms/C. 2118.

Instructions regarding War Diaries and Intelligence Summaries are contained in F. S. Regs., Part II. and the Staff Manual respectively. Title pages will be prepared in manuscript.

WAR DIARY
or
~~INTELLIGENCE SUMMARY~~
(Erase heading not required.)

Army Form C. 2118.

Second Midland Brigade.
ZÜLPICH. JULY.1919.

Place	Date	Hour	Summary of Events and Information	Remarks and references to Appendices
	1919.			
ZULPICH.	13th.		Units held Church Services in the mroning. Sports in the afternoon. The Brigade Commander left for PARIS to witness the VICTORY MARCH.	
	14th.		Units Training in the morning. Sports in the afternoon. Trial Hockey Match at ZULPICH. Brigade Headquarters and 52nd Leicesters.	
	15th.		Units Training in the morning. Hockey Match in the afternoon. Brigade Headquarters V 51st Leicesters at EUSKIRCHEN.	
	16th.		Units Training in the morning. Sports in the afternoon. Brigade Commander returned from PARIS in the morning. Brigade Major suddenly decided that the Officers and men of Brigade Headquarters should go out for early morning runs to prepare themselves for the Brigade Sports. His decision was received with loud applause from all ranks.	
	17th.		Units Training in the morning. Sports in the afternoon. Brigadier General MARINDIN and Mrs MARINDIN visited the Brigade Commander and stayed to lunch. A Lena Ashwell Concert Party gave a concert in the evening at which the Brigadier attended. The members of the party dined at Brigade Headquarters after the Concert.	
	18th.		Units Training in the morning. Brigadier Visited the 51st Leicesters at EUSKIRCHEN. Sports in the afternoon. Cricket Match after tea. Brigade Headquarters V 52nd Leicesters at BESSENICH. Result Brigade Headquarters 25 52nd Leicesters 37. Bowlers Wicket.	

2353 Wt. W2544/1454 700,000 5/15 D. D. & L. A.D.S.S./Forms/C. 2118.

Instructions regarding War Diaries and Intelligence Summaries are contained in F. S. Regs., Part II. and the Staff Manual respectively. Title pages will be prepared in manuscript.

WAR DIARY
or
~~INTELLIGENCE SUMMARY~~
(Erase heading not required.)

Army Form C. 2118.

Second Midland Brigade.
ZULPICH. JULY.1919.

Place	Date 1919.	Hour	Summary of Events and Information	Remarks and references to Appendices
ZULPICH.	19th.		The Official day for Celebration of Peace. The day was observed as a General Holiday. The Brigade Major took two young Officers of Brigade Headquarters to WEISBADEN to celebrate quietly.	
	20 th.		Units held Church Services in the morning. Brigade Commander attended service held by 52nd Leicester The Belgian 1st Regiment of Guides held their races at CREFELD, much to the surprise of everyone the Staff Captain attended. The Brigade Major and the two young Officers returned from WEISBADEN looking extraordinarily fit and sun burnt.	
	21st.		Units Training in the morning. Sports in the afternoon.	
	22nd.		Units Training in the morning. Sports in the afternoon. Brigadier General visited the 1/5th South Staffords in the morning and the Brigade School in the afternoon where he gave a lecture to the students. The Corps Commander visited the 52nd Leicesters.	
	23rd.		Units Training in the morning. Sports in the afternoon. Brigade Commander visited the Trench Mortar Battery in the morning. Rained continously throughout the day.	
	24th.		Units Training in the Morning. Division grant a half holiday for Divisional Horse Show, ROMERHOF. The General attended the horse show.	
	25th.		The General, Lieut Woolley and Captain Troughton motor to COLOGNE and select prizes for the Brigade Sports. Training carried on as usual.	

2353 Wt. W2544/1454 700,000 5/15 D. D. & L. A.D.S.S./Forms/C. 2118.

Instructions regarding War Diaries and Intelligence Summaries are contained in F. S. Regs., Part II. and the Staff Manual respectively. Title pages will be prepared in manuscript.

WAR DIARY

or

~~INTELLIGENCE SUMMARY~~

(Erase heading not required.)

Army Form C. 2118.

Second Midland Brigade.

July, 1919.

ZULPICH.

Place	Date	Hour	Summary of Events and Information	Remarks and references to Appendices
	1919.		Units Training in the morning . Sports in the afternoon.	
ZULPICH.	26th.		The General and Lt.Col.Beecher 52nd Leicesters motor to ANTWERP to inspect the detachment of 52nd Leicesters. Brigade Major Inspected the Brigade Sports Ground at BESSENICH.	
	27th.		Training carried out in the morning. Brigade Headquarters play L.T.M.Battery at Cricket in the afternoon. The German Civilians hold Athletic Sports for Repatriated prisonners in the evening at Zülpich.	
	28th.		Units Training in the morning. Sports in the afternoon. Brigade Headquarters played 1/5th South Staffords at Cricket and 52nd Leicesters played 16th Field Ambulance. Brigadier General Crauford returns from ANTWERP.	
	29th.		Units carry out training in the morning. 51st Leicesters playes 459th Field Coy.R.E. at Cricket. Brigade Headquarters carry out preliminary heats at BESSENICH in the afternoon. Lena Ashwells	
	3		Dramatic Party give "Lady Gorringes Necklace" at ZULPICH Theatre and received a great ovation.	
	30th		Units Training in the morning. Brigadier General visits the Brigade Sports Ground at BESSENICH.	
	31st.		Units Training in the morning. Preliminary Tug-of-War Pulls take place in the afternoon at BESSENICH. 459th Field Coy.R.E., 52nd Leicesters and Brigade Headquarters all reach the finals.	

ZULPICH.
GERMANY.
July, 31st, 1919.

R Cowan Douglas [illegible]

Brigadier General.
Commanding 2nd Midland Brigade.

2353 Wt. W2544/1454 700,000 5/15 D. D. & L. A.D.S.S./Forms/C. 2118.

Instructions regarding War Diaries and Intelligence Summaries are contained in F. S. Regs., Part II. and the Staff Manual respectively. Title pages will be prepared in manuscript.

WAR DIARY
or
~~INTELLIGENCE SUMMARY.~~
(Erase heading not required.)

2nd Midland Brigade.

ZULPICH. J U L Y. 1919.

Army Form C. 2118.

Place	Date	Hour	Summary of Events and Information	Remarks and references to Appendices
	1919.			
(DUREN.)	1st.		Brigade Headquarters moved from DUREN to ZULPICH. Office opened at ZULPICH at 1030 Hours. 51st Leicesters moved from FUSSENICH to EUSKIRCHEN Barracks.	
ZULPICH.	2nd.		1/5th South Staffords moved from DUREN to VETTWEISS arriving at VETTWEISS at 13.00 hours. Brigade Commander and Brigade Major visited 51st Leicesters at EUSKIRCHEN. Detachment of 52nd Leicesters left for ANTWERP. Major L.H.P.HART,D.S.O.in Command.	
	3rd.		1/5th South Staffords moved from VETTWEISS to KOMMERN. Concert in the evening by a Lena Ashwell's party at ZULPICH.	
	4th.		A General Holiday to Celebrate Peace. Brigade Headquarters played the D.A.C.at cricket at NEIDER ELVENICH. The "OWLERS" Concert party gave a concert in the evening.	
	5th.		Units Training and Sports in the afternoon. Brigade Commander visited the 1/5th South Staffords at KOMMERN.	
	6th.		Units held Church Services. Brigade Commander attended service held by 52nd Leicesters. Sports in the afternoon.	
	7th.		Units Training in the morning. Sports in the afternoon. Brigade Commander visited the 51st Leicesters at EUSKIRCHEN Barracks. Brigade Headquarters played Divisional Headquarters Signal Company at BRUHL at 1500 hours.. Divisional Headquarters Signal Company won by an Innings and 21 runs.	

2353 Wt. W2544/1454 700,000 5/15 D. D. & L. A.D.S.S./Forms/C. 2118.

Army Form C. 2118.

Instructions regarding War Diaries and Intelligence Summaries are contained in F. S. Regs., Part II. and the Staff Manual respectively. Title pages will be prepared in manuscript.

WAR DIARY
or
INTELLIGENCE SUMMARY.
(*Erase heading not required.*)

2nd Midland Brigade.
ZULPICH. JULY.1919.

Place	Date	Hour	Summary of Events and Information	Remarks and references to Appendices
	1919.			
ZULPICH.	7th.		South Staffords commenced firing G.M.C on KOMMERN RANGE.	
	8th.		Units Training in the morning. Sports in the afternoon. Practice Hockey Match at 15.00 hours. Teams picked from Brigade Headquarters, L.T.M.Battery and 52nd Leicesters.	
	9th.		Units Training in the morning. The Brigade Commander visited 1/5th South Staffords at KOMMERN. The ZULPICH Hockey XI played the 51st Leicesters at EUSKIRCHEN. Result ZULPICH 2. 51st Leicester 1. The Revd.G.H.Haslett C.F. lectured to 52nd Leicesters, Brigade Headquarters, 2nd Midland L.T.M.Battery and 18th Field Ambulance in the Hall at Officers Club, ZULPICH at 17.30 hours on "Venereal Diseases".	
	10th.		Units Training in the morning. COLOGNE Races. The Brigade Commander and Staff attended. The Staff Captain had a gallop in one race. Miss Sarah Sylvers (the only Y.M.C.A. Lady who has performed before the Grand Fleet) entertained the soldiers in the evening at 17.30 hours in the Hall, ZULPICH.	
	11th.		Units Training in the morning. 1/5th South Staffords held their Sports in the afternoon. The Brigade Commander and Staff attended.	
	12th.		Units Training in the morning. COLOGNE RACES in the afternoon. First Race at 13.00 hours. The Brigade Commander abd Staff attended.	

2353 Wt. W2544/1454 700,000 5/15 D. D. & L. A.D.S.S./Forms/C. 2118.

Instructions regarding War Diaries and Intelligence Summaries are contained in F. S. Regs., Part II. and the Staff Manual respectively. Title pages will be prepared in manuscript.

Army Form C. 2118.

WAR DIARY
or
INTELLIGENCE SUMMARY.
(Erase heading not required.)

Second Midland Brigade.
ZULPICH. JULY.1919.

Place	Date	Hour	Summary of Events and Information	Remarks and references to Appendices
	1919.			
ZULPICH.	13th.		Units held Church Services in the mroning. Sports in the afternoon. The Brigade Commander left for PARIS to witness the VICTORY MARCH.	
	14th.		Units Training in the morning. Sports in the afternoon. Trial Hockey Match at ZULPICH. Brigade Headquarters and 52nd Leicesters.	
	15th.		Units Training in the morning. Hockey Match in the afternoon. Brigade Headquarters V 51st Leicesters at EUSKIRCHEN.	
	16th.		Units Training in the morning. Sports in the afternoon. Brigade Commander returned from PARIS in the morning. Brigade Major suddenly decided that the Officers and men of Brigade Headquarters should go out for early morning runs to prepare themselves for the Brigade Sports. His decision was received with loud applause from all ranks.	
	17th.		Units Training in the morning. Sports in the afternoon. Brigadier General MARINDIN and Mrs MARINDIN visited the Brigade Commander and stayed to lunch. A Lena Ashwell Concert Party gave a concert in the evening at which the Brigadier attended. The members of the party dined at Brigade Headquarters after the Concert.	
	18th.		Units Training in the morning. Brigadier visited the 51st Leicesters at EUSKIRCHEN. Sports in the afternoon. Cricket Match after tea. Brigade Headquarters V 52nd Leicesters at BESSENICH. Result Brigade Headquarters 25 52nd Leicesters 37. Bowlers Wicket.	

2353 Wt. W2544/1454 700,000 5/15 D. D. & L. A.D.S.S./Forms/C. 2118.

Instructions regarding War Diaries and Intelligence Summaries are contained in F. S. Regs., Part II. and the Staff Manual respectively. Title pages will be prepared in manuscript.

WAR DIARY
or
INTELLIGENCE SUMMARY.
(Erase heading not required.)

Army Form C. 2118.

Second Midland Brigade.
ZULPICH. JULY, 1919.

Place	Date	Hour	Summary of Events and Information	Remarks and references to Appendices
	1919.			
ZULPICH.	19th.		The official day for Celebration of Peace. The day was observed as a General Holiday. The Brigade Major took two young Officers of Brigade Headquarters to WEISBADEN to celebrate quietly.	
	20th.		Units held Church Services in the morning. Brigade Commander attended service held by 52nd Leicesters The Belgian 1st Regiment of Guides held their races at CREFELD, much to the surprise of everyone the staff Captain attended. The Brigade Major and the two young officers returned from WEISBADEN looking extraordinarily fit and sun burnt.	
	21st.		Units Training in the morning. Sports in the afternoon.	
	22nd.		Units Training in the morning. Sports in the afternoon. Brigadier General visited the 1/5th South Staffords in the morning and the Brigade School in the afternoon where he gave a lecture to the students. The Corps Commander visited the 52nd Leicesters.	
	23rd.		Units Training in the morning. Sports in the afternoon. Brigade Commander visited the Trench Mortar Battery in the morning. Rained continously throughout the day.	
	24th.		Units Training in the Morning. Division grant a half holiday for Divisional Horse Show, ROHERHOF. The General attended the horse show.	
	25th.		The General, Lieut Woolley and Captain Troughton motor to COLOGNE and select prizes for the Brigade Sports. Training carried on as usual.	

2353 Wt. W2544/1454 700,000 5/15 D. D. & L. A.D.S.S./Forms/C. 2118.

Instructions regarding War Diaries and Intelligence Summaries are contained in F. S. Regs., Part II. and the Staff Manual respectively. Title pages will be prepared in manuscript.

WAR DIARY
or
~~INTELLIGENCE SUMMARY.~~
(Erase heading not required.)

Army Form C. 2118.

Second Midland Brigade.
July, 1919.
ZULPICH.

Place	Date	Hour	Summary of Events and Information	Remarks and references to Appendices
	1919.			
			Units Training in the morning . Sports in the afternoon.	
ZULPICH.	26th.		The General and Lt.Col.Beecher 52nd Leicesters motor to ANTWERP to inspect the detachment of 52nd Leicesters. Brigade Major Inspected the Brigade Sports Ground at BESSENICH.	
	27th.		Training carried out in the morning. Brigade Headquarters play L.T.M.Battery at Cricket in the afternoon. The German Civilians hold Athletic Sports for Repatriated prisoners in the evening at Zülpich.	
	28th.		Units Training in the morning. Sports in the afternoon. Brigade Headquarters played 1/5th South Staffords at Cricket and 52nd Leicesters played 16th Field Ambulance. Brigadier General Crauford returns from ANTWERP.	
	29th.		Units carry out training in the morning. 51st Leicesters playes 459th Field Coy.R.E. at Cricket. Brigade Headquarters carry out preliminary heats at BESSENICH in the afternoon. Lena Ashwells Dramatic Party give "Lady Gorringes Necklace" at ZULPICH Theatre and received a great ovation.	
	30th		Units Training in the morning. Brigadier General visits the Brigade Sports Ground at BESSENICH. Units Training in the morning.	
	31st.		Preliminary Tug-of-War Pulls take place in the afternoon at BESSENICH. 459th Field Coy.R.E., 52nd Leicesters and Brigade Headquarters all reach the finals.	

ZULPICH.
GERMANY.
July, 31st, 1919.

Brigadier General.
Commanding 2nd Midland Brigade.

2353 Wt. W2544/1454 700,000 5/15 D. D. & L. A.D.S.S./Forms/C. 2118.

Army Form C. 2118.

Instructions regarding War Diaries and Intelligence Summaries are contained in F. S. Regs., Part II. and the Staff Manual respectively. Title pages will be prepared in manuscript.

WAR DIARY
or
~~INTELLIGENCE SUMMARY.~~
(Erase heading not required.)

Second Midland Brigade.
ZULPICH. 1919.
August, 1919

Place	Date	Hour	Summary of Events and Information	Remarks and references to Appendices
	1919.			
ZULPICH.	1st.		A General Holiday was given for the Brigade Sports which took place at BESSENICH. The Divisional General, Brigadier and Staff attended. The bands of 1/5th South Staffs and 51st Leicesters and 53rd Gordon Highlanders played during the various events. The Brigadier presented the prizes at the conclusion of the sports and the Unit Championship Cup to the 1/5th South Staffords being the winning Unit. A most enjoyable day andexcellent sports.	
	2nd.		Units Training in the morning. Sports in the afternoon. Brigadier General attended the 2nd Highland Brigade Sports at HAUSEN.	
	3rd.		Units held Church Services in the morning. Sports in the afternoon.	
	4th.		Bank Holiday. Final of Inter Company Cricket Competition. 52nd Leicesters Versus 459th Field Company.R.E. and was played at KOMMERN at 14.30 hours. 459th Field Coy.R.E.won by 10 runs. Brigadier General visited the Cavalry Division Horse Show and IX Corps TATTOO.	
	5th.		Units Training in the morning. Brigade Cross Country Run in the afternoon. 1/5th South Staffords won the Cross Country Run and was presented with the Cup. 52nd Leicesters were second. Staff Captain attended the second day of the Cavalry Division Races.	
	6th.		Units Training in the morning. Sports in the afternoon.Warning order received for the move to England.	

2353 Wt. W2544/1454 700,000 5/15 D. D. & L. A.D.S.S./Forms/C. 2118.

Army Form C. 2118.

Instructions regarding War Diaries and Intelligence Summaries are contained in F. S. Regs., Part II. and the Staff Manual respectively. Title pages will be prepared in manuscript.

WAR DIARY
or
INTELLIGENCE SUMMARY.
(*Erase heading not required.*)

Second Midland Brigade.

Zulpich.
August.1919.

Place	Date 1919.	Hour	Summary of Events and Information	Remarks and references to Appendices
ZULPICH.	7th.		Units Training in the morning. Sports in the afternoon.	
	8th.		Units Training in the morning. Sports in the afternoon. The Brigadier and Staff attended the IX Corps Eliminating Competition for Army Horse Show held at ROMERHOF.	
	9th.		Units Training in the morning. Sports in the afternoon. The "Robin Hoods" (IX CORPS Entertainers) gave a concert in the Hall, ZULPICH in the evening.	
	10th.		Church Services held by Units in the morning. Sports in the afternoon.	
	11th.		Units Training in the morning. Sports in the afternoon. Miss Sarah Sylvers gave an entertainment in the Hall, ZULPICH in the evening at 19.45 hours.	
	12th.		Units Training in the morning. Sports in the afternoon.	
	13th.		Units Training in the morning. Sports in the afternoon.	
	14th.		Units Training in the morning. Sports in the afternoon. Divisional Commander, Brigade Commander and Staff attended 3rd Day of Divisional Sports at ROMERHOF. Preliminary Heats run. The Bands of 51st Leicesters and 1/5th South Staffords gave selections during the various events.	
	15th.		Units Training in the morning. Sports in the afternoon. A concert was given in the evening by the "Darts"	
	16th.		Units Training in the morning. Sports in the afternoon. Semi-Finals and Finals of the Divisional	

Instructions regarding War Diaries and Intelligence Summaries are contained in F. S. Regs., Part II. and the Staff Manual respectively. Title pages will be prepared in manuscript.

WAR DIARY

or

~~INTELLIGENCE SUMMARY~~

(Erase heading not required.)

Second Midland Brigade.
ZULPICH. GERMANY.
August 1919.

Army Form C. 2118.

Place	Date	Hour	Summary of Events and Information	Remarks and references to Appendices
	1919.			
ZULPICH.	16th (Cont)		Sports held at ROMERHOF. Divisional General, Brigadier General and Staff attended. The Divisional Commander distributed the prizes at the close of the Sports to the winning Competitors, and the Unit Championship Cup to the 1/5th South Staffords being the winning Unit. The band of 1/5th South Staffords gave various selections during the sports. The Brigadier General and Staff attended the IX Corps Tattoo in the evening held at NIDEGGEN.	
	17th.		Church Services held by Units in the Morning. The Brigadier General Attended the service of the 52nd Leicesters. Sports in the afternoon.	
	18th.		Units Training in the morning. Sports in the afternoon. Miss Doris Cloud and Party gave a Consert in the Hall, ZULPICH. Brigadier General and Staff attended the Army Horse Show held at COLOGNE.	
	19th.		Units Training in the morning. Sports in the afternoon. Brigadier General and Staff attended the Army Horse Show at MERHEIM, COLOGNE.	
	20th.		Units Training in the morning. Sports in the afternoon.	
	21st.		Units Training in the morning. Sports in the afternoon. Brigadier General visited WIESBADEN.	
	22nd.		Units Training in the morning. Sports in the afternoon.	
	23rd.		Units Training in the morning. Sports in the afternoon. Brigade Major and Staff Captain attended	

Instructions regarding War Diaries and Intelligence Summaries are contained in F. S. Regs., Part II. and the Staff Manual respectively. Title pages will be prepared in manuscript.

WAR DIARY
or
~~INTELLIGENCE SUMMARY~~.
(Erase heading not required.)

Army Form C. 2118.

Second Midland Brigade.
ZULPICH. GERMANY.

Place	Date	Hour	Summary of Events and Information	Remarks and references to Appendices
	1919.			
ZULPICH.	23rd.	(Cont)	the 6th Divisional Dinner in the evening.	
	24th.		Church Services held by Units in the Morning. Brigade Commander attended the service of the 52nd Leicesters at 11.00 hours. Sports in the afternoon.	
	25th.		Units Training in the morning. Brigade Commander and Staff go to Divisional H.Qrs, BRUHL in the morning for Divisional photographs. Farewell Dinner of 2nd Midland Brigade Headquarters held in the evening in the Hall, ZULPICH.	
	26th.		Units Training in the morning. Sports in the afternoon.	
	27th.		Units Training in the Morning . Sports in the afternoon.	
	28th.		Units Training in the Morning. Sports in the afternoon.	
	29th.		Units Training in the morning. Sports in the afternoon. 52nd Leicesters prepare for the move to England. Advance party of the 51st Leicesters leave EUSKIRCHEN. Brigadier General and Staff attend the Races at COLOGNE.	
	30th.		51st Leicesters leave EUSKIRCHEN for England. The Staff Captain and horses of 2nd Midland Brigade Headquarters leave ZULPICH. Brigade Headquarters and 52nd Leicesters prepare for the move.	
	31st.		Brigade Headquarters and 52nd Leicesters leave ZULPICH for England. The Brigade Major and Captain de Winton stay in ZULPICH as rear party.	

2353 Wt. W2544/1454 700,000 5/15 D. D. & L. A.D.S.S./Forms/C. 2118.

Instructions regarding War Diaries and Intelligence Summaries are contained in F. S. Regs., Part II. and the Staff Manual respectively. Title pages will be prepared in manuscript.

WAR DIARY
or
~~INTELLIGENCE SUMMARY~~.
(Erase heading not required.)

SECOND MIDLAND BRIGADE.
ZULPICH. GERMANY.

Army Form C. 2118.

Place	Date	Hour	Summary of Events and Information	Remarks and references to Appendices
			ZULPICH. GERMANY. AUGUST.1919.	
			R Cowan Douglas Capt for Brigadier General. Commanding, Second Midland Brigade.	

2353 Wt. W2544/1454 700,000 5/15 D. D. & L. A.D.S.S./Forms/C. 2118.

BEF

MIDLAND DIV

2 MID. BDE.

51 LEICS. R.

1919 MAR TO 1919 AUG

To: Adjutant General's Office,
BASE.

Herewith, enclosed War Diary of the 51st. Bn. The Leicestershire Regiment, from March 1st. 1919 to March 31st. 1919. Volume 1.

Wm. G. [illegible] Lieut-Col.
Comdg; 51st. Bn. The Leicestershire Regiment,
Euskirchen Barracks,
Germany.
April 9th. 1919.

2505/Gh

1

Army Form C. 2118.

Instructions regarding War Diaries and Intelligence Summaries are contained in F. S. Regs., Part II. and the Staff Manual respectively. Title pages will be prepared in manuscript.

WAR DIARY

~~or~~

~~INTELLIGENCE SUMMARY.~~

(Erase heading not required.)

Euskirchen. 51st Bn Leicestershire Regt.

Place	Date	Hours	Summary of Events and Information	Remarks and references to Appendices
Dunkirk	8/3/19	1600	Battn disembarked & proceeded to West Camp.	
"	9/3/19	1200	Entrained Sand Sidings en route for Cologne	
Cologne	11/3/19	0800	Detrained Bon Tour station. Marched to Siirth, arriving about mid day. Billeted on civil population. Companies scattered.	
Siirth	13/3/19	1030	Battn Inspected by Army Commander.	
"	15/3/19	0900	Took over Transport, Lewis Guns & stores from 1st Bn Leicestershire Regt.	RBW
"	"	1500	Capt H Duke M.O. attached to 51st Bn returned to England. Capt Granger M.O. of 1st Bn takes over duties as M.O. to 51st Bn.	
"	18/3/19	0630	Marched to Cologne entrained en route for Euskirchen.	
Euskirchen	"	1530	Took over part of Kaserne buildings (IX Corps Reception Camp)	
"	22/3/19	0900	Re organisation of Battn. More equal distribution of Companies.	

T2134. Wt. W708—776. 500000. 4/15. Sir J. C. & S.

3

Instructions regarding War Diaries and Intelligence Summaries are contained in F. S. Regs., Part II. and the Staff Manual respectively. Title pages will be prepared in manuscript.

WAR DIARY
or
INTELLIGENCE SUMMARY.
(Erase heading not required.)

Army Form C. 2118.

Place	Date	Hour	Summary of Events and Information	Remarks and references to Appendices
Euskirchen	24 to 29th		Lewis Gun (Theory). Education. Close order drill. Battn Route march (28th). P. & B.T. & games. Sports after on 26th & 29th. Voluntary evening classes for German language. Interior Economy (29th). Squad & Platoon drill.	D.B.

Wm G. Pruslie. Lt Col
Comm 9/51 Bn. Leicestershire Regt.

T2134. Wt. W708—776. 500000. 4/15. Sir J. C. & S.

Instructions regarding War Diaries and Intelligence Summaries are contained in F. S. Regs., Part II. and the Staff Manual respectively. Title pages will be prepared in manuscript.

WAR DIARY

~~or~~

~~INTELLIGENCE~~ ~~SUMMARY.~~

(Erase heading not required.)

Army Form C. 2118.

Place	Date	Hour	Summary of Events and Information	Remarks and references to Appendices
Euskirchen	20/3/19		Lt J W Budd admitted into Hospital	
"	24th	1400	Lecture by M.O. to Battn Venereal disease.	
	25th	1000	C.S.M Ormerod reported. P.&B.T. Instructor	
	26th	-	Lt Budd proceeded to Base. struck of strength.	
	27th	2000	Lt Davis, 2Lt Grimley, 2Lt Richards reported for duty from 1st Bn Leic Regt.	
	27th	1030	Brigade Commander sees officers & staff.	
	29th	1000	Corps Commandant inspects barracks.	
	31st	1400	Officers riding class commences under Batt T. O.	
			Training Summary	
Zulpich	14th to 17th		Arms drill. Company Route marches P.&B.T. Close order drill.	
Euskirchen	19th to 22nd		Interior Economy. - Shortage of utensils. Company Route marches. Close Order drill P.&B.T. & Games.	

T2134. Wt. W708—776. 500000. 4/15. Sir J. C. & S.

To:- A.G.Dept.,
BASE. France.

Euskirchen Barracks.
May 10th. 1919.

CONFIDENTIAL.

Herewith please find War Diary of 51st. Bn. The Leicestershire Regiment, from April 1st/19 to April 30/19 - Volume 2.

Lieut-Col.,
Comdg: 51st. Bn. The Leicestershire Regiment.

Army Form C. 2118.

(1)

WAR DIARY
or
~~INTELLIGENCE~~ SUMMARY
(Erase heading not required.)

Instructions regarding War Diaries and Intelligence Summaries are contained in F. S. Regs., Part II. and the Staff Manual respectively. Title Pages will be prepared in manuscript.

Place	Date	Hour	Summary of Events and Information: Euskirchen Germany. 51st Bn Leicestershire Regt	Remarks and references to Appendices
Euskirchen	1/4/19	1030	Brigade Commander inspects Battalion	
	3/4/19	10 00	Four Officers & 80 OR's attend lecture at Zulpich	
		1000	Lieut Col Crosbie takes over command of Battn from Lieut Col Utterson	
	4/4/19	1000	Brigade Education Officer instructs system of Education to be worked on same lines as 1/5 S Staffs	
	5/4/19	0900	Capt H C Walsh takes over duties of Adjutant vice 2nd Lieut D B Lowe	
	6/4/19	0900	Capt E Pascoe takes over command of A Coy vice Capt S R. Lewis	S.M.S.
			Cyclist & Labour Corps quit barracks & Lieut Col W Mc Crosbie DSO takes charge of same vice Lieut Col Smith.	

Army Form C. 2118.

WAR DIARY
or
~~INTELLIGENCE SUMMARY~~

(Erase heading not required.)

Instructions regarding War Diaries and Intelligence Summaries are contained in F. S. Regs., Part II. and the Staff Manual respectively. Title Pages will be prepared in manuscript.

Place	Date	Hour	Summary of Events and Information	Remarks and references to Appendices
Euskirchen	6th		2nd Lieut G Stevenson appointed Officer i/c messing	J.M.S.
	7th		A Coy commences duty at Weilerswist (Construction of miniature Range)	
	7th	0840	2nd Lt E W Richards + 17 O Rs proceed to Bessenich to form part of a T.M. Battery.	
	8th	0900	Commencement of the erection of Stables in Commernerstrasse	
	8th	1730	Lecture to Battn on temperance (Col Hawkes)	
	9th	10-30	Corps Commander inspects barracks + Transport.	
	10	11.00	Sgt Solley from N Staffs reports to Battn as T. Instructor	
	11	1230.	Weather very dull improves late in the day	
Zulpich	12	14.30	Battn beat 52 Leicesters at football by 2 goals – nil	
Euskirchen	13	10.15.	Good C of E parade	
Zulpich	16	14.30.	2 Officers + 50 O Rs attend lecture on Health + Citizenship	

2449 Wt. W14957/M90 750,000 1/16 J.B.C. & A. Forms/C.2118/12.

Instructions regarding War Diaries and Intelligence Summaries are contained in F. S. Regs., Part II. and the Staff Manual respectively. Title Pages will be prepared in manuscript.

WAR DIARY
or
INTELLIGENCE SUMMARY
(Erase heading not required.)

Army Form C. 2118.

Place	Date	Hour	Summary of Events and Information — Euskirchen Germany — 1st Bn Leicestershire Regt.		Remarks and references to Appendices
			Departures	Arrivals	
Euskirchen	3rd	1000		Lieut Col W. M. Crosbie D.S.O	
	3rd	1100		Major C. E. T. Dixon M.C.	
	6th			Capt H C Walsh M.C.	
	9th	0800	Capt F R Lewis 2nd Lts Stevenson Shaw, & Grainger	Capt E Pascoe.	
	24th	0800	Lieut Col A. T. Le M Utterson D.S.O.		

D B [illegible] Lt Col
a/Cdg 1st Bn. Leicester Regt.

2449 Wt. W14957/M90 750,000 1/16 J.B.C. & A. Forms/C.2118/12.

Army Form C. 2118.

WAR DIARY
or
INTELLIGENCE SUMMARY

(Erase heading not required.)

(3)

Instructions regarding War Diaries and Intelligence Summaries are contained in F. S. Regs., Part II. and the Staff Manual respectively. Title Pages will be prepared in manuscript.

Place	Date	Hour	Summary of Events and Information	Remarks and references to Appendices
Euskirchen	18th	10.30	A D V S inspects animals.	[illegible]
	21	1430	Inter-Coy football commences (organised Bd Coy League)	
	25		Battn lose to Corps at Hockey.	
Zulpich	26	1600.	Battn Officers attend lecture by Commander Viscount Broome R.N. on Naval subjects.	
	~~28th~~	1		
Cologne	28 29	1430	Officers & O.R. attend London Divisional Race meeting at Kalk Cöln	
	30	1030	The Bde Commander inspected Barracks.	
	30	1200	Bde Commander interviews Capt Carelli The latter relieved of command of 'B' Coy	

2449 Wt. W14957/M90 750,000 1/16 J.B.C. & A. Forms/C.2118/12.

Army Form C. 2118.

Instructions regarding War Diaries and Intelligence Summaries are contained in F. S. Regs., Part II. and the Staff Manual respectively. Title Pages will be prepared in manuscript.

WAR DIARY
or
~~INTELLIGENCE SUMMARY~~
(Erase heading not required.)

Euskirchen 1919 — 5/ Bn Leicestershire Rgt

(2)

Place	Date MAY	Hour	Summary of Events and Information	Remarks and references to Appendices
EUSKIRCHEN	15th	1130	G.H.Q. Army of Rhine Inspector of Cookery inspects Battn messing arrangements	
"	14th		3rd Party proceed on Rhine pleasure trip.	
	19th	1000	F.G.C.M. assemble at these H.Q.	
BRUHL	20	1430	Party of 4 officers + 20 OR attend lecture on "Fallacies of Bolshevism"	D.B.L.
EUSKIRCHEN	21	1715	Mr E. Bellingham lectures Battn on "People of the Desert"	
"	23		OC Companys attend lectures "Use of carrier Pigeons"	
"	26th	1430	a/RSM Harvey lectures Battn on "Peace Terms"	
"	27		Lt Crosbie resumes command of this Battn.	
"	27	1730	Brigade Football 'Knock out' competition. A Company 1/5 Staffs beat Bde H.Q. 5 goals to 1.	
"	29	1430	Battn Signal officer lectures on Field cipher	

D B Lowe LT. COL.
COMDG. 5th Bn. LEICESTER REGT.

2449 Wt. W14957/M90 750,000 1/16 J.B.C. & A. Forms/C.2118/12.

Army Form C. 2118.

WAR DIARY
or
~~INTELLIGENCE SUMMARY~~
(Erase heading not required.)

Instructions regarding War Diaries and Intelligence Summaries are contained in F. S. Regs., Part II. and the Staff Manual respectively. Title Pages will be prepared in manuscript.

Euskirchen 1919. 51 Bn Leicestershire Regt.

Place	Date	Hour	Summary of Events and Information	Remarks and references to Appendices
ZINZENICH	MAY 2	1200	Battn inspected by Commander in Chief British Army of Rhine.	
ZULPICH	5	1415	12 officers + 60 OR attend lecture on Naval Subjects	
COLOGNE	7	0930	2 officers attend Cookery demonstrations.	
EUSKIRCHEN	7"		Major Dumbell DSO takes over Command of this Battn	D.B.
"	8"	1700	Bishop of Lichfield lectures Battn on Imperialism ancient + modern.	
"	9"	1130	Brigade Commander lectures Battn on the "Army + the Nation".	
	9"		10 officers + 100 OR proceed on Rhine pleasure Trip	
ZULPICH	11"	1030	Signalling officer + A/Adjt attend lecture on Field Cipher	

2449 Wt. W14957/M90 750,000 1/16 J.B.C. & A. Forms/C.2118/12.

A. G. Base

WAR DIARY

~~or~~

~~INTELLIGENCE SUMMARY.~~

(Erase heading not required.)

Army Form C. 2118.

Instructions regarding War Diaries and Intelligence Summaries are contained in F. S. Regs., Part II. and the Staff Manual respectively. Title pages will be prepared in manuscript.

Euskirchen June 1919 51 Bn The Leicestershire Regt

Place	Date	Hour	Summary of Events and Information	Remarks and references to Appendices
Euskirchen	1.6.19		Lt Col C. H. Dumbell D.S.O. takes over command of Battn	
"	"		Major E. A. Freeman appointed 2nd in Command of 2/4 K.O.Y.L.I.	
"	3.6.19	1000	Ceremonial Parade in honour of H.M. King George V birthday	
"	"		Maj E. A. Freeman rejoins Battn having been wrongly posted.	
"	6.6.19		Lt J. W. Budd (Warwickshire Regt) rejoins Battn from hospital	
"	7.6.19		Extract from Kings birthday honours dated 3.6.1919. Major (Tempy Lt Col) C. H. Dumbell D.S.O. to Brevet Lt Col.	
"	10th	1745	Officers NCO's & men take part part in a discussion on one of the Reconstruction problems viz: Housing.	
"	12th		Capt A. D. Corelli crossposted to 9th Bn Leicestershire Regt	
Buchel	13th		Company officers attend a lecture on "Use of Carrier Pigeons"	
Euskirchen	"		Maj E. A. Freeman proceeded to U.K. to join 1st Bn K.S.L.I	
"	16th		Regimental Sports held. Prizes presented by Brigadier Comdr.	
"	19th		Battn (less two coys) moves to Fussenich by march route on J – 2 day (B & C coys go to Heiberchal on 18th)	
Fussenich	20th		Battn less two coys moves by march route to Schleich area. B. H. Q. Merode.	DB

T2134. Wt. W708—776. 500000. 4/15. Sir J. C. & S.

(2)

WAR DIARY

~~or INTELLIGENCE SUMMARY.~~

(Erase heading not required.)

Army Form C. 2118.

Instructions regarding War Diaries and Intelligence Summaries are contained in F. S. Regs., Part II. and the Staff Manual respectively. Title pages will be prepared in manuscript.

Place	Date	Hour	Summary of Events and Information	Remarks and references to Appendices
	June			
Merode	21st		Difficulties in establishing telephonic communication to Brigade & to Coys	
"	25th		German mark depreciates in value. 10 marks = 2/9.	
"	27th		Winter clothing withdrawn from W.Os, N.C.Os & men of Battn	
"	28th	0900	Battn, less 2 Companies go for short route march.	
"		2030	Phone message received from Brigade – Peace Treaty Signed.	
	30	0630	Battn, less 2 Coys moves (march route) en route for Euskirchen (Stayed one night at Fussenich)!	

[signature]
Lt Col
Comdg 51st Bn The Leicestershire Regt.

a. F. C. 2118.

War Diary.

EUSKIRCHEN July 1919 — 51st. Bn. The Leicestershire Regiment.

Place	date	hour	Summary of Events, and information.
	July		
Euskirchen	1st	1030	Battalion (less two companies) arrive in barracks from Fussenich
"	2nd		Brigade Commander inspects New Officers Mess and Officers Quarters.
Cologne	2nd	0930	Commanding Officer attends Cooking Demonstrations.
Euskirchen	4th		Observed as a General Holiday.
"	4th	1500	B & C Companies rejoin from Herbersthal.
"	7th	1000	Brigade Commander inspects new accommadation of Companies, in barracks.
"	9th	1210	Inspector of Catering inspects Cooking arrangements
"	9th		Lt's Clancy and Farmer join from 53rd.Bn The Leicestershire Regt.,
"	10th	1130	Rev. G.H. Haslett lectures to the Bn.
"	12th		Total amount invested in War Savings by the Bn for the week ending 12th 38024 marks
"	14th		Lt-Col Dumbell having proceeded on leave, Major R.Warner assumes command of the Bn
"	16th		Divisional Commanders Guard taken over by men of this Bn.
"	16th	1000	2/LT Law proceeds for demobolisation.
"	19th	0700	5 Officers and 50 Other Ranks proceed on Rhime Steamer Pleasure Trip.
"	19th		" Peace Day" General Holiday.
"	20th	1400	Officers beat W.O's and Sergeants at cricket.
"	21st	1500	A/Capt Shelton reports for duty from 53rd.Bn.The Leicestershire Regiment.
"	22nd.		Battalion War Savings, Total for 2 weeks 93000 marks.(Record for Rhine Army)
Romerhof	24th		Midland Divisional Horse Show.
Euskirchen	26th		Officers and Other Ranks proceed on day's trip on the Rhine.
"	27th		Battalion paraded for church under Major Dixon.
"	29th		"D" Company cricket team beaten by R.E. Coy by 2 runs.
"	30th		12 men for re-enlistment proceeded to England on furlough.
"	30th	1600	Lt-Col Dumbell returns from leave.
"	31st		Battalion Band attended funeral of murdered A.S.C. Corporal.

(7)

Instructions regarding War Diaries and Intelligence Summaries are contained in F. S. Regs., Part II. and the Staff Manual respectively. Title pages will be prepared in manuscript.

WAR DIARY
or
~~INTELLIGENCE SUMMARY.~~
(Erase heading not required.)

Army Form C. 2118.

Place	Date	Hour	Euskirchen Aug 1919. Summary of Events and Information 51 Bn Leicestershire Regt.	Remarks and references to Appendices
	1919 Aug.			
Euskirchen	1	0830	Dump of enemy bombs exploded, officers mess wrecked, windows broken throughout barracks. 1 officer & 7 men to hospital, slightly hurt	
	1st		2nd Mid Bde Sports at Bessenich	
	2		50 OR of Batt proceed on Rhine pleasure trip	
	4		Photographs taken of Battn by official photographer	
	5		50 OR attended Cavalry Div Races at Chalk	
	5		Brigade cross country race	
	7		D.D.M.S inspected barracks	
	8		All leave stopped	
	9		Lts P. Thompstone, 1 H Kerry left Bn for Lancs Fusiliers & Chinese Labour Corps respectively	
	9		Lt Scoffield proceeded to England on Course	
	10		Draft of 19 men arrived from 3rd Bn England.	
	11		Divnl Sports week starts at Romerhof	
	12		Lt Col Dumbell hands command of Bn over to Major R.W. Warner. Lt Col proceeded to 2nd Bn Notts & Derby Regt Eng.	R.B.

T2134. Wt. W708—776. 500000. 4/15. Sir J. C. & S.

Instructions regarding War Diaries and Intelligence Summaries are contained in F. S. Regs., Part II. and the Staff Manual respectively. Title Pages will be prepared in manuscript.

WAR DIARY
or
~~INTELLIGENCE SUMMARY~~

(Erase heading not required.)

Army Form C. 2118.

(2)

Place	Date	Hour	Summary of Events and Information	Remarks and references to Appendices
Contd Euskirchen	16th		50 O.R. proceed on Rhine pleasure trip	
	18		2 Lt B. Choyce reports for duty from 53 Bn Leic Regt.	
	19		Rate of exchange from 16th to end of Aug. - 10 mks - 2/7.	
	20		Major C.A. Bill (R Warwicks Regt.) assumes command of Battn vice Major Warner.	
	21		2Lt W.E. Styles reports for duty from T.M.B.	
	22	0730	60 OR proceeded on Rhine trip	
	23	0730	70 OR ditto	
	24		Total amount of War Savings for 2 weeks 10,195 marks	W.B.
	27		Capt C.A. Payne joins from 53rd Bn Leic Regt.	
			Capt A.J. McIvor (medical officer) joins the 51st Bn Sherwood For.	
			2 Lt A.S. Taylor rejoins from Midland Divl Signal Coy	
	29	1400	Advance party of incoming unit arrived & took over duties etc	
	30	1350	Battn entrains Euskirchen en route for England.	
	31	2340	Battn detrains at Calais.	

C.A. Bill Lt.Col. ~~Major~~
Comndg 51 Bn Leicestershire Regt.

2449 Wt. W14957/M90 750,000 1/16 J.B.C. & A. Forms/C.2118/12.

BEF

MIDLAND DIV

2 MID. BDE.

52 LEICS. R

1919 MAR to 1919 AUG

52 Leicester

Army Form C. 2118.

Instructions regarding War Diaries and Intelligence Summaries are contained in F. S. Regs., Part II. and the Staff Manual respectively. Title Pages will be prepared in manuscript.

WAR DIARY
or
~~INTELLIGENCE SUMMARY~~

(Erase heading not required.)

Vol I

Place	Date	Hour	Summary of Events and Information	Remarks and references to Appendices
BROCTON CAMP	23/3/19	0100	Departed for Station from Camp	RECG
MILFORD & BROCTON	-do-	0320	Departed from MILFORD & BROCTON Station	RECG
DOVER	-do-	1110	Arrived DOVER	RECG
-do-	-do-	1200	To (No 2 REST CAMP) OIL MILL BARRACKS for Mid-day meal	RECG
-do-	-do-	1300	Left OIL MILL BARRACKS for embarkation. Received Troop Ship Orders	RECG
-do-	-do-	1320	Departed DOVER per "SS ANTRIM"	RECG
DUNKIRK	-do-	1603	Arrived DUNKIRK.	RECG
-do-	-do-	1620	Proceeded to No 3 REST CAMP.	RECG
-do-	-do-	1800	Arrived No. 3 REST CAMP.	RECG
-do-	-do-	1830	Tea at REST CAMP. Encamped for night under Canvas at No 3 REST CAMP	RECG
-do-	24/3/19	0700	Breakfast at No 3 REST CAMP.	RECG
-do-	-do-	1010	Departed for entrainment at No 3 REST CAMP SIDINGS.	RECG
No 3 REST CAMP SDGS. DUNKIRK	-do-	1045	Arrived REST CAMP SIDINGS entrained, and received train movement Orders	RECG
-do-	-do-	1110	Train departed	RECG
St MERRIS	-do-	1400	Halted for dinner	RECG
-do-	-do-	[illegible]	Resumed journey	RECG
BAILLEUL	-do-	2230	Halted for Supper	RECG
-do-	-do-	2330	Resumed journey	RECG
CHARLEROI	25/3/19	1100	Halted for breakfast	RECG
-do-	-do-	1200	Resumed journey	RECG

2449 Wt. W14957/M90 750,000 1/16 J.B.C. & A. Forms/C.2118/12.

GL 2400

SHEET -2-

Instructions regarding War Diaries and Intelligence Summaries are contained in F. S. Regs., Part II. and the Staff Manual respectively. Title Pages will be prepared in manuscript.

WAR DIARY
or
~~INTELLIGENCE SUMMARY~~

(Erase heading not required.)

Army Form C. 2118.

Place	Date	Hour	Summary of Events and Information	Remarks and references to Appendices
HUY	25/3/19	1800	Halted for Tea	RECG
-do-	-do-	1845	Resumed journey	RECG
ZULPICH	26/3/19	0700	Arrived Station	RECG
-do-	-do-	0815	Detained at Station for breakfast	RECG
-do-	-do-	1000	Departed Station for billets	RECG
-do-	-do-		Joined 2nd MIDLAND INFANTRY BRIGADE	RECG
-do-	28/3/19		1 Officer reported for duty i.e. REV. F.J DOVE. Received Transport	RECG
-do-	29/3/19		1 Officer off strength i.e. Capt. J.J. DELANEY R.A.M.C. One officer reported	RECG
			for duty as MEDICAL OFFICER i.e. Lieut. J. GILMOUR R.A.M.C.	RECG

5. 4. 19.

[signature]
Lieut. Colonel.
Commanding 52nd Bn. The Leicestershire Regiment.

2449 Wt. W14957/M90 750,000 1/16 J.B.C. & A. Forms/C.2118/12.

MIDLAND DIVN.

52 Leicesters

12

Army Form C. 2118.

II

Instructions regarding War Diaries and Intelligence Summaries are contained in F. S. Regs., Part II. and the Staff Manual respectively. Title pages will be prepared in manuscript.

WAR DIARY
or
INTELLIGENCE SUMMARY.
(Erase heading not required.)

Hour, Date, Place	Summary of Events and Information	Remarks and references to Appendices
1st Apl 19 ZULPICH	Capt F P DICKINSON M.C. reported for duty 21.3.19 taken on strength from 1-4-19	WHLB
2nd Apl 19 -do-	Inspection of Battalion by C.C. in Market Square ZULPICH Dress – Fighting Order	WHLB
3rd Apl 19 -do-	Lieut C S WOOLLEY reported for duty	
8th Apl 19 -do-	Inspection of Battalion by Corps Commander in ZULPICH	
9th Apl 19 -do-	Lieut F W GRAY & 2/Lieut C A KIRBY proceeded to England for demobilization	WHLB
13th Apl 19 -do-	2/Lieut S SCHOLES proceeded to England sick – Struck off strength. 386 other ranks transferred to this unit on 13-4-19 from 5th 2nd Bn Leicestershire Regt NEMMENICH. Also 11 officers transferred i.e. Capt R L HETT, Capt G BOWS, Lieut E M COPE, Lieut C W G TALLIS, Lieut D ETHERINGTON, Lieut C C RUSCOE, 2/Lieut T B ALLAWAY, 2/Lieut S GLANCY, 2/Lieut F T METCALFE M.C., 2/Lieut W L STUBBS M.C., 2/Lieut D S NEWTON-KING. "B" Company (this unit) transferred from ZULPICH to BESSENICH. "C" Company (this unit) transferred from ZULPICH to NEMMENICH. Capt R L HETT takes over Command of "C" Coy from Capt F W J JONES. Capt F P DICKINSON M.C. takes over Command of "B" Coy from Capt H I CARLICK	WHLB
30th Apl 19	[illegible] transferred to 2nd Mid Bde Light T M Battery at ROVENICH	WHLB

Commanding 52nd Bn Leicestershire Regt

[signature]

(73989) W4141—463. 400,000. 9/14. H.&J.Ltd. Forms/C. 2118/10.

Instructions regarding War Diaries and Intelligence Summaries are contained in F. S. Regs., Part II. and the Staff Manual respectively. Title pages will be prepared in manuscript.

WAR DIARY
or
INTELLIGENCE SUMMARY.
(Erase heading not required.)

Army Form C. 2118.

Hour, Date, Place		Summary of Events and Information	Remarks and references to Appendices
1st Apl 19	ZÜLPICH.	Capt F. P. DICKINSON M.C. reported for duty 31.3.19 taken on strength from 1-4-19	W.M.B.
2nd Apl 19	-do-	Inspection of Battalion by G.O.C. in Market Square ZÜLPICH Dress:- Fighting Order.	W.M.B.
3rd Apl 19	-do-	2/Lieut G.J. WOOLLEY reported for duty	
8th Apl 19	-do-	Inspection of Battalion by Corps Commander in ZÜLPICH	
9th Apl 19	-do-	Lieut F.W. GRAY & 2/Lieut G.A. KIRBY proceeded to England for demobilization	W.M.B.
13th Apl 19	-do-	2/Lieut S. SCHOLES proceeded to England sick - Struck of strength. 386 Other ranks transferred to this Unit on 13.4.19 from 53rd Bn Leicestershire Regt NEMMENICH. Also 11 officers transferred i.e. Capt R.L. HETT, Capt G. BOLUS, Lieut E.M. COPE, Lieut S.W.G. TALLIS Lieut D. ETHERINGTON, Lieut G.C. RUSCOE, 2/Lieut J.B. ALLAWAY 2/Lieut S. GLANCY, 2/Lieut F.T. METCALFE M.C. 2/Lieut W.L. STUBBS M.C 2/Lieut D.S. NEWTON-KING. "B" Company (this Unit) transferred from ZÜLPICH to BESSENICH "C" Company (this Unit) transferred from ZÜLPICH to NEMMENICH Capt R.L. HETT. takes over Command of "C" Coy from Capt F.W.D. JONES. Capt F.P. DICKINSON M.C. takes over Command of "B" Coy from Capt H.I. GARLICK.	W.M.B.
30th Apl 19	-do-	15 Other ranks transferred to 2nd MID BDE Light T.M. Battery at ROVENICH.	W.M.B.

W Dohmm[?]
Lieut Colonel
Commanding 52nd Bn Leicestershire Regt

Confidential

52 Leicesters

War diary

May 1st to 31st

Instructions regarding War Diaries and Intelligence Summaries are contained in F. S. Regs., Part II. and the Staff Manual respectively. Title pages will be prepared in manuscript.

WAR DIARY

or

~~INTELLIGENCE SUMMARY~~.

(Erase heading not required.)

Army Form C. 2118.

Hour, Date, Place		Summary of Events and Information	Remarks and references to Appendices
1.5.19.	ZULPICH.	Drill, Physical Training and bolt drill. - Musketry.	
2.5.19.	ZULPICH. 0900	Inspection by Commander-in-Chief in Market Square, ZULPICH. Dress Marching Order. First line transport present.	
3.5.19.	ZULPICH.	Regimental Classes started. Company and Platoon Training. Recreational Training.	
4.5.19.	ZULPICH.	Church Parades.	
5.5.19.	ZULPICH.	Battalion Drill. Scrubbing of Floors. Inspection of Billets.	
6.5.19.	ZULPICH.	Drill. Physical Traingng and Bolt Drill. Extended Order Drill and Artillery Formation.	
7.5.19.	ZULPICH.	Drill, Bayonet Fighting, and bolt Drill. Bombing.	
8.5.19.	ZULPICH.	Battalion Route March.	
9.5.19.	ZULPICH.	Drill, Physical Training and bolt drill. "B" Company held Sports at BESSENICH.	
10.5.19.	ZULPICH.	Drill, Bayonet Fighting and Bolt Drill. Gas Drill and Saluting.	
11.5.19.	ZULPICH.	Church Parades. "C"Company Sports held at NEMMENICH.	
12.5.19.	ZULPICH.	Battalion Drill. Scrubbing of Floors. "D" Company Sports.	
13.5.19.	ZULPICH.	Drill Physical Training, Bolt Drill. Extended Order Drill.	
14.5.19.	ZULPICH.	Drill, Bayon et Fighting & Bolt Drill. Scrubbing of Floors.	
15.5.19.	ZULPICH.	Battalion Route March.	
16.5.19.	ZULPICH.	Drill, Physical Training and Bolt Drill. Musketry.	
17.5.19.	ZULPICH.	Drill, Bayonet Fighting & Bolt Drill. Gas Drill & Saluting.	
18.5.19.	ZULPICH.	Church Parades.	
19.5.19.	ZULPICH.	Battalion Drill. Lecture by Brigade Education Officer on "PEACE TERMS"	
20.5.19.	ZULPICH.	Drill, Musketry & Physical Training. Extended Order Drill. Artillery Formation. (Platoon in Attack)	
21.5.19.	ZULPICH.	Drill, Musketry & Physical Training. Bayonet Fighting & Bombing.	
22.5.19.	ZULPICH.	Battalion Route March.	
23.5.19.	ZULPICH.	Drill, Physical Training & Bayonet Fighting. Saluting.	
24.5.19.	ZULPICH.	Physical Training. Bayonet Fighting. Interior Economy. Musketry. Battalion Sports. held at BESSENICH.	
25.5.19.	ZULPICH.	Church Parades.	
26.5.19.	ZULPICH.	Battalion Drill. Extended Order. Artillery Formation.	

(73989) W4141—463. 400,000. 9/14. H.&J.Ltd. Forms/C. 2118/10.

Instructions regarding War Diaries and Intelligence Summaries are contained in F. S. Regs., Part II. and the Staff Manual respectively. Title pages will be prepared in manuscript.

WAR DIARY

~~or~~

~~INTELLIGENCE SUMMARY.~~

(*Erase heading not required.*)

Army Form C. 2118.

Hour, Date, Place	Summary of Events and Information	Remarks and references to Appendices
	(c o n t i n u e d)	
27.5.19. ZULPICH.	Drill. Musketry. Physical Training & Bayonet Fighting. Bombing & Lewis Gun.	
28.5.19. ZULPICH.	Drill. Musketry. Physical Training & Bayonet Fighting. Saluting & Lewis Gun.	
29.5.19. ZULPICH.	Drill. Musketry. Physical Training & Bayonet Fighting. Saluting.	
30.5.19. ZULPICH.	Physical Training. Musketry & Lewis Gun. Extended Order. Artillery Formation. Platoon in Attack.	
31.5.19. ZULPICH.	Physical Training. Musketry. Lewis Gunning. Interior Economy.	

C Becher. Lt Col.

Comm'g 52nd Bn The Leicestershire Regt

(73989) W4141—463. 400,000. 9/14. H.&J.Ltd. Forms/C. 2118/10.

Instructions regarding War Diaries and Intelligence Summaries are contained in F. S. Regs., Part II. and the Staff Manual respectively. Title pages will be prepared in manuscript.

WAR DIARY
or
~~INTELLIGENCE~~ SUMMARY.

(*Erase heading not required.*)

Army Form C. 2118.

Hour, Date, Place		Summary of Events and Information	Remarks and references to Appendices
1.5.19.	ZULPICH.	Drill, Physical Training and bolt drill. - Musketry.	
2.5.19.	ZULPICH. 0900	Inspection by Commander-in-Chief in Market Square, ZULPICH. Dress Marching Order. First line transport present.	
3.5.19.	ZULPICH.	Regimental Classes started. Company and Platoon Training. Recreational Training.	
4.5.19.	ZULPICH.	Church Parades.	
5.5.19.	ZULPICH.	Battalion Drill. Scrubbing of Floors. Inspection of Billets.	
6.5.19.	ZULPICH.	Drill. Physical Training and Bolt Drill. Extended Order Drill and Artillery Formation.	
7.5.19.	ZULPICH.	Drill, Bayonet Fighting, and bolt Drill. Bombing.	
8.5.19.	ZULPICH.	Battalion Route March.	
9.5.19.	ZULPICH.	Drill, Physical Training and bolt drill. "B" Company held Sports at BESSENICH.	
10.5.19.	ZULPICH.	Drill, Bayonet Fighting and Bolt Drill. Gas Drill and Saluting.	
11.5.19.	ZULPICH.	Church Parades. "C"Company Sports held at NEMMENICH.	
12.5.19.	ZULPICH.	Battalion Drill. Scrubbing of Floors. "D" Company Sports.	
13.5.19.	ZULPICH.	Drill Physical Training, Bolt Drill. Extended Order Drill.	
14.5.19.	ZULPICH.	Drill, Bayon et Fighting & Bolt Drill. Scrubbing of Floors.	
15.5.19.	ZULPICH.	Battalion Route March.	
16.5.19.	ZULPICH.	Drill, Physical Training and Bolt Drill. Musketry.	
17.5.19.	ZULPICH.	Drill, Bayonet Fighting & Bolt Drill. Gas Drill & Saluting.	
18.5.19.	ZULPICH.	Church Parades.	
19.5.19.	ZULPICH.	Battalion Drill. Lecture by Brigade Education Officer on "PEACE TERMS"	
20.5.19.	ZULPICH.	Drill, Musketry & Physical Training. Extended Order Drill. Artillery Formation. (Platoon in Attack)	
21.5.19.	ZULPICH.	Drill, Musketry & Physical Training. Bayonet Fighting & Bombing.	
22.5.19.	ZULPICH.	Battalion Route March.	
23.5.19.	ZULPICH.	Drill, Physical Training & Bayonet Fighting. Saluting.	
24.5.19.	ZULPICH.	Physical Training. Bayonet Fighting. Interior Economy.Musketry. Battalion Sports.held at BESSENICH.	
25.5.19.	ZULPICH.	Church Parades.	
26.5.19.	ZULPICH.	Battalion Drill. Extended Order. Artillery Formation.	

(73989) W4141—463. 400,000. 9/14. H.&J.Ltd. Forms/C. 2118/10.

Army Form C. 2118.

WAR DIARY

~~or INTELLIGENCE SUMMARY.~~

(*Erase heading not required.*)

Instructions regarding War Diaries and Intelligence Summaries are contained in F. S. Regs., Part II. and the Staff Manual respectively. Title pages will be prepared in manuscript.

Hour, Date, Place		Summary of Events and Information	Remarks and references to Appendices
		(continued)	
27.5.19.	ZULPICH.	Drill. Musketry. Physical Training & Bayonet Fighting. Bombing & Lewis Gun.	
28.5.19.	ZULPICH.	Drill. Musketry. Physical Training & Bayonet Fighting. Saluting & Lewis Gun.	
29.5.19.	ZULPICH.	Drill. Musketry. Physical Training & Bayonet Fighting. Saluting.	
30.5.19.	ZULPICH.	Physical Training. Musketry & Lewis Gun. Extended Order. Artillery Formation. Platoon in Attack.	
31.5.19.	ZULPICH.	Physical Training. Musketry. Lewis Gunning. Interior Economy.	

C Becher. Lt Col.
Comm'g 52nd Leicestershire Regt.

(73989) W4141—463. 400,000. 9/14. H.&J.Ltd. Forms/C. 2118/10.

Army Form C. 2118.

Instructions regarding War Diaries and Intelligence Summaries are contained in F. S. Regs., Part II. and the Staff Manual respectively. Title Pages will be prepared in manuscript.

WAR DIARY
or
INTELLIGENCE SUMMARY

(Erase heading not required.)

Place	Date	Hour	Summary of Events and Information	Remarks and references to Appendices
ZULPICH.	1.6.19.		Church Parades.	
ZULPICH.	2.6.19.		Battn. Drill. Extended Order & Artillery Formation. (Platoon in Attack)	
ZULPICH.	3.6.19.		Drill. Musketry. P.T. & B.F. Bombing and Lewis Gunning.	
ZULPICH.	4.6.19.		Drill. Musketry. P.T. & B.F. Saluting and Lewis Gunning.	
ZULPICH.	5.6.19.		Drill. Musketry. P.T. & B.F. Bombing & Lewis Gunning.	
ZULPICH.	6.6.19.		P.T. Musketry, and Lewis Gun Training. Extended Order. Artillery Formation. (Platoon in Attack)	
ZULPICH.	7.6.19.		P.T. Musketry, and Lewis Gunning. Interior Economy. (Final of the Bde Football Cup),	
ZULPICH.	8.6.19.		Church Parades.	
ZULPICH.	9.6.19.		WHIT MONDAY. No. Training. Officer's Conference. Lecture on Big Game at 1430.	
ZULPICH.	10.6.19.		Drill. Musketry. P.T. & B.F. Bombing and Lewis Gunning. (Replay Bde Football Cup) "C" Coy v "A" Coy 51st Leicesters.	
ZULPICH.	11.6.19.		Drill. Musketry. P.T. & B.F. Saluting & Lewis Gunning.	
ZULPICH.	12.6.19.		P.T. Musketry & Lewis Gun Training. Extended Order. Artillery Formation.	
ZULPICH.	13.6.19.		Drill. Musketry. P.T. & B.F. Saluting & Lewis Gunning. (Lieut. E.M. Cope killed whilst in charge of Ammunition Train Guard. ZULPICH Station) (Special Report rendered.)	
ZULPICH.	14.6.19.		P.T. Musketry & Lewis Gunning. Interior Economy.	
ZULPICH.	15.6.19.		Church Parades.	
ZULPICH.	16.6.19.		Battn. Drill. Extended Order. Artillery Formation. (Platoon in Attack)	
ZULPICH.	17.6.19.		Drill. Musketry P.T. & B.F. Bombing and Lewis Gunning. (Funerals of Lt. E.M. Cope and Pte Andrews at KREMERHOF. EUSKIRCHEN)	
ZULPICH.	18.6.19.		Drill. Musketry. P.T. & B.F. Saluting & Lewis Gunning.	
ZULPICH.	19.6.19.	0300.	Battalion moved to DUREN by Route March. Billetted in HINDENBURG BARRACKS. Arrived at 0730. Took over from 51st Gordons. Relieved Guards.	
DUREN.	20.6.19.		No Training. Interior Economy.	
DUREN.	21.6.19.		-do- -do-	
DUREN.	22.6.19.		Church Parades.	
DUREN.	23.6.19.		Battalion Parade. Bn. Drill. Extended Order. Artillery Formation. (Platoon in Attack)	
DUREN.	24.6.19.		Battn. Parade. Drill Musketry. P.T. & B.F. Bombing and Lewis Gunning.	
DUREN.	25.6.19.		Battn. Parade. " " " " Saluting & Lewis Gunning.	
DUREN.	26.6.19.		Battn. Parade. Bn. Drill. Extended Order. Artillery Formation. (Platoon in Attack)	
DUREN.	27.6.19.		Battn. Parade. Drill. Musketry. P.T. & B.F. Saluting & Lewis Gunning.	
DUREN.	28.6.19.		Battn. Parade. Saluting Drill. Interior Economy.	
DUREN.	29.6.19.		Church Parades.	
ZULPICH.	30/6/19.		Battalion Moved to ZULPICH at 03.30 hours, arrived 07.45.	

C Becher
Lieut. Colonel.
Commanding 52nd. Bn. Leicestershire Regt.,

2449 Wt. W14957/M90 750,000 1/16 J.B.C. & A. Forms/C.2118/12.

Instructions regarding War Diaries and Intelligence Summaries are contained in F. S. Regs., Part II. and the Staff Manual respectively. Title Pages will be prepared in manuscript.

Army Form C. 2118.

~~WAR DIARY~~
~~or~~
~~INTELLIGENCE SUMMARY~~
SPECIAL INTELLIGENCE REPORT.
(Erase heading not required.)

Place	Date	Hour	Summary of Events and Information	Remarks and references to Appendices
Railway Gd. No.2 Sector.	22.6.19.	2300	Sentry on No. 17 Post reported to me at about 2300 hours that a stone was thrown at him from the bushes on the left hand side of the Railway. About 1 minute later the patrol came up, and after challenging ~~them~~ him he asked if ~~they~~ he had thrown any stones, the patrol replied in the negative and passed on to Bridge No. 18 at the end of his beat, about two minutes after the patrol had passed the sentry perceived another form at the side of the rails he challenged and received no reply but heard stones being disturbed. He immediately fired but ~~XXXXXXXXXX~~ apparently with no effect, soon after he heard two shots fired from the wood on the left side of the railway and also heard someone call out. At about 2310 hours I arrived at this post with Lt. Marshall on our tour of inspection of the line and searched the embankment in the vicinity but discovered nothing. Double sentries were posted during the night.	from 2/Lt. H.A. Watson Officer i/c No.2 Sec. Railway Guard. R.W.

R. L. Oddy Capt. & adj.
for Lieut. Colonel.
Commanding 52nd Bn. Leicestershire Regiment.

2449 Wt. W14957/M90 750,000 1/16 J.B.C. & A. Forms/C.2118/12.

Army Form C. 2118.

WAR DIARY
or
~~INTELLIGENCE SUMMARY~~
(Erase heading not required.)

Instructions regarding War Diaries and Intelligence Summaries are contained in F. S. Regs., Part II. and the Staff Manual respectively. Title Pages will be prepared in manuscript.

Place	Date	Hour	Summary of Events and Information	Remarks and references to Appendices
	1919			
ZULPICH.	1st July.		Drill, Musketry. P.T. & B.F. Bombing and Lewis Gunning.	AEW
-do-	2nd -do-		Drill, Musketry. P.T. & B.F. Saluting and Lewis Gunning.	AEW
"	3rd "		P.T. Musketry and Lewis Gunning. Extended Order. Artillery Formation. (Platoon in Attack)	AEW
"	4th "		do do do do do do do do do do	AEW
"	5th "		Drill & Saluting Drill. Interior Economy.	AEW
"	6th "		Church Parades.	AEW
"	7th "		Extended Order Drill. Artillery Formation. (Platoon in attack.)	AEW
"	8th "		Drill. Musketry. P.T. & B.F. Bombing and Lewis Gunning.	AEW
"	9th "		Drill Musketry. P.T. & B.F. Saluting and Lewis Gunning.	AEW
"	10th "		BATTALION ROUTE MARCH.	AEW
"	11th "		P.T. Musketry & Lewis Gunning. Extended Order Drill. Artillery Formation. (Platoon in Attack)	AEW
"	12th "		Drill and Saluting Drill. Interior Economy.	AEW
"	13th "		Church Parades.	AEW
"	14th "		Company and Ceremonial Drill. Boxing. Extended Order Drill. Artillery Formation. (Platoon in Attack)	AEW
"	15th "		Drill. Musketry. P.T. & B.F. Bombing and Lewis Gunning. Boxing.	AEW
"	16th "		Drill. Musketry. P.T. & B.F. Saluting and Lewis Gunning. Boxing.	AEW
"	17th "		BATTALION ROUTE MARCH.	AEW
"	18th "		P.T. Musketry. Lewis Gunning. Boxing. Extended Order Drill. Artillery Formation. (Platoon in Attack)	AEW
"	19th "		Saluting Drill & Boxing. Interior Economy.	AEW
"	20th "		Church Parades.	AEW
"	21st "		Company and Ceremonial Drill. Boxing. Extended Order Drill. Artillery Formation. (Platoon in Attack)	AEW
"	22nd "		Drill. Musketry. P.T. & B.F. Bombing and Lewis Gunning. Boxing.	AEW
"	23rd "		Drill. Musketry. P.T. & B.F. Saluting and Lewis Gunning. Boxing.	AEW
"	24th "		GENERAL HOLIDAY. (Divisional Horse Show)	AEW
"	25th "		P.T. Musketry and Lewis Gunning. Boxing. Extended Order Drill. Artillery Formation. (Platoon in Attack)	AEW
"	26th "		Saluting Drill and Boxing. Interior Economy.	AEW
"	27th "		Church Parades.	AEW
"	28th "		Company & Ceremonial Drill. Boxing. Extended Order Drill. Artillery Formation. (Platoon in Attack)	AEW
"	29th "		Drill. Musketry. P.T. & B.F. Saluting. Lewis Gunning & Boxing.	AEW
"	30th "		Drill. Musketry. P.T. & B.F. Bombing & Lewis Gunning. Boxing.	AEW
"	31st "		Musketry. P.T. Lewis Gunning. Boxing. Extended Order Drill. Artillery Formation. (Platoon in Attack)	AEW

R. L. Oddy Capt & Adj for Lieut. Colonel
Commanding 52nd Bn. Leicestershire Regt

2449 Wt. W14957/M90 750,000 1/16 J.B.C. & A. Forms/C.2118/12.

Instructions regarding War Diaries and Intelligence Summaries are contained in F. S. Regs., Part II. and the Staff Manual respectively. Title pages will be prepared in manuscript.

Confidential

WAR DIARY
&
~~INTELLIGENCE SUMMARY~~

(*Erase heading not required.*)

Army Form C. 2118.

52nd Leic. Regt.

Hour, Date, Place		Summary of Events and Information	Remarks and references to Appendices
1919.			
1st August.	ZULPICH.	Musketry.P.T. Lewis Gunning.Boxing.Extended Order Drill.(Platoon in Attack)	[illegible]
2nd "	"	Saluting Drill. & Boxing.Interior Economy.	[illegible]
3rd "	"	Church Parades.	[illegible]
4th "	"	General Holiday.	[illegible]
5th "	"	Coy and ceremonial Drill.Boxing.Extended Order Drill.Artilley Formation. (Platoon in AttacK)	[illegible]
6th "	"	Drill. Musketry.P.T. & B.F. Saluting.Lewis Gunning & Boxing.	[illegible]
7th "	"	Coy Route Marches.	[illegible]
8th "	"	Drill.Musketry. P.T. & B.F. Bombing & Lewis Gunning and Boxing.	[illegible]
9th "	"	Saluting Drill.Boxing. Interior Economy.	[illegible]
10th "	"	Church Parades.	[illegible]
11th "	"	Coy and ceremonial Drill.Boxing.Coy in attack(Fire Discipline, control etc)	[illegible]
12th "	"	Coy Drill.Musketry. P.T. & B.F. Saluting.Lewis Gunning & Boxing.	[illegible]
13th "	"	Coy Drill.Musketry.P.T. & B.F.Bombing.Lewis Gunning. Boxing.	[illegible]
14th "	"	BATTALION ROUTE MARCH.	[illegible]
15th "	"	Musketry. P.T. &Lewis Gunning. Boxing.Coy in Attack.(Fire discipline,control etc)	[illegible]
16th "	"	Saluting Drill. Boxing. Interior Economy.	[illegible]
17th "	"	Church Parades.	[illegible]
18th "	"	Coy and ceremonial Drill. Boxing. Coy in Attack(Fire discipline,control etc)	[illegible]
19th "	"	Coy Drill.Musketry. P.T. & B.F. Saluting.Lewis Gunning.Boxing.	[illegible]
20th "	"	----ditto--------ditto--------- Bombing. -------ditto--------	[illegible]
21st "	"	" " Saluting. "	[illegible]
22nd "	"	Musketry.P.T. Lewis Gunning.Boxing.Coy in Attack.(Fire discipline contol etc)	[illegible]
23rd "	"	Saluting Drill. Boxing.	[illegible]
24th "	"	Church Parades.	[illegible]
25th "	"	Coy and ceremonial Drill.Boxing.Coy in attack.(Fire discipline etc)	[illegible]
26th "	"	Coy drill.Musketry.P.T. & B.F. Bombing.Lewis Gunning. Boxing.	[illegible]
27th "	"	Musketry. P.T. & Lewis Gunning.Boxing.Coy in Attack.(Fire discipline,control etc.)	[illegible]
28th "	"	" " " " " " " "	[illegible]
29th "	"	Preparing to move to United Kingdom.	[illegible]
30th "	"	" " " "	[illegible]
31st "	"	Moved to United Kingdom.	[illegible]

[illegible] Captain for Lt Colonel Comdg 52nd Bn Leicestershire Regt.

5/9/19.

1559

WO 95/1626 | 8

BEF

MIDLAND DIV

2 MID. BDE.

1/5 S. STAFFS

1919 MAR – 1919 AUG

FROM 46 DIV 137 BDE

a/o/o
50

CONFIDENTIAL.

WAR DIARY.

OF

1/5TH. BN. SOUTH STAFFORDSHIRE REGT.

From 1st. March 1919. To 31st March 1919.

Instructions regarding War Diaries and Intelligence Summaries are contained in F. S. Regs., Part II. and the Staff Manual respectively. Title pages will be prepared in manuscript.

WAR DIARY

or

~~INTELLIGENCE SUMMARY.~~

(*Erase heading not required.*)

Army Form C. 2118.

Place	Date	Hour	Summary of Events and Information	Remarks and references to Appendices
FRESNOY-LE-GRAND	1		Interior Economy. Surgeon-Major A.W.SHEA DSO. T.D. came from 6th Battalion SHERWOOD FORESTERS after serving with them for 24 years to take over duties of Medical Officer.	Burt
	2		After Church Parade the General Officer Commanding 46th Division bade farewell to the Battalion before proceeding to GERMANY.	Burt
	3		Preparing for move, collecting stores and loading them on the train.	Burt
	4	11.00	Battalion entrained with 7 Riding Horses and 2 Light Draught with all Transport vehicles plus 4 G.S. Wagons from the R.A.S.C. Company.	Burt
		12.30	Train left FRESNOY apparently in the wrong direction, towards ST. QUENTIN, but when half-way there, the driver changed his mind, turned about, and proceeded back via FRESNOY - BOHAIN-LE CATEAU and LANDRECIES to MONS, where a hot meal was served about 21.00 hours, the Frontier being crossed at 17.50 hours.	
	5		About 0001 hours, the train left MONS for CHARLEROI, arriving about 08.00 hours, taking a further 20 minutes to pass through the Station. Another hot meal was served, and a move was again made at 10.00 hours, towards NAMUR, along the MEUSE Valley. Very pretty scenery was passed, partly marred by the result of British Air Raids. LIEGE was reached at dusk. It is believed that the Frontier was crossed about 23.40 hours, but the only evidence which is forthcoming, of this, is the Medical Officer's statement that he was awakened at this hour by a garrulous Belgian handing over to a much be-uniformed Bosche, whose friendly advances were promptly repulsed.	Burt
LIBLAR GERMANY	6		Arrived at LIBLAR. After breakfast, the Battalion detrained, and marched via	Burt

D. D. & L., London, E.C.
(A7883) Wt. W809/M1672 350,000 4/17 Sch. 52a Forms/C/2118/14

PAGE 2

Instructions regarding War Diaries and Intelligence Summaries are contained in F. S. Regs., Part II, and the Staff Manual respectively. Title pages will be prepared in manuscript.

WAR DIARY

or

~~INTELLIGENCE SUMMARY.~~

(*Erase heading not required.*)

Army Form C. 2118.

Place	Date	Hour	Summary of Events and Information	Remarks and references to Appendices
LIBLAR GERMANY	6		KOTTINGEN, KIERDORF, BRUGGEN, through very flat country, to GYMNICH, which was recently vacated by the 2nd Battalion SUFFOLK REGIMENT.	Burpt
GYMNICH.	7		Battalion cleaned up. Inspection of Rifles and Interior Economy.	Burpt
	8		The Battalion was visited by Major General T.O. MARDEN, C.B., C.M.G., Commanding the 6th Division, and Brigadier-General CRAWFORD C.M.G., C.I.E. D.S.O. Commanding 18th Infantry Brigade and also by the A.D.M.S. who is obviously a specialist in venereal disease.	Burpt
	9		Church Parades.	Burpt
	10		Company Training during the morning. Brigade Sports at AHREM in the afternoon.	Burpt
	11		Company Training. Battalion Headquarters Mess moved to ~~Count METTENICH~~ Graf V. MANTRE'S SCHLOSS. Warning Orderregarding the transfer of the Battalion to the 16th Brigade, comprising the Young Soldiers' Battalion of the LEICESTERSHIRE REGIMENT, received previously from the Brigadier.	Burpt
	12		Lieutenant J.F.BOURNE MC., Transport Officer, took over from the 11th ESSEX REGIMENT at FRIESHAM, 9 Heavy Draught Horses, 29 Light Draught Horses and 8 Mules.	Burpt
	13		Orders received to move the Battalion to KOMMERN, on the 14th instant. Parades postponed. Packing up commenced, and a billeting party of 4 Officers and 5 N.C.O's proceeded there forthwith.	Burpt

D. D. & L., London, E.C.
(A7883) Wt W809/M1672 350,000 4/17 Sch. 52a Forms/C/2118/14

Army Form C. 2118.

WAR DIARY
or
~~INTELLIGENCE SUMMARY.~~
(*Erase heading not required.*)

Instructions regarding War Diaries and Intelligence Summaries are contained in F. S. Regs., Part II. and the Staff Manual respectively. Title pages will be prepared in manuscript.

Place	Date	Hour	Summary of Events and Information	Remarks and references to Appendices
KOMMERN.	14		Battalion paraded at 07.30 hours, and entrained at LIBLAR for MECHERNICH, where it detrained and Route Marched to KOMMERN, occupying the billets vacated the same day by the 8th Battalion WEST YORKSHIRE REGIMENT(LEEDS RIFLES). 20 Officers and 177 Other Ranks of the 2nd Battalion South Staffordshire Regiment were transferred to this Battalion bringing the Ration Strength up to 1008.	BWP
	15		Interior Economy. Brigadier General W.G. BRAITHEWAITE C.B. C.M.G., D.S.O., Commanding the 16th Infantry Brigade visited the Commanding Officer.	BWP
	16		No Parson, - no Church Parade.	BWP
	17		Rifle Inspections and Re-organization.	BWP
	18		Physical Training. Platoon Training, Fire Control and Arms Drill. Performance of the 'KNOTS'.	BWP
	19		Platoon Training, Arms Drill, training of Junior N.C.O's. Detachments as under were sent to do Guard Duties :- "D" Company. 2 Platoons (Lieut. W.I. AITKEN) FISCHENICH "A" Company 1 Platoon. (Lieut. R. JOWSEY.) SEIGBURG. "C" Company. 1 Platoon. (Lieut. G.E. JONES.) LANGENFELD.	BWP
	20		7 Officers and 65 Other Ranks per Company proceeded to ZULPICH by Motor Lorry to hear a Lecture by the Reverend	BWP

D. D. & L., London, E.C. (A7883) Wt. W809/M1672 350,000 4/17 Sch. 52a Forms/C/2118/14

Instructions regarding War Diaries and Intelligence Summaries are contained in F. S. Regs., Part II. and the Staff Manual respectively. Title pages will be prepared in manuscript.

WAR DIARY
or
~~INTELLIGENCE SUMMARY.~~
(Erase heading not required.)

Army Form C. 2118.

Place	Date	Hour	Summary of Events and Information	Remarks and references to Appendices
KOMMERN	20		HUNTER BOYD on the 'CZECHO-SLAVS'. The Lantern broke down and consequently there were no slides; otherwise, the Lecture was given a very good hearing.	BWR
	21		Company Training and Interior Economy including pay.	BWR
	22		At 11.00 hours, the Battalion Route Marched to MECHERNICH where it halted in the local square, with fixed bayonets, and fell out while the Band played various selections. This action was taken at the request of the Brigadier, who states that there was a probability of a strike among the Civilians in the neighbourhood, and the presence of the Battalion would probably damp the ardour of the leaders, for a disturbance. The Commanding Officer dispensed Justice on wayward Civilians at ZULPICH in the morning and gave a lecture on Musketry in the afternoon.	BWR
	23		Voluntary Church Parades owing to inclement weather.	BWR
	24		Platoon Training and Training of Specialists. A Lecture was given at ZULPICH to 5 Officers and 25 Other Ranks Per Company, by Professor ADAMS, on 'WHAT BELGIUM MEANS TO US.' Major-General G.F. BOYD C.B. C.M.G. D.S.O. D.C.M., late General Officer Commanding 46th Division, visited the Battalion, on taking over command of the Brigade. Snowed all day.	BWR
	25		Company Training as per programme.	BWR
	26		Company Training. Snow.	BWR

D. D. & L., London, E.C.
(A7883) Wt. W809/M1672 350,000 4/17 Sch. 52a Forms/C/2118/14

PAGE 5.

Instructions regarding War Diaries and Intelligence Summaries are contained in F. S. Regs., Part II. and the Staff Manual respectively. Title pages will be prepared in manuscript.

WAR DIARY
or
~~INTELLIGENCE SUMMARY.~~
(Erase heading not required.)

Army Form C. 2118.

Place	Date	Hour	Summary of Events and Information	Remarks and references to Appendices
KOMMERN	26		The 'KNOTS' gave a performance in the evening, in the STAFFORD PAVILION, which was very well attended.	BWP
	27		Company Training.	BWP
	28		Company Training. Snow fell intermittently all day.	BWP
	29		The Battalion Route Marched from KOMMERN via SCHWERFEN - SINZENICH - BURVENICH - thence back to Billets at KOMMERN. Snow.	BWP
	30		Church Parades.	BWP
	31		Company Training. 3 Officers and 20 Other Ranks per Company attended a lecture given by Mr. T.E. WING in the Officers' Club at ZULPICH, - being conveyed there by Lorry.	BWP
			Number of Officers granted leave to United Kingdom during the month:- 23.	
			Number of Other Ranks granted leave to United Kingdom during the month :- ~~40~~. 124	
2nd April,	1919.		[signature] Lt.-Col., Cmdg. 1/5th Bn. S. Staffs. Regt.	

D. D. & L., London, E.C. (A7883) Wt. W803/M1672 350,000 4/17 Sch. 52a Forms/C/2118/14

CONFIDENTIAL.

WAR DIARY

OF

1/5TH BN SOUTH STAFFS REGT.

From. 1st April 1919. To 30th April 1919.

Page 1.

Instructions regarding War Diaries and Intelligence Summaries are contained in F. S. Regs., Part II. and the Staff Manual respectively. Title pages will be prepared in manuscript.

WAR DIARY
or
~~INTELLIGENCE SUMMARY.~~
(Erase heading not required.)

Army Form C. 2118.

Place	Date	Hour	Summary of Events and Information	Remarks and references to Appendices
KOMMERN, Germany.	1.		Company Training.	J.J.L.
	2.		Company Training, - Summer weather. Good Concert in the evening by the 'KNOTS' Concert Party. Four Platoons were sent to relieve the Detachment on Guard at SEIGBURG and LANGENFELD.	J.J.L.
	3.		Company Training. Lecture at ZULPICH by Major A.R. DUGMORE; Subject - 'The Romance of the Beaver and the Newfoudland Caribou.' 4 Officers and 20 Other Ranks proceeded by Lorries.	J.J.L.
	4.		Battalion Inspection by the G.O-C., 2nd Midland Brigade - (Brigadier-General G.F. BOYD, CB. CMG. DSO. DCM.) A very smart turnout by all ranks.	J.J.L.
	5.		Company Training. All Officers, N.C.O's and 25 men per Company, attended lecture in the 'STAFFORD PAVILION' by Lieut. FOXLEY R.N. - Subject:- 'Anti-Submarine Warfare.' Concert was given by the 'KNOTS' Concert Party.	J.J.L.
	6.		Battalion Church Parade on Parade Ground.	J.J.L.
	7.		Company Parades.	J.J.L.
	8.		Battalion Inspection by the Corps Commander, Lieut-General Sir ~~Wm. BRAITHWAITE, CB. CMG. DSO.~~, Walter Braithwaite K.C.B. The Corps Commander was very pleased. Lecture to the Battalion by Captain WEEKES (R.A.M.C.) of the Royal Army Temperance Society.	J.J.L.
	9.		Company Parades. A warm sunny day. Selecting N.C.O's and men for Divisional Guard.	J.J.L.

D. D. & L., London, E.C.
(A10266) Wt W5300/P713 750,000 2/18 Sch. 52 Forms/C2118/16.

Instructions regarding War Diaries and Intelligence Summaries are contained in F. S. Regs., Part II. and the Staff Manual respectively. Title pages will be prepared in manuscript.

WAR DIARY
or
~~INTELLIGENCE SUMMARY~~.

(Erase heading not required.)

Army Form C. 2118.

Place	Date	Hour	Summary of Events and Information	Remarks and references to Appendices
KOMMERN, Germany.	10.		Company Parades. Weather colder. The KNOTS gave a show.	JJ
	11.		Company Parades.	JJ
	12.		A Battalion Route March. KOMMERN - SCHWERFEN - SINZENICH - thence West to Road junction ¼ mile North of 'C' in DURVENICH, South East to SCHWERFEN to billets. Approximately 9½ miles. Football match in the afternoon - Battalion versus RFA. The Battalion won - 3 Goals to 2. The 'KNOTS' gave a very good show in the evening.	JJ
	13.		Inclement weather. Church Parade cancelled on Battalion Parade Ground and held in the STAFFORD PAVILION. Brigadier-General J.V. CAMPBELL VC. DSO. visited the Commanding Officer. Three new Officers joined the Battalion.	JJ
	14.		Company Parades. Musketry etc.	
	15.		Platoon and Company Training. Ordinary parades. 'KNOTS' Concert Party at ZULPICH. Rough weather.	JJ
	16.		Company Parades. 'KNOTS' Concert Party at ZULPICH. Showery weather. Battalion versus 76th R.F.A. at Football. A good win. 5 Goals to 0.	JJ
	17.		Battalion Route March about 6½ miles. KOMMERN - EICKS - FLORSDORF - South side of SCHWERFEN - EICKS - to billets. Very wet. Battalion marched past the Divisional General, between FLORSDORF and SCHWERFEN. Lieut.-Colonel A. WHITE DSO. said farewell to the Battalion	JJ

D. D. & L., London, E.C.
(A10266) Wt W5300/P713 750,000 2/18 Sch. 52 Forms/C2118/16.

Army Form C. 2118.

Instructions regarding War Diaries and Intelligence Summaries are contained in F. S. Regs., Part II. and the Staff Manual respectively. Title pages will be prepared in manuscript.

WAR DIARY
or
~~INTELLIGENCE SUMMARY.~~
(Erase heading not required.)

Place	Date	Hour	Summary of Events and Information	Remarks and references to Appendices
KOMMERN, Germany.	17.		Lieut.-Colonel R.W. MORGAN CMG. DSO. assumed command of the Battalion. The 'KNOTS' Concert Party at night.	[initials]
	18.		Good Friday. Church Parades. The Commanding Officer inspected 'A' and 'B' Companies' Billets and Officers' Chargers. A fine day.	[initials]
	19.		Interior Economy. Kit Inspection. 'KNOTS' Concert Party at night. Farewell show before going on leave.	[initials]
	20.		Easter Sunday. Church Parades. A dull cold day.	[initials]
	21.		Platoon Training - Musketry and Physical Training.	[initials]
	22.		'B' and 'C' Companies - Platoon Training. 'D' Company - Agricultural Work.	[initials]
	23.		'B' and 'D' Companies - Musketry, Physical Training and Gas. 'C' Company - Agricultural Work. The Battalion beat 52nd LEICESTERS at Football by 7 goals to 0.	[initials]
	24.		The Battalion(less 'A' Company) route marched in the morning. in Field Service Marching Order with the Transport. Route : MECHERNICH - KATZVEY - SATZVEY - FIRMENICH - SHAVEN - to billets. No men fell out.	[initials]
	25.		'C' and 'D' Companies - Work on the Rifle Range. 'B' Company - Agricultural Work.	[initials]

D. D. & L., London, E.C.
(A10266) Wt W5300/P713 750,000 2/18 Sch. 52 Forms/C2118/16.

Instructions regarding War Diaries and Intelligence Summaries are contained in F. S. Regs., Part II. and the Staff Manual respectively. Title pages will be prepared in manuscript.

WAR DIARY
or
~~INTELLIGENCE SUMMARY.~~
(*Erase heading not required.*)

Army Form C. 2118.

Place	Date	Hour	Summary of Events and Information	Remarks and references to Appendices
KOMMERN, Germany.	26.		Company Training. and Agricultural Work. The Commanding Officer inspected outlying stations.	
	27.		Church Parades.	
	28.		'B' and 'D' Companies working on KOMMERN Rifle Range under supervision of R.E's. 'C' Company - Agricultural Work. Lecture at ZULPICH by Commander Lord BROOME DSO. RN. on 'Naval Subjects'.	
	29.		'B' and 'D' Companies working on KOMMERN Rifle Range under supervision of R.E's. 'A' Company - Agricultural Work. 'C' Company - Training.	
	30.		'C' and 'D' Companies with 2 Platoons of 'A' Company, working on the Rifle Range under supervision of the R.E's. 'B' Company - 2 Platoons - Training. 2 Platoons - Agricultural Work.	

Lt.-Col.,
Cmdg. 1/5th Bn. South Staffs. Regiment.

D. D. & L., London, E.C.
(A10266) Wt W5300/P713 750,000 2/18 Sch. 52 Forms/C2118/16.

CONFIDENTIAL.

WAR DIARY

OF

1/5TH. BN. SOUTH STAFFS REGT.

FROM 1st. MAY 1919. TO. 31st. MAY, 1919.

Instructions regarding War Diaries and Intelligence Summaries are contained in F. S. Regs., Part II. and the Staff Manual respectively. Title pages will be prepared in manuscript.

WAR DIARY
or
~~INTELLIGENCE SUMMARY.~~
(Erase heading not required.)

Army Form C. 2118.

Place	Date	Hour	Summary of Events and Information	Remarks and references to Appendices
KOMMERN, Germany.	1.		"A" & "B" Companies (2 Platoons) Work on KOMMERN Rifle Range. "D" Company. (2 Platoons) Agricultural Work. (2 Platoons) Training. "May Day." Labour Demonstrations by civil population fizzled out, the Boche enthusiasm being damped by bad weather. Following Officers left to join the 11th. Bn. Somerset Light Infantry, DUNKIRK. Lieut: W.L. Pritchard. " F. Kite. 2/Lieut: L. Morris. " A.E. Murch. " F.G. Surman. " H.D. Deighton MM. Lieut: J.R. Willoughby. Following Officers left to join on being posted to the 17th. Bn. Worcestershire Regt. HAVRE. Lieut: W.A. Lawrence. " G.E. Jones. " G.S. Young MC. " R. Jowsey. 2/Lieut. W.G. Bloom. " W.H.R. Lloyds MC. " J.R. Costley.	B.N.
	2.		Inspection of the Battalion at SINZENICH by the Commanding-in-Chief, "British Army of the Rhine," took place at 11.45 hours.	B.N.
	3.		Educational Classes. Saluting Drill and Interior Economy.	B.N.
	4.		Church Parades.	B.N.
	5.		"B" and "C" Companies. Work on Rifle Range. "A" and "D" Companies. Training. A Lecture on Naval Subjects was given by Commander [illegible] R.N. at ZULPICH. Was attended by 3 Officers and 10 Other Ranks per Company.	B.N.

D. D. & L., London, E.C.
(A10266) Wt.W5300/P713 750,000 2/18 Sch. 52 Forms/C2118/16.

Instructions regarding War Diaries and Intelligence Summaries are contained in F. S. Regs., Part II. and the Staff Manual respectively. Title pages will be prepared in manuscript.

WAR DIARY
or
~~INTELLIGENCE SUMMARY.~~
(Erase heading not required.)

Army Form C. 2118.

Place	Date	Hour	Summary of Events and Information	Remarks and references to Appendices
KOMMERN, Germany.	6.		"A" & "B" Companies worked on Rifle Range making the Stop Butt. "C" & "D" Companies . Training.	
	7.		"A" & "B" Companies, Training. "C" & "D" Companies, Work on Rifle Range. A Lecture on "Citizenship" was given by Major C.W. Haward at ZULPICH. Was attended by 3 Officers and 18 Other Ranks per Company.	
	8.		"A" & "B" Companies work on Rifle Range. "C" & "D" Companies . Training.	
	9.		"C" & "D" Companies work on Rifle Range. "B" Company, Training. "A" Company, Inspection by Commanding Officer.	
	10.		Interior Economy. Saluting Drill for all Companies. Commanding Officer Inspected "B" Company. The Battalion paraded at 11.30 hours in the "Stafford Pavilion" for a Lecture on the "Army and the Nation" by Brigadier-General G.S.G. CRAUFURD CMG. CIE. DSO. ADC. Commanding the 2nd. Midland Brigade.	
	11.		Interior Economy. Saluting Drill.	
	12.		Church Parade.	
	13.		"A" & "B" Companies, Training. "C" & "D" Companies, work on Rifle Range. "A" Company on duty, finding Guards, Piquets, for week commencing to-day.	
	14.		"A" & "B" Companies, work on Rifle Range. "C" Company, Route March. "D" Company's organization tested by the Commanding Officer.	

D. D. & L., London, E.C.
(A10266) Wt W5300/P713 750,000 2/18 Sch. 52 Forms/C2118/16.

Instructions regarding War Diaries and Intelligence Summaries are contained in F. S. Regs., Part II. and the Staff Manual respectively. Title pages will be prepared in manuscript.

WAR DIARY
or
~~INTELLIGENCE SUMMARY~~.
(Erase heading not required.)

Army Form C. 2118.

Place	Date	Hour	Summary of Events and Information	Remarks and references to Appendices
KOMMERN. Germany.	15.		"A" & "B" Companies, (less 1 Platoon) Training. 1 Platoon "B" Coy. Field firing. "C" & "D" Companies, work on Rifle Range. A forest fire broke out at about 20.00 hours on the hills in the vicinity of SATZVEY. The Bosche fire alarm was sounded by permission of the Commanding Officer, but the Fire Brigade failed to turn out owing to the members' fear of being arrested without a pass. The fire burned out at midnight.	R.A.N.
	16.		"A" & "B" Companies. Work on Rifle Range. "C" & "D" Companies, Training, and firing on Miniature Range.	R.A.N.
	17.		Companies at disposal of Company Commanders. to 11.30 a.m. Brigade Education Officer gave a Lecture in the "Stafford Pavilion" on the Peace Treaty.	R.A.N.
	18.		Church Parades.	R.A.N.
	19.		"A" & "B" Companies, work on Rifle Range. "C" & "D" Companies. Training.	R.A.N.
	20.		"A" & "C" Companies, work on Rifle Range. "B" & "D" Companies, Training. A Lecture on "Fallacies of BOLSHEVISM" was given at BRUHL by Lt. Colonel Tysham, which was attended by 4 Officers and 20 Other Ranks of the Battalion.	R.A.N.
	21.		"A" "C" & "D" Companies, work on Rifle Range. "B" Company, Training.	
	22.		"A" C" & "D" Companies work on Rifle Range. "B" Company, Training. IXth. Corps Concert Party gave a performance in the "Stafford Pavilion".	R.A.N. R.A.N.
	23.		"A" "C" & "D" Companies, work on Rifle Range. "B" Company, Training.	R.A.N.

D. D. & L., London, E.C.
(A10266) Wt W5300/P713 750,000 2/18 Sch. 52 Forms/C2118/16.

Instructions regarding War Diaries and Intelligence Summaries are contained in F. S. Regs., Part II. and the Staff Manual respectively. Title pages will be prepared in manuscript.

WAR DIARY
or
~~INTELLIGENCE SUMMARY.~~

(Erase heading not required.)

Army Form C. 2118.

Place	Date	Hour	Summary of Events and Information	Remarks and references to Appendices
KOMMERN. Germany.	24.		EMPIRE Day. Platoon Commanders gave a short address to their Platoons on the BRITISH EMPIRE. The 52nd. Bn. LEICESTERSHIRE Regimental Sports at ZULPICH were attended by a large number of men of the Battalion. They were conveyed there by dog-carts, traps, lorries, wagons, horses and mules, and every other kind of conveyance which the versatile brain of the Transport Officer could conceive.	AN
	25.		Church Parades.	AN
	26.		"A" "B" & "D" Companies, work on Rifle Range. "C" Company, Training, finding Guards and all Picquets etc.	AN
	27.		"A" Company on duty for the week, commencing to-day. "B" "C" & "D" Companies, work on Rifle Range. "A" Company beat Brigade Headquarters at EUSKIRCHEN, in the Brigade Football League, by 5 goals to 1. The irregular Transport again turned out in strength.	AN
	28.		"A" Company, Miniature Range. "B" "C" & "D" Companies, Platoon Training.	AN
	29.		"A" "B" & "C" Companies, Platoon Training. "D" Company, Miniature Range. 50 Other Ranks attended the Divisional Train Gymkhana at ROMER HOF.	AN
	30.		"A" Company, Miniature Range. "B" "C" & "D" Companies, Training.	AN
	31.		Education and Interior Economy. Commanding Officer lectured to Battalion on the overstaying of leave.	AN

Lt.-Col.,
Cmdg. 1/5th. Bn. South Staffs Regt....

D. D. & L., London, E.C.
(A10266) Wt W5300/P713 750,000 2/18 Sch. 52 Forms/C2118/16.

Confidental

War Diary
of
1/5th. Bn. South Staffs Regt

From 1st June, 1919.

To 30th June, 1919

Instructions regarding War Diaries and Intelligence Summaries are contained in F. S. Regs., Part II. and the Staff Manual respectively. Title pages will be prepared in manuscript.

WAR DIARY
or
~~INTELLIGENCE SUMMARY.~~
(Erase heading not required.)

Army Form C. 2118.

Place	Date	Hour	Summary of Events and Information	Remarks and references to Appendices
KOMMERN Germany.	1.		Church Parades- At the Church of England Service an amusing Parson all wreathed in smiles virtually gave us to understand we were a set of complete and hopeless blackguards. *It is to be noted that he was a stranger.*	R.N.
	2.		'D' Company came on duty for the week, finding guards, picquets, etc. 'A' and 'B' Company- Company Training. 'C' Company Firing on the 30 yards range, also Musketry Instruction.	R.N.
	3.		King George the Fifth's Birthday. To commemorate this the Battalion paraded as strong as possible with uncased colours and gave Three Cheers for His Majesty. The remainder of the day was a holiday. The Kings Birthday Honours included the followingawaards to Officers and Other Ranks of the Battalion:- Major. W.J.J.Collas,DSO. — To be Brevet Lieutenant -Colonel. Lieut(Acting Captain) and Adjutant R.Briard. — Awarded Military Cross. 2/Lieut.G.W.Poole. — Awarded Military Cross. 200540.R.S.M.Howse,F. — Awarded Distinguished Conduct Medal. 203284.L/Cpl. Varnam,L.T. — Awarded Distinguished Conduct Medal. 40762.Pte.Clay, H. — Awarded Distinguished Conduct Medal. 200556 C/Sgt Davies, J. — Awarded Meritorious Service Medal.	R.N.
	4.		The Battalion paraded in Field Service Marching Order for a route march of 8 miles. Route-KOMMERN-SCHWERFEN-EICKS-HOSTEL, but owing to the Signals Officer losing his way, for which he blamed the German Map, GLEHN was also included in the march. The Battalion beat the IX Corps troops at cricket at EUXSKIRCHEN.	R.N.
	5.		'A' 'B' & 'C' Companies-Training.	R.N.
	6.		'A' Company Firing on Miniature Range. 'B', 'C' and 'D' Companies Training. Left half of Battalion beat right half Battalion at Cricket. Scores: Right Half. 119. Left Half 123 for 6 wickets. Officers Riding Class was put over the jumps for the first time without mishap to anyone.	R.N.

D. D. & L., London, E.C.
(A10266) Wt W5300/P713 750,000 2/18 Sch. 52 Forms/C2118/16.

Instructions regarding War Diaries and Intelligence Summaries are contained in F. S. Regs., Part II. and the Staff Manual respectively. Title pages will be prepared in manuscript.

WAR DIARY
or
~~INTELLIGENCE - SUMMARY.~~

(*Erase heading not required.*)

Army Form C. 2118.

Place	Date	Hour	Summary of Events and Information	Remarks and references to Appendices
KOMMERN. Germany.	7.		Saluting Drill, Interior Economy and Kit inspections. In the Brigade Knock-out Football Competition 'A' Company drew with 'C' Company 52nd Leicestershire Regiment-2 goals all in the Final at OBERGARTZEM. Major-General G.F.Boyd, CB,CMG,DSO,DCM, late General Officer Commanding,46th Division,took over Command of the Midland Division.	R.N.
	8.		Church Parades. The Senior Chaplain of the Forces preached at the Church of England Service. 'A' Company to be duty Company for the week.	R.N.
	9.		'B' and 'D' Companies- Platoon Training. 'C' Company-Miniature Range and Musketry.	R.N.
	10.		'B','C' and 'D' Companies- Platoon Training -Miniature Range and Musketry.	R.N.
	11.		'B' and 'C' Companies Training. 'D' Company-Miniature Range and Musketry.	R.N.
	12.		'B' Company - Miniature Range. 'C' Company- Outpost Scheme. 'D' Company - Company Training. The Brigadier-General visited the Companies at Training during the morning.	R.N.
	13.		'B' and 'D' Companies-Training. 'C' Company-Miniature Range and Musketry. Three Officers attended a lecture on the use of Carrier Pigeons.	R.N.
	14.		'A' and 'D' Companies. Interior Economy. 'B' and 'C' Vompanies. Educational Examination. The Adjutant, Captain R.Briars, MC, celebrated today his 21st birthday and failed to appear in Mess..	R.N.

D. D. & L., London, E.C.
(A10266) Wt W5300/P713 750,000 2/18 Sch. 52 Forms/C2118/16.

Army Form C. 2118.

WAR DIARY
or
~~INTELLIGENCE SUMMARY.~~
(*Erase heading not required.*)

Instructions regarding War Diaries and Intelligence Summaries are contained in F. S. Regs., Part II. and the Staff Manual respectively. Title pages will be prepared in manuscript.

Place	Date	Hour	Summary of Events and Information	Remarks and references to Appendices
KOMMERN. Germany.	15		Church Parades. The Commanding Officer took all Officers for a technical march in the afternoon. At 18.00 hours, a three mile Cross-Country Run was held, ten men from each Company constituting a team. Result :- 'B', 'C', 'D' 'A'.	R.A.N.
	16		'B' Company on duty for the week. 'A' and 'D' Companies - Educational Training. 'C' Company - Attack Practice. In the afternoon, the preliminary heats for the Sports to be held tomorrow were run off.	R.A.N.
	17		The Battalion moved at 11.20 hours by lorry, to DUREN at 3 hours notice, this being J-3 day. The Sports which were to have been held this afternoon were cancelled, and much love's labour lost over their preparations.	APPENDIX I R.A.N.
DUREN.	18		Companies were at the disposal of Officers Commanding Companies, subject to Guards and Inlying Picquets being found by 'A' and 'B' Companies respectively.	R.A.N.
	19		Company Training.	R.A.N.
	20		Companies at the disposal of Officers Commanding Companies. Lieut.-Col. W.J.J.COLLAS DSO. appointed Commanding Officer of the 51st Bn Devonshire Regt. and left the Battalion to the regret of all ranks.	R.A.N.
	21		Company Training.	R.A.N.
	22		Church Parades for 'A' and 'C' Companies at the Garrison Church, - probably the first occasion on which a Church of England Service has been held in a consecrated building since the Unit proceeded overseas in 1915. These two Companies afterwards marched past the IV Corps Commander(Sir A. GODLEY) on the way back to billets. In the afternoon, several young officers of the Battalion in their best service dress accepted his invitation to a tea-fight, at which they appeared very popular with the ladies of the British Empire Leave Club.	R.A.N.
	23		Company Training.	R.A.N.
	24		Guards Training.	R.A.N.

D. D. & L., London, E.C.
(A10266) Wt W5300/P713 750,000 2/18 Sch. 52 Forms/C2118/16.

Army Form C. 2118.

WAR DIARY
or
~~INTELLIGENCE SUMMARY.~~
(Erase heading not required.)

Instructions regarding War Diaries and Intelligence Summaries are contained in F. S. Regs., Part II. and the Staff Manual respectively. Title pages will be prepared in manuscript.

Place	Date	Hour	Summary of Events and Information	Remarks and references to Appendices
DUREN.	25		A Guard of Honour consisting of 3 Officers and 80 Other Ranks for an Allied Medal Presentation at SPA(BELGIUM) was selected from this Battalion from which it was obviously inferred that the young Guards had not yet reached the standard of smartness set by their war-worn comrades. 'C' Company took over duties of Inlying Picquet from 'B' Company.	R.N.
	26		Company Training.	R.N.
	27		Company Training. 'D' Company found x Guards.	R.N.
	28		Company Training.	R.N.
	29		Church Parades.	R.N.
	30		Company Training.	R.N.

R W Morgan
Lieut.-Colonel,
Cmdg. 1/5th Bn. South Staffs. Regt.

D. D. & L., London, E.C.
(A10266) Wt W5300/P713 750,000 2/18 Sch. 52 Forms/C2118/16.

SECRET 1/5th Bn. SOUTH STAFFS REGT.

APPENDIX I

-o0o-

ORDER No. 260. Copy No. 19.

17th June, 1919.

1. Today is 'J' minus 3 day, and the Battalion will move to DUREN.
50 lorries will be available.
Embussing point KOMMERN - ZULPICH Road. Head CHEN - tail fork road immediately north east of KOMMERN.
DEBUSSING POINT, ZULPICH - DUREN Road, 300 yards south east of junction of ZULPICH - DUREN and NILERAU - DUREN Roads.

2. Upon arrival at DUREN, 'A' Company will take over the following guards :-

Guard	Strength	At present furnished by.
Railway Stn Guard.	2 Officers 48 O.R.	4th, 5th, & 51st Gordon Highlanders.
Captured vehicle park.	1 N.C.O. & 6 men.	51st Gordon Highlanders.
Railhead supply & Corps & Divn'l Pack Train.	2 N.C.O's & 12 men.	-ditto-
Post Office.	2 N.C.O's & 6 men.	-ditto-
Ammunition Dump.	1 N.C.O. & 3 men.	4th Corps H.A.
Prison Guard.	1 N.C.O & 6 men.	-ditto-
R.A.S.C. Guard.	2 N.C.O's & 6 men.	-ditto-
Salvage Dump.	10 O.R.	-ditto-

3. 'A' Company will become inlying picquet, relieving one Company of the 4th Gordon Highlanders.
Arrival in new areas and location of Company Headquarters will be reported to Battalion Headquarters as soon as possible.

3. Officer Commanding 'A' Company will report when Guards, etc. have been taken over.
The 'KNOBS' Concert Party and Battalion Band, under command of 2/Lieut. B.J. KING, will remain at KOMMERN to guard stores left behind at the Quartermaster's Stores.
The Lewis Gun Officer will arrange for the two Headquarters A.A. Lewis Guns, with sufficient ammunition for defensive purposes to be left with this party.

4. The Transport Officer will arrange for the Ammunition to move full.

5. The Battalion Messing Officer will arrange for the Battalion to take one day's preserved rations complete (for consumption on day following move, in addition to unexpired portion of the day's rations.
Every endeavour must be made to prevent losses to the preserved rations occurring on the journey.

6. Iron rations at present stored in the Quartermaster's Stores will be issued to all ranks forthwith.

7. In the event of any disturbance, and fighting taking place, Companies will notify Battalion Headquarters by 10.30 hours daily of the exact number of casualties they have suffered during the preceding 24 hours.
In the case of Officers, the rank, initials and name, and date of casualty will be stated.

8. One blanket per man only will be taken; the second suit of service dress and jerkin will NOT be taken.

9. ACKNOWLEDGE.

Captain.
Adjutant, 1/5th Bn. South Staffs Regt.

Copies issued at..........hours to:-

1. Commanding Officer. 1a. 2nd-in-Command.
2. Officer Commanding 'A' Company.
3. Officer Commanding 'B' Company.
4. Officer Commanding 'C' Company.
5. Officer Commanding 'D' Company.
6. Transport Officer.
7. Quarter master.
8. Signals Officer.
9. Lewis Gun Officer.
10. Messing Officer.
11. Intelligence Officer.
12. Regimental Sergeant-Major.
13. Medical Officer.
14. 2/Lieut. B.J. King. 14a. Headquarters, 2nd Midland Brigade
15. War Diary.
16. War Diary.
17. Retained.

Page. 1.

Instructions regarding War Diaries and Intelligence Summaries are contained in F. S. Regs., Part II. and the Staff Manual respectively. Title pages will be prepared in manuscript.

WAR DIARY
or
~~INTELLIGENCE SUMMARY.~~
(Erase heading not required.)

1/5 S. Staffs

Army Form C. 2118.

Place	Date	Hour	Summary of Events and Information	Remarks and references to Appendices
	July	1919		
DUREN.	1		Day spent in packing up and preparing for move back to KOMMERN.	R.N.
	2		Battalion paraded at 09.40 hours and route marched to WETTVEISS, a distance of about 8 miles, without anyone falling out. The G.-O.-C. watched the march past at KELZ, and complimented the Commanding Officer on the general turnout, particularly of the Transport.	R.N.
WETTVEISS	3		Battalion paraded at 09130 hours and route marched to KOMMERN, a distance of about 10 miles, passing the Brigade Commander before arriving at ZULPICH. On arrival, All Ranks returned to their old billets, but the village was found to be in a very dirty condition, and the Burgermeister was 'gingered up' accordingly. To the deep chagrin of the Medical Officer, the Blue Lamp Room had been pulled down in our absence, and consisted of nothing but a heap of bricks and plaster which the Officers, with the assistance of the Transport, commenced to convert into an 'en tous cas' Tennis Court, on the outskirts of the village.	R.N.
KOMMERN.	4		To celebrate the signing of the Peace Terms on the 28th ultimo, the day was a General Holiday throughout the British Army of the Rhine, and the 'KNOTS' gave a performance in the STAFFORD PAVILION' in the evening. A Committee Meeting decided to hold the Sports on Friday 11th instant. The First Divisional Dance was held at BRUHL.	R.N.
	5		Companies were at disposal of Company Commanders for Interior Economy and Saluting Drill with canes. Much labour was expended in the afternoon by about 20 Officers over the laying down of the new Tennis Court.	R.N.
	6		Church Parades. Very wet. Heavy thunderstorm in the afternoon.	R.N.
	7		Company Training. A Cricket Match between the Battalion and 18th. Field Ambulance resulted in a Win. Score 46 - 25.	R.N.

53 El 6 sheets

D. D. & L., London, E.C.
(A10266) Wt W5300/P713 750,000 2/18 Sch. 52 Forms/C2118/16.

Instructions regarding War Diaries and Intelligence Summaries are contained in F. S. Regs., Part II. and the Staff Manual respectively. Title pages will be prepared in manuscript.

WAR DIARY
or
INTELLIGENCE SUMMARY.
(Erase heading not required.)

Army Form C. 2118.

Place	Date	Hour	Summary of Events and Information	Remarks and references to Appendices
KOMMERN.	7		Lieut: Bourne MC. and Lieut: Burton MC. MM. were selected to carry the Colours on the 14th. inst: in the Victory March thro' PARIS, and left the Battalion with 7 Other Ranks for this purpose.	
			A most ~~eloquent~~ complimentary letter was received from Lt.-General Sir R.C.B. Haking, KCB., KCMG., Chief of the British Armistice Commission, relating to the Guard of Honour found by "B" Company at SPA on the 25th. June 1919.	R.N.
	8.		Company Training and Educational Classes.	R.N.
	9		Company Training and Educational Classes.	
			The Brigadier-General Commanding and the Commanding Officer addressed the Battalion on the following subjects, the keenness ~~of~~ for which seemed to be damped owing to the prospect by a large number of men of early demobilization.	
			1. Voluntary Educational Classes.	R.N.
			2. War Savings.	
	10		Battalion paraded in F.S.M.O. at 09.30 hours for a Route March of 8 miles through Schwerfen Road Junction SW. of Enzen, Obergartzen, Firmenich and back to billets.	
			A Lecture on V.D. was given in the 'STAFFORD PAVILION' at 17.30 hours by the Revd. HASLETT, which was attended by about 12 Officers and 200 Other Ranks. The M.O.'s verdict was to the effect that he could not (even with 30 years' experience) have treated the subject better himself.	R.N.
	11.		Battalion Sports were held in the afternoon.	R.N.
	12		Company Training. ~~No. 2.~~ The 2nd. COLOGNE Race Meeting was attended in the afternoon by several Officers and numerous Other Ranks of the Battalion. 2/Lieutenants J.T. SMITH and J.S. PASLEY proceeded to St. POL to report for duty to the Director of Graves Registration - a melancholy occupation which caused general surprise in attracting even two volunteers.	R.N.
	13		Church Parades. Lt.-Col., R.P. BURNETT DSO. MC. was attached to the Battalion pending an appointment.	R.N.

D. D. & L., London, E.C.
(A10266) Wt W5300/P713 750,000 2/18 Sch. 52 Forms/C2118/16.

Page. 3.

Army Form C. 2118.

WAR DIARY
or
INTELLIGENCE SUMMARY.
(Erase heading not required.)

Instructions regarding War Diaries and Intelligence Summaries are contained in F. S. Regs., Part II. and the Staff Manual respectively. Title pages will be prepared in manuscript.

Place	Date	Hour	Summary of Events and Information	Remarks and references to Appendices
KOMMERN.	14.		The firing of the General Musketry Course by all ranks on KOMMERN Rifle Range, recently completed by German labour, commenced at 08.30 hours with good results which fell off with the advent of rain later in the morning.	P.A.N.
	15.		General Musketry Course.	P.A.N.
	16.		-----ditto-----	P.A.N.
	17.		-----ditto-----	P.A.N.
	18.		-----ditto----- "A" & "B" Companies firing in the morning. "C" & "D" Companies firing in the afternoon. Colour Party returned from its Triumphal March through PARIS.	P.A.N.
	19.		Church Parades.	P.A.N.
	20.		General Musketry Course. "C" & "D" Companies firing in the morning. "A" & "B" Companies firing in the afternoon.	P.A.N.
	21.		General Musketry Course. "A" and "B" Companies firing in the morning, and "C" and "D" Companies in the afternoon.	P.A.N.
	22.		General Musketry Course. Firing Repeats.	P.A.N.
	23.		Part III, General Musketry Course. "C" and "D" Companies firing in the morning, and "A" and "B" Companies in the afternoon.	P.A.N.
	24.		Part III, General Musketry Course. "A" and "B" Companies firing in the morning, and "C" and "D" Companies in the afternoon. Notification received today that the wearing of the British War Medal is now authorized.	P.A.N.
	25.		Part III General Musketry Course. A Lecture was givixn by the Command Paymaster, at EUSKIRCHEN, on the new system of Pay and Mess Books. The Lecture was attended by all 2nds-in-Command of Companies and Company Quartermaster Sergeants.	P.A.N.

D. D. & L., London, E.C.
(A10266) Wt W5300/P713 750,000 2/18 Sch. 52 Forms/C2118/16.

Page 4.

Instructions regarding War Diaries and Intelligence Summaries are contained in F. S. Regs., Part II. and the Staff Manual respectively. Title pages will be prepared in manuscript.

WAR DIARY
or
~~INTELLIGENCE SUMMARY.~~
(Erase heading not required.)

Army Form C. 2118.

Place	Date	Hour	Summary of Events and Information	Remarks and references to Appendices
KOMMERN	26		Firing Part IV General Musketry Course.	R.N.
	27		General Musketry Course completed. Church Parades. The averages for the Course are as follows:- "A" Company: 75.859. "B" Company: 71.71. "C" Company: 65.209. "D" Company: 61.706. Battalion Average: 68.223. No. 6 Platoon "B" Company, obtained the highest average in the Battalion, i.e. 80.538. The 'KNOTS' Concert Party provided an entirely new program which was enthusiastically received. It was attended by the Commanding Officer - who returned that day from leave, - and most of the Officers.	R.N.
	28		Company Training. Battalion furnished the Brigade Guard.	R.N.
	29		Company Training.	R.N.
	30.		Company Training and Educational Classes.	R.N.
	31.		Company Training.	R.N.

R. Neville

Major,
Cmdg. 1/5th Bn. S.Staffs. Regt.

D. D. & L., London, E.C. (A10266) Wt W5300/P713 750,000 2/18 Sch. 52 Forms/C2118/16.

Copy.

A.C./2854.

Headquarters,
1V Corps.

1. I wish to thank the G.O.C. 1V Corps and the Officers Commanding the 1/5th. South Staffordshire Regiment for sending a Guard of Honour to attend at the Ceremonial Parade at SPA today for the presentation of decorations to members of the Allied Armistice Commissions.

2. The Guard of Honour, in spite of the most unfavourable transport and weather conditions, was admirably turned out and very smart on parade, and handled their arms extremely well. Their fine appearance on parade contributed in no small degree to the success of the ceremony, and I will be obliged if you would convey my appreciation to the Commanding Officer of the Battalion.

(sgd) R. HAKING, Lieut:-General,
Chief of the British Armistice Commission.

SPA.
25-6- 1919.

CONFIDENTIAL.

46th Div. mod Hr

1/5th Battalion SOUTH STAFFORDSHIRE REGIMENT.

---oOo---

W A R D I A R Y.

From 1st August, 1919. To 31st August, 1919.

5th Staffs

Instructions regarding War Diaries and Intelligence Summaries are contained in F. S. Regs., Part II. and the Staff Manual respectively. Title pages will be prepared in manuscript.

WAR DIARY
or
~~INTELLIGENCE SUMMARY~~

(Erase heading not required.)

Army Form C. 2118.

Place	Date	Hour	Summary of Events and Information	Remarks and references to Appendices
COMMERN.	AUGUST 1st		Company Training. All men's pay books were withdrawn and the English System of making payments to the men in the Pay and Mess Book was adopted. Brigade Sports were held at "BESSENICH" ,the following results of events enabled the Battalion to bring back the Cup given to the champion Unit in the Brigade. 100yds Lieut.Walton. — 1mile Pte Marsden "C"Coy. 220 " Lieut.Walton. — Putting the weight Lieut. Napier. 440 " Lieut.Walton. — High Jump. Lieut. Napier. ½ mile Pte.Taylor. "D"Coy. — Hurdles. Lieut .Napier. Relay Race. Lieut Walton. — Long Jump. 2/Lt. Wickham-Legge. Pte.Taylor. "D"Coy Sgt.Lee "B" " Cpl. Wilkinson."D"Coy.	R.N.
	2nd		Company Training. Major General G.F.Boyd CB. CMG. DSO. DCM. G.O.C. Midland Division, visited the Battalion, stayed for dinner and a performance of the "KNOTS" Concert Party.	R.N.
	3rd		Church Parades.	R.N.
	4th		To-day being August Bank Holiday no training was carried out. Cricket. Battalion v 1st Batt: M.G.C. at "FLERTZHEIM". Result Win Score 75 - 33. Pte Davies took 5 wickets for 1 run.	R.N.
	5th		Company Training. Battalion won the Cup in BRIGADE CROSS COUNTRY CHAMPIONSHIP. The team were trained by 2/Lt King, and all came home in the first thirteen. Cricket. Officers v Sergeants. Results Officers Won. Scores 91 - 29.	R.N.
	6th		Company Training. Lt.- Col: R.W.Morgan CMG. DSO. who had commanded the Battalion for nearly four months relinquished command to-day to join the 1st Bn South Staffordshire Regt. He took away with him the best wishes of all ranks notwithstanding the fact that the activities of his juniors had been considerably speeded up during his tenure of command, and he was given a hearty send off. Cricket. Battalion v Mid: D.A.C. at "NIEDERELVICH". Result Win. Score. 78 - 29. Sgt Burton took 7 wicket for 14 runs.	R.N.

(A7092). Wt. W12839/M1293. 75,000. 1/17. D. D. & L., Ltd. Forms/C.2118/14.

Army Form C. 2118.

WAR DIARY
or
~~INTELLIGENCE SUMMARY~~
(Erase heading not required.)

Instructions regarding War Diaries and Intelligence Summaries are contained in F. S. Regs., Part II. and the Staff Manual respectively. Title pages will be prepared in manuscript.

Place	Date	Hour	Summary of Events and Information	Remarks and references to Appendices
COMMERN.	August 7th		The Battalion route marched a distance of 8 miles. Route:- KOMMERN.EICKS.FLOISDORF.SCHWERFEN. thence to billets.	R.N.
	8th		Company Training. Major R.P.Burnett DSO. MC. left the Batta ion on being appionted 2nd in Command of the 15th H.L.I. Cricket. Battalion v 77th Siege Batt: R.G.A. Result Win 43-39.	R.N.
	9th		Companies were placed at the disposal of Company Commanders for interior economy and discipline. The following extract from the London Gazette dated the 3rd June 1919, referred to this Batt: the Commanding Officer congratulates the recipient "42137 Cpl EXTON.S. Awarded the D.C.M." Cricket the Battalion drew with Corp Signal Coy Score 111 each.	R.N.
	10th		Church Parades.	R.N.
	11th		Company Training. Midland Divisional Athletic Sports, Polo and Gymkhana week commenced at ROMERHOF which was visited by all available men each day. Cricket. Batt: v 269 Anti-Aircraft Coy. Result Win. Score .59 for 6 declared Sgt Burton took 9 wickets for 7 runs.	R.N.
	12th		Company Training.	R.N.
	13th		Company Training. Cricket. Battalion v 354 Siege Batt: R.G.A. Result WIN. Score 50 - 47.	R.N.
	14th		Company Training. The heats of the Divisional Athletic Sports were held at ROMERHOF. The undermentioned qualified for the finals, 100 yds Lieut Walton. 120 yds Hurdles Lieut Napier. Lieut Wright. 220 yds Lieut Walton. 440 yds Lieut Walton. The final of the ¼ mile open was won by Cpl Shennan.A.G. "B" Coy.	R.N.
	15th		Company Training. Divisional Gymkhana at ROMERHOF at 2-15 pm at which the Battalion gained 48 prizes.	R.N.

(A7092). Wt. W12839/M1293. 750,000. 1/17. D. D. & L., Ltd. Forms/C.2118/14.

PAGE "3"

Instructions regarding War Diaries and Intelligence Summaries are contained in F. S. Regs., Part II. and the Staff Manual respectively. Title pages will be prepared in manuscript.

Army Form C. 2118.

WAR DIARY
or
~~INTELLIGENCE SUMMARY.~~
(Erase heading not required.)

Place	Date	Hour	Summary of Events and Information	Remarks and references to Appendices
COMMERN	August 16th		Company Training. The final events of the Divisional Gymkhana Sports Meeting were heldat ROMERHOF in the afternon. The Battalion was well represented and gained the Challenge Cup given to the Unit scoring the greatest number of points, and Lieut Napier won the Challenge Cup given to the best individual competitor of the Division.	RON.
	17th		Church Parades. Cricket. Battalion v E.Corp Signals. Results WIN. Score, 102 for 3 (declared) 46.	RON.
	18th		Company Training. The whole Battalion were medically inspected. Lieut.- Colonel J.C. Burnett. D.S.O. Duke of Wellingtons Regt. took over command of the Batt: Cricket. Battalion v 140 Siege Batt: R.G.A. Result WIN. Score 69 - 52.	RON.
	19th		Company Training. Cricket. Battalion v 16th Field Ambulance. Result WIN. Score 180 - 40.	RON.
	20th		Company Training.	RON.
	21st		Battalion Route Marched during the morning, leaving billets at 09-30hrs. Route:- KOMMERN. EICKS. HOSTEL. ROGGENDORF. KOMMERN. Dress Fighting Order. Cricket. Battalion v 185 Siege Batt R.G.A. at FLAMMERSHEIM. Result Lost. 54 - 58 for 7 declared	RON.
	22nd		Company Training. 70 Other Ranks under 2/Lt King paraded at 06.15 Hrs marched to MECHERNICH and entrained for BONN whence they started for a trip down the Rhine to COBLENZ and Back. Cricket. - Battalion v. 6th M.G.C. Result:- Win. Score 134 to 114.	RON.
	23rd		Interior Economy and Saluting Drill. Eight Mules were sent to EUSKIRCHEN for sale. Cricket. Battalion v. 6th M.G.C. at KOMMERN. Result, Win. Score 161 for7 declared. 145.	RON.
	24th		Church Parades.	RON.
	25th		Company Training and Educational Classes.	RON.

Instructions regarding War Diaries and Intelligence Summaries are contained in F. S. Regs., Part II. and the Staff Manual respectively. Title pages will be prepared in manuscript.

WAR DIARY
or
~~INTELLIGENCE SUMMARY.~~
(Erase heading not required.)

Army Form C. 2118.

Place	Date	Hour	Summary of Events and Information	Remarks and references to Appendices
	25		A Board of Audit assembled at 10.00 hours to check the Regimental Accounts ending 3 months 31st August, 1919. All Mobilization Equipment packed in accordance with the Sections of A.F.G. 1098 ~~and~~ were returned to ENGLAND via ANTWERP.	R.N.
	26		Company Training and Educational Classes. Captain M.G. Young 'D' Company, took over command of 'A' Company from Lieut. G.L. Brown. 8 Heavy Draught Horses, 1 Pack Mule, were taken to the 24th Veterinary Hospital for dispersal. 5 Officers' Chargers were taken to the Army Animal Collecting Camp at COLOGNE.	R.N.
	27		Company Training and Educational Classes. 25 Mules Mules were taken to the Army Animal Collecting Camp for dispersal.	R.N.
	28		Battalion Route March in the morning. Route: KOMMERN - SCHAVEN - FIRMENICH - SCHWERFEN - EICKS - KOMMERN. Dress: Fighting Order.	R.N.
	29		Company Training and Educational Classes. 70 Warrant Officers, N.C.O's and men proceeded to COLOGNE for final demobilization. The 'KNOTS' Concert Party gave a final show, the proceeds being distributed among the performers. 6 Officers' Chargers were sent to Zulpich for transfer to ENGLAND to rejoin the Battalion on its arrival there.	R.N.
	30		Companies were at the disposal of Company Commanders for Interior Economy and Saluting Drill. 100 Warrant Officers, N.C.O's and men proceeded to COLOGNE for final demobilization in the United Kingdom.	R.N.
	31		Church Parades.	R.N.

J. C. Burnett
Lieut.-Colonel,
Commanding 1/5th ~~Bn.~~ South Staffordshire Regiment.

(A7092). Wt. W12839/M1293. 75,000. 1/17. D. D. & L., Ltd. Forms/C.2118/14.

WO 95/1626/9

MIDLAND DIVISION

LATE 6TH DIVISION

B. H.Q.

3RD MIDLAND INFY BDE

MAR. ~~JAN~~ - AUG 1919

Instructions regarding War Diaries and Intelligence Summaries are contained in F. S. Regs., Part II. and the Staff Manual respectively. Title pages will be prepared in manuscript.

Headquarters, 71st Infantry Brigade.

WAR DIARY

or

~~INTELLIGENCE SUMMARY.~~

(Erase heading not required.)

Page 1. March, 1919.

Army Form C. 2118.

Place	Date	Hour	Summary of Events and Information	Remarks and references to Appendices
EICHHOLZ. GERMANY, Sheet 2.L.	1		Fine day - Warm. 3rd Round 6th Divnl. Football Competition. The match between 9th Norfolk Regt. and 11th Leicestershire Regt. (Pioneers) was postponed until March 2nd owing to break-down of transport. The 1st Leicestershire Regt. drew with 2nd York & Lancs., away - 3 goals all.	
	2		Fine day. Divine Service for all Units in the morning. Replay between 9th Norfolk Regt. and 11th Leicestershire Regt. (Pioneers) ended in a draw - 1 goal all.	
	3		Very nice day. A RHINE paddle boat was chartered for the day and to take a number of Officers and O.R. in the Division up the River from BONN - COBLENTZ and back again. 1st Leicestershire Regt. replayed their match with 2nd York and Lancs. at home and won 2 goals - Nil.	
	4		Wet day. The 51st Sherwood Foresters arrived at BONN TOR Station at 06.00 hours and proceeded to billets in the RODENKIRCHEN - SURTH Area. 9th Norfolk Regt. replayed their match with 11th Leicestershire Regt. (Pioneers) away and lost 3 - 1.	
	5		Very nice day. First day of 6th Divnl. Race Meeting at LIBLAR. There were not many entries from Battalions. No races were won by Infantry.	
	6		Fine day - Showery in the afternoon. Second day of 6th Divnl. Race Meeting at LIBLAR. Battalions continuing Training. Orders received that the Army Commander would inspect the 51st Bn. Sherwood Foresters on 7th March.	
	7		Fine day. The Army Commander, General Sir HERBERT PLUMER, G.C.B., C.M.G., D.S.O., inspected the 51st Bn. Sherwood Foresters at MARIENBURG Barracks in the morning. The Battalion which was made up entirely of "Young Soldiers" were quite steady on Parade and "Marched Past" the Army Commander in a well ordered manner.	
	8		Fine day. The 1st Leicestershire Regt. played the 16th Bde. R.H.A. in the Semi-final of the Divnl. Championship (Association) at BRUHL in the afternoon. It was an excellent game, both sides being equally matched. Result a draw 1 - 1 after extra time had been played.	
	9		Fine day - fairly warm. Divine Service for all Units. Instructions issued to 1st Leicestershire Regt. that all Volunteers and Retainable Officers and men for the Army of Occupation were/....	

D. D. & L., London, E.C. (A8004) Wt. W1771/M2031 750,000 5/17 Sch. 52 Forms/C2118/14

Headquarters, 71st Infantry Brigade.

WAR DIARY

or

~~INTELLIGENCE SUMMARY~~

(Erase heading not required.)

Army Form C. 2118.

Instructions regarding War Diaries and Intelligence Summaries are contained in F. S. Regs., Part II. and the Staff Manual respectively. Title Pages will be prepared in manuscript.

Page 2. March. 1919.

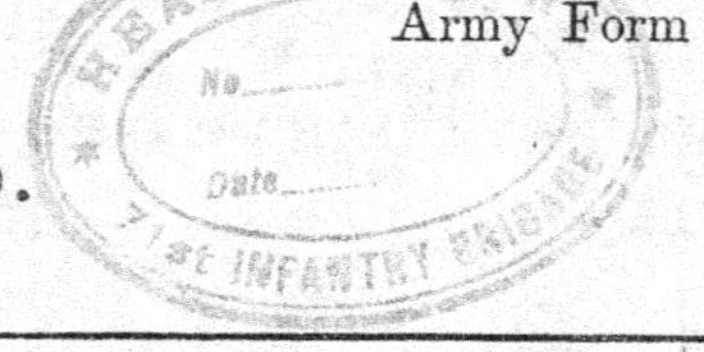

Place	Date	Hour	Summary of Events and Information	Remarks and references to Appendices
EICHHOLZ. GERMANY, Sheet 2.L	9		were to join 11th Leicestershire Regt. (Pioneers) at WEIL/ERWIST on 11th March.	APPENDIX. 1.
	10		Fine day - fairly warm. Brigadier-General Commanding and Staff Captain attended a conference at Divnl. H.Q. in the morning. Semi-final of 6th Divnl. Competition, replay between 16th Bde. R.H.A. and 1st Leicestershire Regt. held in the afternoon. The game was exciting and well contested up to half time when the 16th Bde. R.H.A. were one goal - Nil. The 1st Leicestershire Regt. scored in the 2nd half and extra time had to be played again. During this latter half hour the 1st Leicestershire Regt. attained a marked superiority and eventually won 4 - 1. Amendment to O.O. 411 issued.	APPENDIX. 2.
	11		The 51st Leicestershire Regt. detrained at BONN TOR Station in the morning and proceeded to Billets at SURTH. O.O. 412 issued. Brigadier-General Commanding visited various dumps of War Material in COLOGNE during the morning.	APPENDIX. 3.
	12		Beautiful morning. Amendment to O.O. 412 issued. Final of 6th Divnl. Football Competition played in the afternoon between 1st Leicestershire Regt. and 11th Leicestershire Regt.(Pioneers) on Divnl. H.Q. ground at BRUHL. A very exciting game ensued which ended in a draw 1 all after full time had been played. An extra ¼ hour each was played and during this period the 1st Leicestershire Regt. displayed a marked superiority and eventually earned a well won victory. Result - 1st Leicestershire Regt. 2 goals, 11th Leicestershire Regt. (Pioneers) 1 goal. The 53rd Sherwood Foresters detrained at BRUHL in the morning and proceeded to billets in the town.	APPENDIX. 4.
	13		Dull day. Battalions busy demobilizing and despatching drafts of Retainable men and Volunteers for Army of Occupation to their destinations. Army Commander, General Sir HERBERT PLUMER, G.C.B., C.M.G., D.S.O., inspected the ~~53rd Sherwood Foresters in BRUHL at 11.15 hours~~ 51st Leicestershire Regt. in the afternoon at SURTH. O.O. 413 issued.	APPENDIX. 5.
	14		Very nice day - slight frost. Army Commander, General Sir HERBERT PLUMER, G.C.B., C.M.G., D.S.O., inspected the 53rd Sherwood Foresters in BRUHL at 11.15 hours. 1st Leicestershire Regt. played the 1st Camerons in BONN in the afternoon in the Army Championship. The game was keenly contested and ended in a draw after full time had been played. The Camerons scored during extra time and eventually won 1 - Nil. This was the sixth match the 1st Leicestershire Regt. had played in twelve days and in three of these matches they had had to play extra time so the team was not in the best of condition.	

15th Fine day/....

Instructions regarding War Diaries and Intelligence Summaries are contained in F. S. Regs., Part II. and the Staff Manual respectively. Title pages will be prepared in manuscript.

Headquarters, 71st Infantry Brigade.

WAR DIARY

~~or~~

~~INTELLIGENCE-SUMMARY.~~

(Erase heading not required.)

Page 3. March. 1919.

Army Form C. 2118.

Place	Date	Hour	Summary of Events and Information	Remarks and references to Appendices
EICHHOLZ. GERMANY, Sheet 2.L.	15		Fine day. Battalions busy demobilizing. Nothing to report.	
	16		-do- - do - Capt. BAREFOOT, M.C., reported to take over duties of Staff Captain in relief of Capt. F.W. MUSGRAVE, M.C. to be demobilized.	
	17		Fine cold day. Divisional Commander inspected 9th Norfolk Regt., 1st Leicestershire Regt. and 2nd Sherwood Foresters to say goodbye in the morning. Orders issued for move of 51st Leicestershire Regt. to EUSKIRCHEN and 53rd Sherwood Foresters to SURTH on 18th.	APPENDIX. 6.
	18		Cold day and some rain. 51st Leicestershire Regt. entrained at BONN TOR Station at 0[illegible].00 hrs. for EUSKIRCHEN where they come under orders of 16th Infantry Brigade. 52nd Sherwood Foresters arrived at BONN TOR at 21.00 hours and moved in billets at MARIENBURG coming under orders of 71st Infantry Brigade.	
	19		Fairly fine day. Nothing to report. New Battalions beginning to settle down and commence Training.	
	20		Fairly fine day - some Snow in the evening. Battalions Training as per Programme.	
	21		Fine day Battalions Training. O.O. 415 issued re move of Cadres of 1st Leicestershire Regt. and 2nd Sherwood Foresters on 22nd inst. 250 men of 9th Norfolk Regt. demobilized left by train leaving BRUHL 07.15 hours.	APPENDIX. 7.
	22		Fine day. Cadres of 1st Leicestershire Regt. and 2nd Sherwood Foresters move into BRUHL and join that of 9th Norfolk Regt. Nothing to report.	
	23		Fine day. Battalions Training. Nothing to report.	
	24		Cold day - Some rain. Training by Battalions continued.	
	25		Fine day. Battalions Training. Nothing to report.	
	26.		Cold day - some rain and sleet. O.O. 416 issued re move of Brigade Headquarters and 71st T.M. Battery on 27th inst.	APPENDIX. 8.

RODENKIRCHEN 27th Bde. H.Q./.....

D. D. & L., London, E.C.
(A8004) Wt. W1771/M2031 750,000 5/17 Sch. 52 Forms/C2118/14

Instructions regarding War Diaries and Intelligence Summaries are contained in F. S. Regs., Part II. and the Staff Manual respectively. Title pages will be prepared in manuscript.

Headquarters, 71st Infantry Brigade.

WAR DIARY
or
~~INTELLIGENCE-SUMMARY~~.

(Erase heading not required.)

Page 4. March, 1919.

Army Form C. 2118.

Place	Date	Hour	Summary of Events and Information	Remarks and references to Appendices
RODENKIRCHEN	27		Brigade Headquarters moved to RODENKIRCHEN. Brigadier-General P.C.B. SKINNER, C.M.G., D.S.O., takes over Command of 71st Infantry Brigade, vice Brigadier-General P.W. BROWN, C.M.G., D.S.O.	
	28		Cold day with some snow. Battalions Training. Nothing to report.	
	29		- do - Brigadier-General Commanding and Brigade Major went to Divisional Headquarters in the afternoon to meet the Commander-in-Chief.	
	30		Very cold day - some snow. Battalions attended Divine Service in the morning. Nothing else to report.	
	31		Fairly Fine Day. Battalions Training as usual.	

GENERAL. The reconstitution of the Brigade was gradually effected during the month. The 51st., 52nd. and 53rd Sherwood Foresters arriving in the Area from ENGLAND and relieving the 2nd Sherwood Foresters, 1st Leicestershire Regt. and 9th Norfolk Regt. respectively. The rate of demobilization among these latter Units was greatly increased until at the end of the month they were practically reduced to Cadre strength. Numerous changes took place among the Command and Staff within the Division. Major-General T.O. MARDEN, C.B., C.M.G., commanding the Division being replaced by Major-General Sir C.P.A. HULL, K.C.B., and Brigadier-General P.W. BROWN, C.M.G., D.S.O., Commanding the 71st Infantry Brigade by Brigadier-General P.C.B. SKINNER, C.M.G., D.S.O. These and other changes together with the continuous redistribution of Units and the large number of guards found by Battalions on abandoned War Material (200 in all) rather affected the comfort of the troops and the facilities for training during the month.

The demobilization figures for March were as follows :-

	Officers.	O.Rs.
71st Infantry Brigade Headquarters	2	9
9th Norfolk Regt.	4	338
1st Leicestershire Regt.	1	200
2nd Sherwood Foresters.	3	165
52nd Sherwood Foresters.	-	7
71st T.M. Battery.	-	4

Major,
Brigade Major, 71st Infantry Brigade.

D. D. & L., London, E.C.
(10340) Wt W5300/P713 750,000 3/18 E 2688 Forms C/2118/15.

71st Infantry Brigade.

WAR DIARY for month of MARCH, 1919.

List of APPENDICES.

No. 1. 71st Infantry Brigade O.O. No. 411.
2. Amendment to 71st I.B. O.O. No. 411.
3. 71st Infantry Brigade O.O. No. 412.
4. Amendment to 71st I.B. O.O. No. 412.
5. 71st Infantry Brigade O.O. No. 413.
6. " " " O.O. No. 414.
7. " " " O.O. No. 415.
8. " " " O.O. No. 416.
9. Nominal Roll of Officers.

SECRET.

Copy No. 9.......

71st Infantry Brigade
Operation Order No. 411.
****

1. All Volunteers for, or Retainable Officers and Men for the Army of Occupation from 1st Leicestershire Regt. will proceed to WEILERSWIST on Tuesday, 11th March, where they will join the 11th Leicestershire Regt. (P).

2. Route - BERZDORF - BRUHL and main road to WEILERSWIST. Time of starting at discretion of Commanding Officer. Troops to arrive about 14.00 hours.

3. Men will carry the unconsumed portion of the day's ration and rations for the 12th March will be sent to the 11th Leicestershire Regt. on the afternoon of 11th inst.

4. Pending the result of the Semi-final for the Divisional Football Championship the 1st Leicestershire's Team will not for the present be included in the Officers and Other Ranks proceeding under para. 1.

Should the 1st Leicestershire Regt. win their Match with 13th Bde. R.H.A. on Monday their Team will remain with the Battalion until further orders. Should they lose, members of the Team coming under Categories laid down in para. 1 will proceed with the party for 11th Leicestershire Regt.

5. Three Lorries have been asked for to report at 1st Leicestershire Regt. Headquarters, WESSELING, at 08.00 hours on Tuesday, 11th March.

6. 1st Leicestershire Regt. will report the strength of the party joining 11th Leicestershire Regt. - shewing Officers and Other Ranks - by noon 10th March. This should include Officers and Other Ranks employed on Command who will eventually be transferred to the 11th Leicestershire Regt. (these numbers to be shown separately).

7. ACKNOWLEDGE.

Issued at 07.30 hours.

Captain,
10-3-1919. A/Brigade Major, 71st Infantry Brigade.

DISTRIBUTION.

Copy No. 1. Brigadier-General Commanding.
2. Brigade Major.
3. Staff Captain.
4. 1st Leicestershire Regt.
5. 11th Leicestershire Regt.
6. 6th Division "G".
7. 6th Division "Q".
8. No. 3. Coy. 6th Divnl. Train.
9. War Diary (2).
10. File.

SECRET.

AMENDMENT No. 1 to
71st Infantry Brigade
Operation Order No. 411.

****

W/D

1. All Volunteers for, or Retainable Officers and Men for the Army of Occupation from 1st Leicestershire Regt. will now join 11th Leicestershire Regt. (P) at SECHTEM.

2. Route - EICHHOLZ - SECHTEM.

3. ACKNOWLEDGE.

Captain,
10-3-1919. A/Brigade Major, 71st Infantry Brigade.

Copy to all recipients of 71st Inf. Bde. O.O. No. 411.

App 3

SECRET.

Copy No. 10

71st Infantry Brigade
Operation Order No. 412.

11th March, 1919.

1. All Volunteers and Retainable Officers and Men for the Army of Occupation of 2nd Sherwood Foresters will proceed to join the 11th Leicestershire Regt. (Pioneers) at SECHTEM on 12th March, 1919.

2. Route - GODORF - WESSELING - EICHHOLZ - SECHTEM. Time of start at discretion of Commanding Officer. Party to arrive at SECHTEM before 16.00 hours.

3. All Ranks will carry the unconsumed portion of the day's ration - rations for 13th will be sent to the 11th Leicestershire Regt. on the afternoon of 12th March.

4. Commanding Officer of 2nd Sherwood Foresters will arrange forthwith to relieve all men proceeding to 11th Leicestershire Regt., at present employed on guard, by men liable for demobilization or on the Cadre Strength of the Battalion (i.e. men remaining with the Battalion for the time being).

5. The 52nd Bn. Sherwood Foresters are shortly arriving in the Brigade Area and will on arrival take over sufficient accommodation at MARIENBURG Barracks for 34 Officers and 800 O.R.

6. The 2nd Sherwood Foresters will report as early as possible the number of Officers and O.R. joining the 11th Leicestershire Regt. (P) and also the numbers of Officers and O.R. employed or on Command who will eventually be transferred to that Battalion. These numbers to be shewn separately.

7. Two Lorries have been asked for, to report at MARIENBURG Barracks at 08.00 hours on 12th March for use of party joining 11th Leicestershire Regt. on that date.

8. ACKNOWLEDGE.

Issued at 13.30 hours

J.H. Hamley

Captain,
A/Brigade Major, 71st Infantry Brigade.

DISTRIBUTION.

Copy No. 1. Brigadier-General Commanding.
2. Brigade Major.
3. Staff Captain.
4. 2nd Sherwood Foresters.
5. 51st Sherwood Foresters.
6. 11th Leicestershire Regt. (P).
7. 6th Division "G".
8. 6th Division "Q".
9. No. 3 Coy. 6th Div. Train.
10. War Diary (2).
11. File.

SECRET.

Amendment No. 1 to
71st Infantry Brigade
Operation Order No. 412.
****

1. Reference para. 1. Party will proceed to join 11th Leicestershire Regt. (Pioneers) on 13th inst. and not 12th instant as stated.

2. Rations for 14th instant will be sent to 11th Leicestershire Regt. on afternoon of 13th March. Lorry arrangements will be altered accordingly.

3. ACKNOWLEDGE.

J. H. Hamilton
Captain,
11-3-1919. A/Brigade Major, 71st Infantry Brigade.

Copy to all Recipients of 71st I.B. O.O. No. 412.

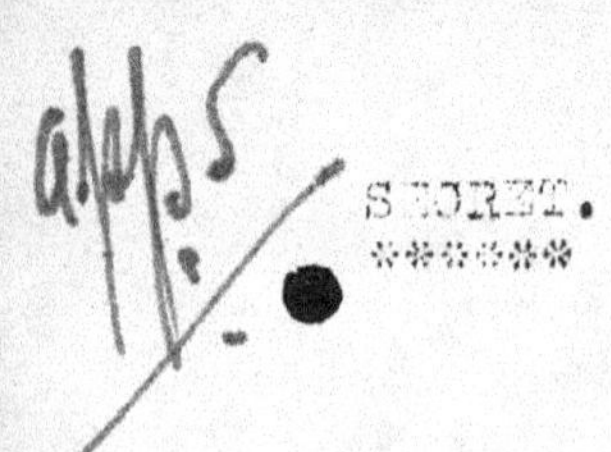

SECRET.
******

Copy No. 8

71st Infantry Brigade
Operation Order No. 413.
****

13th March, 1919.

1. All available, retainable and volunteer Officers and O.R. for Army of Occupation of 9th Norfolk Regt. will entrain to-morrow 14th March at KIERBERG. The train arrives at 12.03 hours and departs at 12.18 hours. Commanding Officer of 9th Norfolk Regt. will arrange for personnel to be on the Station by 11.30 hours.

2. Party will proceed complete with Equipment and Box Respirators and will be rationed up to 15th March inclusive.

3. The detraining Station will be SIEGBURG from where personnel will proceed to join 34th Division. The train will arrive at SIEGBURG at 14.07 hours.

4. ACKNOWLEDGE.

Issued at 19.00 hours

[signature]

Captain,
A/Brigade Major, 71st Infantry Brigade.

DISTRIBUTION.

Copy No. 1. Brigadier-General Commanding.
2. Brigade Major.
3. Staff Captain.
4. 9th Norfolk Regt.
5. 6th Division "G".
6. 6th Division "Q".
7. No. 3 Coy. 6th Div. Train.
8. War Diary (2).
9. File.

SECRET.

Copy No. 14

71st Infantry Brigade
Operation Order No. 414.

17th March, 1919.

1. The following moves will take place to-morrow 18th March at times stated :-

Unit.	From.	To.	Remarks.
51st Leicestershire Regt.	SURTH.	EUSKIRCHEN.	By train leaving BONN TOR Station 10.00 hrs., arrive EUSKIRCHEN 11.47 hrs.
53rd Sherwood Foresters.	BRUHL.	SURTH.	By March Route via BERZDORF - GODORF. Time of starting at discretion of Commanding Officer.

2. Battalions will move complete with transport and stores.

3. The 52nd Sherwood Foresters from EUSKIRCHEN are arriving at BONN TOR Station 17.40 hrs. on same date and after detrainment will proceed with Transport to MARIENBURG Barracks.

4. The 51st Leicestershire Regt. will be at BONN TOR Station by 07.45 hrs. ready to commence entraining at 08.00 hrs.

5. The 53rd Sherwood Foresters will send a billeting party to SURTH forthwith to take over accommodation, paillasses, etc. from 51st Leicestershire Regt.

6. Lorry arrangements will be notified later.

7. Completion of all moves to be reported to this Office with map reference of Headquarters.

8. ACKNOWLEDGE.

Issued at 15.30

J. H. Hamblyn
Captain,
A/Brigade Major, 71st Infantry Brigade.

DISTRIBUTION.

Copy No. 1. Brigadier-General Commanding.
2. Brigade Major.
3. Staff Captain.
4. 9th Norfolk Regt.
5. 1st Leicestershire Regt.
6. 2nd Sherwood Foresters.
7. 51st Leicestershire Regt.
8. 51st Sherwood Foresters.
9. 53rd Sherwood Foresters.
10. 6th Division "G".
11. 6th Division "Q".
12. D.A.D.O.S.
13. No. 3 Coy, 6th Div. Train.
14. War Diary (2).
15. File.

App 7

SECRET

HEADQUARTERS 71st INFANTRY BRIGADE

Copy No. 12

71st Infantry Brigade
Operation Order No. 415.

21st March, 1919.

1. The 1st Leicestershire Regt. and 2nd Sherwood Foresters will move from WESSELING and MARIENBURG respectively to BRUHL to-morrow 22nd March, 1919. Move to take place in the afternoon. Any restrictions as to time of starting and route will be notified if and when received.

2. Three Lorries have been asked for to report to each Battalion Headquarters at a time to be notified later.

3. Billeting Officers of the above mentioned Battalions will meet the Staff Captain in BRUHL at 15.00 hours to-day, when accommodation will be allotted to them.

4. Completion of moves to be reported to this Office by wire.

5. ACKNOWLEDGE.

Issued at 14.30 hrs

J. F. Hamilton
Captain,
A/Brigade Major, 71st Infantry Brigade.

DISTRIBUTION.

Copy No. 1. Brigadier-General Commanding.
2. Brigade Major.
3. Staff Captain.
4. 1st Leicestershire Regt.
5. 2nd Sherwood Foresters.
6. 9th Norfolk Regt.
7. Midland Division "G".
8. Midland Division "Q".
9. 17th Field Ambulance.
10. No. 3 Coy. 6th Div. Train.
11. D.A.P.M.
12. War Diary (2). ✓
13. File.

SECRET.

71st Infantry Brigade
Operation Order No. 416.

Copy No......16........

1. 71st Infantry Brigade Headquarters & 71st T.M. Battery will move to RODENKIRCHEN to-morrow 27th March 1919.
Route - WESSELING - GODORF - SURTH.

2. The Starting point will be the road junction at 4.C.24.08. Brigade Headquarters will pass this point at 10.20 hours and 71st T.M. Battery at 10.22 hours.

3. 71st T.M. Battery will detail an Officer or N.C.O. to meet the Staff Captain at Burgomaster's Office, RODENKIRCHEN at 10.00 hrs. to-morrow 27th March, 1919.

4. Brigade Headquarters will close at EICHHOLZ at 12.00 hours and open at RODENKIRCHEN at same hour on 27th March.

5. 1 Lorry will report at 71st T.M. Battery Headquarters at 09.00 hours to-morrow.

6. ACKNOWLEDGE.

Issued at...15.00 hours...

Captain,
26-3-1919. A/Brigade Major, 71st Infantry Brigade.

Copy No. 1. B.G.C.
2. B.M.
3. S.C.
4. 9th Norfolk R.
5. 1st Leic. Regt.
6. 2nd Sher. Fors.
No. 7. 51st Sher.Fors.
8. 52nd Sher.Fors.
9. 53rd Sher.Fors.
10. 71st T.M.B.
11. 17th Field Ambles.
12. No. 3 Coy. Train.
No. 13. Mid.Div."G".
14. Mid.Div."Q".
15. D.A.P.M.
16. War Diary(2)
17. File.

71st Infantry Brigade.

ROLL OF OFFICERS SERVING ON 31st MARCH, 1919.

Brigadier-General P.C.B.SKINNER, C.M.G., D.S.O.	Brigade Commander.
Major A. WEYMAN, M.C.	Brigade Major.
Captain G.W.N. BAREFOOT, M.C.	Staff Captain.
Captain L.F. LAMPARD.	Brigade Educational Officer. (on leave)
Lieut. E.L. HAYNE, M.C.	Intelligence Officer. (on leave)

ATTACHED.

Brigadier-General P.W. BROWN, C.M.G., D.S.O.		Gordan Highlanders. (late B.G.Commanding).
Captain J.F. TAMBLYN, M.C.	(East Surrey Regt).	Acting Brigade Major.
Captain B.M. ARMSTRONG, M.C.	(4th Traffic Control Squadron).	P.R.O.
Lieut. J.C. ROWBOTHAM,	(Norfolk Regt).	Brigade Transport Officer.
Lieut. J.V. TAILBY, M.C.	(Leicestershire Regt.)	Brigade Lewis Gun Officer.
Lieut. H. COY.	(Leicestershire Regt.)	Civil Staff Captain.
Lieut. C. MORGAN.	(Royal Engineers).	Brigade Signal Officer.

CONFIDENTIAL.

Headquarters "A"
Midland Division.

Herewith War Diary of Headquarters of 3rd Midland Brigade for the month of April 1919.

Please acknowledge.

Brigadier General.
Commanding 3rd Midland Brigade.

3rd Midland Brigade.

WAR DIARY for month of April, 1919.

List of APPENDICES.

No.1. 3rd Midland Brigade Provisional Instructions.
2. 3rd Midland Brigade Order No.417.
3. War Diary (Miscellaneous).
4. Nominal Roll of Officers.
5. Special Order of the Day.

@@@@@@@@@@@@@@@@@@@@@@@

Headquarters, 3rd Midland Brigade.

WAR DIARY
or
~~INTELLIGENCE SUMMARY.~~
(*Erase heading not required.*)

Army Form C. 2118.

Instructions regarding War Diaries and Intelligence Summaries are contained in F. S. Regs., Part II. and the Staff Manual respectively. Title pages will be prepared in manuscript.

Page 1. April, 1919.

Place	Date	Hour	Summary of Events and Information	Remarks and references to Appendices
RODENKIRCHEN	1		The Brigadier-General Commanding and Brigade Major visited the Arsenal, COLOGNE and various Forts and Dumps in and outside COLOGNE where the Brigade provides Guards, and inspected the Guards. The Cadres of 6th Division transferred from Brigades and put under Command of Brigadier-General BRAIGHTHWAIGHTE.	Names of Towns & Villages can be found in Sheet 2.L. GERMANY 1/100.000.
	2		The Brigadier-General Commanding and Brigade Major visited Fort VII and the Powder Magazine COLOGNE and inspected the Guards.	
	3		Arrangements started for removal of rifles, machine guns and swords from the Arsenal COLOGNE to Fort V11. This work is to be carried out by 52nd Sherwood Foresters.	
	4.		A large number of rifles and rifle racks moved from Arsenal to Fort VII. Brigadier-General Commanding and Brigade Major went to look for Training Grounds immediately East of the RHINE. The whole country is cultivated and no ground was found S. of COLOGNE capable of training anything larger than ½ Company.	
	5.		Brigade Headquarters moved from RODENKIRCHEN to a big house on outskirts of COLOGNE, Sheet 2.L., 3.C.2.7. 600 Officers and O.R. (200 from each Battalion) went on a River trip by Steamer up the RHINE towards COBLENTZ. A perfect day for it.	
	7.		Platoon and Recreational training.	
	8.		Brigadier General Commanding inspected 52nd Sherwood Foresters in Mass formation at MARIENBURG Barracks. The Battalion was well turned out though very weak owing to the big Guards which it is finding.	
	9.		The Brigadier General Commanding inspected 51st Sherwood Foresters at RODENTHAL. Battalion was well turned out.	
	10.		The Brigadier General Commanding inspected 53rd Sherwood Foresters at SURTH. Battalion was well turned out but improvement is required in their Transport. The Battalion is entirely a young soldiers Battalion, some of the boys being small and very young. All three Battalions are very badly off for N.C.Os, also for Pioneers, Tailors, and Shoemakers. (Most of these having been demobilized in England before the Battalion came out) 51st Battalion have neither drums/.........	

Headquarters, 3rd Midland Brigade.

Army Form C. 2118.

WAR DIARY

~~or~~

~~INTELLIGENCE SUMMARY.~~

(*Erase heading not required.*)

Instructions regarding War Diaries and Intelligence Summaries are contained in F. S. Regs., Part II. and the Staff Manual respectively. Title pages will be prepared in manuscript.

April, 1919.

Place	Date	Hour	Summary of Events and Information	Remarks and references to Appendices
			drums nor band. 52nd and 53rd Battalions have drums only.	
MARIENBURG (Cologne).	11.		Brigadier-General P.W.Brown, C.M.G., D.S.O., left the Brigade to join the 1/4th Gordons as Battalion Commander. Captain J.F.Tamblyn, M.C. South Surrey Regt. left the Brigade.	
	12.		The General Officer Commanding IX Corps inspected Battalions as under :- 51st and 52nd Sherwood Foresters at MARIENBURG Barracks at 10.30 hours. 53rd Sherwood Foresters at SURTH at 12.00 hours. The Divisional Commander, Major-General Sir AMYATT HULL, K.C.B. was also present. Battalions were drawn up in Mass with 1st line Transport on parade and were all well turned out.	
	13.		Lieut-Colonel F.G.Spring, D.S.O. arrived to take over Command of 52nd Sherwood Foresters from Lieut-Colonel G.C.Lambten, D.S.O.	
	14.		The Brigadier-General Commanding visited 51st Bn.,Sherwood Foresters at training.	
	15.		The Brigadier-General Commanding visited 53rd Bn.,Sherwood Foresters at training. Lieut.J.C.Rowbottom, M.C. Bde.Transport Officer, 3rd Midland Brigade, left to be Demobilized. Provisional Instructions re action to be taken in the case of Civil Riot issued (No.G.5665)	APPENDIX No.1.
	16.		The Brigadier-General Commanding visited 52nd Bn.,Sherwood Foresters at training. Lieut-Colonel W.B.Thornton, D.S.O. arrived to take over the Command of 51st Bn.,Sherwood Foresters from Lieut-Colonel H.M.Milward, D.S.O.	
	17.		Brigade Operation Order No.417 issued. 52nd Bn.,Sherwood Foresters to move to BRUHL.	APPENDIX No.2.
	18.		Good Friday.	
	19.		The Divisional Commander paid a surprise visit to 53rd Bn.,Sherwood Foresters at SURTH. Amendment No.1 to Brigade Operation Order No.417 issued. Battalions warned to push on with Musketry as one Battalion may have to go away to Classification Ranges about the middle of May.	
	20.		51st Bn.,Sherwood Foresters handed over guard of Powder Magazine to 52nd Bn.Sherwood Foresters.	

21. Guards/..........

D. D. & L., London, E.C. (A8004) Wt W1771/M2031 750,000 5/17 Sch. 52 Forms/C2118/14

Headquarters, 3rd Midland Brigade.

WAR DIARY
or
~~INTELLIGENCE SUMMARY.~~

Army Form C. 2118.

Instructions regarding War Diaries and Intelligence Summaries are contained in F. S. Regs., Part II. and the Staff Manual respectively. Title pages will be prepared in manuscript.

Page 3. April, 1919.

(*Erase heading not required.*)

Place	Date	Hour	Summary of Events and Information	Remarks and references to Appendices
MARIENBERG (Cologne(.	21.		Guards(as under) over Forts found by 52nd Sherwood Foresters, relieved by 1st Northern Brigade. Arsenal, COLOGNE..............................2 Officers 25 O.Rs. Fort V11.......................................2 " 25 " Powder Magazine, RADENTHAL......................4 " 63 " Bon Tor Station, COLOGNE,(E.F.C. dump). 2 N.C.Os. 8 men. Banhof Bontor, COLOGNE. 2 " 8 " VOLKSGARTEN. " 2 " 8 " VORGEBIRG Strasse " 2 " 8 " TOTAL:- Officers 6. O.Rs. 128. The guard at the triangle Bonner Strasse cancelled. 52nd Bn.,Sherwood Foresters to prepare a scheme for defence of the 4 railway bridges at BRUHL, (Not to use more than one Company of 120 Other Ranks) in case of Civil Riot. 53rd Bn.,Sherwood Foresters Sports at SURTH.	
	22.		52nd Bn.,Sherwood Foresters moved to BRUHL to billets in the ALUMNET and SEMINARY. The General Officer Commanding inspected 51st Bn.,Sherwood Foresters marching through GODORF.	
	23.		The Brigadier-General visited BRUHL to inspect the billets of 52nd Bn.,Sherwood Foresters.	
	24.		Lieut-Colonel.F.G.Spring, D.S.O. Commanding 52nd Sherwood Foresters and Brigade-Major met G.S.O.2 Division at BRUHL, and visited the big ammunition dumps just outside the town to render a plan of defence in case dump is attacked by a mob. Garrison of two platoons was considered necessary in normal times, to be reinforced by two more platoons in case of a riot or civil disturbance.	
	25.		The Brigadier-General Commanding inspected the demobilization registers of units.	
	26.		Units training.	
	28.		Lecture by Commander Viscount Broome, R.N. on Naval subjects. London Division Races - 200 from this Brigade attended.	

29. The Brigadier/.......

D. D. & L., London, E.C.
(A8004) Wt W1771/M2031 750,000 5/17 Sch. 52 Forms/C2118/14

Instructions regarding War Diaries and Intelligence Summaries are contained in F. S. Regs., Part II. and the Staff Manual respectively. Title pages will be prepared in manuscript.

Headquarters, 3rd Midland Brigade.

WAR DIARY

~~or~~

~~INTELLIGENCE SUMMARY.~~

(*Erase heading not required.*)

Page 4. April, 1919.

Army Form C. 2118.

Place	Date	Hour	Summary of Events and Information	Remarks and references to Appendices
MARIENBERG (Cologne).	29.		The Brigadier-General Commanding reconnoitred part of the area which ~~we are~~ This Brigade is responsible for in case of Civil disturbance or riot (BRUHL, ECKDORF, GLUCK), the big coal mines on the high ground near ECKDORF and GLUCK are the chief features. Warning order received that the Commander in Chief, British Army of the Rhine, would inspect two battalions on 2nd May. Special instructions in case of riot or disturbance on May 1st issued to units.	
	30.		The Brigadier-General Commanding reconnoitred mining area of KIERBERG, GLUCK, for which this Brigade is responsible in case of Civil disturbance. Drafts from 1st Midland Brigade joined Battalions as under:- 51st Bn.,Sherwood Foresters...............195 Other Ranks from 2/4 Duke of Wellington Regt. 52nd Bn.,Sherwood Foresters...............200 " " " 2/4 K.O.Y.L.I. Regt. 53rd Bn.,Sherwood Foresters...............195 " " " 5th K.O.Y.L.I. "	
			<u>GENERAL.</u> <u>EDUCATION</u> - Great interest has been taken in Education throughout the month. One hour per day is compulsory. Educational training is confined to Group A work - elementary - but voluntary classes are held in other subjects and are very popular. Foreign language classes are popular. <u>TRAINING</u> - Chiefly musketry. Some excellent 30 yards Ranges have been built by each Battalion. Gas drill is also carried out at least twice per week. Both training and Education were greatly interfered with during the first three weeks of April by the numerous Guards which had to be found. <u>RECREATION</u>- In addition to Football (Rugby and Association) and Hockey, two steamer trips were made up the Rhine towards COBLENTZ. These are very popular.	

[signature] Major.
Brigade Major, 3rd Midland Brigade.

D. D. & L., London, E.C. (A8004) Wt W1771/M2031 750,000 5/17 Sch. 52 Forms/C2118/14

Appendix No 1.

SECRET.

3rd Midland Brigade

G5665

Action to be taken in the event of Civil Riot or Insurrection.

PROVISIONAL INSTRUCTIONS.

A. On receipt of the message from Brigade Headquarters "Civil Riot. Take Precautions", the following action will be taken :-

1. All Troops at training, on Working Parties or at Games, will be recalled to Barracks or Billets.
All individual Officers and Other Ranks, who may be away from their quarters, on becoming aware that disturbances are impending, through the sounding of the "Alarm" by Buglers or other means, will return at once to their Units.

2. Units will be prepared to move at twenty minutes notice.
Dress - Marching Order with Steel Helmets and Box Respirators.

3. An additional 50 rounds S.A.A. per man will be held ready to issue to the Troops immediately they parade. Water Bottles will be filled.

4. Lewis Gun and S.A.A. Limbered G.S. Wagons will be packed, and Cookers will be held in readiness. Animals will be harnessed but not hooked in, and Transport will be held ready to move in twenty minutes.

5. All Battalion Stores and Heavy Kit will be packed up ready to transfer to a Brigade Depot, - (MARIENBURG BARRACKS).

6. Parties will be detailed by each Unit of equivalent strength to each of the Detachments and Guards found by that Unit - other than the Brigade Headquarters Guard, - and hold ready to reinforce those Detachments or Guards.

7. Battalions will each detail a Guard of 1 Officer, 2 N.C.Os. and 12 Rank & File for duty at the Brigade Depot, and a Party to remain at the Depot to include the following :-

Quartermaster and Quartermaster's Personnel.
Orderly Room Staff.
Regimental Tradesmen.
3 Signallers.
6 Runners and Despatch Riders.
3 Rank and File for General Duties.
2 Cooks.

Brigade Headquarters and Trench Mortar Battery will detail a Depot Party in proportion.
The O.C., 52nd Sherwood Foresters will detail an Officer not below the rank of Captain to Command the whole party left at the Brigade Depot.

8. Visual Signal ~~Sections~~ Stations ensuring communication between each Unit and Brigade Headquarters, and between MARIENBURG BARRACKS and Fort VII, will be manned and kept manned until permission is given to dismiss or the Unit moves off.

9. The Guards at/......

9. The Guards at -

BAHNHOF BONN TOR (ALTERBURGER WALL).
KOBLENTZ STRASSE.
VORGEBIRGS STRASSE.
VOLKSGARTEN.

will be prepared to concentrate in the Area between the BONNER WALL and BISCHOFS WEG, and together with the Guard already there, to defend the E.F.C. Depot, Stores and Railway Trucks.
Two Officers will be detailed by the O.C., 52nd Sherwood Foresters to take Command of these combined Guards if required. These Officers will reconnoitre beforehand the above Area, with a view to its defence.

D. On receipt of the message from Brigade Headquarters "Civil Riot. Take Action" -

1. Units will parade at once. An additional 50 round S.A.A. per man will be issued, Transport Animals will be hooked in, and, failing orders to the contrary, the Brigade will concentrate at the Brigade Depot (MARIENBURG BARRACKS).

2. Detachments and Guards detailed already, will be sent direct to reinforce existing Detachments and Guards as may be ordered.

3. The Battalion Stores and Heavy Kit of Units will be conveyed to the Brigade Depot by Lorry, so soon as Lorries can be made available, and in the meantime those Stores must be left under Guard at the Headquarters of Units.

4. Visual Signal Stations no longer required in consequence of the above moves will be closed down.

5. Brigade Headquarters will be established at the Brigade Depot (MARIENBURG BARRACKS).

6. The Guards referred to in para. A.9. above, will concentrate as therein directed, and the Officers detailed will take over their Command.

7. All Detachments and Guards will adopt any necessary measures for defence and will be prepared to defend themselves if attacked.

8. Whilst engaged in suppressing disturbances, troops will parade always with fixed bayonets. Fire will be controlled, and if an Officer is present will only be opened on the orders of that Officer. Fire, if opened, is to be effective.

A. M. Tyrman
Major,
Brigade Major, 3rd Midland Brigade.

15-4-1919.

DISTRIBUTION.

Brigadier-General Commanding.
Brigade Major. ✓
Staff Captain.
Brigade Signal Officer.
51st Sherwood Foresters.
52nd Sherwood Foresters.
53rd Sherwood Foresters.
Trench Mortar Battery.
Brigade Civil Staff Captain.
Midland Divn. "G") for information.
" " "Q")
War Diary (2)
File.

SECRET.
****

AMENDMENT No. 1. to
3rd Midland Brigade Order No. 417.

1. 3rd Midland Brigade Order No. 417 dated 17-4-1919 is amended as follows :-

2. 52nd Sherwood Foresters will move from MARIENBURG Barracks on 22nd April, 1919, and will be clear of Barracks by 10.00 hrs. on that day.

3. On April 20th, 1919, 52nd Sherwood Foresters will take over the Guards in the Powder Magazine from 51st Sherwood Foresters. Arrangements re relief to be made direct between Battalions concerned.

4. On April 21st, 1919, 52nd Sherwood Foresters will hand over to 53rd Northumberland Fusiliers all Guards mentioned in 3rd Midland Brigade Order No. 417, para. 3, and also the Guards at the Powder Magazine, RADERTHAL. Arrangements re relief of Guards to be made direct between Battalions concerned.

5. Relief of Guards will be reported to this Office.

6. ACKNOWLEDGE.

Issued at..11.00 hrs...........

Major,
Brigade Major, 3rd Midland Brigade.

19-4-1919.

Copy to all Recipients of 3rd Midland Brigade Order No. 417.

SECRET. Appendix No 2 Copy No.....15.....

3rd Midland Brigade.
~~Operation~~ Order No. 417.

1. The 52nd Sherwood Foresters will move from MARIENBURG BARRACKS, MARIENBURG, on 21st April, 1919, by March Route to billets in BRUHL.

2. The Barracks at MARIENBURG will be taken over by the 53rd Northumberland Fusiliers.

3. Guards as under will be relieved by 53rd Northumberland Fusiliers on 20th April, 1919 :-

Fort VII.	-	1 Platoon with Lewis Gun (not less than 2 Officers and 25 O.R.)
Arsenal, COLOGNE.		- do -
VORGEBIRGS STRASSE, COLOGNE.	-	2 N.C.Os. and 8 Men.
BANHOF, BONN TOR, COLOGNE.	-	-do-
VOLKSGARTEN.	-	-do-
E.F.C. Dump, COLOGNE.	-	-do-
Triangle, BONNER STRASSE COBLENTZER STRASSE, COLOGNE.		-do-
Arsenal - Fort VII.		Working Party - 1 Officer 30 O.R.

4. All arrangements re relief of Guards and Barracks to be made direct between 52nd Sherwood Foresters and 53rd Northumberland Fusiliers.

5. The relief of the Guard of 51st Sherwood Foresters in the Powder Magazine is not yet settled.

6. All orders as regards the Guards will be handed over together with such information as regards stores on charge as is available.

7. Billeting Parties will report to Town Major, BRUHL on Saturday 19th April, 1919.

8. ACKNOWLEDGE.

Issued at..23-30 hrs.......

Major,
17-4-1919. Brigade Major, 3rd Midland Brigade.

DISTRIBUTION.

Copy No. 1. Brig.Genl. Commdg.
2. Brigade Major.
3. Staff Captain.
4. Bde. Signal Officer.
5. Civil Staff Captain.
6. 51st Sherwood Foresters.
7. 52nd Sherwood Foresters.
8. 53rd Sherwood Foresters.

Copy No. 9. 3rd Midland T.M. Battery.
10. No. 3 Coy. Train.
11. 17th Field Ambulance.
12. Midland Division "G".
13. " " "Q".
14. 1st Bde., Northern Div.
15. War Diary (2).
16. File.

W A R D A I R Y. APPENDIX 3.

Miscellaneous.

Capt, Brevt. Major A.Weyman, MC.	Took over duties of Brigade Major vice Capt.J.Tamblyn, MC,East Surrey Regt, A/B.M. 1.4.19.
Brig-Genl.P.W.Brown, CMG,DSO.	To 1/4 Gordons 11.4.19.
Capt.J.Tamblyn, MC. East Surrey Regt.	On leave to U.K. 11.4.19.
Lieut.J.C.Rowbottom, MC.	Demobilized, 15.4.19.
Capt.D.McCallum, MC.	Took over duties of Staff Capt. vice Capt.G.W.N.Barefoot, MC. R.I.Fusileers. 15.4.19.
Capt.G.W.N.Barefoot, MC. R.I.Fusileers.	To 1X Corps A/D.A.A.G. 28.4.19.

@@@@@@@@@@@@@@@@@@@@@@@@@@@@@@@@@

3rd Midland Brigade.

ROLL OF OFFICERS. APPENDIX No.4.

Brigadier-General P.C.B.SKINNER,C.M.G.,D.S.O.	Brigade Commander.
Major A. WEYMAN, M.C.	Brigade Major.
Captain D. McCALLUM, M.C.	Staff Captain.
Captain C.F.LAMPARD.	Brigade Education Officer.

ATTACHED.

Captain J.F.TAMBLYN, M.C.(East Surrey Regt.)	Late A/Brigade Major (On Leave).
Lieutenant J.V.TAILBY, M.C.(Leicester Regt.)	Brigade Lewis Gun Officer.
Lieutenant H. COY. (Leicestershire Regt.)	Civil Staff Captain.
Lieutenant C. MORGAN. (Royal Engineers.)	Brigade Signal Officer.
Lieutenant R. WATSON, M.C. (Sherwood Foresters)	Relief for B.L.G.Officer.

@@@@@@@@@@@@@@@@@@@@@@@@@@@@@@@

Appendix No 5.

SPECIAL ORDER OF THE DAY.

Now that the demobilization of the greater part of the British Expeditionary Force and the reforming of our Peace Garrisons at home and abroad necessitates the ~~making~~ breaking up of the 71st Infantry Brigade (commencing to-morrow), I desire to place on record my very high appreciation of the services of All Ranks from the highest to the lowest and to thank all from the bottom of my heart for their unfailing support, cheerful endurance of hardship and marked devotion to duty on every occasion.

I have now had the honour and pleasure of Commanding the Brigade for 19 months and during that period we have had our share of hard knocks. The Milestones of the period were the victorious attack at CAMBRAI on 20th November, 1917, followed 10 days later by the Enemy's Counter-attack, when the steadiness of the Brigade North of MARCOING (all troops on their right having temporarily been driven back) was most marked: the Enemy's Offensive on March 21st and 22nd, 1918, when the Brigade suffered such heavy casualties, but maintained its position in the Corps line until relieved in the evening of the latter date: the Enemy's Offensive against the Channel Ports in April, 1918, when the Brigade, composed mainly of new drafts, fought with its usual gallantry South of MONT KEMMEL, earning the special thanks of the Commander of the Division to which it was attached: and lastly the victorious advance from September 18th to October 30th which resulted in the Enemy suing for an Armistice.

Between these different dates were the discomforts and hardships of the seemingly never-ending Trench Warfare, demanding almost as high a standard of Valour and Determination as the more active phases.

We all deplore the loss of many gallant friends, who so worthily upheld the fine traditions of their Regiments and who will never be forgotten. Those who are left may with certainty look back with pride in years to come on the part they played in the 71st Infantry Brigade.

Once again I thank you for the support and help you have at all times given me and, whatever the future may hold for you, I wish you all the very best of luck - Goodbye and God Speed.

Brigadier-General,
Commanding 71st Infantry Brigade.

10-3-1919.

CONFIDENTIAL.

Headquarters "A",
Midland Division.

Herewith War Diary of Headquarters of 3rd Midland Brigade for the month of May, 1919.

Please acknowledge.

Brigadier-General.
Commanding 3rd Midland Brigade.

2/6/19.

Headquarters, 3rd Midland Brigade.

Original Copy

Army Form C. 2118.

WAR DIARY
or
~~INTELLIGENCE SUMMARY~~.

(Erase heading not required.)

Instructions regarding War Diaries and Intelligence Summaries are contained in F. S. Regs., Part II. and the Staff Manual respectively. Title pages will be prepared in manuscript.

Page 1. May, 1919.

Place	Date	Hour	Summary of Events and Information	Remarks and references to Appendices
MARIENBURG	1		Training and Education. Location of Units of the Brigade is as under:- Bde. Headquarters - KASTANIEN ALLEE, MARIENBURG. 51st Sherwood Foresters - RODENKIRCHEN. 52ns Sherwood Foresters - BRUHL. 53rd Sherwood Foresters - SURTH. 3rd Midland T.M.Battery - RODENKIRCHEN.	
	2		Training and Education.	
	3		Training and Education.	
	5.		The Commander in Chief, British Army of the Rhine (General Sir W. Robertson, K.C.B.,K.C.M.G., D.S.O., A.D.C.) inspected 51st and 53rd Sherwood Forestrs at SURTH. Battalions marched past in column or route after the inspection. The Commander in Chief was very pleased indeed with the steadiness on parade and turn out of troops and transport and announced his intention of inspecting 52nd Sherwood Foresters at an early date. The Corps and Divisional Commanders were also present.	
	6		The Brigadier General Commanding visited the 52nd Sherwood Foresters at BRUHL, inspected one company organised in accordance with O.B. 1919, also visited the Ranges.	
	7		Training and Education for all Units.	
	8		Training and Education for all Units. Lieut.J.V.Tailby, M.C., 1st Leicestershire Regt.attached Bde.H.Qs. as Brigade Lewis Gun Officer left for England to be Demobilized. 3rd Midland Brigade No.G.5866 (Provisional Defence Scheme in the event of Civil Dusturbance) ISSUED.	APPENDIX No. 1.
	9		The Brigadier General Commanding inspected one company 51st Sherwood Foresters organised in accordance with O.B.1919, and then visited 53rd Sherwood Foresters.	
	10		Training and Education for all Units.	
	12		The Brigadier General Commanding and Lieut-Colonel W.B.Thornton, D.S.O. (Comdg. 51st Sherwood Foresters) went down to GEMUND to inspect the training areas which we are going to in June.	

(GEMUND/.........

D. D. & L., London, E.C. (A8004) Wt W1771/M2031 750,000 5/17 Sch. 52 Forms/C2118/14

Instructions regarding War Diaries and Intelligence Summaries are contained in F. S. Regs., Part II. and the Staff Manual respectively. Title pages will be prepared in manuscript.

Headquarters, 3rd Midland Brigade.

Army Form C. 2118.

Page 2

WAR DIARY

or

~~INTELLIGENCE SUMMARY~~. May, 1919.

(Erase heading not required.)

Place	Date	Hour	Summary of Events and Information	Remarks and references to Appendices
MARIENBURG			(GEMUND is about 35 miles South South West of COLOGNE.	
	12-14		All Units Training and Education. The first half of May has been very fine and warm, the 7th and 14th having been really hot. Training has been carried out three hours daily, especial attention being paid to Musketry. Each Battalion has two or three excellent minature ranges (30 yards). One hour a day Educational training has been compulsory. Recreational training has been carried out in the afternoons.	
	15		Training.	
	16		Marshal Foch visited the army area, coming down by river from COBLENTZ to BONN to COLOGNE. He left BONN at 0900 hours reaching COLOGNE at 1100 hours. His steamer the BISMARCK was escorted by the English and French Naval Flotillas (some 24 craft), also by three squadrons of aeroplanes. It was a glorious day and the scene was most spectacular. Troops in the vicinity of the Rhine lined the banks and cheered as the Marshal went by. 53rd Sherwood Foresters were just north of WEISS. 51st Sherwood Foresters at RODENKIRCHEN. 3rd Midland T.M.Battery at do. H.Qs, 3rd Midland Brigade at MARIENBURG.	
	17		About ~~7.30 hours~~ 720 [handwritten] all ranks went up the Rhine from BONN to COBLENTZ on a pleasure steamer.	
	19		Training and Recreation.	
	20		Training and Recreation. A most interesting lecture on the Fallacies of Bolshevism was given by Lieut-Colonel Wysham at BRUHL. Representatives of each Battalion were present.	
	21		The Brigadier General Commanding visited Trench Mortar training grounds to watch the Battery practice with dummy shells and went on to SURTH to inspect a company of 53rd Sherwood Foresters.	
		19.30	Warned that the Brigade may possibly have to move to LIBLAR, LECHINICH area in relief of 1st Midland Brigade. This will not take place before 23rd May and only then if the Germans refuse to sign the Peace Terms, in which case the army will move forward. Battalions warned.	

22 Brigadier/....

D. D. & L., London, E.C. (A8004) Wt W1771/M2031 750,000 5/17 Sch. 52 Forms/C2118/14

Headquarters, 3rd Midland Brigade.

Army Form C. 2118.

WAR DIARY
or
~~INTELLIGENCE SUMMARY~~.

Instructions regarding War Diaries and Intelligence Summaries are contained in F. S. Regs., Part II. and the Staff Manual respectively. Title pages will be prepared in manuscript.

Page 3

May, 1919.

(Erase heading not required.)

Place	Date	Hour	Summary of Events and Information	Remarks and references to Appendices
MARIENBURG.	22		Brigadier General Commanding, Brigade Major and Staff Captain visited 1st Midland Brigade H.Qs. at LECHINICH to discuss possible move. Defence Scheme in the event of Civil Disturbances issued. (G.5954).	APPENDIX No. 2.
		19.30	Warned to send a company 200 strong to ANTWERP on 23rd May for duty under Base Commandant. Owing to short notice, 51st Sherwood Foresters detailed to find the company.	
	23	17.30	100 men entrained EUSKIRCHEN for ANTWERP, remainder to follow on 28th May.	
	24		Training.	
	25		3rd Midland Brigade Order No.418 issued re move in case enemy does not sign the peace terms.	APPENDIX No. 3.
	18.25		The French X Army Horse Show at WIESBADEN. A few vacancies for Officers and Other Ranks were allotted to this Brigade and were eagerly filled.	
	25-27		The Brigadier General Commanding, Brigade Major and Lieut-Colonel F.G.Spring, D.S.O. visited the training area SCHEMIDTHEIM - BLANKENHEIMER - MARMEGEN to arrange billets in case camp is not ready for first week in June.	
	28		Training and Education. The remaining 100 Officers and men of 51st Sherwood Foresters for guards left for ANTWERP.	
	29		Training and Education. The Divisional Train held a Gymkhana at ROMERHOFF near LIBLAR. General Skinner and Colonel Milward rode in races as did several other officers of the Brigade, and a special train was provided to take troops over.	
	30		River trip up the Rhine from BONN to COBLENTZ. 600 went from this Brigade, lovely day and most enjoyable trip.	
	31		Lieut-Colonel H.M.Milward, D.S.O. 2nd in Command of 51st Sherwood Foresters left to take over command of 2/4th K.O.Y.L.I. in 1st Midland Brigade. Sir Harry Johnson was to lecture on AFRICA to this Brigade at 11.30 hours, but never turned up. Of the last five lectures by outside lecturers four have been cancelled at the last minute and in this case the lecturer never turned up.	

General/.....

Headquarters, 3rd Midland Brigade.

Army Form C. 2118.

Instructions regarding War Diaries and Intelligence Summaries are contained in F. S. Regs., Part II. and the Staff Manual respectively. Title pages will be prepared in manuscript.

WAR DIARY
or
~~INTELLIGENCE SUMMARY.~~

Page 4 May, 1919.

(*Erase heading not required.*)

Place	Date	Hour	Summary of Events and Information	Remarks and references to Appendices
			GENERAL REMARKS.	

Training.

The perfect weather throughout the month has been most helpful for training. Training has been devoted to Platoon and Section training, Musketry and Lewis Gun fire on the 30 yards ranges: (of which there are 8 in the Brigade) P.T. Gas Drill. The Brigade Signal Class which commenced on 5th May has done good work.

Education.

The Education work has on the whole greatly improved, but is still hampered through lack of instructors. Illiterate and backward men still receive special attention. Voluntary classes have been popular. Educational tours round the sights of COLOGNE organised by the Brigade have proved very popular.

Recreational Training.

Many matches have been played between various units and sports have been held.

Major.
Brigade Major, 3rd Midland Brigade.

D. D. & L., London, E.C.
(A8004) Wt W1771/M2031 750,000 5/17 Sch. 52 Forms/C2118/14

3rd Midland Brigade.

WAR DIARY FOR MONTH OF MAY, 1919.

List of APPENDICES.

No.1. 3rd Midland Brigade No.G.5866. Provisional Defence Scheme in the event of Civil Disturbance.
2. 3rd Midland Brigade No.G.5954. Defence Scheme in the event of Civil Disturbance.
3. 3rd Midland Brigade Order No.418.
4. Nominal Roll of Officers on Brigade Headquarters.
5. Ration Strength of Brigade on 31/5/19.

****

Appendix I.

HEADQUARTERS
No. 95866
Ortr.
71st INFANTRY BRIGADE

S E C R E T.

Ref.
GERMANY.
1/100000
Sheet 8L.

3rd Midland Brigade.

Provisional Defence Scheme in the event of Civil Disturbance.

1. The Brigade will be responsible for:-

(a) Local defence of the Brigade Area.
(b) Special protection of BRUHL with its railway bridges and of the main roads leading from it, as far as the Brigade boundaries.
(c) Maintainance of order in the mining areas VOCHEM - KIERBURG - GLUCK - ECKDORF.
(d) Defence of the Army Ammunition Dump at VOCHEM.
(e) Protection of 17th Field Ambulance at BERZDORF and No.3 Coy., Divisional Train at PINGSDORF.
(f) Safety of the Railway Bridges at WEILERSWIST (in the event of disturbances on a large scale.)

2. In the case of disturbances outside the Divisional Area, the Brigade may be required to assist the VI Corps in quelling disturbances in COLOGNE and towards KENDENICH and HURTH.

3. In the event of civil disturbance arising, the following general action will be taken.

(i) <u>52nd Sherwood Foresters.</u>

(a) The guard at the VOCHEM Army ammunition Dump will be reinforced by the remainder of the company, and all measures taken for the defence of the Dump.

(b) The company detailed for the defence of the Railway Bridges at BRUHL will take up its dispositions in accordance with the scheme prepared.

(c) One company will be detailed to maintain order in the ECKDORF - BADORF - PINGSDORF villages and mines, and in the GLUCK mine.

(d) One company (less one platoon) will maintain order in VOCHEM - KIERBURG and the KIERBURG mine.

(e) One platoon will be sent to No.17 Field Ambulance for its defence.

(f) Troops engaged in maintaining order in outlying villages and mines will picquet and patrol the roads from BRUHL.

<u>NOTE.</u> - The 1st Midland Brigade are responsible for the protection of the LIBLAR - BRUHL road, as far as the LIBLAR - KIERBURG railway inclusive, and for the mining areas, and mines alongside this railway from LIBLAR to HEIDE inclusive.

(g) Battalion Headquarters will be devoted to the preservation of order within BRUHL itself, and in this the personnel at Divisional headquarters, who will be organised by the Camp Commandant, will assist. Divisional Headquarters personnel, as soon as organised will report to, and come under the orders of the O.C. 52nd Sherwood Foresters.

(ii) <u>53rd Sherwood Foresters.</u>

(a) Will complete the guard at the Chemical Factory at RODENKIRCHEN up to the strength of one platoon under an officer.

(b) Will despatch one platoon to GODORF to picquet, and patrol the road to COLOGNE, and to BRUHL so far as No.17 Field Ambulance.

(c) Will hold two companies in immediate readiness, to reinforce or relieve 52nd Sherwood Foresters, in the BRUHL area.

(iii) 51st Sherwood Foresters.

The battalion will be held in immediate readiness to move as required, and will complete the Guard at Brigade Headquarters up to the strength of one platoon under an officer.

(iv) 3rd Midland Trench Mortar Battery.

Will hold a mobile section of 4 Mortars with ammunition, ready to move as required.

(v) Brigade Headquarters.

Until the development of the situation in any direction necessitates a move, will remain at its present Headquarters.

4. The 500th Field Company R.E. and one company 11th Leicestershire Regiment (Pioneers) at WEILERSWIST unless withdrawn for special reasons by Divisional Headquarters, will come under the orders of the 3rd Midland Brigade; the defence of the Railway Bridges at WEILERSWIST and the maintainance of order and communications in the WEILERSWIST area, under the senior officer on the spot, are allotted to the above troops.

5. In the event of the troops referred to in para 4. being withdrawn by Divisional Headquarters it may be necessary for the O.C. 52nd Sherwood Foresters to despatch a company to WEILERSWIST, this company being replaced in the BRUHL area by a company of the 53rd Sherwood Foresters from SURTH.

6. Should the situation demand it, the heavy kit and surplus stores of all units will be transferred to a Brigade depot in BRUHL. This depot will be at the SEMINARY.

On receipt of the message from Brigade Headquarters "Civil disturbance. Get ready" the following measures will be taken:

(i) All troops at training, on working parties, or at games, will be recalled to billets.

All individual officers and other ranks who may be away from their quarters, on becoming aware that disturbances are impending, through the sounding of the "Alarm" by buglers, or other means, will return at once to their units.

(ii) Units will be prepared to move at twenty minutes notice. Dress "Marching Order".

(iii) An additional 50 rounds S.A.A. per man will be held ready to issue to the troops immediately they parade. Water bottles will be filled.

(iv) Lewis Guns and S.A.A. Limbers and G.S. Wagons will be packed, and cookers will be held in readiness.

Animals will be harnessed but not hooked in, and transport will be ready to move in twenty minutes.

(v) Surplus stores and heavy kit will be packed up ready to transfer to the Brigade Depot.

(vi) Battalions will each detail a guard of one officer, two N.C.O.s and 12 rank and file for duty at the Brigade Depot., and a party to remain at the Depot, to include the following:-

Quarter Master and Quartermaster's personnel.
Regimental Tradesmen.
Orderly Room Staff.
3 Signallers.
6 Runners and despatch riders.
6 Rank and File for general duties.
2 Cooks.

Brigade Headquarters and Trench Mortar Battery in proportion.

The O.C. 52nd Sherwood Foresters will detail an experienced officer to command the whole party left at the Brigade Depot.

(vii) Visual Signal Stations ensuring communication between each unit and Brigade Headquarters will be manned until the unit moves off, or permission is given to dismiss.

9. ......

8. On receipt of the message from Brigade Headquarters "Civil Disturbance. Take action" ;
(i) The various guards and detachments referred to in para.8 above ~~para. 3a~~, will move as soon as possible to their posts, after the additional 50 rounds S.A.A. per man has been issued.
(ii) Units and portions of units not detailed for any definite task will remain standing by, pending the receipt of orders from Brigade Headquarters.

9. If, owing to absence of any warning of impending disturbance, no "Get ready" message is sent, units will act as soon as possible on the receipt of the "Take action" message; and C.O.s will take measures on the spot in the event of a disturbance breaking out before any message has been received, reporting steps taken to Brigade Headquarters.

10. "D" Coy. (8 Guns), 8th Battalion Machine Gun Corps may be available to assist in this Brigade Area.
On arrival it will be billeted in the village of MELCHENICH and half the company (4 Guns) will probably be allotted to the O.C. 52nd Sherwood Foresters, for the defence of the BRUHL bridges, and VOCHEM Ammunition Dump.

11. Artillery, if available, will be accommodated in the outskirts of BRUHL or in the village of RONDORF.

12. Whilst engaged in supressing disturbances, troops will parade always with fixed bayonets.
Fire will be controlled, and if an officer is present, will only be opened on the orders of that officer.
Fire, if opened, is to be effective.

[Signature]
Major,
8/3/1919. Brigade Major, 3rd Midland Brigade.

Distribution:-
Brigadier-General Commanding.
Brigade Major.
Staff Captain.
Civil Staff Captain.
Brigade Signal Officer.
51st Sherwood Foresters.
52nd Sherwood Foresters.
53rd Sherwood Foresters.
3rd Midland T.M.Battery.
17th Field Ambulance.
No.3. Coy. Divl. Train.
Midland Division. "G".
Midland Division Camp Commandant.
C.R.A.
8th Bn. M.G.C.
11th Leicestershire Regt.
509th Field Company. R.E.

Appendix No 2

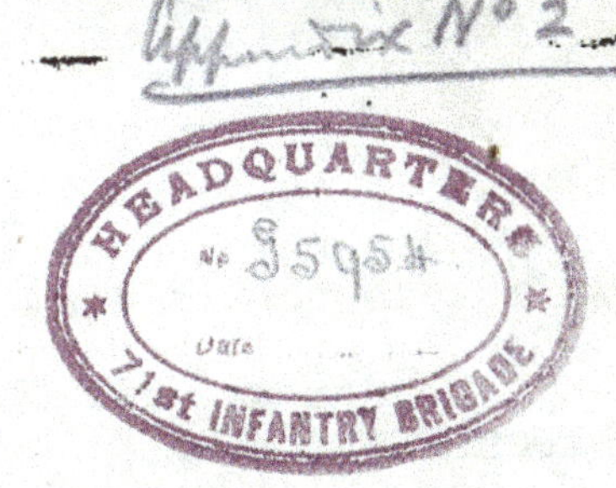

S E C R E T.

3rd Midland Brigade.

Reference
GERMANY
1/100000
Sheet 8 L.

Defence Scheme in the event of Civil Disturbance.

1. The Contingencies to be guarded against are:-

(a) Local Industrial riots, or anti-British demonstrations.
(b) An organised rising by the inhabitants against the British throughout the whole Area of Occupation.

It is possible that previous warning, if any, of these events may be very short.

2. In the case of (a).
Immediate action will be taken:-
A. By the troops within the disturbed Area:-
(i) To safeguard points of Special importance, such as the Railway Bridges at BRUHL, the Army Ammunition Dump at VOCHEM, etc.
(ii) To suppress the disturbance.

B. By the troops outside the disturbed Area.
(iii) To isolate the Area of disturbance.
(iv) To hold themselves in readiness to suppress sympathetic riots within their own Area, and to be ready to reinforce troops in the disturbed area.

In the case of (b) Immediate action will be taken to
(i) Safeguard points of special importance
(ii) To keep open certain avenues of Communication; So far as they lie within the Divisional Area, as follows:-

(a) The DUREN-EUSKIRCHEN Railway.
(b) The EUSKIRCHEN-BRUHL-COLOGNE-Railway.
(c) The BONN-COLOGNE-Railway.
(d) The DUREN-EUSKIRCHEN Road.
(e) The EUSKIRCHEN-BRUHL Road.
(f) The ZULPICH-BRUHL-COLOGNE Road.
(g) The BONN-COLOGNE Road.

3. In the event of trouble either under (a) or (b) Battalions will be responsible respectively for the maintainance of order, and of Communication within the area shown on attached map.

The village and industrial Areas of RODENKIRCHEN,-RONDORF-MESCHENICH and IMMENDORF being inclusive to the 51st Sherwood Foresters.

Those of SURTH-WEISS-GODORF and BERZDORF to the 53rd Sherwood Foresters (less one Company).

And the remainder of the Brigade Area to the 52nd Sherwood Foresters, reinforced by one Company of the 53rd Sherwood Foresters.

4. The 1st Midland Brigade are responsible for the protection of the LIBLAR-BRUHL Road, so far as the LIBLAR-KIERBURG Railway inclusive, and for the mining areas, and mines alongside this Railway from LIBLAR to HEIDE inclusive.

5. In the event of disturbance either under (a) or (b) in para 1 above the following Special Steps will be taken.

(i) <u>52nd Sherwood Foresters.</u>
(a) The Guard at the VOCHEM Army Ammunition Dump will be reinforced by the remainder of the Company, and all measures taken for the defence of the Dump

(b)-----------

(b) The Company detailed for the defence of the Railway Bridges at BRUHL will take up its dispositions in accordance with the Scheme proposed.

(c) One Company will be ~~taken~~ detailed to maintain order in the ECKDORF-BADORF-PINGSDORF villages and mines, and in the GLUCK mine.

(d) One Company (less one Platoon) will maintain order in VOCHEM-Kierburg and the KIERBURG Mine.

(e) One Platoon will be sent to No.17 Field Ambulance for its defence.

(f) A party will be detailed to maintain order within the Town of BRUHL itself, in this the personnel at Divisional Headquarters, who will be organised by the Camp Commandant will assist. Divisional Headquarters personnel, so soon as organised, will report to, and come under the orders of the Officer Commanding 52nd Sherwood Foresters.

(ii) 53rd Sherwood Foresters.

(a) Will complete the guard at the Chemical Factory at RODENKIRCHEN up to the strength of one Platoon under an Officer.

(b) Will detail one Company to relieve immediately the Company of the 52nd Sherwood Foresters referred to in (d) and (e) of (i) above. This latter Company when relieved will be at the disposal of the Officer Commanding 52nd Sherwood Foresters for use as required.

(c) Will detail one Company, complete with transport, as a mobile column ready to proceed wherever required.

(III) 51st Sherwood Foresters.

(a) Will complete the Guard at Brigade Headquarters up to the strength of one Platoon under an Officer.

(b) Will hold Two Companies complete with transport, in immediate readiness, to move as mobile Column wherever required.

(iv) 3rd Midland Trench Mortar Battery.

Will hold a Mobile Section of 4 Mortars ready to move as required.

(v) 3rd Midland Brigade Headquarters.

Until the development of the Situation necessitates a move, will remain at its present Headquarters.

6\. In addition to the above measures, Officers Commanding Battalions will

(a) Patrol the Communications referred to in para 3 above, and guard all bridges, railway crossings on main roads, etc, within their respective areas.

(b) Arrange for the defence of essential billets, and for stores to be collected in a central spot if necessary, within the Battalion Area, under guard.

(c) Select a place in which Prisoners Rioters, etc, can conveniently be confined and guarded.

(d) Arrange Alarm Posts beforehand for all troops.

(e) In accordance with the Situation, detail an inlying Picquet ready to support any threatened point.

7\. The above instructions assume a situation in which Battalions will remain within their own Areas, or at least within the Brigade Area, but the Brigade may be required to be concentrated, or to move out of its Area, in which case all Surplus Kit and heavy stores of Units will be collected at Brigade Depot at the Seminary BRUHL.

3.----------------

8. In the event of the concentration of heavy stores at a Brigade Depot each Battalion will detail a guard of one Officer, two N.C.Os. and 12 Rank and File for duty at the Depot and a party to remain there to include the following:-

Quartermaster and Quartermaster's Personnel.
Regimental Tradesmen.
Orderly Room Staff.
5 Signallers.
6 Runners and Dispatch Riders.
6 Rank and File for General Duties.
2 Cooks.
Brigade Headquarters and Trench Mortar Battery in proportion.

The Officer Commanding 52nd Sherwood Foresters will detail an experienced Officer to Command the whole party left at the Brigade Depot.

9. In the event of the Brigade having to move out of its own Area it may be required to operate with one or more Battalions in COLOGNE (South)

10. Normal precautions to be taken to ensure the success of the Defence Scheme are

(a) That Battalions reconnitre their areas, know all bridges and points to be defended, and make arrangements beforehand for their defence.
(b) That all Ranks know what to do, and where to go on the Alarm being given, and that they are practised in manning their Alarm Posts.
(c) That S.A.A. Grenades, etc, are kept under guard, and that rifles in billets are properly protected.
(d) That wireless, visual and pigeon communications are fixed beforehand and capable of being quickly manned on the Alarm being given, or a Precautionary Period being ordered.
(e) That escorts for Ration wagons to and from refilling point are arranged for.

11. The following Signal will be used to give the Alarm.

(i) Bugles will sound the "Alarm"; this call will be taken up by all buglers within hearing.
(ii) Strombus Horns will be sounded, and Maroons, if available, fired.
(iii) Units will be warned by Telephone visual signals, mounted orderly or Runner.
(iv) The following Light Signals will be used:-

Red Verey Lights	------	Alarm.
Green " "	------	S.O.S.
White " "	------ -	Answering Signal.

The S.O.S. Signal will be used by any detachment or Post to show that help is required.

12. On receipt of the message from Brigade Headquarters "Civil Disturbance. Get Ready" the Following ~~precautions will~~ measures will be taken:

(i) All troops at Training, on Working parties, or at games, will be recalled to billets.

All individual Officers and other Ranks who may be away from their quarters, on becoming aware that disturbances are pending, through the sounding of the "Alarm" by buglers, or other means, will return at once to their Units

(ii) Units will be prepared to move at twenty minutes notice. Dress "Marching Order"

(iii) An additional 50 rounds S.A.A. per man will be held ready to issue to the troops immediately they Parade. Water bottles will be filled.

(iv) Lewis Guns and S.A.A. Limbers, G.S. Wagons will be packed and Cooker will be held in readiness.

Animals will be harnessed but not hooked in, and transport will be ready to move in twenty minutes.

(v) Surplus stores and heavy kit will be packed up ready to transfer to the Brigade Depot.

(vi) Visual Signal Stations ensuring communication between each unit and Brigade Headquarters will be manned until the Unit moves off, or permission is given to dismiss.

13---------------

13. On receipt of the message from Brigade Headquarters " Civil Disturbance. Take action." ;

(i) The various guards and detachments referred to in para 3 above will move as soon as possible to their posts, after the additional 50 rounds S.A.A. per man has been issued.

(ii) Units and portions of Units not detailed for any definite task will remain standing by, pending the receipt of orders from Brigade Headquarters.

14. If, owing to absence of any warning of impending disturbance, no "Get Ready" message is sent, Units will act so soon as possible on the receipt of the "Take Action" message; and Commanding Officers will take measures on the spot in the event of a Disturbance breaking out before any message has been received, reporting steps taken to Brigade Headquarters.

15. The 509th Field Company R.E. and one Company 11th Leicestershire Regiment (Pioneers) at WEILERWIST unless withdrawn for special reasons by Divisional Headquarters, will come under the orders of the 3rd Midland Brigade; The defence of the Railway bridges at WEILERWIST and the maintainance of order and Communications in the WEILERWIST area, under the Senior Officer on the spot, are alloted to the above Troops.

16. In the event of the troops referred to in para 15 being withdrawn by Divisional Headquarters it may be necessary for the Officer Commanding 52nd Sherwood Foresters to dispatch a Company to WEILERWIST, this company being replaced in the BRUHL area if required by a Company of the 53rd Sherwood Foresters from SURTH.

17. "D" Company (8guns), 6th Battalion Machine Gun Corps may be available to assist in this Brigade Area.

On arrival it will be billeted in the village of MESCHENICH and half the Company (4 Guns) will probably be alloted to the Officer Commanding 52nd Sherwood Foresters, for the defence of the BRUHL bridges, and VOCHEM Ammunition Dump.

18. Artillery, if available, will be accomadated in the outskirts of BRUHL or in the village or RONDORF.

19. Whilst engaged in suppressing disturbances, troops will parade always with fixed bayonets.

Fire will be controlled, and if an Officer is present, will only be opened on the orders of that Officer.

Fire, if opened, is to be effective.

A. Weyman
Major.
Brigade Major, 3rd Midland Brigade.

22nd May 1919.

Distribution:-
- Brigadier General Commanding.
- Brigade Major. ✓
- Staff Captain.
- Civil Staff Captain.
- Brigade Signal Officer.
- 51st Sherwood Foresters.
- 52nd Sherwood Foresters.
- 53rd Sherwood Foresters.
- 3rd Midland T.M. Battery.
- 17th Field Ambulance.
- No.3 Coy. Divl. Train
- Midland Division "G"
- Midland Division Camp Commandant.
- C.R.A.
- 6th Bn. M.G.C.
- 11th Bn. Leicestershire Regt.
- 509th Field Company.

Reference para 3 Maps referred to issued to Battalions only.

Appendix 3

SECRET.
Ref.Sheet 59.

3rd Midland Brigade Order No.418 dated 25/5/1919.

1. If the peace negotiations fail notice of the termination of the Armistice in 72 hours will be given to the Germans. The Day on which the Armistice ceases will be called J Day. On that Day the three leading British Corps advance into neutral territory.

2. In this event 3rd Midland Brigade will move to 1st Midland Brigade area in accordance with attached ~~time~~ move table.

3. The object of the move of the Midland Division is to guard the communication by road, and railway along the WEISWEILER - DUREN - COLOGNE line.

4. On completion of the move the Brigadier General Commanding 3rd Midland Brigade will administer the present 1st and 3rd Midland Brigade areas.

5. In notifying J day by telegram to all concerned the following code will be used.

26 May - B
27 May - C
28 May - D
29 May - E
30 May - F
31 May - G
1 June - H
2 June - I
3 June - J

etc. etc.

Thus if J day were to be 1st June the following telegram would be sent in clear to all concerned " Reference 3rd Mid. Bde. No. 418 dated 25th May J day will be H".

6. 3rd Midland Brigade will be responsible for the administration and rationing of the affiliated battery R.F.A., and also "D" Coy. Machine Gun Battalion from the date on which they join 3rd Midland Brigade.group.

7. Each battalion will leave a guard of not less than one platoon to guard surplus kit.

8. Advanced parties will be sent on one day ahead to arrange for billets.

9. Distances on the line of march will be maintained in accordance with "Notes on March Discipline 'A' " (this office G5969 dated 24/5/1919.)

10. Administrative arrangements are being issued to units of 3rd Midland Brigade.

11. Acknowledge.

[signature]

Major,
Brigade Major, 3rd Midland Brigade.

25/5/1919.

Distribution:-

Brigadier General Commanding.
Brigade Major.
Staff Captain.
Signal Officer.
Civil Staff Captain.
51st Sherwood Foresters.
52nd Sherwood Foresters.
53rd Sherwood Foresters.
3rd Midland T.M.Battery.
509th Field Coy. R.E.
18th Field Ambulance.
No.3 Coy. Divl. Train.

Midland Division. G.
" " Q.
1st Midland Brigade.
C.R.A. Midland Division.
C.R.E. " "
A.D.M.S. " "
D.A.P.M. " "
War

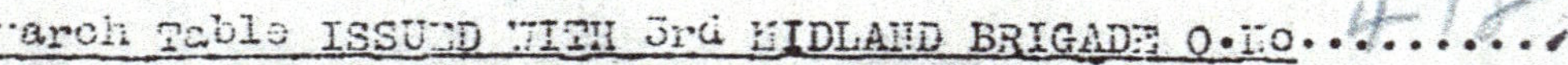

March Table ISSUED WITH 3rd MIDLAND BRIGADE O.No. 4.18

Date.	Unit.	From	To.	Remarks.
J.- 2 Day.	3rd Midland Brigade Headquarters.	MARIENBURG	LECHENICH.	
J - 2 Day	3rd Midland T.M.Battery.	RODENKIRCHEN	BRUHL.	
J - 2 Day	51st Sherwood Foresters.	RODENKIRCHEN	BRUHL.	
J - 1 Day	51st Sherwood Foresters.	BRUHL	LECHENICH	To be clear of BRUHL by 08.00 hours.
J - 1 Day	53rd Sherwood Foresters.	SURTH.	LIBLAR	Not to enter BRUHL before 08.30 hours.
J - 1 Day	D Coy.Machine Gun Bn.	ERP.	GYMNICH	To march via HERRIG. No restriction as to time.
J - 1 Day	1 Section 18th Field Ambulance.	BERZDORF.	BLESSEM	Not to enter BRUHL before 09.00 hours.
J - 2 Day	No.3 Coy.Train.	BRUHL.	ARHEM.	As may be necessary.

52nd Sherwood Foresters
1 Battery R.F.A. (to be detailed by G.O.C. R.A.)
509 Field Coy. R.E.

Will remain in present billets.

3rd Mid. Bde. No.3999.

Administrative Instructions issued in connection with 3rd Midland Brigade Order No. ~~120~~ 418 dated 25th May 1919.

---

1. SURPLUS BAGGAGE. Each unit will be provided with the following Motor Lorries to assist in carrying out the move.

Brigade Headquarters 2 Motor Lorries (to include L.T.M.B.?

Infantry Battalions 3 Motor Lorries.

This Transport will not be sufficient to move all surplus baggage etc. belonging to units. Arrangements will, therfore, be made for a store in each unit area, and surplus baggage etc. will be collected later as far as possible. Those surplus stores will be concentrated to avoid unnecessary guards. Each battalion will leave one platoon to guard the dump. All guards will be issued with three full days rations.

2. TRANSPORT - TRENCH MORTAR BATTERIES. The G.S. Limbers belonging to the D.A.C. will remain with the 3rd Midland T.M.Battery.

3. AMMUNITION. All units will move with full echelons.

4. SUPPLIES. The normal system of supplies will be taken into use the day the move commences. Divisional Railhead and the new refilling point will be notified later.

5. DIVISIONAL TRAIN. Each Infantry Btigade will be accompanied by its own Brigade Company of the Train, sufficient supply wagons being attached to each Brigade Company to carry rations for Artillery Battery affiliated to the Brigade.

6. CIVIL STAFF CAPTAINS AND P.R.O. 3rd Midland Brigade Sub-area Civil Staff Captain will remain with 3rd Midland Brigade. P.R.O. from 2nd Midland Brigade is being attached temporarily for duty to 3rd Midland Brigade.

7. DIVISIONAL RECEPTION CAMP will be prepared to move to DUREN.

8. D.A.D.O.S. will probably move to DUREN.

9. DIVISIONAL CANTEEN and the "FANCIES" are remaining in their present site pending further orders.

10. DIVISIONAL HOSTEL COLOGNE. is remaining in present site.

11. DIVISIONAL EMPLOYMENT COMPANY. will probably move to KREUZEAN.

[signature]
Major,
Brigade Major, 3rd Midland Brigade.

25/5/1919.

Distribution:-

Brigadier General Commanding.
Brigade Major.
Staff Captain.
Brigade Signal Officer.
51st Sherwood Foresters.
52nd Sherwood Foresters.
53rd Sherwood Foresters.
3rd Midland T.M.Battery.
No.3 Coy. Div. Train.

SECRET.

Reference
Sheet 59.

1. Reference march table attached to 3rd Midland Brigade Order No.418 dated 25/5/19. line 6 (unit D.Coy. Machine Gun Battalion) for "J-I day" read "J.day".

2. Acknowledge.

L.R. Watson Lieut
Capt.

26.5.19. for Brigade Major.3rd.Midland Brigade.

Distribution.

Brigadier General Commanding.
Brigade Major.
Staff Captain.
Brigade Signal Officer.
Civil Staff Captain.
Midland Division"G".
Midland Division"Q"
1st.Midland Brigade.
6th.Bn. Machine Gun Corps.
D.Coy.6th.Machine Gun.Corps.

SECRET.
******

Addendum No. 2 to 3rd Midland Brigade Order No. 418 dated 25th May 1919.

The following instructions are issued in continuation of Administrative Instructions issued in connection with 3rd Midland Brigade Order No. 418 dated 25th May 1919.

1. AMMUNITION.

(a) Dumps. R.A.Ammunition, S.A.A., Grenades etc. are established at
VOCHEM
LONGERICH.

(b) Units will demand by wire to reach this office by 1200 daily.

2. SUPPLIES.

(a) Iron Rations have been drawn by units. These will be issued to every officer and man on receipt of wire notifying J day.

(b) Railhead. will move to DUREN.

(c) REFILLING POINT for
R.A.
Mob. Vet. Section.
3rd Midland Brigade Group.
} ROHERHOFF.

(d) Petrol Tins. will be made up to normal establishment forthwith.

3. TRAFFIC CONTROL.

The present system of Military Police Patrol in the Corps Area will continue. Whenever weather permits, cross country tracks will be used by Horse Transport and Infantry. All units will take steps to ensure that when halted, columns are clear of the road, and transport halted as close to the near side of the road as possible.

4. CASUALTIES - RETURN "A". Battalions which have suffered 50 casualties or more, and machine gun battalions 25 casualties or more, will wire the approximate casualties to ~~Division~~ Brigade by 0800 hours daily. If at least 50 more casualties have occured in the battalion, or at least 25 in the Machine Gun Battalion, during the night, a fresh wire will be sent next morning. Casualties will be reported by phases, commencement of the phase will be notified from Division Headquarters. Daily Casualty wire will include numbers already reported since the commencement of the phase, and will begin with the following words:- "Estimated casualties from (here insert date of cammencement of phase)."

RETURN "B" An accurate statement will be sent in giving the rank initials, and names of ~~the~~ officers and the date of the Officer's casualty. Also the number of other ranks, as soon as the information is is obtainable. If any General Officers, Staff Officers or Commanding Officers become a casualty, the fact will at once be reported by wire to Brigade H.Q. containing if possible, a brief statement of how the casualty occured.

5. MEDICAL ARRANGEMENTS. The division is vacating No.11 Stationary Hospital, DUREN, and No. 42 Stationary Hospital EUSKIRCHEN. A reserve of medical Stores is at No. 47 M.A.C. NORD HOTEL, EUSKIRCHEN.

6 PRISONERS OF WAR CAGE. Divisional Cage will be at KREUZAU, exact site will be notified later.

L. K. Watson Lieut.,
A/Staff Captain, 3rd Midland Brigade.

Distribution:-
Brigadier-General Commanding.
Brigade Major.
Staff Captain.
Brigade Signal Officer.
51st Sherwood Foresters.
"D" Coy. 6th M.G.C.
52nd Sherwood Foresters.
53rd Sherwood Foresters.
3rd Midland T.M.Battery.
No. 3. Coy. Div. Train.

3rd Midland Brigade.

ROLL OF OFFICERS.

APPENDIX No.4.

Brigadier-General P.C.B.SKINNER, C.M.G.,D.S.O.	Brigade Commander.
Captain (Bt.Major) A.WEYMAN, M.C.	Brigade Major.
Captain G.W.N.BAREFOOT, M.C.	Staff Captain.
Captain C.F.LAMPARD. (Norfolk Regt.)	Brigade Education Officer.

ATTACHED.

Lieut. C.MORGAN, (Royal Engineers)	Brigade Signal Officer.
Lieut. H.COY, (Leicestershire Regt.)	Civil Staff Captain.
Lieut. R.WATSON, M.C. (Sherwood Foresters)	Bde.Lewis Gun Officer.

8/5/19. Lieut.J.V.TAILBY, M.C.(Leicestershire Regt.) Demobilized.

****

APPENDIX No.5.

RATION STRENGTH OF 3rd MIDLAND BRIGADE ON 31/5/19.

	Officers.	Other Ranks.
Brigade Headquarters.	7.	154.
51st Sherwood Foresters.	33.	519.
52nd Sherwood Foresters,	29.	688.
53rd Sherwood Foresters.	40.	621.
3rd Midland T.M.Battery.	4.	29.

****

Headquarters, "A".,

Midland Division.

3rd Midland Brigade No.G. ~~21~~ 31.

Herewith War Diary for the month of June, 1919.

[signature]

Lieut-Colonel.
Commanding 3rd Midland Brigade.

3.7.19.

Instructions regarding War Diaries and Intelligence Summaries are contained in F. S. Regs., Part II. and the Staff Manual respectively. Title pages will be prepared in manuscript.

Headquarters, 3rd Midland Brigade.

Army Form C. 2118.

WAR DIARY
or
~~INTELLIGENCE SUMMARY.~~

Page 1. June, 1919.

(Erase heading not required.)

Place	Date	Hour	Summary of Events and Information	Remarks and references to Appendices
MARIENBURG	1		Brigade situated in billets as follows :- Bde. Headquarters MARIENBURG (Cologne) 51st Sherwood Foresters, RODENKIRCHEN 52nd Sherwood Foresters, BRUHL. 53rd Sherwood Foresters, SURTH. Brigade Signal School, FORT V111. 3rd Midland T.M.Battery, RODENKIRCHEN.	
	2		Training and Education.	
	3		General holiday except for the King's Birthday Parade. Bde. H.Qs, 51st & 53rd Sherwood Foresters 3rd Mid. T.M.B. and Bde. Signal School paraded on Golf Links COLOGNE 09.30 hours. 52nd Sherwood Foresters paraded at BRUHL.	
	4&5		Preparations for move to the Training Area. 3rd Midland Brigade Order 419 issued .	APPENDIX No.1.
	6		Training and Education. Southern Division Races at KALK, COLOGNE. A number of Officers and O.Rs. from the Brigade were present.	
	7		Brigade Major and Staff Captain made entraining arrangements at BRUHL re move to Training Areas.	
	8		All baggage loaded on lorries and entrained at BRUHL - roughly 150 tons of baggage allotted for.	
SCHMIDTHEIM	9		Brigade entrained at BRUHL at 10.00 hours and 12.00 hours for SCHMIDTHEIM X Training area arriving at SCHMIDTHEIM at 14.00 hours and 16.50 hours respectivily. Camp not quite ready but the Advanced Parties had done very good work on it. Lorries met trains at SCHMIDTHEIM and all baggage was got to Camp on the same evening.	X about 20 miles S.S.W. EUSKIRCHEN.
	10		The day was spent improving the Camp.	
	11		Training and Education.	
	12,13 & 14.		Platoon and Company Training, each Battalion having a different area daily. The country affords excellent facilities for training of all sorts. 51st and 53rd Sherwood Foresters held Sports in afternoon of 14th June. A sports meeting to consider arrangements re the "Efficiency Cup" vide this office No.G.6999.	APPENDIX No.2.

16/.......

D. D. & L., London, E.C. (A8004) Wt W1771/M2031 750,000 5/17 Sch. 52 Forms/C2118/14

Army Form C. 2118.

Headquarters, 3rd Midland Brigade.

WAR DIARY
or
~~INTELLIGENCE SUMMARY.~~

(*Erase heading not required.*)

Page 2. June, 1919.

Instructions regarding War Diaries and Intelligence Summaries are contained in F. S. Regs., Part II. and the Staff Manual respectively. Title pages will be prepared in manuscript.

Place	Date	Hour	Summary of Events and Information	Remarks and references to Appendices
SCHMIDTHEIM	16		3rd Midland Brigade Order No.420 issued for moves re "J" day, should J day occur while this Brigade is in Camp at SCHMIDTHEIM.	APPENDIX No.3.
	17	8.30 1130	Wire from Division that J day would be 20th June. Units warned. The Duke of Portland K.G. Lord Lieutenant of Nottinghamshire, and the GOC. Division visited the Brigade to see the Sherwood Foresters. The Battalions were formed up on three sides of a square, 51st Sherwoods on left, 52nd Sherwoods in centre and 53rd Sherwoods on right, and after inspection marched past by Companies. The Duke expressed his keen appreciation of the parade.	
	18	0430 1800	52nd Sherwood Foresters entrained at SCHMIDTHEIM for LIBLAR, destination BRUHL. The train arrived 1½ hours late at SCHMIDTHEIM. Bde. H.Qs. No 3 Coy Train and T.M.Battery entrained for LIBLAR arriving at 22.15 hours, there was also a great deal of baggage of 51st and 53rd Sherwoods on the train, so that the work of clearing the baggage from the station was not finished till about 05.00 19th inst, although the train was unloaded by 03.00 hours 19th June.	
LECHENICH	19	08.30 18.00	51st Sherwood Foresters entrained for LIBLAR. 53rd Sherwood Foresters entrained for LIBLAR. Location of Brigade group on completion of moves is as follows :- Bde. H.Qs.) 52nd Sherwood Foresters, BRUHL. No.3 Coy Train ARHEM (4) T.M.Battery.) LECHENICH (1) 53rd Sherwood Foresters, LIBLAR(2) 51st Sherwoods) B Sec. 18th Field Ambulance BLESSEM(3) attached in accordance with Midland Division Order No. 5. C/77 Bde.R.F.A. BORR (5) D Coy M.G.Batt., GYMNICH (6). Billets are good. All baggage except for Camp stores was brought up from SCHMIDTHEIM to Units billets. All moves were carried through without a hitch	Germany Sheet 1L. 1/100,000 (1) N.5. (2) O.5. (3) O.5. (4) N.5. (5) N.6. (6) N.4.
	20		"J" Day measures taken to protect railways and bridges in accordance with 3rd Mid. Bde.No.G. 7053. Brigadier-General Commanding visited BRUHL and inspected the arrangements for defence of the bridges at BRUHL, with the O.C. 52nd Sherwood Foresters.	APPENDIX No.4.
	21		Brigadier-General Commanding inspected arrangements for defence of LIBLAR-EUSKIRCHEN railway with O.C. 53rd Sherwood Foresters.	

22/......

D. D. & L., London, E.C.
(A8004) Wt W1771/M2031 750,000 5/17 Sch. 52 Forms/C2118/14

Headquarters, 3rd Midland Brigade.

Army Form C. 2118.

Instructions regarding War Diaries and Intelligence Summaries are contained in F. S. Regs., Part II. and the Staff Manual respectively. Title pages will be prepared in manuscript.

Page 3

WAR DIARY
~~or~~
~~INTELLIGENCE~~ SUMMARY.

June, 1919.

(*Erase heading not required.*)

Place	Date	Hour	Summary of Events and Information	Remarks and references to Appendices
LECHENICH	22) 23)		52nd and 53rd Sherwood Foresters finding railway guards in accordance with appendix No.4.	
	24		Midland Division Orders No.7 and No.8 received re moves of Division into area occupied previous to J - 3 day when peace is signed, and re moves of R.A. to practice camp for TRaining. 3rd Midland Brigade Order No.421 issued. Railway guards taken off.	APPENDIX No.5.
	25 26&27		Standing by for news that Peace has been signed.	
	28	16.00	News received that peace has been signed.	
		18.00	Guns on river front just North of HOHENZOLLERN Bridge, COLOGNE, fired a salute of 101 guns (2 batteries of Field Guns of London Division fired the salute). There was a big crowd and great enthuasiasm. Civilian population took little interest in the procedure though many came to look on.	
		19.30	Units notified that A day is 30th June. Units of this Brigade move to SCHMIDTHEIM Camp on B & C days. (1st and 2nd July.)	
	30		53rd Sherwood Foresters dumped baggage at the station preparatory to moving 06.00 hours 1st July D Coy. M.G. Battn. moved from GYMNICH to WEILER (7) and DISTERNICH (8)	Sheet 1L (7) N 6. (8) M 6.

Major,
Brigade Major, 3rd Midland Brigade.

D. D. & L., London, E.C. (A8004) Wt W1771/M2031 750,000 5/17 Sch. 52 Forms/C2118/14

3rdn Midland Brigade

WAR DIARY FOR MONTH OF JUNE, 1919.

List of Appendices.

No.1. 3rd Midland Brigade Order No.419.
2. Sports meeting re "Efficiency Cup" No.G.6999.
3. 3rd Midland Brigade Order No.420.
4. 3rd Midland Brigade No.7053 ref "J" day measures.
5. 3rd Midland Brigade Order No.421.
6. Nominal Roll of Officers on Brigade Headquarters.
7. Ration Strength of Brigade on 30/6/19.

@@@@@@@@@@@@@@@@@@@@@@@@@

Reference.
Sheet 8L Germany
and Euskirchen

Appendix 1

3rd Midland Brigade Order No.419 dated 4/6/19.

1. (a) 3rd Midland Brigade, B, Section 18th Field Ambulance, and No. 3 Coy Train, will move to the training Camp at SCHMIDTHEIM in accordance with detailed instructions which will be issued later.

(b) 3rd Midland Brigade (less Transport) will move on 9th June by train, entrain at BRUHL.

(c) Transport will move by road staying at LECHINICH and ROGGENDORF.

2. 1st Midland Brigade is moving one Battalion (les one Company) to "47¾=BRUHL in releif of 53nd Sherwood Foresters.

3. The responsibility for the defence of BRUHL and of that part of the BONN-COLOGNE railway which is within the Divisional Area is being taken over by the G.O.C. 1st Midland Brigade.

4. 53nd Sherwood Foresters will hand over to the Battalion of the 1st Midland Brigade which takes over billets at BRUHL the following:

(a) 3rd Midland Brigade defence Scheme in case of Civil Disturbances and Midland Division No.G.30/1/1(333).
(b) Orders re guarding of the Railway Bridges at BRUHL 3rd Midland Brigade No.G.3590/1.
(c) Scheme for defence of Army Ammunition Dump VOCHEM.

5. 1st Midland Brigade is releiving the u/m guards:

Place	at present found by.	Date of releif.
(a) VOCHEM Army Ammunition Dump.	53nd, S.F.	7th or 8th,
(b) RODENKIRCHEN Chemical Factory. (Sheet 8L.36.35.00)	53rd S.F.	8th

Guides for both guards will be sent to Headquarters 53nd Sherwood Foresters, at the SEMINARY. BRUHL. at a time to be notified later. Completion of releif to be reported to Brigade Headquarters by wire.

(6) Administrative instruction for the moves are attached.

(6) Transport moves will take place as soon as possible in the early morning to avoid the heat of the day.

Attention is directed to Notes on March Discipline.

(7) Battalion Cyclists will proceedby road on 9th. with the limbers which are being retained by the Battalions vide Administrative instructions para 8.(J).

(9) Acknowledge.

4th. June 1919.

G.M. Burefoot Captain.
Staff Captain.
Major.
Brigade Major, 3rd Midland Brigade.

DISTRIBUTION.

Brigadier General Commanding.
Staff Captain.
1st Sherwood Foresters.
3rd Sherwood Foresters.
Midland Division "G"
1st Midland Brigade.
A.P.M. Midland Division.
No.3 Coy Train.
War Diary. (2) (3)

Brigade Major.
Brigade Signal Officer.
53nd Sherwood Foresters.
3rd Midland T.M. Battery.
Midland Division "Q"
A.D.M.S. Midland Division.
Area Commandant, Schmidtheim.
B. Section, R.F.A.
Brigade Office. (2)

Administrative Instructions to accompnay Brigade Operation Order No. 419.

****

Maps: GERMANY 2L 1/100000
EUSKIRCHEN Sheet.

1. ADVANCED PARTIES.

(a) The following admanced parties of the 3rd Midland Brigade will proceed by train to SCHMIDTHEIM on Friday 6th inst.

Bde. H.Q.	1 Offr.	6 O.R.s	
T.M.B.	1 "	4 "	
Each Infy. Bn.	3 "	70 "	(Approx) 2 platoons also to include some Bn. Pioneers.
No. 3 Coy. Train	1 "	6 "	
Field Amb.	1	6 "	

2. TRANSPORT.

(a) The transport of the Brigade Group will proceed by road and stage as follows:

Friday 6th. LECHENICH.
Saturday 7th. ROGGENDORF.
Sunday 8th SCHMIDTHEIM. (Final destination)

(b) The Brigade Column will march under orders of O.C. No.3 Coy. Div. Train.
(c) Hour of starting 1500 hours.
(d) Starting point - road junction Sheet 2L 4B 10.00
(e) Order of March - 52nd Sherwood Foresters, No. 3 Coy. Div. Train, E Section 18th Field Ambulance, 53rd Sherwood Foresters, 51st Sherwood Foresters, Bde. H.Q.
(f) Strict March Discipline will be observed and the following distances maintained:
Between transport of Units - 100 yards.
Between each section of 12 vehicles - 50 yards.
Transport will halt every 10 minutes to the Clock hour and all personnel will dismount and at once loosen girths.
(g) Baggage wagons will report to units by 0900 hours 5th inst. and will march with Battalions' transport.
(h) The following personnel and vehicles will proceed:
Bde. H.Q. 1 Offr. 28 O.R.s - All vehicles and transport of Bde. H.Q. and Signal Section. [illegible])
Each Infy. Bn. 1 Offr. 27 O.R.s 29 animals (including 6 limbered G.S. Wagons, 2 Water Carts, and 4 Cookers. 1 Maltese Cart 1 Officers Mess Cart
No. 3 Coy. Train. 2 Offrs. 66 O.R.s 63 Animals and all vehicles (to include supply and transport wagons.)
Section of F.A. 1 Offr. 18 O.R.s 27 Animals to include riders.
T.M.B. 1 N.C.O. and 1 Limber.
(i) The numbers of officers and O.R.s and animals may be varied provided that the numbers as laid down for each unit are not exceeded.
(j) Remainder of the vehicles will remain behind and proceed by road on Monday 9th inst., brigaded under the B.T.O. and will stage at the same places as the advanced transport.
(k) The limber left behind by the T.M.B. will draw rations for Brigade Headquarters as well as T.M.B.
(l) Owing to the hilly nature of the country, units will ensure that their transports are not overloaded.

3. RATIONS.

Rations will be carried as follows:
(a) Rations for transport proceeding by road will be carried by No. 3 Coy. Div. Train for consumption on the 8th. Rations for consumption on the 7th. will be carried by units, rations for consumption on the 9th. will be delivered at SCHMIDTHEIM Camp by M.T.
(b) Rations for advanced party.
Advanced party will entrain with rations for consumption on the 7th. RATIONS for 8th & 9th will be delivered to SCHMIDTHEIM
(c) Rations for main party.
Main party will entrain on the 9th inst. with rations for consumption on the 10th. after which date Corps are arranging to deliver supplies.

6. <u>STORES, KITS, (continued).</u>

Any stores or baggage that cannot be moved to the Camp on the 9th inst. will be collected and stored in the SEMINARY, BRUHL. A storeman from each unit will be left in charge of any stores dumped. Arrabgements will be made for these stores to be guarded by the 1st Midland Brigade incase of necessity.

supplies to BLENKENHEIM on SCHMIDTHEIM Stations

~~(d) Rations for 8th and 9th will be delivered at SCHMIDTHEIM.~~

(d) All Units will take Iron Rations in bulk. These will not be issued till firther orders.

4. ENTRAINING STRENGTHS.

Units will wire Entraining Strengths as follows by 1800 hours 5th inst.:

(1) Strength of officer, O.R. of advanced party.
" " " " " road party.
(3) " " " " " main body.

The main body will entrain at BRUHL Station on Monday 9th inst. and will proceed by train to SCHMIDTHEIM. Trucks are being provided to carry 120 tons of baggage, stores etc. which will include Brigade Headquarters, Infantry Battalions, Divisional Train and Field Amb.

Further entraining instructions will be issued later.

5. LORRIES.

The following lorries will report to units on the 9th.

7 lorries per Battalion. to take stores, kit etc. to the station at BRUHL.

1 lorry. T.M.B.
3 Field Ambulance.
2 No. 3 Coy. Div. Train.
3 Brigade Headquarters.

6. STORES, KITS, etc.

Units will arrange to divide their stores into the following categories:

(1) Arms, Ammunition and Military Equipment.
(2) Furniture, washing bowls, crockery etc.
(3) Recreational kit, Educational books etc.
(4) Training Stores, targets and apparatus.
(5) Q.M. Stores, spare boots and clothing.

In the event of there not being enough accommodation on the train at BRUHL for all, it will be loaded on the precedence given above.

7. LOADING PARTIES.

O.C. 52nd Sherwood Foresters will detail a working party of 3 officers and 60 O.R.s to assist in unloading lorries and loading train. other units will send parties by lorries who will be responsible for the safe-guarding of their stores, and for unloading and loading.

Units will be responsible for off-loading their own stores at the detraining point.

8. TENTS AND EQUIPMENT.

Under arrangements to be made by IX Corps tents will be delivered to SCHMIDTHEIM on Friday 6th inst. D.A.D.O.S. will arrange for a representative to take over these tents on arrival. The off-loading ~~party~~ will be carried out by the advanced parties. Tents will be issued to each unit in accordance with the scale laid down in para. 5. of Midland Division No. Q 40/3 and G.R.O. 3365.

One store tent will be issued to each Infantry Battalion.

9. TRANSPORT FOR REMOVAL OF TENTAGE, STORES, etc., FROM THE STATION TO THE CAMP SITE.

IX Corps have been asked to provide 12 lorries to be at SCHMIDTHEIM Station from the 7th. to the 9th inst. to convey stores from the station to the Camp.

CAMP FURNITURE........

10. CAMP FURNITURE.
Spray Baths, and other Government property that cannot be collected and stored will be handed over to the charge of the Burgermeister and a list will be forwarded to Brigade Headquarters by 1800 hours 10th stating articles so handed over.

Camp Commandant SCHMIDTHEIM, will arrange to have all tables, chairs and forms already requisitioned collected and handed over to D.A.D.O.S. representative for issue to the troops on arrival by S[illegible]day morning 7th inst.

As it is expected that the full quantity of Camp furniture will not be available by the 7th inst. units will take with them by train all available tables, chairs, and benches that are the property of the government.

11 SANITATION.

As there has not been time to complete the preparation of the Camp, each unit will be responsible for the construction of temporary incinerators, until such time as permanent ones can be erected.

12. WATER ARRANGEMENTS.

As it is not possible to complete the laying of the water supply to the Camp, the C.R.E. will arrange for 4 GARFORTH LORRIES, to be sent to the Camp not later than Friday the 6th inst. These lorries will be under the direct orders of the Camp Commandant, who will arrange for their distribution as required.

13. Acknowledge.

Captain,
Staff Captain, 3rd Midland Brigade.

Distribution:-
Brigadier General Commanding
Staff Captain.
Brigade Transport Officer.
52nd Sherwood Foresters.
3rd Midland T.M.Battery.
Midland Division. "G".
A.D.M.S. Midland Division.
Area Commandant, SCHMIDTHEIM.
B Section, 18th Field Ambulance.
Brigade Office (2)
Brigade Major.
Brigade Signal Officer.
51st Sherwood Foresters.
53rd Sherwood Foresters.
Midland Division "Q".
1st Midland Brigade.
D.A.P.M. Midland Division.
Nod.3 Coy. Div. Train.
War Diary. (2)

Brigadier-General Commanding.
Brigade Major.
Staff Captain.
Brigade Signal Officer.
Brigade Transport Officer.
"B" Section 18th Field Ambulance.
D.A.P.M. Midland Division.
Area Commandant SCHMIDTHEIM.
1st Midland Brigade.
51st Sherwood Foresters.
52nd Sherwood Foresters.
53rd Sherwood Foresters.
3rd Midland T.M.Battery.
Midland Division "Q"
No. 3 Coy. Div. Train.
A.D.M.S. Midland Division.
Brigade Office (2) War Diary (2).
Midland Division. "G".

Reference Brigade Operation Order No. 410 and Administrative Instructions.

The Advanced Parties of the Brigade Group will entrain at BRUHL Station at 1000 hours, arriving at SCHMIDTHEIM at 1810 hours.

All parties must arrive at BRUHL Station by 0915 hours.*

The Officer i/c of each party will report to the Staff Captain at the entraining point, and bring a copy of his entraining strength with him.

The whole of the advanced parties will be under the command of Capt. MUDGE, 52nd Sherwood Foresters.

On arrival at SCHMIDTHEIM, the officer i/c party will report to area Commandant, SCHMIDTHEIM, and will erect the Camp under his orders.

Officer i/c party will be responsible for unloading of D.A.D.O.S. Stores at SCHMIDTHEIM. Tents, included in the above will have to be used for the accommodation of the advanced party.

Rations for consumption 8-9th will be placed in the train under arrangements made by Division.

Officer i/c party will be responsible that these rations are properly distributed on arrival. Rations for consumption 7th will be carried by the parties to the train.

The following lorries will report as stated:

Unit.	Place.	Time.	No.
Brigade Headquarters.	MARIENBURG.	0800 hrs.	1
51st Sherwood Foresters.	RODENKIRCHEN.	0800 hrs.	3 (to be shared by T.M.B.)
53rd Sherwood Foresters.	SURTH.	0800 hrs.	3

Officer Commanding 52nd Sherwood Foresters will detail a working party of 1 Offr. and 35 O.R.s to report to D.A.D.O.S. representative at BRUHL Station at 0700 hours to-morrow to load stores.

Acknowledge.

G.W.M. Barfoot
Captain,
Staff Captain, 3rd Midland Brigade.

5.6.1919.

*Map. Ref. of station: Sheet 2L. 4B 37.18 (close to MT workshops)

Amendments to Administrative Instructions to accompany Brigade Operation Order No. 419.

Para.2. sub-para (h) should read as follows:

(h) The following personnel and vehicles will proceed:
<u>Bde. H.Q.</u> 1 Offr. 22 O.R.s All vehicles and transport of Brigade Headquarters and Signal Section.
<u>Each Infantry Bn.</u> 1 Offr. 27 O.R.s 29 Animals (including Pack Animals and Riders) 1 Maltese Cart, 1 Officers Mess Cart, 8 Limbered G.S. Wagons, 2 Water Carts, and 4 Cookers.
<u>No. 3 Coy. Train.</u> 2 Offrs. 66 O.R.s 68 animals and all Vehicles (to include supply and transport wagons).
<u>Section of Field Ambulance.</u> 1 Offr. 18 O.R.s 27 animals to include riders.
<u>T.M.B.</u> 1 N.C.O. and 1 Limber.

Delete para.3 and substitute:-

Rations will be carried as follows:

(a) <u>Rations for Advanced transport</u> proceeding by road will be carried by No. 3 Coy. Div. Train for consumption on 7th. 8th and 9th after which date rations will be delivered in the new area.

(b) <u>Rations for advanced Party.</u> Rations for consumption 7th., 8th., and 9th. will be placed on the train under Divisional arrangements. The senior officer of the Advanced Party will be responsible for the distribution of these rations.

(c) <u>Rations for main party.</u> Main party will entrain on the 9th inst. with rations for consumption on the 10th. after which date Corps are arranging to deliver supplies to BLANKENHEIM or SCHMIDTHEIM Stations.

(d) All units will take Iron Rations in bulk. These will not be issued till further orders.

[signature] Captain,
Staff Captain, 3rd Midland Brigade.

<u>Distribution:-</u>

Brigadier-General Commanding
Brigade Major.
Staff Captain.
Brigade Signal Officer.
Brigade Transport Officer.
51st Sherwood Foresters.
52nd Sherwood Foresters.
53rd Sherwood Foresters.
3rd Midland T.M.Battery.
A.D.M.S. Midland Division.
Area Commandant SCHMIDTHEIM.
"B" Section, 18th Field Amb.
Mid. Div. "Q"
1st Midland Brigade.
D.A.P.M. Midland Division.
No. 3 Coy. Div. Train.
Brigade Office (2).
War Diary (2).

S P O R T S .

Appendix No. 2

1. A meeting of the Brigade Sports Committee was held H.Q. 52nd Sherwood Foresters, on 13th June, to decide on the events to be included in the "efficiency Competition".

2. Rules:-

(a) All events to be teams only.
(b) Each team to be furnished by one Company or its equivalent.
(c) All points scored by a company to count towards the aggregate of its unit-i e. Battalion or R.E. etc.
(d) Brigade Headquarters.)
T.M.Battery.) To count as one Company.
B.Section.18th Field Ambulance)

No.3.Coy. Train. do.
93rd. Field Coy. R.E. do.
One Infantry Battalion to count as five Companies.

(e) Winning team of each event to score 12 points.
2nd. " " " " " " " 10 " .
3rd " " " " " " " 8 " .
4th. " " " " " " " 6 " .
5th. " " " " " " " 4 " .
6th. " " " " " " " 2 " .

3. The following events to be part of the Competition

(a) Relay Race. Teams of 6 each.
To consist of 1 officer, C.S.M. or C.Q.M.S. 1 Sergeant 1 corporal 1 L/Cpl, 1 Private.
To run in any order.
Distances Two, 220 yards,
Three 440 yards,
One, 880 yards,

(b) Cross Country Run Teams of 15.
Distance---3 miles. There will be three counts at finishing post, marks per man. 1st Count, 3 marks,
2nd Count, 2 marks,
3rd Count 1 mark.
The time allowed for each count to be fixed as soon as the course is decided.

(c) Tug of War, Teams of 10.
Not to be above average of 11½ stone. Pulls 12 foot
Best of three pulls.

(d) Falling Plate Competition, (Probably in ~~Filed~~ Field Firing Range)
Section Teams. Strength of sections 1 N.C.O. 6 men.
Further details to be arranged.

(e) Lewis Gun Competition. Section Teams.
Competition to include, coming into action--- Fire Control-- three changes of drums-
Marks to be allotted for coming into action---fire control--- changes of drums-- No of targets hit--- number of rounds not expended.

(f) Runners Race., Teams of four,
Across Country, distance about one mile, to include 2 or 3 changes of messages. (Verbal and written).

(g) Football Competition, Six aside.
10 minutes each way. goals count 2 points.
corners count 1 point.
(Off side rule 2 men instead of three).

(h) Rifle Grenade Competition.
Each Team, 1 Rifle Section (to include 2 R:G.'s).
Strength of Sections, 1 N.C.O. 6 men.
Scheme.--- Attack on M.G. Nest.
Details will be worked out later.

(i) Bayonet Foghting.- Spring Bayonets-
Section teams on the knock-out system
Strength of Sections N.C.O. 6 men.

(j). Cricket. Company Teams.

(k). Basket Ball. Team of five.

(l). Tabloid Sports.

Long Jump. High Jump. Three forward Jumps.
Three Backward Junps. Sprint 80 yards.
Backward Race. 50 yards. Relay Race. 50 yards.

4. Representatives were in favor of a Brigade Sports Meeting at which finals for events 3 A.B.C.G.and K.could take place in addition to other events.

5. It may be necessary to wait till this Brigade moves to Musketry Camp,to comple e some events in the ~~different~~ efficiency competitions.

6. Forecast of dates.

(a). Brigade Efficiency Competition,either end of fourth week at Schmidtheim Camp,or during fifth week.

(b) Brigade Sports about the same time.

Major.
14th June.1919. Brigade Major,3rd.Midland Brigade.

- -

Distribution.

General Officer Commanding.
Briagde Major.
Staff Captain.
51st Sherwood Foresters.
52nd Sherwood Foresters.
53rd Sherwood Foresters,
3rd Midland T.M.Battery.
B.Section 18th Field Ambulance.
No.3.Coy.Train.
93rd.Field Coy.R.E.
Brigade Office.(4).

SECRET.
Ref. Sheet 59.
& EUSKIRCHEN Sheet.

Appen No 3.

3rd Midland Brigade Order No.420 dated 16/6/19.

1. If the peace negotiations fail notice of the termination of the Armistice in 72 hours will be given to the Germans. The day on which the Armistice ceases will be called J Day. On that day the three leading British Corps advance into neutral territory.

2. In this event 3rd Midland Brigade will move by train to 1st Midland Brigade area in accordance with attached tables A and B.

3. The object of the move of the Midland Division is to guard the communication by road, and railway along the WEISWEILER - DUREN - COLOGNE line.

4. On completion of the move the Brigadier General Commanding 3rd Midland Brigade will administer the present 1st and 3rd Midland Brigade areas.

5. In notifying J Day by wire to all concerned the following code will be used.

20 June - A
21 June - B
22 June - C
23 June - D
24 June - E
25 June - F
26 June - G
27 June - H
28 June - I
29 June - J

Thus if J day were to be 26th June the following telegram would be sent in clear to all concerned "Reference 3rd Midland Brigade No.420 dated 16th June, J day will be G.

6. 3rd Midland Brigade will be responsible for the administration and rationing of the affiliated battery R.F.A., and also "D" Coy. Machine Gun Battalion from the date on which they join 3rd Midland Brigade group.

7. 52nd Sherwood Foresters will arrange to relieve the u/m guards. Completion of relief to be reported to this office.

Guard.	Strength.	Found by	Date of relief.	Remarks.
VOCHEM Army Amm. Dump.	2 Off. 12 N.C.Os 48 men.	1st Mid. Bde(probably 1/5 K.O.Y.L.I.	J - 1 day.	
COLOGNE DEUTZ Guard.	1 Off. 2 N.C.Os 6 men.	do.	J day.	The guard in situation on J day will remain on till relief detailed are available to take over their duties.
Midland Div.Pack Train.	1 N.C.O. 4 men.	do.	J - 1 day.	Guard will report to BADRT EIFEL TOR Station near Southern Bridge COLOGNE at 16.00 hrs.

8. Administrative Instructions are being issued to units of 3rd Midland Brigade group.

9. 93rd Field Coy. R.E. will remain behind and move under orders to be issued by C.R.E.

10 acknowledge

HEADQUARTERS No. G/7041 Date. 71st INFANTRY BRIGADE

16.6.19.

[signature]
Major.
Brigade Major, 3rd Midland Brigade.

P.T.O.

Distribution.

Brigadier General Commanding.	Midland Division "G".
Brigade Major.	" " "Q".
Staff Captain.	1st Midland Brigade.
Signal Officer.	C.R.A. Midland Division.
Brigade Transport Officer.	C.R.E. " "
51st Sherwood Foresters.	A.D.M.S. " "
52nd Sherwood Foresters.	D.A.P.M. " "
53rd Sherwood Foresters.	6th Battn. M.G.C.
3rd Midland T.M.Battery.	D Coy. 6th Bn. M.G.C.
93rd Field Coy. R.E.	War Diary 2.
B Sec.18th Field Amb.	Bde. office file. 2.
No.3 Coy. Divl. Train.	

TABLE "A". **to accompany 3rd Midland Brigade Order No.420.**

Date.	Unit.	From.	To.	Remarks.
J - 2 day.	52nd Sherwood Foresters.	SCHMIDTHEIM.	BRUHL.	
J - 2 day.	3rd Midland T.M.Battery.	do.	LECHENICH.	
J - 2 day.	No.3 Coy. Mid. Div. Train.	do.	ARHEM.	
J - 2 day.	3rd Midland Brigade H.Qs.	do.	LECHENICH.	
J - 1 day.	53rd Sherwood Foresters.	do.	LIBLAR.	
J - 1 day.	51st Sherwood Foresters.	do.	LECHENICH.	
J - 1 day.	B Sec. 18th Field Ambulance.	do.	BLESSEM.	
J day.	D Coy. Machine Gun Battalion.	ERP.	GYMNICH.	To march via HERRIG. To be clear of HERRIG before 16.00 hrs.

Table "B" to accompany 3rd. Midland Brigade Order No.420.

Serial No.	Unit.	No.of Train.	Allotment of covered wagons for men.	Allotment of covered wagons for horses.	Flats.	Entraining Station.	Detraining Station.
1.	52.Sherwood Foresters.	1.	23.	7	9.	SCHMIDTHEIM	LIBLAR.
2.	Brigade Headquarters.	2.	3.	3	3.	do	do
3.	3rd.Mid.T.M.Battery.	2.	1.	1	1.	do	do
4.	No3.Coy Train.	2.	4.	7	10.	do	do
5.	51.Sherwood Foresters.	3.	18.	7	9.	do	do
6.	B.Sect.18.Field Ambu.	3.	2.	2	3.	do	do
7.	53.Sherwood Foresters.	~~3~~.4	21.	7	9.	do	do

Remarks. (1). Each Train consists of 1 coach for officers.30 covered wagons and 17 Flats.

(2). The accomodation has been allotted as far as possible on the basis of 30 per covered wagon.

(3). All transport to travel fully loaded. Each Flat takes four axles.

(4). Time of departure of trains will be notified later.

All petrol tins will be carried full of water.
An additional water cart will be issued to each Infantry Battalion by G.H.Q. on demand if required.

The No. 3 Coy. Train will deliver rations for consumption 19th to Units this afternoon. In the case of 52nd Sherwood Foresters Bde. H.Q. and T.M.B. supply wagons of these units will park full with No. 3 Coy. train and will be delivered as available.
These units will arrange to send a representative to report to No. 3 Coy. train and look after supply wagons.

SECRET.

ADMINISTRATIVE INSTRUCTIONS TO ACCOMPANY BRIGADE OPERATION ORDER No. 420.

****

1. AMMUNITION. (a) All Echelons will move full.
(b) All Units will demand ammunition requirements by wire to reach Brigade Headquarters by 0900 hours daily.
(c) DUMPS R.A. Ammunition, S.A.A., Grenades etc., are established at
VOCHEM
LONGERICH.

2. Rations will be arranged as follows:
Rations for consumption J-1 day will be carried by troops entraining on J-2 days.
Troops entraining on J-1 day will carry the unexpired portions of the days rations with them.
Rations for J day will be delivered in new area in the usual way and on arrival of troops travelling on J-1 day.
On receipt of these Instructions every officer and man will be issued with Iron Rations.
The No. 3 Coy. Train will deliver rations for consumption tomorrow at 0600 hours. Refilling point 3rd Midland Bde. ROHERHOF.

3. ADVANCE PARTIES.
The following advance parties will be detailed to proceed in advance of their Units as follows:-
Advance parties for troops proceeding on J-2 days proceed by civilian train leaving SCHNI THEIM at 4.10 today.
For troops proceeding on J-1 day the advanced parties will proceed with troops proceeding on J-2 days 2nd train).
Units will send parties as follows:- Battalions 1 officer 1 N.C.O. and 1 man per H.Q. and each Coy. Other Units 1 officer or Senior N.C.O. and 1 man.

4. REAR PARTIES. 1 officer (optional) 1 N.C.O. and 5 men per battalion and a suitable party from Bde. H.Q. F.A. 3 Coy. Train and T.M.B. will remain behind to guard any surplus baggage left behind.

5. BAGGAGE. All baggage will be divided into two headings:-
(a) Essential kit consisting of mobile stores, kit bags blankets, and all S.A.A. and Grenades.
(b) Surplus kits surplus Q.M.Stores Recreational kit and Educational kit.
Baggage under heading (a) will proceed by train with troops.
Baggage under heading (b) will remain behind under charge of rear party., and will be concentrated as close together in the case of the 3 battalions as possible. In the case of Bde. H.Q., No. 3 Coy. Train, F.A., will be concentrated in the store tent of F.A.
Lists of all tents, furniture and tonnage of surplus kit left behind will be forwarded to Bde. H.Q. by 0900 hours 21st Inst.
There will probably be the following accommodation on No. 2 Train on J-2 days for the baggage of all units of the Brigade Group as under:
Battalions 3 trucks each.
Bde H.Q. and T.M.B. 1 truck.
F.A. and Coy. Train 1 truck.
Units will arrange to send baggage guard with their kit who will be responsible for loading and unloading and must travel in the same wagons.
Baggage under heading (a) will arrive at Northern side of the station. On receipt of these orders Units must commence dumping kits at the place marked for them at the station.

6. ENTRAINING OF TRANSPORT. All transport will be loaded and will be entrained on the southern side of the station and must be at the station 3 hours before departure of train. On arrival at station officer in charge will report to the Staff Captain, who will show him where transport is to be parked and he will then outspan and move his animals to their entraining point

7. UNLOADING PARTIES. Each battalion will furnish a loading party of 75 O.R.s. under 2 officers and a proportion of N.C.O.s. as there is only a small ramp for loading vehicles. All vehicles will have to be manhandled into ramp and loaded endways on to the flats and then manhandled to the furthest end of the train.Units will arrange to detail a similar unloading party on arrival at destination. 53rd Sherwood Foresters will arrange for a party of I officer and 50 O.R.s. to be at station 3 hours before departure of 2nd train on J-2 days to help entrain transport Bde.H.Q., T.M.B., and No.3 Coy. Train. 5Ist Sherwood Foresters will detail I officer and 30 O.R.s. to entrain transport of Section of I8th Field Ambulance in No. 3 train.

8. LORRIES. There will be 6 lorries at the disposal of Brigade for removal of kits to station, these will be allotted by the Staff Captain on arrival.

At detraining point the following lorries will be available for conveyance of stores to billots:-

Bde. H.Q. and T.M.B.	2
Battalions.	3
F.A.	I
No. 3 Coy Train.	I

IO. ENTRAINING OF PERSONNEL. All personnel will entrain on the nothern side of the station. Each unit will detail an officer to act as entraining officer. This officer will report to the Staff Captain at entraining point 50 minutes before train is due to start and should be in possession of complete entraining strength showing officers O.R.s. horses, vehicles. All troops must be at entraining point 45 minutes before train is due to start.

II.STRIKING OF CAMP. All tents will be struck and stores, they will be concentrated as much as possible in the care of each unit in cookhouses and store tents or marquees, due regard being to access from roads. Bde. H.Q. and No. 3 Coy. Train will store their tents with section I8th Field Ambulance. A list of all tents stores to be furnished to the Camp Commandant and copies to this office.
XX
I2. LEAVE PARTIES. will proceed by train from Duren or Cologne. In case of necessity they will be accommodated at Duren in the Divisional Reception Camp after it moves to Duren, and at the Reception Camp BRUGLEMAN HOUSE? COLOGNE.

I3.TRAFFIC CONTROL. 2nd Lieut. J.A. PHILLIPS? Ist Bn. M.G.C. is in charge of IX Corps Traffic Control. The D.A.P.M. Midland Division? will select control posts in the new Divisional area, and will report selected sites to Midland Division "A". The present system of

Military Police Patrol in the Corps Area will continue. Whenever weather permits, cross country tracks will be used by horse transport and Infantry. All Units will take steps to ensure that when halted columns are clear of the road and transport halted as close to the near side of the road as possible.

I4.CASUALTIES - RETURN "A" Battalions which have suffered 50 casualties or more, and the Machine Gun Battalion 25 casualties or more will wire the approximate casualtiesto by hours daily. If at least 50 more casualties have occurred in the Battalion, or 25 in the Machine Gun Battalion, during the night, a fresh wire will be sent next morning. Casualties will be reported by phases, commencement of phase will be notified from Division Headquarters Daily casualty wire will include numbers already reported since the commencement of the phase, and will begin with the following words:-
"Estimated casualties from (here insert date of commencement of phase)."

I5. Medical arrangements. The Division will vacate to No.II Station Hospital, Duren, and No. 42 Station Hospital, Euskirchen. Reserve of drugs, Dressings, etc., at Serum, obtained from No. I3 base Medical Stores, Zulnner Strasse, (near Uber Ring) Cologne.
I000 Stretchers and "000 Blankets are held in reserve at 47 N.A.C. Nord Hotel, Euskirchen, for issue if required.

I6. PRISONERS OF WAR CAGE. IX Corps cage will be at the Sugar Factory, Euskirchen. The D.A.P.M. will arrange to establish a Divisional Cage at Kreuzau, exact site will be notified later.

I7. DETRAINING. The detraining will be carried out under orders of the Brigade Major. On arrival at detraining point, the entraining officer of each unit will report to the Brigade Major for orders and act as detraining officer.

I8. GAGGAGE WAGONS will rejoin units today.

I9. Acknowledge.

J. Lumb Beauford
Captain.
Staff Captain 3rd Midland Brigade.

I7-6-I9I9.

Distribution:-

Brigadier General Commanding
Brigade Major
Staff captain
Signal Officer
Brigade Transport Officer
5Ist Sherwood Foresters
52nd Sherwood Foresters
53rd Sherwood Foresters
3rd Midland T.M.Battery.
93rd Field Coy. R.E.
"B" Sect. I8 th F.A.
No. 3 Coy. Div. Train.
Camp Commandant.
Bde. Q.M.S.

Midland Division "G"
" " "Q"
Ist Midland Brigade.
C.R.A. Midland Division.
CRR.E. Midland Division.
A.D.M.S. Midland Division.
D.A.P.M. Midland Division.
6th Bn. M.G.C.
D Coy. 6th Bn. M.G.C.
War Diary 2
Bde. office. "

SECRET.

ADDENDUM No.1

to 3rd Midland Brigade Order No.420. dated 10/6/19.

1. (a) 3rd Midland Brigade H.Qs will close at the SCHLOSS at SCHMIDTHEIM at 16.00 hours, 18th June, and will open at the SCHLOSS at LECHENICH at 23.00 hours the same day.

(b) The Staff Captain will remain behind at H.Qs. 51st Sherwood Foresters to superintend the entraining, and will proceed on the 4th train.

(c) The Brigade Major will superintend the detraining, and will travel on the first train.

2. Trains depart on J - 2 and J - 1 day as under :-

J-2 day	1st Train	arrives	SCHMIDTHEIM at	03.00 hours.
	" "	departs	do.	05.54 "
	" "	arrives	LIBLAR	09.08 "
	2nd "	arrives	SCHMIDTHEIM	16.30 "
	" "	departs	do.	18.07 "
	" "	arrives	LIBLAR	21.09 "
J-1 day	3rd "	arrives	SCHMIDTHEIM	03.00 "
	" "	departs	do.	05.54 "
	" "	arrives	LIBLAR	09.08 "
	4th "	arrives	SCHMIDTHEIM	16.30 "
	" "	departs	do.	18.07 "
	" "	arrives	LIBLAR	21.09 "

Units will commence loading baggage and transport immediately each train arrives at SCHMIDTHEIM.

3. The Officer commanding each train will ensure that there is a guard of 1 Officer, 1 N.C.O. and 6 men, who will travel as near the engine as possible, and will be ready to take action in the event of emergency.

4. Acknowledge.

To all recipients of 3rd Midland Brigade Order No.420.

17.6.19.

[signature]
Major.
Brigade Major, 3rd Midland Brigade.

appen H

SECRET.

WARNING ORDER.

Reference 2L & 1L. 1/100,000

1. From J Day inclusive measures for the Defence of the following will be taken to guard against Civil disturbance, and attempts on the part of the civil population to interrupt the lines of communication.

2. 52nd Sherwood Foresters will be responsible for the defence of :-

(a) KIERBERG.

(b) VOCHEM Ammunition Dump.

(c) The KALSHEUREN - EUSKIRCHEN Line from KIERBERG inclusive to VOCHEM inclusive.

(d) The defence of BRUHL Railway Bridges.

(e) The COLOGNE - BONN line within the Divisional boundaries.

The troops to be detailed for the above are as follows :-

for (a) and (c) 2 platoons altogether.

for (b) 1 company.

for (d) 1 company (of which 2 platoons may remain in billets till required).

for (e) see para 4.

3. 53rd Sherwood Foresters will be responsible for the defence of:-

(a) LIBLAR telegraph and telephone offices.

(b) The Railway bridge E by S of LIBLAR.

(c) The KALSHEUREN - EUSKIRCHEN Line from point on the railway sheet 2L 5A 08.05 to KIERBERG exclusive.

O.C. 53rd Sherwood Foresters will report the number of troops required to safeguard the above.

4. The Railway lines mentioned above will from J Day inclusive be guarded by picquets at essential points (e.g. bridges, subways, level crossings or junctions), with patrols (mounted bicycle or on foot) working between them.

5. The instructions re defence of VOCHEM Ammunition Dump, BRUHL Bridges, and BONN - COLOGNE Railway are the same as previously issued to 52nd Sherwood Foresters when in the BRUHL area prior to the move to SCHMIDTHEIM.

6. Further instructions will be issued.

7. Acknowledge.

Major.

18.6.19. Brigade Major, 3rd Midland Brigade.

(for distribution see back).

Appen 5

SECRET.

3rd Midland Brigade Order No:421 dated 24/6/19.

Reference Sheet 59 EUSKIRCHEN Sheet.

1. In the event of peace being signed without further advance, orders may be expected for all troops to resume normal dispositions, when the organisation of areas and Civil administration which existed prior to J - 3 day will be resumed.

2. 3rd Midland Brigade Group will move to SCHMIDTHEIM Camp by T.U. TRain in accordance with attached move Table.

3. Guards found by this Brigade will be relieved by 1st Midland Brigade as follows :-

Day of Relief.	Guard.	Found by.	Relieved by.	Remarks.
B day.	No.3 Coy. Train. ROMERHOF.	51st Sherwood Foresters.	T.M.B. 1st Mid.Bde.	Present Guard to withdraw at Reveille and proceed on No.3 Train.
do.	VOCHEM.	52nd Sherwood Foresters.	5th K.O.Y.L.I.	Relief to take place by 12.00 hours.
do.	EIFEL TOR.	52nd Sherwood Foresters.	do.	Present Guard to withdraw 09.00 hours.
do.	No.3 Coy. Train, BRUHL.	52nd Sherwood Foresters.	do.	Present Guard to withdraw at Reveille.
do.	No.1 Coy.Train HAUSWEILER.	53rd Sherwood Foresters.	do.	Present Guard to withdraw at 10.00 hours and proceed by civilian train to SCHMIDTHEIM.

4. B Coy. Machine Gun Battn. will move as follows :-

A day.	from GYMNICH	to	ERP.	To be clear of GYMNICH by 08.30 hrs and march via HERRIG.
B day.	from ERP.	to	MECHERNICH	To be clear of ERP by 07.30 hours No restriction as to route.

5. No.4 Coy. Divn.Train will march from FRAUWULLERSHEIM to ARHEM on B day. To be clear of FRAUWULLERSHEIM by 08.00 hours No restriction as to route.

6. The Brigade Major will supervise the entraining at BRUHL and LIBLAR and will travel on the last train. The Staff Captain will supervise detraining at SCHMIDTHEIM.

7. Completion of moves and reliefs of guards to be reported to Brigade H.Qs. by wire.

8. Acknowledge.

A. Ferguson
Major,
Brigade Major, 3rd Midland Brigade.

24.6.19.

DISTRIBUTION.

Brigadier General Commanding.	Midland Division G.
Brigade Major.	" " Q.
Staff Captain.	1st Midland Brigade.
Brigade Signal Officer.	C.R.E.)
Brigade Transport Officer.	C.R.A.) Midland Division.
51st Sherwood Foresters.	A.D.M.S.)
52nd Sherwood Foresters.	D.A.P.M. " "
53rd Sherwood Foresters.	6th Bn. M.G.C.
3rd Midland T.M.Battery	D Coy. 6th Bn. M.G.C.
B Sec. 1[illegible]th Field Amb.	O.C. Mid. Divn.Train.
No.3 Coy. Divn. Train.	Area Commandant, SCHMIDTHEIM.
4 Coy. Divn. Train.	

Serial No.	Day.	Unit.	No. of Train.	Allottment of Covered wagons for men.	Allottment of Covered Wagons for horses.	Flats.	Entraining Station.	Detraining Station.
1.	A-day.	53rd Sherwood Foresters.	1.	21.	7.	9.	LIBLAR.	SCHMIDTHEIM.
2.	do.	51st Sherwood Foresters.	2.	18.	7.	9.	do.	do.
3.	do.	B Sec. 18th Field Amb.	2.	2.	2.	3.	do.	do.
4.	B day.	Bde. H.Qs.	3.	3.	4.	3.	do.	do.
5.	do.	T.M.B.	3.	1.	1.	1.	do.	do.
6.	do.	No. 3 Coy. Div. Train.	3.	4.	7.	10.	do.	do.
7.	do.	52nd Sherwood Foresters.	4.	23.	7.	9.	BRUHL.	do.

REMARKS.

(1) Each train consists of one coach for Officers, 30 covered wagons, 17 flats.
(2) The accomodation has been allotted as far as possible on the basis of 30 per covered wagon.
(3) All Transport to travel fully loaded. Each flat takes four axles.
(4) Time of departure of trains will be notified later.
(5) Battalions will arrange that all their baggage travels on their own train.

SECRET.

ADMINISTRATIVE INSTRUCTIONS TO ACCOMPNAY BRIGADE OPERATION ORDER No. 421.

****

1. SUPPLIES.

(a) Normal system will continue to be adopted until units have resumed their original dispositions.

(b) Iron Rations now in the possession of officers and men will be recollected and stored under Units arrangements in the Quartermaster's Store.

(c) Advanced parties for SCHMIDTHEIM Camp will take rations up to and for the 25th instant. They will subsequently be rationed direct under arrangements to be made by Divisional Train. All units will wire exact Numbers of advanced parties to Brigade Headquarters on receipt of these Orders.

(d) Railhead will probably move to WEILERWIST on the 26th instant.

(e) Refilling Points will be those previous to the move to DUREN area.

2. LORRIES.

Each unit will be provided with the following Motor Lorries to assist in carrying out the move.

Brigade Headquarters	2	(to include T.M.B.)
51st Sherwood Foresters.	3	
52nd Sherwood Foresters.	3	
53rd Sherwood Foresters.	3	
"B" Section 18th.Field Amb.	1	
No. 3 Coy. train.	1	
No. 4 Coy. Train.	1	
D Coy. M.G.C.	1	

Time and place of rendezvous will be notified later.

3. SURPLUS BAGGAGE.

In the event of the transport provided being insufficient to complete the move of surplus stores, a guard will be left a wire sent to Brigade Headquarters notifying transport required to complete. Guards will be issued with two days rations.

4. TRANSPORT.

All units moving to SCHMIDTHEIM Camp will take with them on the train Baggage Wagons.

All transport will entrain loaded; petrol cans will be filled.

5. TENTAGE.

All tents drawn by Units for guarding Railway Lines, etc., will be returned to D.A.D.O.S. or the units from which they were borrowed.

Units will notify Brigade Headquarters when all tents have been handed over.

6. CIVIL ADMINISTRATION.

Sub-areas will be those prior to the move to DUREN. 1st Brigade Sub-area Civil Staff Captain and P.R.O. will return to LECHENICH on "E" day. 2nd Brigade Sub-area - Brigadier Commanding 2nd Brigade will resume charge of Civil Administration on "E" day. C.R.A. will resume charge of No- 3 Sub-area on "E" day, Civil Staff Captain and P.R.O. returning to Bruhl on that day.

The day on which the Divisional Staff Captain will hand over to the Highland Division will be notified later.

7. LEAVE PARTIES.

Normal procedure will be resumed.

8. Divisional Reception Camp, D.A.D.O.S., Divisional Clothing Company, Canteen, Clean Clothing Store, "Fancies" and Divisional Hostel will remain in their present position.

9. TRAFFIC CONTROL.

D.A.P.M. Midland Division will withdraw all his Control Posts and Military Police from the DUREN area arranging direct with the Highland Division D.A.P.M. for their reliefs reporting completion to Division "A".

10. ENTRAINING.

Instructions will be issued later.

11. LOADING and UNLOADING PARTIES.

Each battalion will furnish a party of 3 officers and 75 other ranks for loading and unloading transport. Trench Mortar Battery will supply 1 officer and 25 other ranks for loading and unloading transport of Brigade Headquarters, T.M.B. and No. 3 Coy. Train. O.C. 51st Sherwood Foresters will furnish a suitable loading and unloading party for transport of "B" Section 15th Field Ambulance. Officers in charge of parties will report to the Brigade Major at the entraining point and the Staff Captain at the detraining point. Units will detail a suitable loading and unloading party to load and unload baggage; the officer I/C those parties will report to the Brigade Major and Staff Captain at entraining and detraining points respectively.

12. BAGGAGE WAGONS. Will rejoin units tomorrow 25th instant.

13. Acknowledge.

[signature] Captain.
Staff Captain 3rd Midland Brigade.

June 24th 1919.

Distribution:-

Brigadier General Commanding.
Brigade Major.
Staff Captain.
Brigade Signal Officer.
Brigade Transport Officer.
51st Sherwood Foresters.
52nd Sherwood Foresters.
53rd Sherwood Foresters.
3rd Midland T.M.Battery.
"B" Section 15 Field Ambulance.
No. 3 Coy. Train.
No. 4 Coy. Train.

Midland Division "G",
" " "Q",
1st Midland Brigade.
C.R.E. Midland Division.
C.R.A. Midland Division.
A.D.M.S. " "
D.A.P.M. " "
8th Bn. M.G.C.
D Coy. 8th Bn. M.G.C.
O.C. Mid. Divn. Train.
Area Commandant DUREN.

-- 2 --

SECRET.

C.481/1

Amendment No.I to 3rd Midland Brigade Order No.481 dated 24/6/19.

I. Reference para 3 of Order No.481:-

All guards will be relieved on C day.

2. Cancel para 4 of Order No. 481, and substitute D Coy. Machine Gun Battalion will move as follows.

A day from GYMNICH to WEILER and DISTERNICH	To be clear of GYMNICH by 08.30 hours and march via HARRIG.
B day from WEILER and DISTERNICH to MECHERNICH.	To move off not later than 08.00 hours. No restriction as to route.

3. Reference para 8 of Order No. 481:-

No. 4 Coy. Divisional Train will move on C day.

4. Reference move table attached to Order No. 481:-

For A day read B day.

For B day read C day.

5. Acknowledge.

28th June, 1919.

Major,
Brigade Major, 3rd Midland Brigade.

Distribution.

To all recipients of 3rd Midland Brigade No. 481.

Reference para. 10 of ADministrative Instructions to accompany Brigade Operation Order No. 421.
****

Entraining arrangements will be as follows:-

No.	Train.	From.	To.	Loads.	Departs.	Arrives destination.
1	"B" day.	LIBLAR.	SCHMIDTHEIM.	0600	0828	1158
2	"B" day	LIBLAR	SCHMIDTHEIM	1800	2054	0013
3	"C" day	LIBLAR	SCHMIDTHEIM	0600	0828	1158
4	"C" day	~~LIBLAR~~ BRUHL	SCHMIDTHEIM	1800	2054	0013

TRANSPORT BAGGAGE.

All transport and baggage will be at the loading siding (i.e., the same place as baggage was unloaded on arrival) 30 minutes before loading times as stated above. All G.S. Wagons will be kept together in front of transport and loaded first.

In the case of Battalion loading at BRUHL, all baggage and transport will be near ramp at BRUHL station sheet 2LAB.25.19. 30 mins before loading time.

PERSONNEL.

All personnel will be at the station 45 minutes before train is due to depart and will be entrained at least 15 minutes before departure of train. Each Unit will detail an officer to act as entraining officer who will report to the Brigade Major 50 minutes before departure of train with the exact entraining strength of Officers, Other Ranks, Horses and Vehicles. This Officer will also act as detraining officer on arrival of train at detraining point and will report to the Staff Captain on arrival.

Units will report by wire by 1800 hours 27th inst., the numbers of trucks they intend to use on their train for baggage.

Acknowledge.

G.W. Beaufort
Captain.
Staff Captain 3rd Midland Brigade.

June 26th 1919.

Distribution:-

Brigadier General Commanding.
Brigade Major.
Staff Captain.
Brigade Signal Officer.
Brigade Transport Officer.
51st Sherwood Foresters.
52nd Sherwood Foresters.
53rd Sherwood Foresters.
3rd Midland T.M.Battery.
"B" Section 18 Field Ambulance.
No. 3 Coy Train.
No. 4 Coy Train.
Midland Division "G"
" " "Q"
1st Midland Brigade.
C.R.E. Midland Division.
C.R.A. " "
A.D.M.S. " "
D.A.P.M. " "
8th Bn. M.G.C.
D Coy. M.G.C.
O.C. Mid. Div. Train.
Area Commandant SCHMIDTHEIM.

3rd Midland Brigade.

ROLL OF OFFICERS.

APPENDIX No.6.

Brigadier-General P.C.B.SKINNER, C.M.G.?D.S.O.	Brigade Commander.
Captain (Bt.Major) A.WEYMAN, MC.	Brigade Major.
Captain G.W.N. BAREFOOT, MC,	Staff Captain.
Captain C.F.LAMPARD. (Norfolk Regt).	Brigade Education Officer.

ATTACHED.

Lieut. C. MORGAN, (Royal Engineers).	Brigade Signal Officer.
Lieut. H. COY, (Leicestershire Regt.)	Civil Staff Captain.
Lieut. R. WATSON, M.C. (Sherwood Foresters).	Bde. Lewis Gun Officer.
Lieut. J.M.JORDON, (Sherwood Foresters).	Brigade Transport Officer.

@@@@@@@@@@@@@@@@@@@@@@

APPENDIX No.7.

RATION STRENGHT OF 3rd MIDLAND BRIGADE ON 30/6/19.

	Officers.	Other Ranks.
Brigade Headquarters.	4.	60.
51st Sherwood Forésters.	53.	868.
52nd Sherwood Foresters.	46.	821.
53rd Sherwood Foresters.	57.	826.
3rd Midland T.M.Battery.	4.	35.

@@@@@@@@@@@@@@@@@@@@@@@@@@@@@

Headquarters, 3rd Midland Brigade.

Army Form C. 2118.

WAR DIARY

or

~~INTELLIGENCE SUMMARY.~~

(Erase heading not required.)

Instructions regarding War Diaries and Intelligence Summaries are contained in F. S. Regs., Part II. and the Staff Manual respectively. Title pages will be prepared in manuscript.

Page1. July , 1919.

Place	Date	Hour	Summary of Events and Information	Remarks and references to Appendices
LECHENICH Area.	1	0829	53rd Sherwood Foresters left LIBLAR for SCHMIDTHEIM Training Camp. All baggage and transport entrained in under the hour.	
		0930	Brigadier General Commanding went on leave to England. Lt-Col.Spring, DSO.,Comdg. 52nd Sherwood Foresters temporarily assumes Command of the Brigade.	
		1800	51st Sherwood Foresters and B Sec. 18th Field Ambulance left LIBLAR Stn. for Camp.	
	2	0829	Bde. H.Qs.,T.M.B., and No.3 Coy. Train lsft LIBLAR for Camp.	
		1935	52nd Sherwood Foresters left BRUHL Stn . for Camp.	
SCHMIDTHEIM.	3) 4) 5)		Camp at SCHMIDTHEIM. Platoon Training and Recreation for all units also one hours education per man per day.	
	4		A most successful officers dance was given by the Division H.Qs. at the Kaisers Schloss, BRUHL.	
	7		Capt & Adjt. W.Boyd Orr, MC, 51st Sherwood Foresters left with a party of 4 O.Rs per Battalion to represent this Brigade at the VICTORY March PARIS on the 14th July.	
	8 9 10		Platoons and Company Training, Recreation and Education. do do do do do do do do A party of 34 Officers and 370 O.Rs went by special train to COLOGNE to visit the Races.	
	11	1730	Mounted Paper Chase over a good course. Very Popular.	
	12		30 Officers and 400 O.Rs went by special train to COLOGNE Races. 53rd Sherwood Foresters Sports.	
	13		Lt-Col. R.E.Power, DSO, 53rd Sherwood Foresters and 1 Officer and 1 O.R. per Battn. left for PARIS by special train to see the VICTORY March as spectators.	
	14		51st Sherwood Foresters Sports. The weather for the last 4 days has been bitterly cold and very wet. Heavy rainstorms coming over about every 2 hours. There was an exceptionally heavy thunder-storm on 12th July in the afternoon.	

/15 Rev.......

D. D. & L., London, E.C.
(A8004) Wt W1771/M2031 750,000 5/17 Sch. 52 Forms/C2118/14

Headquarters, 3rd Midland Brigade.

Army Form C. 2118.

Instructions regarding War Diaries and Intelligence Summaries are contained in F. S. Regs., Part II. and the Staff Manual respectively. Title pages will be prepared in manuscript.

Page 11.

WAR DIARY
or
~~INTELLIGENCE SUMMARY.~~

(*Erase heading not required.*)

July, 1919.

Place	Date	Hour	Summary of Events and Information	Remarks and references to Appendices
SCHMIDTHEIM.	15		Rev. Haslett visited the Brigade to lecture to all Units on 14th and 15th - Subject:- Venereal Disease.	
	16		Lt-General Sir Walter Braithwaite, K.C.B., Comdg. IX Corps, and Brig-Gen. Montgommery, Brig-Gen G.S. visited the Camp and inspected it. They visited all Bns. at Training, lunched at Bde.H.Qs, and than paid a short visit to 52nd Sherwood Foresters Sports.	
	17		Brigadier-General Commanding returned from leave.	
	16-19		Training and Education.	
	19		3rd Midland Brigade Horse Show. Very sucessful except for a severe thunderstorm at 15.00 hours which wet some of the vehicles. Most of the horses were got into marquees. The transport exibits were very good indeed, especially 51st S.F., 52nd S.F., and Bde. H.Qs. The Horse Show was open to the entire Brigade Group and included a hurdle race and a four furlong race.	
	20) 21)		Preparations for the Brigade Sports which are to take place 22nd July.	
	22		Pouring wet day. Sports postponed to 23rd July.	
	23		do do do do 26th July.	
	24		Midland Division Horse Show at ROMERHOF near LECHENICH.	
	25		53rd Sherwood Foresters Battalion Field Day.	
	26		Brigade Sports. Great enthusiasm and a very successful day, each unit winning one of the chief events.	
	28		Training and Education.	

/29..............

D. D. & L., London, E.C.
(A8004) Wt W1771/M2031 750,000 5/17 Sch. 52 Forms/C2118/14

Instructions regarding War Diaries and Intelligence Summaries are contained in F. S. Regs., Part II. and the Staff Manual respectively. Title pages will be prepared in manuscript.

Headquarters, 3rd Midland Brigade.

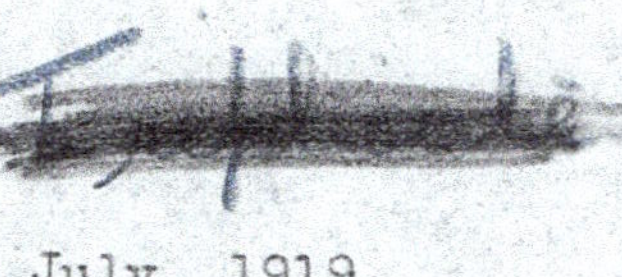

Army Form C. 2118.

WAR DIARY

~~or~~

Page 111. ~~INTELLIGENCE SUMMARY.~~ July, 1919.

(*Erase heading not required.*)

Place	Date	Hour	Summary of Events and Information	Remarks and references to Appendices
	29		Midland Division Order No.9 received reference move from SCHMIDTHEIM to area RODENKIRCHEN - SURTH - BRUHL - WEILERWHIST Camp. Warning Order issued to all units.	APPENDIX 1
	30 } 31 }		Training and Education.	

Captain,
for Brigade Major, 3rd Midland Brigade.

D. D. & L., London, E.C.
(A8004) Wt W1771/M2031 750,000 5/17 Sch. 52 Forms/C2118/14

3rd Midland Brigade.

WAR DIARY FOR MONTH OF JULY, 1919.

List of Appendices.

No.1. 3rd Midland Brigade WARNING ORDER dated 29th July.
2. Nominal Roll of Officers. on Brigade Headquarters.
3. Ration Strength of Brigade on 31/7/19.

@@@@@@@@@@@@@@@@@

SECRET. G.180/1.

Amendment No.1.
to.
3rd Midland Brigade WARNING ORDER dated 29/7/19.

Reference above order, para1, location of Brigade Group on completion of moves, for B Sec. 13th Field Ambulance - "BERSDORF", read "BLESSEM."

Acknowledge.

Staff Captain,
30th July, 1919. for Brigade Major, 3rd Midland Brigade.

Appendix No 1

WARNING ORDER. G.180.

1. The 3rd Midland Brigade Group will move to the Area RODENKIRCHEN - SURTH - BRUHL - WEILERWIST.

Transport will march by road on 4th August, staging at ROGGENDORF and LECHENICH on nights of 4th and 5th respectively.

Personnel will proceed by train on 6th and 7th August.

The following will be the disposition of Brigade Group on arrival in new area:-

Unit.	LOCATION.
Brigade Headquarters.	MARIENBERG.
51st Sherwood Foresters.	WEILERWIST CAMP.
52nd " "	BRUHL.
53rd " "	RODENKIRCHEN.
3rd Midland T.M.Battery.	do.
509th Field Coy.R.E.	WEILERWIST.
B Sec. 18th Field Ambulance.	BERSDORF.
No. 3 Coy. Divl. Train.	BRUHL.

2. Advance parties as under will proceed to new area under arrangements to be made by Os.C. Units to arrange billets.

Brigade Headquarters.	1 Offr. 6 O.Rs.
Battalions.	1 Offr. 20 O.Rs.
T.M.Battery.	1 Offr. 6 O.Rs.
509th Field Coy.R.E.	1 Offr. 10 O.Rs.
No. 3 Coy. Divl. Train.	1 Offr. 10 O.Rs.
B Sec.18th Field Amb.	1 Offr. 6 O.Rs.

3. Transport will move as light as possible.

4. The Brigade Group will be as follows:-

3rd Midland Brigade. B.Sec. 18th Field Ambulance.

509th Field Coy.R.E. No. 3 Coy. Divl. Train.

5. ACKNOWLEDGE.

[signature] Capt for

Staff Captain,

29th July,1919. for Brigade Major,3rd Midland Brigade.

DISTRIBUTION:-

Brigadier General Commanding.
Staff Captain.
Midland Division "G".
1st Midland Brigade.
D.A.P.M. Mid.Div.
All units Brigade Group.
Brigade Major.
Brigade Signal Officer.
Midland Division "Q".
A.D.M.S. Mid.Div.
Area Commandant SCHMIDTHEIM.
✓ War Diary (2).

3rd Midland Brigade.

ROLL OF OFFICERS. APPENDIX No.2.

Brigadier-General P.C.B.SKINNER, C.M.G.,D.S.O.	Brigade Commander.
Captain (Bt. Major) A. WEYMAN, MC.	Brigade Major.
Captain G.W.N. BAREFOOT, MC.	Staff Captain.
Captain C.F. LAMPARD. (Norfolk Regiment).	Brigade Education Officer.

<u>ATTACHED</u>.

Lieut. C. MORGAN, (Royal Engineers).	Brigade Signal Officer.
Lieut. H. COY, (Leicestershire Regt.)	Civil Staff Captain.
Lieut. R. WATSON, MC. (Sherwood Foresters).	Bde. Lewis Gun Officer.
Lieut. J.M. JORDON,(Sherwood Foresters).	Brigade Transport Officer.

@@@@@@@@@@@@@@@@@@

APPENDIX No.3.

RATION STRENGTH OF 3rd MIDLAND BRIGADE ON 31/7/19.

	Officers.	Other Ranks.
Brigade Headquarters.	4	80.
51st Sherwood Foresters.	51	853.
52nd Sherwood Foresters.	44	809.
53rd Sherwood Foresters.	58	773.
3rd Midland T.M.Battery.	3	35.

@@@@@@@@@@@@@@@@@@@@@@@@@@@@@

Instructions regarding War Diaries and Intelligence Summaries are contained in F. S. Regs., Part II. and the Staff Manual respectively. Title pages will be prepared in manuscript.

Army Form C. 2118.

Headquarters, 3rd Midland Brigade.

WAR DIARY
or
~~INTELLIGENCE SUMMARY.~~

(*Erase heading not required.*)

Page I. August, 1919.

Place	Date	Hour	Summary of Events and Information	Remarks and references to Appendices
SCHMIDTHEIM	I-2		Brigade Gymkhana - 2 very successful afternoons.	
	I.		3rd Midland Brigade Order No.422 and Administrative Instructions reference move to new Area ' issued.	Appendix I.
	3.		Movement Table and Amendment to same to be attached to order 422 issued.	
			Cross Country run for Brigade - a large attendence, including G.O.C. Midland Division.	
	4-5.		Transport started by road to new Area. Preparations for Move.	
	5.		Preparations for Move.	
Cologne - Bruhl Area.	6.		Bde.H.Q. proceeded to MARIENBERG by train from SCHMIDTHEIM arriving about I7.00 hours.	
			53rd Sherwood Foresters. " " RODENKIRCHEN " " " " " " "	
			3rd Mid.T.M.B. " " " " " " " " " "	
			52nd Sherwood Foresters. " " BRUHL " " " " " I5.00 "	
			No.3 Coy.Train. " " PINGSDORF " " " " " " "	
	7.		51st Sherwood Foresters. " " (Musketry Camp) WEILERWIST) " " " " " I3.00 "	
			509th Field Coy R.E. " " WEILERWIST " " " " " " "	
	8.		Brigadier General Commanding visited 51st Sherwood Foresters.	
	II.		Ist day of Midland Division recreational week at ROMERHOF.	
	I2.		Midland Division Officers Fancy Dress Dance at Kaiser's Schloss BRUHL. Gymkhana at ROMERHOF.	
	I4.		Sports at ROMERHOF.	
	I5.		Gymkhana "	
	I6.		Finals of Sports, Boxing, and inter Company Cricket (I8th Field Ambulance V C Coy.53rd Sher.Fers) at ROMERHOF. 53rd Sherwood Foresters won the Cricket, and were 3rd best Unit in the Division.	
	I8.		Orders received that the 3rd Midland Brigade and 6th M.G.Battalion are to proceed to IRELAND about 28th August. On Arrival Hqrs 3rd Midland Brigade will be disbanded.	
	I8-I9.		The Army Horse Show at COLOGNE.	
	20.		Preparations for the Move.	
	23-24.		Equipment sent to BRUHL Station and loaded on Equipment Train for England.	
	25.		Horses for ENGLAND left by train.	

/26 ....

D. D. & L., London, E.C. (A8004) Wt W1771/M2031 750,000 5/17 Sch. 52 Forms/C2118/14

3rd Midland Brigade.

WAR DIARY FOR MONTH OF AUGUST, 1919.

List of Appendices.

No. 1. 3rd Midland Brigade Order No.422 dated 1st August.
" 2. Nominal Roll of Officers on Brigade Headquarters.
" 3. Ration Strength of Brigade on 28/8/1919.

@@@@@@@@@@@@@@@@@@@@@@

Instructions regarding War Diaries and Intelligence Summaries are contained in F. S. Regs., Part II. and the Staff Manual respectively. Title pages will be prepared in manuscript.

WAR DIARY ~~or~~ ~~INTELLIGENCE SUMMARY.~~

(*Erase heading not required.*)

Army Form C. 2118.

Page 2.

August, 1919.

Place	Date	Hour	Summary of Events and Information	Remarks and references to Appendices
COLOGNE-~~BRUH~~ BRUHL Area.	26.		General Officer Commanding IX Corps visited all Battalions in turn and Brigade Headquarters to say Good-bye to Officers Commanding and the Brigadier General Commanding.	
	27.		General Boyd C.B. C.M.G. D.S.O. D.C.M. inspected each Battalion in turn and made a farewell speech. Battalions paraded as under forming 3 sides of a square. 10.30 am. 53rd Sherwood Foresters RODENKIRCHEN. 11.05 am. 51st " " WESSELING. 11.35 am. 52nd " " BRUHL. The General Officer Commanding the Division was very pleased indeed with the turn out, especially that of 51st Sherwood Foresters which was excellent. 51st Sherwood Foresters held some excellent swimming sports in baths in the Rhine at WESSELING.	
	28.	11.45	53rd Sherwood Foresters left BRUHL station for Kilworth Camp FERMOY Ireland via Calais. Owing to the engine breaking down the train left one hour late. *Orders received for H.Qrs 3 Midland Bde to go to KINMEL Camp RHYL (Wales) and instead of Ireland*	*Ans.*
	29.	10.46	52nd Sherwood Foresters left BRUHL for BALLYKINLAR Ireland - via CALAIS - Brigade Signal Section rejoined Divisional Headquarters.	
	30.	10.46	51st Sherwood Foresters left BRUHL for BALLYKINLAR Ireland via CALAIS. They cheered theGeneral most enthusiastically as the train went out of the station.	

A W Seymour Major

Brigade Major, 3rd Midland Brigade.

D. D. & L., London, E.C.
(A8004) Wt W1771/M2031 750,000 5/17 Sch. 52 Forms/C2118/14

Ref. EUSKIRCHEN Sheet.
Germany I.L. I/100.000

COPY No. 18

SECRET. 3rd Midland Brigade Order No. 422 dated I/8/19.

I. 3rd Midland Brigade Group will move to the Area RODENKIRCHEN - SURT BRUHL - WEILERSWIST CAMP on 6th and 7th August. Transport by road, staging at ROGGENDORF and LECHENICH on nights 4th and 5th August, and relieve Ist Midland Brigade at BRUHL and WEILERSWIST CAMP. Ist Midland Brigade on reli will move to Area LIBLAR - GYMNICH - ERP.

2. Advance parties Ist Midland Brigade consisting of one Platoon per Battalion will move by rail to SCHMIDTHEIM on August 6th, where they will come under the orders of the Camp Commandant, and will find the necessary guards for the Camp under his orders.

3. Brigade Groups mentioned in this order consist of the following :-

Ist Midland Brigade Group.	3rd Midland Brigade Group.
Ist Midland Brigade.	3rd Midland Brigade.
459th Field Coy. R.E.	509th Field Coy. R.E.
H.qs. I8th Field Amb.	B Sec. I8th Field Amb.
No. 4 Coy. Divl. Train.	No. 3 Coy. Divl. Train.

4. Table of movements will be issued later.

5. Completion of moves will be wired to Brigade H.Qrs.

6. All Units will wire Map Locations and addresses of their Headquarter on arrival.

7. Brigade H.Qrs. will close down at the Schloss SCHMIDTHEIM at 08.00 hours 6th instant, and re-open at 27 KASTANIEN ALLEE MARIENBURG at I2 mid-d 6th instant.

8. Administrative Instructions are being issued.

9. ACKNOWLEDGE.

[signature]
Staff Captain,
For Brigade Major, 3rd Midland Brigade.

Ist August, I9I9.

DISTRIBUTION.

Copy No. I. Brigadier General Commanding.
" " 3. Staff Captain.
" " 5. Midland Division "G".
" " 7. Ist Midland Brigade.
" " 9. D.A.P.M. Mid.Div.
" " II. 5Ist Sherwood Foresters.
" " I2. 52nd " "
" " I4. 3rd Midland T.M.Battery.
" " I6. B Sec. I8th Field Amb.
" " I8. War Diary.

Copy No. 2. Brigade Major.
" " 4. Brigade Signal Offr.
" " 6. Midland Division "Q".
" " 8. A.D.M.S. Mid.Div.
" " I0. Area Commandant SCHMI H
" " I3. 53rd Sherwood Foreste
" " I5. No.3 Coy.Divl. Train.
" " I7. 509th Field Coy.R.E.
" " I9. War Diary.

@@@@@@@@@@@@@@@@@@@@

ADMINISTRATIVE INSTRUCTIONS TO ACCOMPANY 3rd MIDLAND BRIGADE OPERATION ORDER NO. 422.

SECRET.

Ref: MUENCHEN Sheet
GERMANY BL 1/100000.

1. Tents, Camp Equipment and Stores.

Units will leave all camp stores and furniture behind and all tents standing. Lists of all stores left behind will be made out in triplicate, one copy to be retained by unit, one copy to be given to Camp Commandant and receipt obtained, and one copy sent to this office.

2. Cleanliness of Camp and Billets.

All units will ensure that their Camp or billets are left scrupulously clean and certificates to this effect obtained either from 1st Midland Brigade Advance Party or Camp Commandant. These certificates will be retained by Units.

3. Transport.

(a) The transport of the Brigade Group will proceed by road and will stage as follows:

Night of 4th – 5th ROGGENDORF.
" " 5th – 6th LECHENICH.
" " 6th – 7th Final destination.

(b) Brigade Column will march under the orders of O.C. No. 3 Coy. Divisional Train.

(c) Hour of starting – 0800 hours.

(d) Starting Point: Junction of HARMAGEN-SCHMIDTHEIM and HECHEN-SCHMIDTHEIM roads.

(e) Order of March:
No. 3 Coy. Train; Bde. H.Q.; T.M.B.; 51st., 52nd., 53rd., Sherwood Foresters; 503th Field Coy. R.E.; "B" Sec. 18th F.A..

(f) Strict March Discipline will be observed and following distances maintained:

Between transport of Units 100 yards.
Between each section of 12 Vehicles 50 yards.

Transport will halt every 10 minutes to the clock hour, and all personnel will dismount and at once loosen girths. All petrol tins will be carried full of water.

(g) Baggage waggons will report to units by 0900 hours 2nd. inst and will march with Battalion transport.

(h) Each Unit will detail one special N.C.O. or man who will draw rations for transport each day on arrival supply lorries.

(i) O.C. No. 3 Coy. Train will arrange for billets on the night of 4th – 5th at ROGGENDORF direct with Burgomaster, LECHENICH, (who administers ROGGENDORF) and billets for night of 5th – 6th with Civil Staff Captain, 1st Midland Brigade, LECHENICH.

4. RATIONS.

The following will be rationing arrangements of Brigade Group.

(a) Rations for transport proceeding by road. –
Units will refill twice on 3rd inst. and transport will march with rations for consumption 4th and 5th. On arrival at ROGGENDORF,

/rations.

rations for consumption 6th will be issued and on arrival at LECHENICH rations for consumption 7th.

(b) Rations for Advance Parties -
Units will make their own arrangements.

(c) Rations for Main Party.-
Units proceeding on 6th will carry rations for consumption 7th inclusive.
Units proceeding 7th will be rationed up to 7th inclusive.

(d) Units transport will draw from Refilling Point, BRUHL rations for consumption 8th for whole Brigade on the 7th inst. at a time to be arranged by Supply Officer, 3rd Midland Brigade. This will be the normal procedure from 7th onwards.

(e) Rations for personnel of Institutes and Camp Commandant and Staff-
The above personnel will be rationed by the Brigade until the 7th inclusive, after which date Division will make necessary arrangements

5. CANTEEN STORES.

The weekly Brigade allotment will be drawn by units on arrival in new area under arrangements to be made by Lieut. PRICE, Brigade Canteen Officer.

6. BRIGADE BATHS.

Brigade Baths will close on Sunday 3rd inst. after which date no bathing will take place. N.C.O. i/c Baths will have all clean and dirty clothing done up in bundles, and exact amount of each will be reported to this office. N.C.O. i/c Baths will obtain a certificate from Camp Commandant that all fittings etc. are complete in baths. Men employed on bathing duty will rejoin their units by 1800 hours 4th inst.

7. EMPLOYED MEN WITH INSTITUTES.

All men employed with Y.M.C.A., Church Army, and Salvation Army Institutes will join their Battalions before entrainment under arrangements to be made direct between units and Institutes concerned.

8. LORRIES.

Six lorries will be available to move stores from Camp to Station and will be allotted by Staff Captain. These lorries will report on the morning of the 5th inst.

The following lorries will be available for carrying kit of units from detraining station to their billots:-

Each Battalion	. . . . . .	6 Lorries.
Brigade H.Q. } T.M.B. }	. . . .	3 "
"B" Sec. 18th F.A.	. . . .	1 Lorry.
No. 3 Coy. Train	. . . .	1 "
509th Field Coy. R.E.	. .	2 Lorries.

9. KITS.

Units will arrange to have all kits and baggage they wish to take stacked ready for removal to station as soon as possible. All kits, when moved will be dumped on the Southern side of the station at the place allotted to each unit. Notice boards will mark this space.

10. LOADING AND UNLOADING PARTIES.

Each unit will arrange for a suitable loading and unloading party to be at the station. Dates and times at which these parties are to report will be notified later. The officer i/c this party will report to Staff Officer present who will give him instructions.

53rd Sherwood Foresters will detail 1 N.C.O. and 15 men to load and unload Brigade Headquarters.

11. Entraining instructions will be issued later.

12. CAMP COMMANDANT, WEILERWIST CAMP.

O.C. 51st Sherwood Foresters will detail an officer to act as Camp Commandant, WEILERWIST CAMP, who will take over from Camp Commandant, 1st Midland Brigade. He will sign for all stores, ammunition etc. handed over and forward list of stores taken over direct with receipts to this office. This officer will be responsible for this Camp. 51st Sherwood Foresters will wire name of officer selected to this office as soon as possible.

13. ACKNOWLEDGE.

1/8/1919.

[signature] Captain,
Staff Captain, 3rd Midland Brigade.

Distribution:-

Brigadier-General Commanding.
Staff Captain.
Brigade Major.
Brigade Signal Officer.
Mid. Div. "G"
Mid. Div. "Q".
1st Midland Brigade.
A.D.M.S. Midland Division.
Area Commandant, SCHILDTHEIM.
51st Sherwood Foresters.
52nd Sherwood Foresters.
53rd Sherwood Foresters.
3rd Midland T.M.Battery.
509th Field Coy. R.E.
"B" Section 10th Field Amb.
No. 3 Coy. Train.
N.C.O.i/c Baths.
Supply Officer, 3rd Midland Bde.
S.M.O. 3rd Midland Brigade.
War Diary (2)
"G"

War Diary

DATE.	Serial No.	Unit.	No. of Train.	Train Accommodation. Personnel Offrs.	O.Rs.	(allotted) Baggage.	Entraining Station.	Detraining Station.	Destination.	Remarks.
6 Aug.	1.	Bde.H.Qs.	1.	5.	100.	8 tons.	SCHMIDTHEIM.	BRUHL.	ARINBURG.	By march route from BRUHL.
6 "	2.	52nd Sherwood Foresters.	1.	29.	583.	42 tons.	do.	do.	BRUHL.	
6th"	3.	53rd Sherwood Foresters.	1.	33.	570.	20. "	do.	do.	RODENKIRCHEN.	By march route from BRUHL.
6 "	4.	T.M.B.	1.	4.	30.	2 "	do.	do.	do.	do.
6 "	5.	No.3 Coy Train	1.	6	6.	5 "	do.	do.	~~BERSDORF~~ PINGSDORF.	do.
7 "	6.	51st Sherwood Foresters.	2.	31.	670.	35 "	do.	WEILERSWIST.	~~CAMP.~~ WEILERSWHIST CAMP	By march route from WEILERHIST.
7 "	7.	509 Field Coy. R.E.	2.	2.	70.	4. "	do.	do.	do.	

(1) 1st Train will accommodate 71 Offrs. 1289 O.Rs, 77 tons of baggage. 2nd Train will accommodate 33 Offrs, 740 O.RS. 39 tons of baggage.
As these trains will only carry the exact amount of baggage, units are asked ~~that~~ for strict care must be taken that only that amount be taken to the station.
(2) Numbers of trucks not yet known. These will be allotted to Bns. on the basis of 30 men per covered wagon at the Station.
(3) Train Times as follows :-
1st Train loads SCHMIDTHEIM 08.30 departs 09.20 arrives BRUHL 13.37 hours. 6th Aug
2nd Train loads SCHMIDTHEIM 09.45 departs 10.22 arrives WEILERWHIST 13.38 hours. 7th Aug
(4) Entraining instructions are being issued.

Table of Movements to accompany 3rd Midland Brigade Order No. 422 dated I/8/I9.

3rd August, I9I9.

[signature]
Staff Captain,
For Brigade Major, 3rd Midland Brigade.

Brigadier-General Commanding.
Staff Captain.
51st Sherwood Foresters.
52nd Sherwood Foresters.
53rd Sherwood Foresters.
1st Midland Brigade.
Mid. Div. "Q"
A.D. .S. Mid. Div.
Camp Commandant SOMMIDTHIL.

Brigade Major.
Brigade Signal Officer.
3rd Midland T....Battery.
509th Field Coy. R.E.
"D" Section 15th F.A.
No. 3 Coy. Train.
Mid. Div. "G"
D.A.P.M. Mid. Div.
War Diary (2)

"5" ✓

Reference Table of Movements accompanying Brigade Operation Order No. 422.

Main body of the Brigade Group will proceed by rail on the 6th and 7th insts.

All baggage will be dumped on the Southern side of the station at the sites allotted and will be loaded from that side. Baggage must be stacked ready for loading 1st train by 0700 hours 6th inst. and 2nd train by 0800 hours 7th inst.

All personnel will entrain from northern side.

Each unit will detail an entraining and detraining officer who will report to Staff Captain or his representative at the station with exact entraining strengths, 45 minutes before train is due to start.

Entrainment of personnel will be carried out in following order, the head of the leading unit will be at the station gates at 0830 hours.-

Brigade Headquarters.
3rd Mid. T...Battery.
No. 3 Coy. Train.
52nd Sherwood Foresters.
53rd Sherwood Foresters.

The same instructions will be observed for 2nd. train loading on 7th inst. O.C. 51st Sherwood Foresters will be responsible for the entraining and detraining of baggage and personnel of that train.

Loading parties for troops proceeding on first train will report to Staff Captain at southern side of station by 0700 hours 6th inst. Those for troops entraing on 7th inst. at 0800 hours.

ACKNOWLEDGE.

3/8/1919.

G.W.Barfoot Captain,
Staff Captain, 3rd Midland Brigade.

3rd Midland Brigade.

Roll of Officers. Appendix No.2.

Brigadier-General P.C.B. Skinner, C.M.G., D.S.O.	Brigade Commander.
Captain (Bt. Major) A.Weyman, M.C.	Brigade Major.
Captain G.W.N. Barefoot M.C.	Staff Captain.
Captain C.F. Lampard. (Norfolk Regiment).	Brigade Education Officer.

ATTACHED.

Lieut. C.Morgan (Royal Engineers).	Brigade Signal Officer.
Lieut.H.Coy, (Leicestershire Regt).	Civil Staff Captain.
Lieut.R.Watson,M.C. (Sherwood ForestersX.	Brigade Lewis Gun Officer.
LieutzJ.M.Jordan. (Sherwood Foresters).	Brigade Transport Officer.

@@@@@@@@@@@@@@@@@@@@@@@@@@@@@

APPENDIX No.3.

RATION STRENGTH OF 3rd MIDLAND BRIGADE on 28/8/19.

	Officers.	Other Ranks.
Brigade Headquarters.	4.	80.
51st Sherwood Foresters.	51.	853.
52nd Sherwood Foresters.	44.	809.
53rd Sherwood Foresters.	58.	775.
3rd Midland T.M.Battery.	3.	35.

@@@@@@@@@@@@@@@@@@@@@@@@@@@@@@@@

MIDLAND DIVISION
(LATE 6TH DIVISION)

~~3RD MID'D INFY BDE~~

51ST BN NOTTS & DERBY REGT

MAR - JLY 1919

M

51 N & Derby

Instructions regarding War Diaries and Intelligence Summaries are contained in F. S. Regs., Part II. and the Staff Manual respectively. Title pages will be prepared in manuscript.

WAR DIARY
or
~~INTELLIGENCE SUMMARY.~~
(Erase heading not required.)

Army Form C. 2118.

Hour, Date, Place	Summary of Events and Information	Remarks and references to Appendices
0830 28.2.19 Brocton Camp	Bn paraded in readiness to proceed overseas was addressed by G.O.C. 208th Inf. Bde (Gen Wessel)	
1015 .. Milford Station	Bn entrained for Dover. 37 Officers & 587 other ranks	Mar – July 1919
1700 .. Dover	Bn detrained & marched to Oil Mill where it stayed the night. Officers accomodated at No 3 Rest Camp. (South Front Barracks 2/Lt King [illegible].	
1215 1.3.19 ..	Bn embarked on S.S. Antrim for Dunkirk	
1600 1.3.19 Dunkirk	Bn disembarked & proceeded to No 3 Rest Camp	
0830 2.3.19 3.3.19 ..	Bn paraded & marched to Sand Siding where it entrained for the front passing through Bailleul, Armentières, Lille, Liege, & Namur.	
0730 4.3.19	Bn detrained at Bonntor Station near Cologne & was met by 2nd Sherwoods band, marched to Rodenkirchen & billetted there.	
5.3.19 Rodenkirchen	The whole day was spent in settling down in billets & cleaning up.	
6.3.19 ..	Bn reorganised into four Companies & Bn Headquarters.	
1030 7.3.19 ..	Bn paraded & marched to Marienburger Barracks where it was inspected by the 2nd Army Commander (Gen Plumer) who complimented the C.O. on the smart appearance of the Bn.	
8.3.19.	Morning spent in completing the reorganisation of the Bn. Afternoon devoted to games	
10.3.19.	Training carried out under company arrangements. 2/Lt Franklin proceeded to Marienburger Barracks with the Transport Section for instruction with the 2nd Bn The Sherwood Foresters.	

Instructions regarding War Diaries and Intelligence Summaries are contained in F. S. Regs., Part II. and the Staff Manual respectively. Title pages will be prepared in manuscript.

WAR DIARY
or
INTELLIGENCE SUMMARY.
(*Erase heading not required.*)

Army Form C. 2118.

Hour, Date, Place	Summary of Events and Information	Remarks and references to Appendices
11.3.19 Rodenkirchen	The C.O. lectured to the Bn on March Discipline, afterwards short route march by companies	
12.3.19 "	Bn took over the following Guards from 2nd Bn The Sherwood Foresters The Arsenal, Vorgebirge Strasse, Volksgarten, Fort 8, Magazine and Bonton Station. Drill + guard mounting parades in the morning	
13.3.19	The Bn took over the Guard at Bde Hdqrs from 1st Leicesters Parades as yesterday	
14.3.19	Mobilization equipment taken over from 2nd Bn The Sherwood Foresters Parades as usual.	
15.3.19	Training carried out as usual.	
16.3.19	No Church Parade in the morning but Voluntary Service in the evening Maj. Edwards gave an address in Education Room.	
17.3.19	Officers + N.C.Os Lewis gun class started. St. Patricks Day	
18.3.19	Training as usual.	
19.3.19	Training as usual. 439 Field Coy R.E. were to have played the Bn at football today, but as they were changing station the game was not played.	
20.3.19	Training as usual. Hockey match played against 52nd Bn Sherwoods. Score 6-4 for the Bn.	
21-3-19	Training as usual. All subaltern officers were taken on a tactical exercise by the Commanding Officer. Lt C. G. J. Raynor R.A.M.C. reported to 19th Field Ambulance Capt. J. F. M. Wigley R.A.M.C. reported to this unit for duty.	

(9 29 6) W 3332—1107 100,000 10/13 H W V Forms/C. 2118/10.

Instructions regarding War Diaries and Intelligence Summaries are contained in F. S. Regs., Part II. and the Staff Manual respectively. Title pages will be prepared in manuscript.

WAR DIARY

or

INTELLIGENCE SUMMARY.

(Erase heading not required.)

Army Form C. 2118.

Hour, Date, Place		Summary of Events and Information	Remarks and references to Appendices
RODENKIRCHEN	22-3-19	Training as usual. Football match played against No 8 Vet. Hospital Result – draw 1 goal each. Guards at Fort VIII & Arsenal relieved by 53rd Bn The Sherwood Foresters. Proff. Adkins lectured on "The Origin of the War" at 1100 hours.	
	~~23-3-19~~		
	23-3-19	Church Parades in morning. R.C. parade in RODENKIRCHEN church C of E in Education Rooms. Football in afternoon	
	24-3-19.	Training & recreation as usual.	
	25-3-19.	Route march in morning. Hockey match in afternoon with 53rd Bn The Sherwood Foresters at MARIENBURGHER BRKS. Score 6-1 for the Bn.	
	26-3-19.	Training as usual. Football match was to have been played against 53rd Bn The Sherwood Foresters but was cancelled.	
	27-3-19	Training as usual. T/Maj. K. W. Maxwell M.C. reported from 15th Bn Sherwood Foresters. Afternoon. Hockey match against 53rd Bn Sherwood Foresters. Result draw 2 all.	
	28-3-19.	Muster parade at 0915. Instruction in Shooting & Lecturing started under 2/Lt Larkam, Lt A.C. Fairbrother M.C. 2/Lt C.B.O. Brodick, 2/Lt L. Bromham. Lt W.J. Hinter M.C. reported from 8th Bn Sherwood Foresters. 2/Lt W Edom reported from 139 Trench Mortar Battery. A VI Football match in afternoon against	
	29-3-19	Training as usual. Afternoon Football match against 47th Div R.E. Result 3-1 against. Lt & Q.M. Spare 9th London Regt reported.	
	30-3-19	Church Parades as last Sunday	
	31-3-19	Training & recreation as usual	

[illegible signature]
LIEUT. COL.
[illegible] BATTN. THE NOTTS & DERBY REGT.

(9 29 6) W 3332—1107 100,000 10/13 H W V Forms/C. 2118/10.

ORDERLY ROOM
No. 2B560
DATE 2.4.19

ROLL OF OFFICERS.

51st.Bn.Sherwood Foresters.

Lieut.Colonels.
Lt.Col.A.B.Wayte.D.S.O.

Majors.
Major K.W.Sorrell.M.C.

Lieutenants.
Lt. H.F.F.Coggin
W.H.N.Dent.
A.S.Read.
G.N.D.Whyte.
T.Mason.
G.M.Humphry.
E.S.W.Thomas.
F.W.Llewelyn.
J.F.Russell.
C.Shirley.
H.Hickman.M.M.
E.E.Scotton.
H.G.Taylor.
M.E.Williams.
H.Edson.
G.W.M.Hare.
A.C.Fairbrother.M.C.
W.J.Winter.M.C.

Adjutant.
Cpt.W.Boyd-Orr.M.C.

Qr.Mr.
Lt.&.Q.M.A.J.DUNN.

Attached.
Medical Officer.
Cpt.J.E.M.Wigley.

Captains.
Cpt.W.R.Perry.
J.I.Spicer.
F.J.Jennion.
C.H.Peart.
E.S.C.Vaughan.M.C.

2/Lieutenants.
2/Lt.C.Franklin.
E.Flewitt.
W.Collins.
C.A.Turner.
R.W.Larkam.
A.Mackintosh.M.C.
H.de Loney.
H.W.Fitzgerald.
C.Sunday.
E.Graver.
H.W.King.
C.H.Winterbottom.
C.W.Hall.
B.Bornby.M.C.
W.J.Howard.
C.Haworth.
C.O.Bradish.
L.Bromham.

A Wayte
Lieut.Col.
Comdg.51st.Bn.SHERWOOD FORESTERS.

31-3-19.

4 HQ

Instructions regarding War Diaries and Intelligence Summaries are contained in F. S. Regs., Part II. and the Staff Manual respectively. Title pages will be prepared in manuscript.

WAR DIARY
or
INTELLIGENCE SUMMARY.
(Erase heading not required.)

Army Form C. 2118.

Hour, Date, Place	Summary of Events and Information	Remarks and references to Appendices
1-4-19 RODENKIRCHEN	Training & Recreation as usual. Lt R A Wood reported from 139th L.T.M. Battery.	
2-4-19	Training as usual. Recreation in afternoon	
3-4-19.	Training as usual. Afternoon Bn played 53rd Bn at Hockey Result lost 10-5	
4-4-19	Training as usual. ~~Effect~~ Col H. M. Milward DSO reported from 2nd Bn The Sherwood Foresters & assumed command. Football match against 47th Div Signals Result lost 5-1	
5-4-19	Bn proceeded on a pleasure trip up the Rhine Left Cologne 0900 & returned 1615. 2/Lt J M Wilde reported from 105th T.M. Battery	
6-4-19	Church parades as usual.	
7-4-19	Training & recreation as usual	
8-4-19	Route march in morning. Lt King Gloucester Regt lectured on Post Bellum Army.	
9-4-19.	Bn inspected by Brigadier General Skinner Commanding 3rd Midland Brigade. Football match was to have been played with M.L. Detachment at Cologne but they could not turn up.	
10-4-19	Training & recreation as usual	

Instructions regarding War Diaries and Intelligence Summaries are contained in F. S. Regs., Part II. and the Staff Manual respectively. Title pages will be prepared in manuscript.

WAR DIARY
or
INTELLIGENCE SUMMARY.
(Erase heading not required.)

Army Form C. 2118.

Hour, Date, Place	Summary of Events and Information	Remarks and references to Appendices
11-4-19 RODENKIRCHEN	Training recreation as usual	
12-4-19	Bn paraded at 1030 & marched to [illegible] Barracks where it was inspected by the Corps Commander. Afternoon football match against No 8 Veterinary Hospital Result lost 4-0. Lieut J. Powell, D.S.O. reported from 8th Bn The Sherwood Foresters	
13-4-19	Church parades in morning. Afternoon recreation	
14-4-19	Training as usual.	
15. 4. 19.	Training as usual.	
16. 4. 19.	Training as usual. 2/Lt. J.H. Smith MC reported from 8th. Sherwood Foresters. 9 O.Rs. reported from 11th Bn Leicestershire Regt.	
17. 4. 19.	Lt Col. Thornton D.S.O. reported on 16th inst. & assumed command of the Bn vice Lt Col. Milward who assumed duties of 2nd in command.	
18. 4. 19	Training as usual.	
19. 4. 19	2nd Lt Winterbottom proceeded to England on duty	

(9 29 6) W 3332—1107 100,000 10/13 H W V Forms/C. 2118/10.

Instructions regarding War Diaries and Intelligence Summaries are contained in F. S. Regs., Part II. and the Staff Manual respectively. Title pages will be prepared in manuscript.

WAR DIARY
or
INTELLIGENCE SUMMARY.

(Erase heading not required.)

Army Form C. 2118.

Hour, Date, Place		Summary of Events and Information	Remarks and references to Appendices
20.4.19.	Rodenkirchen	Church Parades as usual.	
21.4.19	"	Training as usual. Capt. N.G. Smith reported from 15th Sherwood Foresters.	
22.4.19.	"	Route march in morning.	
23.4.19	"	Training as usual.	
24.4.19	"	Training as usual. Lt. Hare G.O.M. proceeded to England on Educational Course. 2/Lt. W. Collins proceeded for demobilization.	
25.4.19	"	Training as usual.	
26.4.19	"	~~Training~~ Church Parades as usual.	
27.4.19.	"	Training as usual.	
28.4.19	"	Training as usual. Capt. H.C.V. Warneford M.C. and Capt. J.D. Johnston. M.C. reported from 3rd Bn. Sherwood Foresters	
29.4.19.	"	Training as usual.	
30.4.19	"	Training as usual.	

[signature] Lieut.-Col.
Comdg. 51 Bn. Sherwood Foresters.

Instructions regarding War Diaries and Intelligence Summaries are contained in F. S. Regs., Part II. and the Staff Manual respectively. Title pages will be prepared in manuscript.

WAR DIARY
or
INTELLIGENCE SUMMARY
(Erase heading not required.)

Army Form C. 2118.

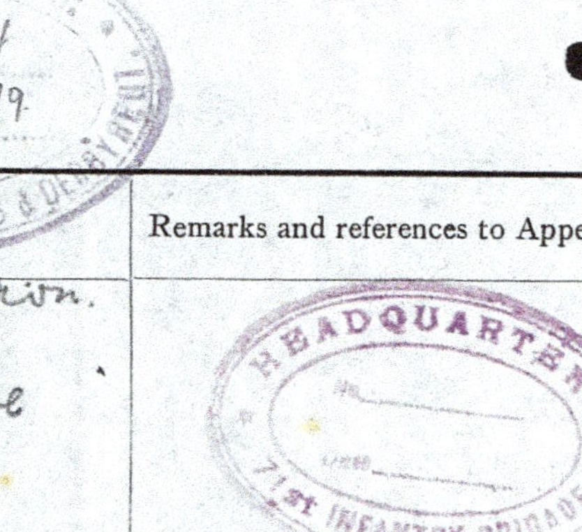

Hour, Date, Place		Summary of Events and Information	Remarks and references to Appendices
1.5.19	Rodenkirchen	Training as usual. Capt. J.C. Spicer proceeded to Mid. Divn. for duty as Camp Commandant	HEADQUARTERS 71st INFANTRY BRIGADE
2.6.19.	"	Training as usual. The Bn concert Party "The Nibs" gave their first concert.	
3.6.19	"	Training as usual	
4.5.19	"	Church Parades. Bn football XI v 509th Field Coy. – Won 5-2.	
5.5.19	"	Bn marched to Surth for inspection by G.O.C. in C. Bn shield competition commenced in afternoon. Lt. G.N.D. Whyte resumed duties as messing officer. 2/Lt. G.H. Winterbottom returned from duty in England.	
6.5.19	"	Training as usual. Message from G.O.C. in C expressing his appreciation of the bearing, steadiness on parade, and turn out, both of troops & transport, when inspected yesterday. Lt. Read reported for duty to A.D.R.T. Cologne.	
7.5.19	"	Training as usual.	
8.5.19	"	Training as usual.	
9.6.19	"	Training as usual. G.O.C. Bde inspected "B" Coy in organisation. Hockey Match: Bn v IX Corps Hdqrs. – Lost 3-8.	
10.5.19	"	Training as usual.	
11.5.19	"	Church Parades.	
12.5.19	"	Training as usual. Lt. Col. W.B. Thornton D.S.O. proceeded on Bde. duty; Lt. Col. Hon Milward D.S.O. assumes command of the Bn.	

Instructions regarding War Diaries and Intelligence Summaries are contained in F. S. Regs., Part II. and the Staff Manual respectively. Title pages will be prepared in manuscript.

WAR DIARY
or
INTELLIGENCE SUMMARY
(Erase heading not required.)

Army Form C. 2118.

Hour, Date, Place		Summary of Events and Information	Remarks and references to Appendices
12.5.19	RODENKIRCHEN.	Lts W. J. Winter, M.E. Williams, C.P.O. Bradish & 2/Lts. G.A. Turner, L.H.W. Fitzgerald proceeded to 2/8th Bn Worcester Regt Cherbourg.	
13.5.19.	"	Route march in morning. Lt. J.M. White reported to 3rd. Mid. Trench Mortar Battery for duty.	
14.5.19	"	Training as usual. Lt Col Thornton returned from Bde. duty & re-assumes command of Bn.	
15.5.19	"	Training as usual. Capt. J.E.M Wigley. R.A.M.C. proceeded to England.	
16.5.19	"	Bn paraded to cheer Marshal Foch, as he passed down the Rhine. Capt. C. Dean. R.A.M.C. reported for duty as Medical Officer.	
17.5.19	"	Bn. proceeded on pleasure trip up the Rhine.	
18.5.19	"	Church Parades.	
19.5.19	"	Training as usual	
20.5.19	"	Route March	
21.5.19	"	Training as usual.	
22.5.19		5 Offs & 35 O.Rs. proceeded on pleasure trip up the Rhine.	
23.5.19		Training as usual.	
24.5.19		Traing as usual. Lt E.S.W. Thomas appointed a/Ass/Adjt. vice Lt Coggin apptd. Education Officer. Lt E.S.C. Vaughan proceeded for duty to IX Corps Hostel.	
25.5.19		Church Parades. Capt. Warneford M.C. proceeded to England to attend course at Harrow.	

1247 W 3299 200,000 (E) 8/14 J.B.C. & A. Forms/C. 2118/11.

Instructions regarding War Diaries and Intelligence Summaries are contained in F. S. Regs., Part II. and the Staff Manual respectively. Title pages will be prepared in manuscript.

WAR DIARY
or
INTELLIGENCE SUMMARY
(Erase heading not required.)

Army Form C. 2118.

Hour, Date, Place		Summary of Events and Information	Remarks and references to Appendices
25.5.19	RODENKIRCHEN.	Capt. W.R. Perry proceeded to England, and struck off strength of Bn.	
26.5.19	"	Training as usual.	
27.5.19	"	Route March. Capt. J.R.H. Mollan. M.C. (Ramc) reported for duty as Medical Officer, thereby relieving Capt. C. Dean. M.C. (Ramc).	
28.5.19	"	Training as usual.	
29.5.19	"	Training as usual.	
30.5.19		Bn proceeded on Rhine pleasure trip.	
31.5.19	"	Training as usual. Lt. J.W. Sandall. reported from 11th Bn Leicestershire Regt.	

[signature] Lieut. Col.
Comdg. 51st Battn. The Notts & Derby Regt.

1247 W 3299 200,000 (E) 8/14 J.B.C. & A. Forms/C. 2118/11.

Instructions regarding War Diaries and Intelligence Summaries are contained in F. S. Regs., Part II. and the Staff Manual respectively. Title Pages will be prepared in manuscript.

WAR DIARY
or
INTELLIGENCE SUMMARY
(Erase heading not required.)

Army Form C. 2118

Place	Date	Hour	Summary of Events and Information	Remarks and references to Appendices
RODENKIRCHEN.	1.6.19		~~Training~~ Church Parades as usual.	
	2.6.19		Training as usual.	
	3.6.19		Kings birthday. Brigade Parade on Cologne Golf Course. Rest of day - holiday. G.O.C. 3rd Mid. Bde. message of appreciation on turnout of Bn.	
	4.6.19		Training as usual.	
	5.6.19		Training as usual. 2/Lt. E. Graves proceeded to 257th Area Employment Coy.	
	6.6.19		Training as usual.	
	7.6.19		Training as usual.	
	8.6.19		Sunday. No church parade owing to Bn moving.	
	9.6.19		Bn. moved to Summer Camp at Schmidtheim. Lt. J. Mason proceeded to Mid. Div. for temporary attachment vice Capt. J. J. Spicer.	
	10.6.19		Training as usual. 2/Lt. A.J. Dunn proceeded to Midland Div. 9.6.19	
	11.6.19		Training as usual.	
	12.6.19		Training as usual.	
	13.6.19		Training as usual.	
	14.6.19		Training as usual	
	15.6.19		Church Parades.	
	16.6.19		Training as usual.	
	17.6.19		Bn. inspected by Duke of Portland. Div. Commander expresses pleasure at turn out & soldierly bearing of the Bde.	
	18.6.19		Training as usual.	
LECHENICH	19.6.19		Bn moved to Lechenich	
	20.6.19		Companies at disposal of Coy. Commanders.	

Army Form C. 2118

Instructions regarding War Diaries and Intelligence Summaries are contained in F. S. Regs., Part II. and the Staff Manual respectively. Title Pages will be prepared in manuscript.

WAR DIARY
or
INTELLIGENCE SUMMARY
(Erase heading not required.)

Place	Date	Hour	Summary of Events and Information	Remarks and references to Appendices
LECHENICH	21.6.19		Training as usual. Lt. Hare reported from Course at Oxford.	
	22.6.19		Church Parades.	
	23.6.19		Training as usual.	
	24.6.19		Training as usual.	
	25.6.19		Training as usual.	
	26.6.19		Training as usual. Major H.C. Stephen (N'land Fus) taken on strength of Bn. and assumes duties of 2nd in Command.	
	27.6.19		Training as usual.	
	28.6.19		Training as usual	
	29.6.19		Church Parades.	
	30.6.19		Training as usual.	

[signature] LIEUT. COL.,
COMMDG. 51st BN. THE SHERWOOD FORESTERS

3.7.19.

1875 Wt. W593/826 1,000,000 4/15 J.B.C. & A. A.D.S.S./Forms/C. 2118.

51st NaD

Instructions regarding War Diaries and Intelligence Summaries are contained in F. S. Regs., Part II. and the Staff Manual respectively. Title pages will be prepared in manuscript.

WAR DIARY
or
INTELLIGENCE SUMMARY
(Erase heading not required.)

Army Form C. 2118.

	Hour, Date, Place	Summary of Events and Information	Remarks and references to Appendices
1.7.19	Lechenich	Bn. moved to Schmidtheim.	
2.7.19	Schmidtheim	Bn. arranging camp, cleaning up etc.	
3.7.19	"	do. do. do.	
4.7.19	"	General Holiday to commemorate the signing of peace.	
5.7.19	"	Bn parade. Capt. F. J. Jamion, Manchester Regt. Struck off strength of Bn.	
6.7.19	"	Church parades.	
7.7.19	"	Parades as usual.	
8.7.19	"	Parades as usual. Lieut. G.W.M. Hare proceeded on IX Corps for course in "method"	
9.7.19	"	Parades as usual.	
10.7.19	"	Bn. parade.	
11.7.19	"	Parades as usual. Lt. W. J. Howard proceeded to 9th Bn Cheshire Regt.	
12.7.19	"	Parades as usual.	
13.7.19	"	Church parades	
14.7.19	"	Parades as usual. Lecture by Rev. G. H. Haslett. B.A.	
15.7.19	"	Parades as usual.	
16.7.19	"	Parades as usual.	

1247 W 3299 200,000 (E) 8/14 J.B.C. & A. Forms/C. 2118/11.

Army Form C. 2118.

Instructions regarding War Diaries and Intelligence Summaries are contained in F. S. Regs., Part II. and the Staff Manual respectively. Title pages will be prepared in manuscript.

WAR DIARY
or
INTELLIGENCE SUMMARY

(Erase heading not required.)

Hour, Date, Place		Summary of Events and Information	Remarks and references to Appendices
17.7.19	Schmidtheim	Bn. Parade.	
18.7.19	"	Parades as usual.	
19.7.19	"	Parades as usual.	
20.7.19	"	Church Parades.	
21.7.19	"	Parades as usual.	
22.7.19	"	Bn. Parade.	
23.7.19	"	Parades as usual.	
24.7.19	"	Parades as usual.	
25.7.19	"	Bn. Parade.	
26.7.19	"	2nd. Midland Bde. Sports.	
27.7.19	"	Church Parades.	
28.7.19	"	Parades as usual.	
29.7.19	"	Parades as usual.	
30.7.19	"	Bn. Parade.	
31.7.19	"	Bn. Parade.	

H. C. Hopkins[?] Major.
Commanding 51st Bn.The Sherwood Foresters.

1247 W 3299 200,000 (E) 8/14 J.B.C. & A. Forms/C. 2118/11.

MIDLAND DIVISION
(LATE 6TH DIVISION)

3RD MID'D' BDE (INFY)

52ND BN NOTTS & DERBYS.

~~JAN. - JLY 1919~~

1917 NOV — 1919 JULY

52nd Sherwood Foresters

Instructions regarding War Diaries and Intelligence Summaries are contained in F. S. Regs., Part II. and the Staff Manual respectively. Title pages will be prepared in manuscript.

WAR DIARY
or
INTELLIGENCE SUMMARY.
(*Erase heading not required.*)

Army Form C. 2118.

War Vol I

Place	Date	Hour	Summary of Events and Information	Remarks and references to Appendices
5th Ashford Kent	17th Nov 1917		On 17th Nov 1917 the 278th Infantry T.R. Battn became the 52nd Grad. Bn Notts	
			& Derby Regt under the graduated system of training for which only recruits of	
			between 18 & 19 years of age were accepted, & a 5th Coy was formed.	
			The Companies were graduated according to age & drafted overseas on	
			reaching the age of 19 years. A new company from the 53rd Young Soldiers Battn	
			replacing it in the Graduated Bn.	
			The first station was at Ashford Kent, where the men were billeted & the Bn	
			formed part of the 200 Bde under Brigadier Gen E H Gorges C.B. The Bde consisted	
			of the 52 Northumberland Fus & 52 West Yorks & 52 Notts & Derby & the Cambridge Territorials	
			The Battn was commanded by Col the Earl of Radnor C.I.E. Strength of Bn about 1000	
			Training areas in the vicinity were very fair; but digging instruction was	
			difficult owing to the [illegible] of the [illegible], various parks were placed	
			at the disposal of the Bde. Musketry Ranges were at Rye in Sussex.	
			The Battn were fully [illegible] & was included in the Home Defence Scheme.	
	Jan 1918		Early in Jany the Bde was inspected on the line of march by Field Marshal	
			Sir John French.	

A6945 Wt. W11422/M1160 350,000 12/16 D. D. & L. Forms/C./2118/14.

5th Sherwood Foresters. Sheet 2

Instructions regarding War Diaries and Intelligence Summaries are contained in F. S. Regs., Part II. and the Staff Manual respectively. Title pages will be prepared in manuscript.

WAR DIARY
or
INTELLIGENCE SUMMARY.
(Erase heading not required.)

Army Form C. 2118.

Place	Date	Hour	Summary of Events and Information	Remarks and references to Appendices
5th Ashford	10th		On the 10th of Jany the Earl of Radnor relinquished his command & Maj J. A. [illegible]	
Kent	Jany 1918		having assumed command from 2nd in command.	
— " —	18 Jany		On the 18th Jany Bt Lt Colonel & Temporary Lt Col [illegible] DSO [illegible] Regt	
			arrived & appointed to command the Battn	
			The following officers commanded coys "A" Coy Capt P. A. [illegible] Manc Regt, "B" Coy	
			Lt K M Sinclair Arg & Suthd Hrs, "C" Coy Capt H W Royle Manc Regt, "D" Coy	
			Maj L G Bird DSO Lanc Fus, "E" Coy Capt [illegible] 5th S Staffs Regt	
			Adjutant Capt R [illegible] Manc Regt & Capt J R Jones Manchester Regt as 2nd Major.	
			Lewis guns were issued to the Battn about this time.	
— " —	14 Feby 1918		On the 14th Feby 1918 "A" Coy the senior coy proceeded overseas to join the E.F. in	
			France & disembarked at Calais. A new coy from the Y.S. Bn joined the same	
	15th Feby		day	
Clipstone Camp	22nd Feby 1918		On the 22nd Feby the Battn moved to Clipstone Camp, Nottingham after handing over	
Nottingham			the whole of their Mobilization Equip to the Southern Command, and took over	
			similar stores from the 1/5th Norfolk [illegible]. Forming part of [illegible]	

A6945 Wt. W11422/M1160 350,000 12/16 D. D. & L. Forms/C./2118/14.

52 Sherwood Foresters

Sheet 3

WAR DIARY
or
INTELLIGENCE SUMMARY.
(*Erase heading not required.*)

Army Form C. 2118.

Instructions regarding War Diaries and Intelligence Summaries are contained in F. S. Regs., Part II, and the Staff Manual respectively. Title pages will be prepared in manuscript.

Place	Date	Hour	Summary of Events and Information	Remarks and references to Appendices
Clipstone Camp Nottingham	22 Feby 1918		but attached temporarily to the 207th Bde	
			Capt C. Gregory Kane has arrived & took over charge & payment of B Coy	
			In spite of the severe weather the health of the troops was excellent.	
			Training continued for 17 days	
Redmires Camp Sheffield	11th March 1919		On this date the Battn (less E Coy) moved to Redmires Camp 7 miles W of Sheffield. E Coy under Capt W.T. Cowap proceeding on detachment to Silkstone Camp near Barnsley. The transport arrangements on arrival at Sheffield were extremely bad, no provision of any description having been made for the removal of the Bn stores from the station to camp. The 1st Line transport being already fully loaded. Arrangements had to be made there & then with the local M.T. Corps who kindly came to the rescue. Darkness & a Zeppelin raid put an end to the operations for the night.	
	12th March 1918		Training recommenced. Redmires Camp was very well built with a splendid training ground & well suited for summer training, but the weather was apt to be severe in winter. Rifle ranges were at Totley about 6 miles	

A6945 Wt. W11422/M1160 350,000 12/16 D. D. & L. Forms/C./2118/14.

52nd Sherwood Foresters.

Sheet 4

Army Form C. 2118.

Instructions regarding War Diaries and Intelligence Summaries are contained in F. S. Regs., Part II. and the Staff Manual respectively. Title pages will be prepared in manuscript.

WAR DIARY
or
INTELLIGENCE SUMMARY.
(*Erase heading not required.*)

Place	Date	Hour	Summary of Events and Information	Remarks and references to Appendices
Redmires Camp Sheffield	12 March 1918		distant, where men were billeted during their Musketry course	
			The training was considerably hampered by the fact that the R.E. who had	
			been in the camp before, had been ordered to fill in all their trenches &	
			bombing pits. The detachment at Silkstone under Capt. Crump were somewhat	
			better situated, the destruction of trenches etc not having been completed.	
—"—	18th March		The dispatch of drafts was somewhat hampered by outbreaks of measles	
			& scarlet fever, but nothing serious. 'B' Coy was drafted fully equipped to 5th [illegible]	
—"—	22nd March		Owing to the urgent call for reinforcements for France, it was decided by	
			War Office to draft all men who had 6 months training & were over 18 yrs	
			[illegible] months overseas at once. This involved the immediate equipping & dispatch	
			of C, D & E Coys & owing to the urgent nature of the call C & D Cos were unable	
			to be granted Embarkation leave. It was found possible to allow E Coy to proceed	
			on leave for 4 clear days. This Coy was recalled from Silkstone & dispatched on leave	
—"—	27 March 1918		on 27th March. Although E Coy marched out of Redmires camp to proceed on leave	
			& C & D Cos being under orders could not go, there was not a single absentee in	
			these two Cos when they paraded to leave for overseas. This reflected very great	

A6945 Wt. W11422/M1160 350,000 12/16 D. D. & L. Forms/C./2118/14.

52 Sherwood Foresters

Sheet 5

Army Form C. 2118.

WAR DIARY
or
INTELLIGENCE SUMMARY.
(*Erase heading not required.*)

Instructions regarding War Diaries and Intelligence Summaries are contained in F. S. Regs., Part II. and the Staff Manual respectively. Title pages will be prepared in manuscript.

Place	Date	Hour	Summary of Events and Information	Remarks and references to Appendices
Rimms Camp	1918 27th March		credit on all concerned	
Sheffield	28th March		C & D Co about 350 strong proceeded to Folkestone for overseas, on arrival at Calais they marched to the Rest Camp about 4 miles distant, owing to the glut of reinforcements there was no accommodation or rations for these men on arrival. The men slept that night on the sand & without blankets. The officer who commanded this draft reported that in spite of this that there was not the least sign of discontent, all taking it in good spirit. All these men were immediately drafted up country & were in the fighting line within 14 days, & many were returned wounded within a short period.	
~~[illegible]~~	~~18th~~		~~A new B Coy arrived from the [illegible]~~	
~~[illegible]~~	14th April		E Coy proceeded overseas & were sent intact to the 10th Lincolns. This Coy joined its new HQrs in the fighting line during an engagement near Armentieres which was being drenched with gas & heavy artillery & suffered 36 casualties in the town of Armentieres before reaching their HQrs, they however pushed on reported, they were still kept intact as a Coy & the opportunity of 10th	

A6945 Wt. W11422/M1160 350,000 12/16 D. D. & L. Forms/C./2118/14.

52nd Sherwood Foresters

Sheet 6

Army Form C. 2118.

Instructions regarding War Diaries and Intelligence Summaries are contained in F. S. Regs., Part II. and the Staff Manual respectively. Title pages will be prepared in manuscript.

WAR DIARY
or
INTELLIGENCE SUMMARY.
(Erase heading not required.)

Place	Date	Hour	Summary of Events and Information	Remarks and references to Appendices
Redmires Camp Sheffield	1918 14 April		Lincolns reported they fought extremely well at Kemmel after the withdrawl from Armentières	
	15th April		A new B Coy arrived from the Y S Batt	
	22 April		As the Battn was under orders to camp at Welbeck & there was another outbreak of measles at Redmires the new C Coy due to arrive was ordered to proceed direct to Welbeck. This Coy after about 1 week at Welbeck was sent to Totley for their recruits musketry course.	
— " —	4th May		Battn proceeded by Route March to Welbeck for Summer Camp billeting at Eckington on the night 4/5th May & marched into Welbeck Camp on the morning of the 5th	
Welbeck Camp near Worksop	5th May		The 208th Bde concentrated at Welbeck Camp under Command of Brigadier Gen F J W Dancell, the Bde being composed of 51st & 52nd Notts & Derby & 51st & 52nd KOYLI	
— " —	18th May		All men of A Coy who had reached the age of 19 years & 6 months & details of other Cos who had been in quarantine owing to measles proceeded overseas.	
			Training grounds of every description were available at Welbeck & all ranks	

5/2 Sherwood Foresters.

Instructions regarding War Diaries and Intelligence Summaries are contained in F. S. Regs., Part II, and the Staff Manual respectively. Title pages will be prepared in manuscript.

WAR DIARY
or
INTELLIGENCE SUMMARY.
(Erase heading not required.)

Army Form C. 2118.

Sheet 7

Place	Date	Hour	Summary of Events and Information	Remarks and references to Appendices
Welbeck Camp	18 May		seemed imbued with one idea ("hard & fast training)	
Nr Worksop	to			
— do —	15 June		All men who had been rejected for service overseas on physical grounds or delayed	
			training were now transferred to "A" Coy with a view to their doing special	
			training to make them fit & so successful was this scheme that at least 80 per	
			cent of these men were drafted overseas at [illegible] dates.	
			The new D & E Co's which arrived on this date were of very poor physique & many	
	to		just a few weeks over 18 years of age but improved rapidly with a [illegible]	
			system of graduated training	
			All musketry training was carried out at Wormald Green near Ripon with	
			the exception of [illegible] firing at Clipstone Camp Range.	
— do —	1st July		B Coy now proceeded overseas C Coy following on the	
— do —	14th July		14th July. All the Co's previously mentioned received the highest praise	
			from the C in C in France for the gallant manner in which they fought & all	
	to		ranks concerned for the manner in which their training had been carried out.	
			(This is corroborated by captured Hun dispatches which stated it was	

A6945 Wt. W11422/M1160 350,000 12/16 D. D. & L. Forms/C./2118/14.

52nd Sherwood Foresters

Instructions regarding War Diaries and Intelligence Summaries are contained in F. S. Regs., Part II. and the Staff Manual respectively. Title pages will be prepared in manuscript.

WAR DIARY
or
~~INTELLIGENCE SUMMARY~~.
(Erase heading not required.)

Army Form C. 2118.

Sheet 8

Place	Date	Hour	Summary of Events and Information	Remarks and references to Appendices
	1918			
Welbeck Camp	14 Jul.		Englands young Home Army which turned the scale against them	
Nr Worksop			~~A~~ new B Coy arrived. (A Coy remaining a Cadre Coy) This was of very fine physique, but as in all others & throughout the training three platoons were made of the fitter men & 1 platoon of men of lower physique so that they might be trained under a graduated system suitable to their physique individually.	
			This system proved a great success & there were no men ever discharged by T.M.B. on account of physical breakdown during training. A number	
	16		of men with flat feet were supplied with special boots obtained from a private firm; these men were mostly trained as transport men & proved a great success & were drafted as such.	
			The following is a list of names that are known to have received military awards for good service during the operations since 21st March chiefly for	
	Aug 18 ~~Aug 18~~		Lewis Gun work	
			No 6/15150 L/Cpl Brown promoted Sergt. — No 6/19344 Pte Lawes, W.G. D.C.M. — No 6/12572 Pte Crosaley M.M.	
			No 6/15554 . Wilson do do — Pte Hartley promoted Cpl	
			No 6/15025 Pte Faddin to D.C.M. — No 6/7094 . Fawdry P.G. to promoted Sgt	

A6945 Wt. W11422/M1160 350,000 12/16 D. D. & L. Forms/C./2118/14.

It is believed that there were others whose names are not to hand

Instructions regarding War Diaries and Intelligence Summaries are contained in F. S. Regs., Part II. and the Staff Manual respectively. Title pages will be prepared in manuscript.

WAR DIARY
or
~~INTELLIGENCE SUMMARY.~~
(Erase heading not required.)

Army Form C. 2118.

Sh[illegible] 9

Place	Date	Hour	Summary of Events and Information	Remarks and references to Appendices
			In January 1918 a War Savings Association was started & by September over £3,000 had been subscribed & permission	
	July 14th		was granted to have the Battalion's name inscribed on an Aeroplane	
			During the period of training at Welbeck special attention was given to training of Section leaders in wood	
			fighting, the ground being particularly suitable for this purpose, in fact the main idea was that the men should be trained	
			on the lines the circumstances demanded in France. The method of crossing a river being practically carried out	
Welbeck Camp			under a smoke barrage & to show that the training had good results a young Officer who left the Battalion to go to	
Nr Worksop			France wrote to the Adjutant & said how useful the training he had received at Welbeck had been to him since he	
			had been in France as they were fighting in practically the same sort of country as at Welbeck. During	
			this period the Brigade was inspected by Gen Sir W Robertson on Norton Common. The Brigade was drawn up in	
			line of Battalions in mass fully mobilized with 1st Line Transport. Notification was received	
			from War Office that the War Cabinet had decided that after Aug 31st no soldier under 19 years of age should be sent on	
			Active Service Overseas. About this time quite an alarming epidemic of influenza broke out in Camp, so	
			steps were taken to isolate the cases ~~[illegible]~~. There were no serious results. At the end of August	
	August 31st		the Battalion took part in Divisional Field Operations near Welbeck & Carburton lasting 48 hours.	
	Sept		At the end of September the Battalion moved to Clipstone Camp where training was continued	
			Armistice Day. The Battalion was on its training area when news arrived that the Armistice had been signed. After	
	to		completing the manoeuvres in which the Battalion was engaged, orders were received to attend a Thanksgiving	
	Dec 21		Service on the Brigade Parade Ground. Training was carried on but all the spirit had gone out of the men	

A6945 Wt. W11422/M1160 350,000 12/16 D. D. & L. Forms/C./2118/14.

WAR DIARY
or
~~INTELLIGENCE SUMMARY.~~
(*Erase heading not required.*)

Instructions regarding War Diaries and Intelligence Summaries are contained in F. S. Regs., Part II. and the Staff Manual respectively. Title pages will be prepared in manuscript.

Army Form C. 2118.

Sheet 10

Place	Date	Hour	Summary of Events and Information	Remarks and references to Appendices
	Sept to Dec 21st		& it seemed as if the men felt there was no special object for which to train. During this period the first orders for demobilization were received, the Coal miners being the first to go. About 100 were demobilized up to 21st Dec.	
	Dec 22nd		The Battalion moved by rail to Preston Camp. A more undesirable place for a Graduated Battalion could hardly have been chosen especially during the winter as there was no place for amusement except Y.M.C.A. The C.O. instituted a Regimental Cinema which was open every evening from 18 hrs & was much appreciated by the men.	
1919	Dec to Feb 11th		Training was almost at a standstill during this period owing to the 12 days Xmas leave, bad weather & to not having a proper ground & most of the time was devoted to Coy Route Marches & Education. The order that men could be demobilized came as quite a surprise. This greatly disorganised the Battalion as quite 75% of the NCOs left. None of the A IV had any idea that demobilization would affect them —	
	Feb 11th		An order from War Office dated Feb 8th was received that Graduated Battalions & Y.S. Battalions would shortly be sent to form part of the Army of Occupation & from the date of the letter they would no longer be T.R. Battalions but would become Service Battalions & be reorganised as such under W.E. Part VII A. The 5th Coy was transferred to 7 Coy, being about the same age & the Battalion was formed into 4 Coys & sent on draft leave. Here was a problem, demobilization, mobilization, reinforcement for Post Bellum Army to be carried out at the same time. A great percentage of the Sgts & Cpls had been demobilized & others were expecting to go any day. It was now that the benefit of the Junior NCOs School which had been run in the Battalion since Ashford was felt. About 30 most promising A IV L/Cpls were promoted Cpls & a few made Sgts & CQMS & taking everything into consideration it proved a great success — About 150 of the men re-enlisted in the Post Bellum Army for different periods	

A6945 Wt. W11422/M1160 350,000 12/16 D. D. & L. Forms/C./2118/14.

Instructions regarding War Diaries and Intelligence Summaries are contained in F. S. Regs., Part II. and the Staff Manual respectively. Title pages will be prepared in manuscript.

WAR DIARY
or
~~INTELLIGENCE SUMMARY.~~
(Erase heading not required.)

Army Form C. 2118.

Sheet 11

Place	Date	Hour	Summary of Events and Information	Remarks and references to Appendices
	1919			
Brocton Camp	Feb 19th		Orders were received from War Office to speed up mobilization of the Battalion. The deficiency in Sgts & Rank & file were applied for & promised, but none arrived. 22 Officers were demobilized & others waiting to go. These deficiencies were made up by Officers from other Battalions. Altogether 450 WOs, NCOs & men were demobilized & 150 re-enlisted	
	Feb 26th		Orders were received on this date that the Battalion would entrain at Brocton Stn at 04:00 hrs & proceed overseas	
			Orders were received to continue our reorganization but owing to no personnel arriving nothing could be done except that 10 NCOs available for demobilization were compulsorily retained until they could be ~~released~~ & [illegible]	
			Before proceeding Overseas the Battalion was inspected by Gen Sir W. Robertson	
	March 3rd		The Battalion paraded at 02.00 hrs & marched to Brocton Stn where they entrained. Strength 34 Officers 562 O.R.	
			The following is a list of Officers who proceeded with the Battalion	
			Lt Col G.C. Hamilton, DSO. Worcester Regt Commanding Offr. Lieut I Hodgkinson RAMC	
			Major C.A. Bell R Warwick Regt 2nd in Command	
			Capt & Lt T. Crump S. Staffordshire Regt Adjutant	
			2/Lt R. Light Sherwood Foresters Asst Adjutant	
			Capt & QM. J.R. Jones Manchester Regt Quartermaster	
			Lieut C.F. Mattocks Gloucester " Signalling Officer	
			Lieut Greenwood ~~Transport~~ Lincoln " Transport "	
			2 Lt A. Jewell Sherwood Foresters L.G. Officer	

A6945 Wt. W11422/M1160 350,000 12/16 D. D. & L. Forms/C./2118/14.

Instructions regarding War Diaries and Intelligence Summaries are contained in F. S. Regs., Part II. and the Staff Manual respectively. Title pages will be prepared in manuscript.

WAR DIARY
or
~~INTELLIGENCE SUMMARY.~~
(Erase heading not required.)

Army Form C. 2118.

Sheet 11 9

Place	Date	Hour	Summary of Events and Information	Remarks and references to Appendices
			A Coy. — C. Coy.	
			Capt C. J. McDonnell Sherwood Foresters — Capt H. W. Royle Manchester Regt	
			" A.A. Dean " — " B.H. Challinor Lincoln	
			Lieut A.L. Dibb Lincoln Regt — Lieut S. Barton Cheshire	
			" A.G. Dent Sherwood Foresters — " L.E. Brown Northumberland Fusiliers	
			2/Lt ~~A. [illegible]~~ G.H. Robinson " — 2/Lt W.S. Jenson Sherwood Foresters	
			" C. Blamires Lincoln Regt — " J. Harper Lincoln Regt	
			2/Lt A. Brazzler "	
			" J. Hildreth " — " A. Marshall "	
			B. Coy.	
			Capt C. Spicer M.C. Sherwood Foresters — D. Coy	
			Lieut A. Barnsley Gloucester Regt — Capt A.H. Jackson R. Fusiliers	
			" C.K. Hanson M.C. Sherwood Foresters — " Cox Sherwood Foresters	
			2/Lt R.F. ~~[illegible]~~ Cassnell " — Lieut F.L. Parker Lancaster Regt	
			Lieut A.L. Newton " — 2/Lt A.A. Charlton Lincoln	
			" A. Nicholls "	

A6945 Wt. W11422/M1160 350,000 12/16 D. D. & L. Forms/C./2118/14.

Instructions regarding War Diaries and Intelligence Summaries are contained in F. S. Regs., Part II. and the Staff Manual respectively. Title pages will be prepared in manuscript.

WAR DIARY
or
~~INTELLIGENCE~~ SUMMARY.
(*Erase heading not required.*)

Army Form C. 2118.

Sheet 12

Place	Date	Hour	Summary of Events and Information	Remarks and references to Appendices
	1919		Capt C. Gregory & Lt A.R. Carruthers remained with Rear Party with instructions to join the Battalion on completion of duty	
March 1st			The Battalion arrived at Dover at 12.00 hrs & immediately embarked on H.M.T. Antrim & sailed for Dunkirk at 13.00 hrs with the 51st Sherwood Foresters. The Battalion arrived at ~~Dov~~ Dunkirk at 17.00 hrs & proceeded to the Rest Camp about 3 miles distant where the men were provided with a good hot meal & accommodated in Tents.	
March 2nd			The Battalion paraded at 6.30 hrs & marched to Sand Siding & entrained. Blankets & fuel were issued & 3 days rations taken on the train. About 18 men were allotted to each Truck & they were soon very comfortably settled. The train left Sand Siding at 13.00 hrs. A halt of one hour was made at Menin where at 17.30 to [illegible] where a hot meal was served to all Ranks. The men were very interested while passing through the War Zone in the Armentières District where their dear brothers & fathers had recently been fighting & they expressed great bitterness when they saw the destruction caused. It was very fortunate that it was daylight when passing through the old fighting area & it gave the men some idea of what the War meant.	
March 3rd			Arrived at Charleroi about 6.00 hrs where another meal was served & continued the journey via Namur Huy. Several halts were made where meals were served, everything being prepared for the Battn arrival	
March 3rd			The Battalion arrived at Euskirchen at 10.00 hrs where they detrained at 11.00 hrs & marched to Euskirchen Barracks. The Battalion was attached to the 16th Brigade 6th Division	
Euskirchen March 4, 5, 6			The Battalion carried on training	

A6945 Wt. W11422/M1160 350,000 12/16 D. D. & L. Forms/C./2118/14.

Instructions regarding War Diaries and Intelligence Summaries are contained in F. S. Regs., Part II. and the Staff Manual respectively. Title pages will be prepared in manuscript.

WAR DIARY
or
~~INTELLIGENCE SUMMARY.~~
(Erase heading not required.)

Army Form C. 2118.

Sheet 13.

Place	Date	Hour	Summary of Events and Information	Remarks and references to Appendices
Euskirchen	7/3/19		The Battalion paraded at 11.00 hrs for inspection by the Army Commander, Sir H. Plumer & the Battalion marched past in Column of Route. Sir H. Plumer congratulated the C.O. on the turnout of the Battalion & the manner in which they handled their arms & he informed the Brigade Commander that he was most favourably impressed with all he had seen	
"	8/3/19 to 11/3/19		Received Transport & Mobilization Equipment from K.O.Y.L.I. Training carried on.	
"	11/3/19		Received orders from Brigade to hold Battalion in readiness to proceed to Marienburg Barracks, Cologne within 48 hrs	
	12/3/19		Capt Trahife M.C. RAMC relieved Lt I Hodkinson RAMC. The latter was a great loss to the Battalion as he knew almost every man & had made a study of their physical capabilities	
"	12/3/19 to 15/3/19		Carried on training including a Battalion Route March	
			Received orders that the Battalion would proceed to Cologne on 18th & would be relieved by the 51st Pioneers	
	18/3/19		The Battalion was ordered to move by rail from Euskirchen to Marienburg Barracks Cologne in the same train that brought the 51st Pioneers on relief. The Battalion was ordered to entrain at 12.45 owing to delays of the	
Cologne			entraining & detraining by the 51st Pioneers the Battalion did not leave Euskirchen until 18.00 hrs. The Battalion with 1st Line Transport & Baggage only took one hour to entrain. The Battalion commenced to detrain at Bonn Tor Station at about 21 hrs & everything was in Barracks by midnight. The 2nd Btn Sherwood Foresters met the Battn at the Station with their Drums & played them to Barracks which was appreciated	

A6945 Wt. W11422/M1160 350,000 12/16 D. D. & L. Forms/C./2118/14.

Army Form C. 2118.

Instructions regarding War Diaries and Intelligence Summaries are contained in F. S. Regs., Part II. and the Staff Manual respectively. Title pages will be prepared in manuscript.

WAR DIARY
or
INTELLIGENCE SUMMARY.
(Erase heading not required.)

Sheet 14

Place	Date	Hour	Summary of Events and Information	Remarks and references to Appendices
Marienburg			by all ranks. The Battalion transferred to the 7th Brigade.	
Barracks Cologne	18/3/19		Devoted to settling down	
	19/3/19		Brigadier Gen P. Brown Commanding 7th Brigade visited the Battalion. Training was recommenced	
	20/3/19		Pte Compton D Coy died at Euskirchen C.C.S. Battalion Route March	
	22/3/19		Major Gen Hull Commanding Midland Division visited the Battalion & Transport. *	
			D Coy proceeded to occupy the Arsenal & other Guards in Cologne on War Material, also Fort VII &	
			Fort VIII in the suburbs of Cologne	
	27/3/19		The Adjutant met with an accident by falling from his horse & proceeded to Hospital	
	28/3/19		Training & Education started in full swing.	
			The Battalion continued to find Guards & Extra Guards were found for a Train at Bonn[?]	
			& one for Brigade HQ.	
	30/3/19		Brig General Skinner having taken over Command of the Brigade visited the Battalion	
			G. Clarke[?] Lt Col 52nd Sherwood Foresters 3/4/19.	

Instructions regarding War Diaries and Intelligence Summaries are contained in F. S. Regs., Part II. and the Staff Manual respectively. Title pages will be prepared in manuscript.

WAR DIARY
or
~~INTELLIGENCE SUMMARY.~~
(*Erase heading not required.*)

52nd Sherwood Foresters Army Form C. 2118.

Place	Date	Hour	Summary of Events and Information	Remarks and references to Appendices
	1919 April			
Cologne	1st		The Battalion continued to find Guards in Cologne	
	3rd		The removal of all German Rifles etc was started from the Arsenal to Fort VII. This was carried out by the Battalion	
	5th		The Battalion paraded over 200 strong for a trip on the Rhine. Started from Barracks at 07.30hrs in Trams for Hohenzollern Bridge whence the Boat started. We were accompanied by the 51st & 53rd Sherwood Foresters. Siebenburg was reached about 13.00hrs when a the boat turned downstream & reached Hohenzollern Bridge about 16.00hrs. The weather was perfect & the trip was much enjoyed by all	
	8th		The Battalion with 1st Line Transport was inspected by B.G.C. 3rd Midland Brigade & afterwards marched past in column of fours. The B.G.C. complimented the Battalion on their smart appearance, the handling of arms being especially good. In the afternoon a visit was paid by the Chief of the Serbian, Japanese, Portuguese & Brazilian Missions who inspected Barracks & stables	
	12th		The Battalion was inspected by the Corps Commander who expressed himself as very pleased with all he saw. The Battalion was drawn up in Mass with on Marienburg Barracks Square the 51st on the right & 52nd on the left with respective Transports in	

A6945 Wt. W11422/M1160 350,000 12/16 D. D. & L. Forms/C./2118/14.

Instructions regarding War Diaries and Intelligence Summaries are contained in F. S. Regs., Part II. and the Staff Manual respectively. Title pages will be prepared in manuscript.

WAR DIARY
or
INTELLIGENCE SUMMARY.
(*Erase heading not required.*)

Army Form C. 2118.

Place	Date	Hour	Summary of Events and Information	Remarks and references to Appendices
	April			
Cologne.			After the inspection each Battalion marched past in column of fours. A letter was later received from B.G.C. 3rd Midland Brigade thanking all concerned for the excellent turnout of the Battalion.	
	15th		Lt Col Spring DSO. lately commanding 33rd Infantry Brigade took over Command of the Battalion vice Lt Col G.C. Lambton DSO.	
	16th		The Transport was inspected by Officer Commanding Divisional Train who was very favourably impressed with all he saw. Orders were received that the Battalion was to vacate Marienburg Barracks & ~~some~~ move to Brühl	
	19th-20th		The Bonn Tor Guard arrested two Germans who amongst others were seen trying to steal stores from a Train. The remainder although fired on escaped.	
	~~22nd~~		~~The Battalion moved to Brühl by March Route arriving~~ R.	
	20th		The Battalion ~~relieved~~ relieved the Guard at the Powder Magazine from 51st Foresters	
	21st		All Guards were relieved by the 53rd Northumberland Fusiliers	
	22nd		The Battalion moved to Brühl by March Route arriving about 12-45 hrs. A & B Coys proceeded to the Seminary & C & D to the Hospital with H.Q. at the latter Place. The Transport except Officers chargers were all in the open behind the Hospital.	

A6945 Wt. W11422/M1160 350,000 12/16 D. D. & L. Forms/C./2118/14.

Instructions regarding War Diaries and Intelligence Summaries are contained in F. S. Regs., Part II. and the Staff Manual respectively. Title pages will be prepared in manuscript.

WAR DIARY
or
INTELLIGENCE SUMMARY.
(*Erase heading not required.*)

Army Form C. 2118.

Place	Date	Hour	Summary of Events and Information	Remarks and references to Appendices
Bruhl	April 30th		The Battalion paraded 300 strong under Major Hill to raid the village of Badorf for Arms etc. The work was carried out under the direction of the D.A.P.M. Bruhl. On arriving at Badorf a man was detailed to a house to see that all the inmates kept in one room & did not leave the house. The Houses were then searched in turn by an Officer Military Police & German Civil Police. Although a thorough search was made very little was found. During the afternoon 200 NCOs & men from 2/4 KOYLI arrived as reinforcements. They were posted to Companies with a view to making all Companies effective strength equal.	

[illegible] Lt. Colonel,
Comdg. 52nd Bn. The Notts & Derby Regt.

Instructions regarding War Diaries and Intelligence Summaries are contained in F. S. Regs., Part II, and the Staff Manual respectively. Title pages will be prepared in manuscript.

WAR DIARY
or
INTELLIGENCE SUMMARY.
(Erase heading not required.)

Army Form C. 2118.

Place	Date	Hour	Summary of Events and Information	Remarks and references to Appendices
Bruhl Germany	1919 1st May		Head Qrs C + D Coy at Almuit A + B Coy at Seminar	
	4th		Maj C.H. Dumbell D.S.O. N. Fus. reported his arrival as 2nd in Command	
	5th		Lt Col G C Lambton D.S.O. proceeded on leave to U K	
	6th		D Coy furnished two platoons to take over the charge of Vochem Army Amn Dump	
	7th		Maj C.H. Dumbell D.S.O. ordered to report to 51st [illegible] + take over temporary Cmd	
	8		Musketry + Lewis Gun practice carried out on 30 x Ranges daily by Coys	
			Lt R Light proceeded to U K on 14 days leave	
	13th		Two platoons B Coy relieved D Coy on guard at Army Ammunition Dump	
	14th		Lieut F L Parker proceeded to U K on 14 days leave	
	6th		Musketry + Lewis Gun practice carried out daily by Coys on 30 x ranges	
	19		277 Offrs + OR on trip up the Rhine to Coblenz	
	20th		Two platoons C Coy relieved B Coy on guard at Army Ammn Dump Vochem	
	21st		Capt G J McDonnell took over duties of acting Adjt vice Capt W T Crop resigned the appointment.	
	22nd		Lt Col G C Lambton D.S.O. appointed to command 11th Leicester Batt. Bruhl	

A6945 Wt. W11422/M1160 350,000 12/16 D. D. & L. Forms/C./2118/14.

Instructions regarding War Diaries and Intelligence Summaries are contained in F. S. Regs., Part II. and the Staff Manual respectively. Title pages will be prepared in manuscript.

WAR DIARY
or
INTELLIGENCE SUMMARY.
(*Erase heading not required.*)

Army Form C. 2118.

Place	Date	Hour	Summary of Events and Information	Remarks and references to Appendices
Bruhl.	26/5/19	0900	~~Lieut Col. F. Spring D.S.O. Commanding 52nd Sherwood Foresters proceeded to inspect the camping ground at [illegible] Schnitheim.~~	
"	27/5/19	0920	No 12277 Pte A Rhodes accidently killed by Steam Tram near Kaiser Strasse.	
"	28/5/19	11.55	"B" Coy. 3 Officer's 120 other ranks furnished funeral party to bury Pte Roades in Cologne. (Place of burial Sudfriedhof Honninger Weg).	
"	28/5/19	0845	Commanding Officer inspected "A" & "D" Coys. ~~at 0900~~ in fighting Order. The Companies after inspection took up their Defensive positions and were visited by the Commanding Officer. "A" Coy. ECKDORF Area. "D" KIER-BERG Area.	
	30/5/19	/	Major C.H. Dumbell. D.S.O. Appointed to Command 51st Bn Leicestershire Regt.	

F. Spring
Lt Col.
COMMANDING 52nd BATT. THE SHERWOOD FORESTERS.

A6945 Wt. W11422/M1160 350,000 12/16 D. D. & L. Forms/C./2118/14.

(1)

Instructions regarding War Diaries and Intelligence Summaries are contained in F. S. Regs., Part II. and the Staff Manual respectively. Title pages will be prepared in manuscript.

WAR DIARY
or
INTELLIGENCE SUMMARY.
(*Erase heading not required.*)

Army Form C. 2118.

Place	Date	Hour	Summary of Events and Information	Remarks and references to Appendices
Bruhl.	3/6/19	0930.	The Battalion paraded as Strong as possible to Celebrate the Birthday of His Majesty King George V. The Battalion was drawn up in Close Column of Companies, and Carried out the various movemts of Ceremonial drill, giving three Cheers for His Majesty the King. Completing the Ceremony by a march past. The Commanding Officer (Lieut Colonel F.G. Spring C.M.G. D.S.O.) taking the Salute. There were a number of German Spectators present.	
"	6/6/19	0830	An advance party Consisting of 3 Officers, and 85 Other Ranks, und the Command of Captain J.B. Mudge M.C. proceeded to Schmidtheim, for the purpose of preparing the Battalion Training Camp.	
	"	1500.	1 Officer (Lieut H.R. Greenwood). and 35 Other ranks proceeded by road to Schmidheim with Animals and Vehicles (3 days march).	
"	9/6/19	0900	1st Party of Battalion, Consisting of 3 Officers, and 300 Other ranks under the Command of Major C.A. Bill. proceeded by first train to Schmidtheim, Arriving about 1459hrs.	

(A9475) Wt W2358/P360 600,000 12/17 D. D. & L. Sch. 52a. Forms/C2118/15.

Instructions regarding War Diaries and Intelligence Summaries are contained in F. S. Regs., Part II. and the Staff Manual respectively. Title pages will be prepared in manuscript.

2/

WAR DIARY
or
INTELLIGENCE SUMMARY.
(Erase heading not required.)

Army Form C. 2118.

Place	Date	Hour	Summary of Events and Information	Remarks and references to Appendices
Bruhl.	9/6/19	1200.	The remainder of the Battalion Consisting of 25 Officers and 350 other ranks under the Command of the Commanding Officer (Lieut-Colonel F.G. Spring C.M.G. D.S.O.) proceeded by Second train to Schmidtheim. Arriving about 1629 hours.	
"	"	15 00	1 Officer (Lieut M.T. Hurndall M.C.) and 22 other ranks Transport proceeded by road to Schmidtheim. (3 days march).	
Schmidheim	14/6/19	0900	Battalion Practice Ceremonial Parade. for Visit of His Grace The Duke of Portland. The Battalion was drawn up in Close Column of Companies. North of Trench Motor Battery Camp for this parade. Movements Carried out:– General Salute, Wheel, march past by Companys. The Commanding Officer taking the Salute, Battalion reformed and marched back to Camp.	
"	16/6/19	0830	Brigade Practice Ceremonial parade for His Grace The Duke of Portland. Movements Carried out as above, Salute taken by Brigadier General P.A.S. Skinner C.M.G. D.S.O. Commanding 3rd Midland Brigade.	

3

Instructions regarding War Diaries and Intelligence Summaries are contained in F. S. Regs., Part II. and the Staff Manual respectively. Title pages will be prepared in manuscript.

WAR DIARY
or
INTELLIGENCE SUMMARY.
(*Erase heading not required.*)

Army Form C. 2118.

Place	Date	Hour	Summary of Events and Information	Remarks and references to Appendices
Schmidheim	17/6/19	1130	Brigade Ceremonial Parade to receive His Grace The Duke of Portland, KG. The Brigade formed up in three Sides of a Square 51st Bn Sherwood Foresters on the right, 52nd Bn Centre, 53rd Bn on the left. Brigadier General P.A.S. Skinner. Commanding 3rd Midland Brigade, Commanded the parade. The Duke Arrived about 1200 hours and was received with the General Salute, He Afterwards inspected the Brigade, and addressed them, Saying how proud and pleased he was at having the honour of reviewing and Speaking to them.	
			The Brigade formed up in Close Column of Companies, and afterwards marched passed by Coys, His Grace taking the Salute.	
"	"	1300	Battalion received orders to Strike Camp and be prepared to move back to Bruhl the following morning.	
"	18/6/19	0700	Battalion entrained at Schmidheim for Bruhl. on Arrival at Liblar the Bn. detrained and proceeded to Bruhl by march route. Arriving in billets about 1550 hours. "A" Company. took over the Guard duties of Vochem Ammunition Dump, according to Defence Scheme issued.	

(A9175) Wt W2358/P360 600,000 12/17 D. D. & L. Sch. 52a. Forms/C2118/15.

4

Instructions regarding War Diaries and Intelligence Summaries are contained in F. S. Regs., Part II. and the Staff Manual respectively. Title pages will be prepared in manuscript.

WAR DIARY
or
INTELLIGENCE SUMMARY.
(*Erase heading not required.*)

Army Form C. 2118.

Place	Date	Hour	Summary of Events and Information	Remarks and references to Appendices
Bruhl	19/6/19	0900	"C" Company took over the undermentioned Guards:–	
			Cologne Deutz, Eifel Tor, Rodenkirchen Chemical Works, Midland Div. Train.	
			1 officer. 1 Sgt. 6 Ptes. 1 Cpl. 4 Ptes. 1 Sgt. 1 Cpl. 7 Ptes 1 Cpl 3 Ptes.	
"	20/6/19	0930	"B" Company took up Defensive position on Bruhl Railway Bridges. } According to	
			D ~ do ~ Kierberg ~ do ~ } Defence	
"		11 00	All positions were inspected by the General Officer Commanding } Schemes issued.	
			3rd Midland Brigade. (Brigadier General P.A.S. Skinner C.M.G. D.S.O.) He was accompanied	
			on his inspection by the Commanding Officer, Brigade Major, Adjutant, and	
			OCs "B" and "D" Companies.	
"	24/6/19	1300	An Advance party of 3 Officers and 73 Other ranks under the Command of	
			Captain H W Royle. proceeded to Schmidheim to prepare training Camp	
			for the Battalion.	
	"		All Defence Guards on Railway Bridges Etc. ~~[illegible]~~ were withdrawn	

Bruhl
1st July 1919.

[signature] Lieut: Colonel
Commanding 52nd Sherwood Foresters

(A9475) Wt W2358/P360 600,000 12/17 D. D. & L. Sch. 52a. Forms/C2118/15.

Instructions regarding War Diaries and Intelligence Summaries are contained in F. S. Regs., Part II. and the Staff Manual respectively. Title pages will be prepared in manuscript.

WAR DIARY or INTELLIGENCE SUMMARY.

(*Erase heading not required.*)

Sheet I 52 N&D

Army Form C. 2118.

Place	Date	Hour	Summary of Events and Information	Remarks and references to Appendices
Bruhl	2/4/19	1935 hrs.	The Battalion under the Command of Major C. A. Bill, entrained at Bruhl for Schmidtheim Training Camp, Arriving at Schmidtheim Railway Station at 0013 hrs 3/4/19. B Company carried out the duties of unloading at Station, "C" Company off loading in Camp.	
			Lieut. Colonel G. G. Spring C.M.G. D.S.O. took over Command of 3rd Midland Brigade during the absence of Brigadier Gen. P. A. B. Skinner. C.M.G. D.S.O. on leave in U.K. Major C. A. Bill assumed temporary Command of the Battalion	
Schmidtheim	13/7/19	14 00	Preliminary Heats for Battalion Sport.	
~ " ~	14/7/19	"	~ do ~	
	15/7/19	11 15	Lt. Gen. Sir W. P. BRAITHWAITE. K. C. B. Inspected the Battalion on Area "A", Afterwards inspecting the Battalion Institutes, Workshops, and Company lines. He also attended the Battalion Sports meeting during the afternoon.	
		1400	Battalion Sports were held on ground opposite 3rd Mid. Bde. Trench Mortar Battery lines. Prize Winners in each event are shown below:-	
			100 Yds flat Race 1st Sergt. Shaw. 2nd Pte Mellor. 3rd Pte Broughton.	

(A9475) Wt W2358/P360 600,000 12/17 D. D. & L. Sch. 52a. Forms/C2118/15.

Instructions regarding War Diaries and Intelligence Summaries are contained in F. S. Regs., Part II. and the Staff Manual respectively. Title pages will be prepared in manuscript.

WAR DIARY
or
INTELLIGENCE SUMMARY.
(*Erase heading not required.*)

Army Form C. 2118.

II

Place	Date	Hour	Summary of Events and Information	Remarks and references to Appendices
			Prize Winners Continued	
Schmidtheim	15/7/19	14.00	440 yds flat. 1st Sergt Shaw. 2nd Sergt Wood. 3rd Pte Harral.	
			1 Mile " 1st " Wood. 2nd Lieut. Casswell. 3rd " Winterton.	
			220 yds " 1st " Shaw. 2nd Pte Darley. 3rd " Mellor.	
			Officers Race 100 yds 1st Lieut. Street. 2nd Lieut Robinson. 3rd Lieut. Marsh.	
			Pillow Fight 1st Pte Moore. 2nd L/Cpl Stanley. 3rd L/Cpl Carr.	
			Relay Race Coy. teams. Distance (3) 220 yds (2) 440 yds. (1) 880 yds. 1st C. Coy. 2nd D Coy.	
			Tug O War. 110 Stone. 1st D Coy. 2nd Hd. Qr. Coy.	
			Basket Ball Competition. 1st Hd. Qr. Coy. 2nd A Coy.	
			Football Six a Side. 1st A Coy. 2nd Hd. Qr. Coy.	
			Bun + Flour Race. 1st Pte Lowe. 2nd Pte Brayton. 3rd Pte Gittins.	
			Sack Race. 1st Lieut McNarney. 2nd Pte Slade.	
			Three Legged Race. 1st Pte Passy + Wild. 2nd Pte Evans + Hazard. 3rd Pte Swift + Smith.	
~ do ~	19/7/19		The Battalion was successful in carrying off Prizes as enumerated below.	
			at 3rd Mid. Bde. Horse Show. 2nd Champion Mule stripped. 1st Officers Chargers	
			under 15 hands. 1st Cooker + pair. 1st Maltese Cart. 1st Officers Jumping Competition.	
			2nd Officers Chargers over 15 hands. 2nd Pair Pack Mules. 3rd G. S. Limber + pair.	

(A9475) Wt W2358/P360 600,000 12/17 D. D. & L. Sch. 52a. Forms/C2118/15.

Instructions regarding War Diaries and Intelligence Summaries are contained in F. S. Regs., Part II. and the Staff Manual respectively. Title pages will be prepared in manuscript.

WAR DIARY
or
INTELLIGENCE SUMMARY.
(Erase heading not required.)

Army Form C. 2118.

III

Place	Date	Hour	Summary of Events and Information	Remarks and references to Appendices
			Horse Show Continued	
Schmidthen	19/7/19		3rd Pair Heavy Draught Horses.	
			3rd Water Cart & pair.	
			The Battalion was successful in Carrying of Prizes as enumerated below, at 3rd	
~ do ~	26/7/19		Mid Bde Sports.	
			1st 100 yds Flat Race. Sergt Shaw. 2nd Six a side Football. "A" Coy.	
			1st 220 yds ~ " ~ " Shaw. 2nd Tug o War. "D" Coy.	
			1st 440 yds ~ " ~ " Shaw.	
			1st Basket Ball Competition Hqr. Coy. Team.	
			1st Filling the Bucket Pte Moore & Parks.	
			1st Three legged Race. Pte Possey & Wild.	
			1st Bun & Flour Race " Pettins.	

[signature]
LT. COL.
COMMANDING 52nd BATT. THE SHERWOOD FORESTERS.

(A9175) Wt W2358/P360 600,000 12/17 D. D. & L. Sch. 52a. Forms/C2118/15.

MIDLAND DIVISION
(LATE 6TH DIVISION)

3RD MID'D INFY BDE

53RD BN NOTTS & DERBYS.

MAR - JLY 1919

53rd Bn Notts & Derby Regt

Instructions regarding War Diaries and Intelligence Summaries are contained in F. S. Regs., Part II. and the Staff Manual respectively. Title pages will be prepared in manuscript.

WAR DIARY
or
~~INTELLIGENCE SUMMARY.~~
(Erase heading not required.)

Army Form C. 2118.

Vol #I

Place	Date	Hour	Summary of Events and Information	Remarks and references to Appendices
CATTERICK	8.3.19	21.30	Entrained at CATTERICK BRIDGE for DOVER.	
DOVER	9.3.19	10.00	ARRIVED at DOVER and detrained (Lt.Col. Bond C.M.G. D.S.O. joined the battn) marched to rest Camp for dinner.	
DOVER	9.3.19	13.00	Embarked for DUNKERQUE passage smooth	
DUNKERQUE	9.3.19	16.30	Disembarked and marched to No 3 CAMP. Stayed the night. Accommodation, men in tents, officers in huts.	
DUNKERQUE	10.3.19	12.00	Marched from Camp to Siding and entrained.	
DUNKERQUE	10.3.19	13.00	Left DUNKERQUE en route for ~~Cologne~~ BRÜHL	
EN ROUTE	11.3.19			
BRÜHL	12.3.19	09.00	arrived at BRÜHL and detrained, marched to billets	
BRÜHL	13.3.19		Cleaning up and straightening billets.	
BRÜHL	14.3.19	11.15	Inspection by ARMY COMMANDER.	
BRÜHL	15.3.19		training and sports. Took over transport and surplus stores from 9th NORFOLK REGT.	
BRÜHL	16.3.19	10.00	Church parade	
BRÜHL	17.3.19		Training and packing of stores etc for move to SÜRTH	
BRÜHL	18.3.19	10.00	Marched of, en route for SÜRTH	
SÜRTH	18.3.19	12.30	Arrival at ~~Surth~~ SÜRTH	
SÜRTH	19.3.19		Cleaning up and arrangement of billets.	
SÜRTH	20.3.19		Cleaning up and training and sports in afternoon	
SÜRTH	21.3.19	10.00	ROUTE MARCH and sport in afternoon	
SÜRTH	22.3.19		Interior Economy and sport in afternoon	
SÜRTH	23.3.19	09.30	Church parade	
SÜRTH	24.3.19		training and sports in afternoon	
SÜRTH	25.3.19		training and sports in afternoon	

1/4/19

[signature] Major
53rd Notts & Derby Regt

D. D. & L., London, E.C.
(10540) Wt W5300/P713 750,000 3/18 E 2688 Forms/C2118/16.

53rd Bn NOTTS & DERBY REGT.

Instructions regarding War Diaries and Intelligence Summaries are contained in F. S. Regs., Part II. and the Staff Manual respectively. Title pages will be prepared in manuscript.

WAR DIARY
or
~~INTELLIGENCE SUMMARY.~~
(Erase heading not required.)

Army Form C. 2118.

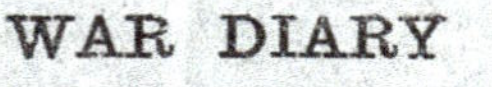

Place	Date	Hour	Summary of Events and Information	Remarks and references to Appendices
CATTERICK	8.3.19	21.30	Entrained at CATTERICK BRIDGE for DOVER.	
DOVER	9.3.19	10.00	ARRIVED at DOVER and detrained (Lt. Col. BOND. C.M.G. D.S.O. joined the battn.) marched to rest Camp for dinner.	
DOVER	9.3.19	13.00	Embarked for DUNKERQUE passage smooth.	
DUNKERQUE	9.3.19	16.30.	Disembarked and marched to NO. 3 CAMP. stayed the night. Accommodation men in tents officers in huts	
DUNKERQUE	10.3.19	12.30	Marched from Camp to Siding and entrained	
DUNKERQUE	10.3.19	13.00	Left DUNKERQUE en route for BRÜHL	
EN ROUTE	11.3.19			
BRÜHL	12.3.19	09.00	Arrival at BRÜHL detrained and marched to billets	
BRÜHL	13.3.19		Cleaning up and straightening billets	
BRÜHL	14.3.19	11.15	Inspection by ARMY COMMANDER.	
BRÜHL	15.3.19		Training and sports took over transport and surplus stores from 9th NORFOLK REGT.	
BRÜHL	16.3.19	10.00	Church parade	
BRÜHL	17.3.19		Training and packing of stores etc for move to SÜRTH	
BRÜHL	18.3.19	10.00	Marched off en route for SÜRTH	
SÜRTH	18.3.19	12.30	Arrival at SÜRTH	
SÜRTH	19.3.19		Cleaning up and arrangement of billets	
SÜRTH.	20.3.19		Cleaning up, training and sports in afternoon	
SÜRTH	21.3.19	10.00	ROUTE MARCH and sports in afternoon	
SÜRTH	22.3.19		Interior economy and sports in afternoon	
SÜRTH	23.3.19	09.30	Church parade	
SÜRTH.	24.3.19		Training and sports in afternoon	
SÜRTH	25.3.19		Training and sports in afternoon.	

1/4/19. [signature] Major
53rd Notts & Derby Regt.

D. D. & L., London, E.C.
(10349) Wt W5300/P713 750,000 3/18 E 2688 Forms/C/2118/16.

53rd NOTTS & DERBY REGT.

Army Form C. 2118.

WAR DIARY
or
INTELLIGENCE SUMMARY.

(*Erase heading not required.*)

Instructions regarding War Diaries and Intelligence Summaries are contained in F. S. Regs., Part II. and the Staff Manual respectively. Title pages will be prepared in manuscript.

Place	Date	Hour	Summary of Events and Information	Remarks and references to Appendices
CATTERICK	8.3.19	21.30	Entrained at CATTERICK BRIDGE for DOVER.	
DOVER	9.3.19	10.00	Arrived at DOVER and detrained (Lt Col. BOND. CMG. DSO joined the battn.) Marched to rest Camp for dinner.	
DOVER.	9.3.19	18.00	Embarked for DUNKERQUE passage smooth.	
DUNKERQUE	9.3.19	16.30	Disembarked, marched to No3 Camp stayed the night Accommodation men in tents, officers in huts.	
DUNKERQUE	10.3.19	12.00	Marched from Camp to siding and entrained	
DUNKERQUE	10.3.19	13.00	Left DUNKERQUE en route for BRÜHL	
EN ROUTE	11.3.19			
BRÜHL	12.3.19	09.00	Arrived at BRÜHL detrained and marched to billets	
BRÜHL	13.3.19		Cleaning up and straightening billet	
BRÜHL	14.3.19	11.15	Inspection by ARMY COMMANDER	
BRÜHL	15.3.19		Training and sports took over transport and surplus stores from 9th NORFOLK REGT.	
BRÜHL	16.3.19	10.00	Church parade	
BRÜHL	17.3.19		Training and packing of stores etc for move to SÜRTH	
BRÜHL	18.3.19	10.00	Marched off enroute for SÜRTH.	
SÜRTH	18.3.19	12.30	Arrived at SÜRTH	
SÜRTH	19.3.19		Cleaning up and arrangement of billets	
SÜRTH	20.3.19		Cleaning up, training and sports in afternoon	
SÜRTH	21.3.19	10.00	ROUTE MARCH, sports in afternoon	
SÜRTH	22.3.19		Interior economy and sports in afternoon	
SÜRTH	23.3.19	09.30	Church parade	
SÜRTH	24.3.19		Training and sports in afternoon	
SÜRTH	25.3.19		Training and sports in afternoon	

1/4/19. [illegible] Major
53rd Notts & Derby Regt

D. D. & L., London, E.C.
(10340) Wt W5300/P713 750,000 3/18 E 2688 Forms C/2118/16.

53rd. Bn NOTTS & DERBY REGT.

WAR DIARY

or

~~INTELLIGENCE SUMMARY.~~

(Erase heading not required.)

Army Form C. 2118.

Instructions regarding War Diaries and Intelligence Summaries are contained in F. S. Regs., Part II. and the Staff Manual respectively. Title pages will be prepared in manuscript.

Place	Date	Hour	Summary of Events and Information	Remarks and references to Appendices
SÜRTH.	26.3.19		Training and Sports in afternoon	
SÜRTH.	27.3.19	1000	ROUTE MARCH and Sports in afternoon	
SÜRTH.	28.3.19		Training and Sports in afternoon	
SÜRTH	29.3.19		Interior Economy and sports in afternoon	
SÜRTH	30.3.19	09.30	Church Parade	
SÜRTH	31.3.19		Training and Sports in afternoon	

1/4/19.

[illegible] Major
53rd Notts & Derby Regt

D. D. & L., London, E.C.
(10340) Wt W5300/P713 750,000 3/18 E 2688 Forms C/2118/15.

53rd Bn NOTTS & DERBY REGT.

Army Form C. 2118.

WAR DIARY
or
~~INTELLIGENCE SUMMARY.~~

(*Erase heading not required.*)

Instructions regarding War Diaries and Intelligence Summaries are contained in F. S. Regs., Part II. and the Staff Manual respectively. Title pages will be prepared in manuscript.

Place	Date	Hour	Summary of Events and Information	Remarks and references to Appendices
SÜRTH	26.3.19		Training and Sports in afternoon	
SÜRTH	27.3.19	10.00	ROUTE MARCH and Sports in afternoon	
SÜRTH	28.3.19		Training and Sports in afternoon	
SÜRTH	29.3.19		Interior Economy and Sports in afternoon	
SÜRTH	30.3.19	09.30	Church parade	
SÜRTH	31.3.19		Training and Sports in afternoon	

K. Woodhouse Major
53rd Notts & Derby Regt
1/4/19.

D. D. & L., London, E.C.
(10340) Wt W3300/P713 750,000 3/18 E 2688 Forms C/2118/18.

53rd Bn NOTTS & DERBY REGT.

Army Form C. 2118.

WAR DIARY
or
INTELLIGENCE SUMMARY.
(Erase heading not required.)

Instructions regarding War Diaries and Intelligence Summaries are contained in F. S. Regs., Part II. and the Staff Manual respectively. Title pages will be prepared in manuscript.

Place	Date	Hour	Summary of Events and Information	Remarks and references to Appendices
SÜRTH	26 3/19		Training and Sports in afternoon	
SÜRTH	27 3/19	10.00	ROUTE MARCH and sports in afternoon	
SÜRTH	28 3/19		Training and Sports in afternoon.	
SÜRTH	29 3/19		Interior economy and sports in afternoon	
SÜRTH	30 3/19	09.30	Church parade.	
SÜRTH	31 3/19		Training and Sports in afternoon	

1/4/19. [illegible] Major
53rd Notts & Derby Regt.

D. D. & L., London, E.C.
(10348) Wt W5300/P713 750,000 3/18 E 2888 Forms C/2118/15.

53rd Bn SHERWOOD FORESTERS.

Army Form C. 2118.

WAR DIARY
or
~~INTELLIGENCE SUMMARY.~~
(Erase heading not required.)

Instructions regarding War Diaries and Intelligence Summaries are contained in F. S. Regs., Part II. and the Staff Manual respectively. Title pages will be prepared in manuscript.

Place	Date	Hour	Summary of Events and Information	Remarks and references to Appendices
SÜRTH	1/4/19		Training in the morning Sports in the afternoon	
do.	2/4/19		do. do. do. do.	
do.	3/4/19		do. do. do. do.	
do.	4/4/19		do. do. do. do. Lecture at RODENKIRCHEN by MAJ. A.J. DUGMORE.	
do.	5/4/19		do. do. do. do. Part Bn trip up river to LINZ.	
do.	6/4/19	09.30	Church parade.	
do.	7/4/19		Training in the morning Sports in the afternoon.	
do.	8/4/19		do do do do.	
do.	9/4/19		do do do do Lecture at RODENKIRCHEN by Maj. EARL GREY	
do.	10/4/19	10.30	Inspection by Brig. Gen. Comdg. 71st Bde. Sports in the afternoon. Demonstration at WITTERSCHLICK RANGE.	
do.	11/4/19		Training in the morning Sports in the afternoon.	
do.	12/4/19	12.0	Inspection by Corps Commander Sports in the afternoon	
do.	13/4/19	09.30	Church parade.	
do.	14/4/19		Training in the morning Sports in the afternoon.	
do.	15/4/19		do. do. do. do.	
do.	16/4/19		do. do. do. do.	
do.	17/4/19		do. do. do. do	
do	18/4/19		Part Bn river trip to COBLENZ. Voluntary church.	

D. D. & L., London, E.C.
(10340) Wt W5300/P713 750,000 3/18 E 2688 Forms/C/2118/16.

53rd Bn SHERWOOD FORESTERS.

WAR DIARY
or
~~INTELLIGENCE SUMMARY.~~
(Erase heading not required.)

Army Form C. 2118.

Instructions regarding War Diaries and Intelligence Summaries are contained in F. S. Regs., Part II. and the Staff Manual respectively. Title pages will be prepared in manuscript.

Place	Date	Hour	Summary of Events and Information	Remarks and references to Appendices
SÜRTH	19/4/19		Training and Sports in afternoon.	
do	20/4/19	10.00	Church parade	
do	21/4/19		Battalion Sports.	
do	22/4/19		Battalion Route March and Sports in afternoon.	
do	23/4/19		Training and Sports in afternoon	
do.	24/4/19		Training and Sports. Lecture at RODENKIRCHEN by Rev. Canon J.J. BARFITT	
do	25/4/19		do do in afternoon	
do	26/4/19		do do do.	
do	27/4/19	11.00	Church parade.	
do	28/4/19		Training and Sports in afternoon	
do	29/4/19		Training and Sports.	
do	30/4/19		Training and Sports.	

K. Woolhouse. Major
53rd Sherwood Foresters.

D. D. & L., London, E.C.
(10340) Wt W5300/P713 750,000 3/18 E 2688 Forms/C/2118/16.

53rd SHERWOOD FORESTERS.

Army Form C. [illegible]18.

WAR DIARY

or

~~INTELLIGENCE SUMMARY~~.

(Erase heading not required.)

Instructions regarding War Diaries and Intelligence Summaries are contained in F. S. Regs., Part II. and the Staff Manual respectively. Title pages will be prepared in manuscript.

Place	Date	Hour	Summary of Events and Information	Remarks and references to Appendices
SÜRTH	1/6/19	5 1030	Training and sports C.O's ~~inspection of all coys.~~ Battn. parade.	
"	2/6/19		Training and sports C.O.'s inspection of all coys.	HEADQUARTERS INFANTRY BRIGADE
"	3/6/19		Training and sports.	
"	4/6/19	09.30	Church parade.	
"	5/6/19		Inspection by the Army Commander Sports in afternoon.	
"	6/6/19		Training and sports.	
"	7/6/19		Training and sports.	
"	8/6/19		Training and sports. ~~Lecture on carrier pigeons~~	
"	9/6/19		Training and sports Lecture on carrier pigeons at BRÜHL.	
"	10/6/19		Training and sports.	
"	11/6/19	09.30	Church parade	
"	12/6/19		Training and sports.	
"	13/6/19		Training and sports. Lecture by Mr. POUNDS on THE BRITISH EMPIRE.	
"	14/6/19		Training and sports. Battn Boxing tournament in evening	
"	15/6/19		Training and sports. Battn. Boxing tournament in evening	

D. D. & L., London, E.C.
(20340) Wt W5300/P713 750,000 3/18 E 2688 Forms/C/2118/16.

Army Form C. 2118.

.53rd SHERWOOD FORESTERS. WAR DIARY

~~or INTELLIGENCE SUMMARY.~~

(Erase heading not required.)

Instructions regarding War Diaries and Intelligence Summaries are contained in F. S. Regs., Part II. and the Staff Manual respectively. Title pages will be prepared in manuscript.

Place	Date	Hour	Summary of Events and Information	Remarks and references to Appendices
SÜRTH	16/6/19		Training and Sports.	
"	17/6/19		Training and Sports. Part Battn river trip up RHINE to COBLENZ and back.	
"	18/6/19	09.30	Church parade.	
"	19/6/19		Training and sports.	
"	20/6/19	9.00	ROUTE MARCH. Sports in afternoon. Lecture by Lt. Col. TYSHAM at BRÜHL.	
"	21/6/19	10.00	Inspection by B.G.C. of "C" Coy. Remainder training. afternoon sports.	
"	22/6/19		River trip up RHINE to COBLENZ and back. Remainder training and sports.	
"	23/6/19		Training and sports. ~~Lecture by MR. J. REID~~	
"	24/6/19		Training and sports. Lecture by MR. J. REID at SÜRTH.	
"	25/6/19	09.30	Church parade.	
"	26/6/19		Training and Sports.	
"	27/6/19		Training and sports. ~~Lecture by MR. F. J. KIRWAN.~~	
"	28/6/19	09.00	Battn. ROUTE MARCH. Lecture by MR. F. J. KIRWAN.	
"	29/6/19		Training and sports. Lecture at RODENKIRCHEN by SIR HARRY JONSTON.	
"	30/6/19		Training and sports. RIVER trip up RHINE to COBLENZ and back.	
	31/5/19		Training & Sports	

6/6/19 W. Power Lt Col Cdg 53rd Sherwood Foresters — R. Woolhouse Major 53rd Sherwood Foresters.

D. D. & L., London, E.C. (10540) Wt W5300/P713 750,000 3/18 E 2688 Forms C/2118/16.

53rd. SHERWOOD FORESTERS.

Army Form C. 2118.

WAR DIARY
or
~~INTELLIGENCE SUMMARY.~~
(*Erase heading not required.*)

Instructions regarding War Diaries and Intelligence Summaries are contained in F. S. Regs., Part II. and the Staff Manual respectively. Title pages will be prepared in manuscript.

Place	Date	Hour	Summary of Events and Information	Remarks and references to Appendices
SÜRTH	1/6/19 ~~09.15~~	09.15	CHURCH PARADE	KW
"	2/6/19		Training and sports in afternoon	KW
"	3/6/19	09.30	Kings birthday. Parade of Brigade on COLOGNE GOLF LINKS, RODENKIRCHEN	KW
"	4/6/19		Parade until 09.30 remainder of day birthday holiday	KW
"	5/6/19		Training and sports in afternoon.	KW
"	6/6/19		Training and packing of kit for SCHMIDTHEIM.	KW
"	7/6/19		Packing of kit and cleaning of billets etc.	KW
"	8/6/19		Packing of kit and cleaning of billets etc.	KW
"	9/6/19		Move of the battalion to SCHMIDTHEIM.	KW
SCHMIDTHEIM	10/6/19		Settling in the camp.	KW
"	11/6/19		Training and sports	KW
"	12/6/19		Training and sports	KW
"	13/6/19		Training and sports	KW
"	14/6/19	09.00	Battalion parade, training and sports in afternoon	KW
"	15/6/19	10.00	Church parade	KW
"	16/6/19	09.00	Brigade parade, remainder of day training and sports.	KW
"	17/6/19	11.00	Brigade parade and inspection by Rt Hon DUKE OF PORTLAND K.G., G.C.V.O.	KW
"	18/6/19		Packing up for move to LIBLAR.	KW

D. D. & L., London, E.C.
(10340) Wt W5300/P713 750,000 3/18 E 2688 Forms C/2118/16.

53rd SHERWOOD FORESTERS.

Army Form C. 2118.

WAR DIARY
or
~~INTELLIGENCE SUMMARY.~~
(Erase heading not required.)

Instructions regarding War Diaries and Intelligence Summaries are contained in F. S. Regs., Part II. and the Staff Manual respectively. Title pages will be prepared in manuscript.

Place	Date	Hour	Summary of Events and Information	Remarks and references to Appendices
LIBLAR	19/6/19		Move of battalion to LIBLAR.	KW
"	20/6/19		posting of picquets on Ry. line and important points, remainder of battalion training	KW
"	21/6/19		A and D Coys. on picquet duty, remainder of battalion training and sports.	KW
"	22/6/19	09.30	Church parade.	KW
"	23/6/19		A and D Coys. on picquet duty, remainder of battalion training and sports.	KW
"	24/6/19		do do do do do do do	KW
"	25/6/19		Withdrawal of picquets. Training and sports.	KW
"	26/6/19		Training and sports.	KW
"	27/6/19		Training and sports	KW
"	28/6/19		Training and Sports	KW
"	28/6/19	22.30	Received official message that Peace was signed.	KW
"	29/6/19	09.30	Church parade	KW
"	30/6/19		Packing up for move to SCHMIDTHEIM. Cleaning of billets.	KW

K Woolhouse Major
53rd Sherwood Foresters.

W Bassett Lt Col
Cdg 53rd Sherwood Foresters

D. D. & L., London, E.C.
(10340) Wt W3300/P713 750,000 3/18 E 2688 Forms/C2118/16.

53rd SHERWOOD FORESTERS.

Army Form C. 2118.

WAR DIARY
or
~~INTELLIGENCE SUMMARY.~~
(Erase heading not required.)

Instructions regarding War Diaries and Intelligence Summaries are contained in F. S. Regs., Part II. and the Staff Manual respectively. Title pages will be prepared in manuscript.

Place	Date	Hour	Summary of Events and Information	Remarks and references to Appendices
LIBLAR	1/7/19		Move of battalion back into Camp at SCHMIDTHEIM.	K.W.
SCHMIDTHEIM	2/7/19		Settling into Camp.	K.W.
"	3/7/19		Training and Sports in afternoon.	K.W.
"	4/7/19		General holiday	K.W.
"	5/7/19		Inspection of Camp and sports.	K.W.
"	6/7/19	10.15	CHURCH PARADE	K.W.
"	7/7/19		Training and Sports in afternoon	K.W.
"	8/7/19		Training and Sports in afternoon	K.W.
"	9/7/19	0900	Battalion parade. Sports in afternoon	K.W.
"	10/7/19		Training and Sports in afternoon	K.W.
"	11/7/19		Training and Sports in afternoon	K.W.
"	12/7/19		Training and Sports in afternoon (battalion sports)	K.W.
"	13/7/19	10.00	CHURCH PARADE	K.W.
"	14/7/19		Training and sports in afternoon	K.W.
"	15/7/19		Training and sports in afternoon	K.W.
"	16/7/19		Inspection by Corps Commander. Sports in afternoon	K.W.
"	17/7/19		Training and Sports in afternoon.	K.W.

D. D. & L., London, E.C.
(10340) Wt W5300/P713 750,000 3/18 E 2688 Forms C/2118/16.

53rd SHERWOOD FORESTERS

Army Form C. 2118.

WAR DIARY
or
~~INTELLIGENCE SUMMARY.~~ KW
(Erase heading not required.)

Instructions regarding War Diaries and Intelligence Summaries are contained in F. S. Regs., Part II. and the Staff Manual respectively. Title pages will be prepared in manuscript.

Place	Date	Hour	Summary of Events and Information	Remarks and references to Appendices
SCHMIDTHEIM	18/7/19		Training and Sports in afternoon	KW.
"	19/7/19		General holiday. Brigade horse show	KW.
"	20/7/19	10.00	CHURCH PARADE.	KW.
"	21/7/19		Training and sports	KW
"	22/7/19		Training and sports	KW
"	23/7/19		Training and sports	KW
"	24/7/19		Holiday. Divisional horse show at ~~Ro[illegible]hof~~. ROMERHOF	KW
"	25/7/19		Training and sports	KW
"	26/7/19		Brigade sports	KW
"	27/7/19	10.00	CHURCH PARADE	KW
	28/7/19		Training and Sports	KW
	29/7/19		Battalion tactical scheme. Sports in afternoon	KW
	30/7/19		Training and Sports.	KW
	31/7/19		Training and sports.	KW.

K. Worthouse[?] Major
53rd Sherwood Foresters

W. Power[?] Lt. Col.
Cdg 53rd Sherwood Foresters

D. D. & L., London, E.C.
(10340) Wt W5300/P713 750,000 3/18 E 2688 Forms/C/2118/15.

www.ingramcontent.com/pod-product-compliance
Lightning Source LLC
Chambersburg PA
CBHW080819010526
44111CB00015B/2577
9781474506298